The Development of Logic in Adulthood

Postformal Thought and
Its Applications

The Plenum Series in Adult Development and Aging

SERIES EDITOR:
Jack Demick, *Suffolk University, Boston, Massachusetts*

ADULT DEVELOPMENT, THERAPY, AND CULTURE
A Postmodern Synthesis
Gerald D. Young

THE AMERICAN FATHER
Biocultural and Developmental Aspects
Wade C. Mackey

THE DEVELOPMENT OF LOGIC IN ADULTHOOD
Postformal Thought and Its Applications
Jan D. Sinnott

HANDBOOK OF AGING AND MENTAL HEALTH
An Integrative Approach
Edited by Jacob Lomranz

HANDBOOK OF CLINICAL GEROPSYCHOLOGY
Edited by Michel Hersen and Vincent B. Van Hasselt

HANDBOOK OF PAIN AND AGING
Edited by David I. Mostofsky and Jacob Lomranz

HUMAN DEVELOPMENT IN ADULTHOOD
Lewis R. Aiken

PSYCHOLOGICAL TREATMENT OF OLDER ADULTS
An Introductory Text
Edited by Michel Hersen and Vincent B. Van Hasselt

The Development of Logic in Adulthood

Postformal Thought and Its Applications

Jan D. Sinnott

Towson University
Baltimore, Maryland

Plenum Press • New York and London

Library of Congress Cataloging-in-Publication Data

Sinnott, Jan D.
    The development of logic in adulthood : postformal thought and its
applications / Jan D. Sinnott.
        p.   cm. -- (Plenum series in adult development and aging)
    Includes bibliographical references and index.
    ISBN 0-306-45723-7
    1. Adulthood--Psychological aspects. 2. Cognition--Age factors.
3. Logic.   I. Title.   II. Series.
    BF724.55.C63S55   1998
    155.6--dc21   97-51715
                                                                      CIP

Cover illustration: M. C. Escher's "Drawing Hands" ©1997 Cordon Art B.V.
Baarn, The Netherlands. All rights reserved.

ISBN 0-306-45723-7

© 1998 Plenum Press, New York
A Division of Plenum Publishing Corporation
233 Spring Street, New York, N.Y. 10013

http://www.plenum.com

10 9 8 7 6 5 4 3 2 1

Printed in the United States of America

To those who keep teaching me to live in balance,
and to understand,
especially my life partner Lynn
and my children James, Gwenn, Kiersten, and Gavyn

Preface

This book is a result of my desire to understand how some adults grow wiser as they grow older. My tools are those of my own field of expertise, that of cognitive life-span developmental psychology; but my theories rest on all the accumulated knowledge of psychology, philosophy, the life sciences, and the natural sciences. Beyond my purpose of understanding, in the abstract, the phenomenon of adult wisdom (which, as this book describes, I now have accomplished in part), I have another purpose: to share this knowledge. I want as many of us as possible to understand, as the wise ones seem to understand, how we are cocreators of our own worlds and of the world we share with each other. I have come to believe that acting on such an understanding can lead to more skilled behavior and less suffering for individuals and for humanity. I hope that sharing my theory and understanding will provide a life-long gift of increasing awareness to individuals as well as providing stimulating possibilities for researchers, students, and practitioners in psychology and many related fields.

To accomplish this task I have focused the book on four goals. First, I describe on a personal and theoretical level how my theory of postformal thought came to be created. Second, I offer a brief summary of the years of research and scholarship that form the background of the theory. Next, I make several applications of the theory to number of fields in order to show its potential utility both in everyday life and in professional life. Finally, I discuss interventions, that is, how one might teach postformal thought and use it to live in balance. This "living in balance" means living wisely, orchestrating the needs of mind, heart, spirit, body, and others in our lives, in spite of the conflicting demands that all of us face in adulthood.

To reach these goals, I have organized the book into three main sections, each of which is preceded by an introductory chapter. Chapter 1, the introductory chapter, describes a rationale for my Theory of Postformal Thought. I describe how the theory was created as my own life experience led to realizations about the nature of adult logic. This may give the reader better insight into "where I am coming from" and what the lenses are through which I view the reality of the logic of adult development.

Part I (Chapters 2–7) explains the nature of postformal thought and describes how it develops. Chapter 2 outlines the limits of traditional approaches to understanding adult logical development. Such approaches come from the evolution of the field itself. Postformal thought has several intellectual ancestors and several allied ideas, all of which channel its direction. Middle and old age are also unique developmental times of life with tasks that demand a more advanced and sophisticated logic. New fields such as the "new" physics (relativity theory and quantum physics), chaos theory, complexity theory, and general systems theory suggest richer theoretical approaches to thinking about our cognitive growth.

Chapter 3 describes what characterizes postformal thought. The unique thinking operations of postformal thought are explored, and it is discussed as a special form of intelligence. Postformal thought is related to thinking characteristic of the new physics. In terms of problem-solving theory, postformal thought solves *ill*-structured problems. It is part of complex learning and appears to be like "wisdom," as wisdom is popularly defined.

Chapter 4 discusses the *development* of such complex thinking. It seems that the multiple truths to which we are exposed when we have social interactions with others form the foundation of this skill. Adult developmental tasks such as generativity are not simply "cognitive" or "emotional" but bridge all these areas of human experience. To be part of a culture demands that individuals use a cognition that goes beyond the individual, one that reflects a reality cocreated with others.

Chapter 5 explores the new physics models underlying postformal adult logic. Such models are extended to the study of life-span development in general. Chapter 6 explores General Systems Theory as another basis for postformal thought. General Systems Theory is defined and described briefly with special focus on change processes. Chapter 7 introduces the reader to the new theories of chaos, complexity, and self-organizing systems, including them among the theories of the new biology. This chapter shows how adult logical development, as part of a self-organizing system, has characteristics of these new approaches.

Part II (Chapters 8–12) summarizes some of the research that describes the most interesting relations between postformal thought and pertinent variables. Chapter 8 tells the story of the first research projects, those done with the motivation of understanding why seemingly intelligent, highly functioning adults looked illogical on many traditional tests. What else might they be doing?

Chapter 9 gives examples of some interview studies in which respondents were able to talk in more detail about what they were thinking. Formalized "thinking aloud" studies found the same postformal operations as the initial studies did. They also gave greater insight into the process of this complex logic.

Chapter 10 describes some differences among younger, middle-aged, and older respondent groups. These groups differed in use of formal logic, postformal operations, steps to solution of problems, and crucial errors. Age groups also differed in compensatory strategies, that is, in ways to get around their problem-solving weaknesses.

In Chapter 11 the factors of emotions, intention, goal clarity, and availability of a problem-solving heuristic are related to use of postformal operations. Traditional measures such as physical health, memory, and vocabulary are also related to this complex logic. Problem context influenced the logical operations used. Probe questions led to a deeper understanding of respondents' richly textured thinking processes. An experiment on the influence of minor manipulations on the complexity of logical thought that is articulated is presented in this chapter.

In the case studies of Chapter 12, we see the utility of postformal thought. It then became interesting to consider some special subsamples which would likely make use of such complex thought.

Part III (Chapters 13–20) focuses on application of the Theory of Postformal Thought to certain areas of life in the "worlds" of individuals, of couples, of families, and of cultures. How is this thinking used in those several worlds?

Chapter 13 starts this examination by applying the theory to education. We examine the nature of learning and the way teachers teach. Master teachers are specialists at postformal logic. The theory can speak to the question of how learning institutions are structured. Still focused on learning, Chapter 14 examines how we might reinvent the university (and other adult learning centers) to stimulate postformal thought in adults.

In Chapters 15 and 16 we consider postformal thought in the multiperson group. First we see the challenges of the workplace. There are intragroup and intergroup conflicts there, as well as organizational change. At the end of the chapter, the focus is on administrators who deal with these changing multiple realities as a part of their job. In Chapter 16 the focus on our interest is the couple or the family. There is an interplay among cognitive postformal skills and intimate relationships, in times of joy, distress, and healing, over the life course of the relationship.

Spiritual development and the search for meaning are important forces in individual lives. The relationship between postformal thought and these experiences is the topic of Chapter 17. Does an aware spirituality grow with complex cognitive abilities? Some testable hypotheses are outlined. The question of how individuals can live in balance, juggling the demands of mind, emotion, body, *spirit,* and significant others, is addressed.

Creativity is the subject of Chapter 18. Broader definitions of creativity link postformal thought to creative thought. Postformal thought regulates stimulation overload from the many elements that must be synthesized in the creative response. A similar process is necessary to prevent fragmentation in the complex postmodern self. The complex thought necessary for creating aspects of the self is exemplified through a discussion of sex or gender role development over the lifespan.

Chapter 19 addresses the connection between postformal thought and healing of four very different sorts: healing the mind; healing the body; healing international conflict; and healing the environmental wounds of the planet. Psychopathology can be postformal; the postformal psychotherapist is the one best equipped to work with all types of psychopathology. The principles of mind–body medicine always demand, by their very nature, postformal medical care. Conflict resolution demands the ability to juggle the multiple logical realities of the parties to the conflict. Healing the earth requires slipping from larger to smaller-scale logical realities about environmental processes.

Some uses of postformal thought in the theories and activities of humanistic psychology are discussed in Chapter 20, the last chapter in Part III. The cognitive problems posed by thinking "humanistically" and by addressing existential issues are discussed. Some practical examples of postformal-thought-based humanistic psychology techniques are offered including discussions of guided imagery, mind–body medicine, and creative intentionality.

The final section of the book, Part IV, including Chapters 21 and 22, points the way to the next steps in our learning about complex adult logic. Chapter 21 offers the challenge "Can we *teach* adults to use complex postformal thought?" Some examples of activities suitable for the classroom and other settings are offered. Finally, in Chapter 22, the questions are raised: "How can we live 'in balance,' juggling demands of mind, heart, spirit, body, and others? Can the postformal, complex logic of adulthood help?" The book ends with references, appendices, and indexes.

Acknowledgments

While all the lessons of life have helped me create this theory and this book, there are some specific persons, events, and institutions that were most directly helpful. I am grateful to my life partner, Lynn Johnson, for her own visionary thinking, for her encouragement to me to think through these ideas to their conclusions and implications, and for her challenges to me to make my theory more practical. Lynn is a living example of postformal thought in action. Thank you to daughter Kiersten and son Gavyn for making life richer and more lively, for challenging my views, and for having patience with their book-writing parent. Thanks to son James and daughter Gwenn for their older wisdom and for their feedback about college, graduate school, and their worlds of work and family. They see in fresh ways, and they have the heart to help create the future. Thanks to my parents, to other relatives, and to friends for their thoughts, their challenges, their caring, their willingness to risk, and their examples over the years. All these members of my local "family" provide the daily support that make the creation of a theory and a book possible.

Thanks, too, to my larger professional, intellectual, and spiritual "family" who helped in the formation of ideas, the growth of soul, and the stimulation of chaotic creativity. Former professors, wise teachers, and current colleagues (too numerous to mention by name) have challenged the ideas and the systems within psychology, education, research, spirituality, and all the many applied fields to which I refer in this book. They have helped to inspire the creation and augmentation of my theories, and have helped me "nest" those theories in the world of perennial wisdom.

I would like to thank Towson University (formerly Towson State University) for its support through research and conference grants, assigned time grants, and sabbaticals during my career there. Thank you to Roger Fink who chaired our Psychology Department during the time I was working on this book, and to our secretarial and library support staff. I am grateful to my friends and colleagues and students and interns from many departments in many universities (local, national, and international) who talked over ideas with me. It was possible for me to see Postformal Thought in action and application as we discussed the frivolous and the profound, talked about "Missing Links" and "dead bugs," and wondered at Harvard Conferences, at home, and at work whether such a thing as adult cognitive development could coexist with the unskilled behavior of real human beings.

Thanks to all the other universities and research institutions that have been home to me and to my ideas over the years. My graduate school faculty at Catholic University planted many seeds of ideas that are now bearing fruit. Colleagues at the University of Maryland, College Park, assisted me as I developed some of my ideas while I was supported by funding from the National Institutes of Health. A postdoctoral fellowship from the Public Health Service made it possible to do further work at the Gerontology Research Center of the National Institute on Aging of the National Institutes of Health, so that I could gain experience in the laboratory of Dave Arenberg.

I am especially grateful to the innovative and visionary research teams, workshop participants, creative discussion groups, and symposia panelists who gathered together with me for a wide range of purposes at many times and places in the world, and stimulated my thinking while doing so. They have helped me to think as a global citizen who can reach into the past and the future, can see the "big picture" more successfully.

The support and help of Plenum Editor Eliot Werner and Plenum's support staff have been very much appreciated. And thank you to Jack Demick, the editor of this series, for his support and friendship now and over the years.

Only by our working together can we cocreate the reality of our lives and our universe. The logic of adulthood teaches us this truth. May we all develop the postformal wisdom that allows us to consciously accomplish this creation with the intention to act in the service of good. This has been and is my hidden agenda in doing this research and in writing this book.

Contents

PART II. SOME RESEARCH TO SUPPORT THE THEORY: STUDIES OF COMPLEX POSTFORMAL THOUGHT

Introduction

Creation of a Theory and
the Purpose of This Book

When the great innovation appears, it will almost certainly be in muddled, incomplete and confusing form. To the discoverer . . . it will be only half understood. . . . For any speculation which does not at first glance look crazy, there is no hope.

NEILS BOHR

The theory I am about to offer you, the reader, is a complex one with revolutionary implications for the way we conceptualize adult thought. It is one that I am convinced is immensely important and useful. The complexity of this theory is due to its power to synthesize many fields in psychology, other sciences, and the humanities as well. Its importance is partly due to that same feature, for the theory I am about to offer you is a way to describe how humans balance mind, heart, soul, and the needs of others, over time. This theory provides a cognitive vantage point for a "general theory" of psychological–social–spiritual life-span development.

The importance of this theory also stems from the fact that at this point in history, at this point in the story of the human species, we very much desire the kind of synthetic, "big picture" understanding that a unifying theory can bring to the way we see ourselves as human beings. We have spent centuries taking the human experience apart in analytical ways; it seems that we now want to synthesize ideas about our minds, hearts, bodies, spirits, and our links with other humans in order to see ourselves whole again.

1

The theory I am about to offer you is also extremely useful. Name a situation in which adults are interacting with each other and developing over time, and I will show you a situation in which this theory can be applied. Whether your interest is in developing good teachers, in counseling couples, in training experts, in understanding mystics, in resolving conflicts, in becoming a better manager, in examining health care decisions, in ending family conflicts—whatever the area, this theory can offer new insights and interventions.

Most of all—and most important—this theory can stimulate good questions. As Ashley Montagu (personal communication, August 1995) has said, the function of a professor (and, I think, a good theorist) is to rush into your mind and leave it in shambles, then straighten it out together with you. I cannot yet offer the answers to all the questions raised in this book, but I hope you can join with me in thinking about the answers we do have and in entertaining some of those questions that have incomplete answers.

In this chapter, I will share with you how this theory of postformal thought, a theory of adult logical development, came into being. Considerable work has been done over two decades to test the parameters and implications of the theory. Considerable time has been spent exploring just a few of the applications. I will consider these with you in this book. The several purposes of this book will be summarized as a conclusion to this chapter.

First, though, I invite you on a journey over the very different paths of thought that jointly led to the creation of this theory and that again led away, in several directions, as the theory was applied. In a possibly apocryphal story, Winston Churchill is said to have sent a pudding back to the kitchen one day, rejecting it because "it had no theme." The "pudding" of my widely varying scholarly activities does have a single theme and a single heart, and that is the understanding of postformal thought.

CREATION OF A THEORY OF ADULT LOGICAL DEVELOPMENT

I invite you to imagine yourself sitting with me in a quiet study carrel of the National Institutes of Health Library of Medicine, looking out the narrow window at the very green grass running riot during a wet and steamy day of a Washington, DC, summer. It is the mid-1970s. I have recently finished my doctoral dissertation. I had been curious about how individuals develop the ability to know objective reality. In my dissertation, I attempted to discover what happens to Piagetian logical abilities as people reach maturity and old age. On the basis of my data, the answer to my question was that mature adults performed badly on these several Piagetian logical tasks, at least in terms of passing complex Piagetian formal operations; they performed significantly worse than younger respondents, worse than teenagers. My data fit with results of prior studies, my dissertation was publishable (an important issue for academics and researchers), and everyone was satisfied but me.

Far from feeling satisfied, I felt confused and depressed, almost as though something were missing. Scientifically speaking, I *had* been cheering for the wrong side: I had wanted to find that the complex thinking of younger and older respondents was *equivalent*. In fact, I had specifically set up my study to use "everyday" kinds of formal operations problems stated in a normal context (not an abstract, scientific one) to get around what I thought were prior researchers' mistakes of testing mature adults with physics-, math-, or chemistry-contexted formal problems. My thinking was that mature adults would show the cognitive abilities they really had if they were given problems that were like those they encountered in daily life. But my mature respondents still did poorly. These data were disappointing to me for scientific reasons, but also for reasons that were partly personal and that I had never discussed with my dissertation committee.

My dissertation committee knew nothing about my middle-aged and older relatives. I had never thought to share information about them. My large, ethnic family was blessed (or, on bad days, cursed) not only with parents and grandparents but also with great-grandparents in healthy numbers, and even with great-great-grandparents, not to mention older aunts, uncles, cousins (of the first, second, third, and other degrees), and lots of other members holding roles by marriage. Most lived relatively near each other so that we could see them at family gatherings. They not only matured gracefully and enjoyed retirement, but also tended to remain with us into their 90s.

Not all these people were perfect. Some of these middle-aged and older relatives were masterful complainers and manipulators. Some were less gifted and less ethical than others; many had limited formal years of education and were men or women of few words. After all, many of the grandparents had been immigrants from Eastern Europe with the hardships that entailed, and none of them had the luxury of money or time to pursue their primary interests in the face of economic necessity.

But most of my mature and older relatives were very bright, creative, practical, and, yes, logical people. They invented things that were technologically sophisticated (for the times) and that later someone else would patent and successfully market. Some of them were wise. Many philosophized and narrated stories centered on their favorite themes. They told rich and complex stories of their lives. They had endless debates in which they built logical castles and defended them with ease. And they had friends who did the same—friends not so different from my talented research subjects who held professional jobs and advanced degrees and did logical things in the outside world. I was certain that my relatives were quite logical. But even with my "everyday" problems, I could not get my respondents to look logical on my potentially life-span Piagetian problem-solving test. They did poorly on Piaget's formal logic problems. What was going on here? What was I missing? Perhaps my own logical thinking was already deficient; after all, I was 32 years old.

While all this dissertation writing and disappointment was going on, I had been raising two young children, working on contracts for pay, taking part in social change efforts (remember, this was the sixties and seventies), trying to understand systems of spiritual development, pursuing a lifelong interest in that area, and reading all I possibly could about Piaget's theory. Before Piaget died, he seemed on the brink of thinking about some "next stage" of logical thought that might be a hallmark of adulthood in the way that formal logical thought was the hallmark achievement of adolescence. Piaget said no more about that "next stage," but the hint felt enough like a nod of approval from an authority to permit even a new researcher like me to consider the possibility of adult later-life stages of cognitive development. What might a new stage be? Looking at my own children, I tried to imagine what their performance would look like if now, in elementary school, they took logical tests meant for preschoolers. Giving this imaginary exercise a try, I imagined they would make errors on the easy tests, not because they *lost* the logical skill but because they were doing *something else more sophisticated* that did not allow the simplistic "right" test answers to emerge. Hmmmm. Interesting possibility. How could I study that?

I had also been reading all that I could in the "new physics" of relativity theory and quantum physics and general systems theory. With all the things I had crammed into my busy life, I had long felt that I shifted entire realities many times a day. I felt as though I were living in several somewhat contradictory situations in the sense of the contradictions of Newtonian physics versus new physics, creating many worlds for myself to inhabit. Here in the new physics was a way of conceptualizing my own and others' developing-over-time reality. I had been focused on cognitive epistemology à la Piaget; what about the way "objective" reality is known in the new physics? For that matter, what about the approaches of cognitive scientists analyzing solutions to ill-structured problems? What about the social–cognitive realities, the consensus realities, of several people developing together? These were just a few of my many intriguing questions.

So now I was sitting in the Library of Medicine, confused. I was struggling with the disappointing knowledge that my respondents, who were mature and older adults, did not look logical on Piagetian problems. In real life, though, they—like my relatives—seemed very logical and competent in scientific formal operational reasoning. But I knew from watching my own reality shift logically that development of that logic-shifting sort was going on in everyday life with me as I passed through adulthood. I knew from watching my children that people seldom look so inarticulate and "illogical" as when they are much wiser than your questions and when they despair of your ever understanding the world in the complex ways they can employ. And I knew from the ideas of general systems theory, chaos and complexity, and the new physics that there are *very* logical ways of addressing what we can know about the physical world that still appear to be *il*logical. These ways of thinking about the physical world demand that you use *process-oriented* general systems theory or its offshoots, and in doing so you can see reality simultaneously through the eyes of Newton *and* Einstein *and* self-regulating chaotic processes.

Slowly, a new set of research questions came together on that day in the library and on the days that followed: Find out what what respondents *are* thinking, in response to a problem. Describe the logic of that thinking. If it has a logic, see whether it bears any resemblance to thinking in the new physics, to ill-structured problem-solving theory or to thinking about what is traditionally said to develop in maturity, namely, wisdom. If a special mature adult thought exists, see what relates to its presence or absence. If it exists, see what it is good for. If it is useful, see how it can be taught. I came to call the answers I found to these new questions the Theory of Relativistic Postformal Thought, or Postformal Thought for short. That Theory of Postformal Thought is the focus of this book.

This modest menu of questions and insights forms the underpinning of my Theory of Relativistic Postformal Thought and the results and applications you will read about in this book. Each step of the logic and details of the theory itself will be described in chapters to follow.

TESTING THE THEORY OF RELATIVISTIC
POSTFORMAL THOUGHT

From 1975 to the present, I have pursued answers to the questions mentioned above. Qualitative and quantitative research studies of all sorts including experimental and nonexperimental studies have been carried out in a number of different locations with the support of a postdoctoral fellowship, sabbaticals, and grants. Refinements in the theory have followed each part of the research process. Results have always suggested new questions.

Creation and testing of a new theory always follows the same steps and logic. First, the researcher uses past research or theory or experience to stimulate a logical leap to a provisional statement that some new law or regularized phenomenon has been recognized. Descriptive data are gathered. If the original hunch still appears valid, relations between the phenomenon of interest and other concomitant phenomena are sought. If interest is still merited, potential causal relations are hypothesized and tested. At each step, a new layer is added to the geology of the theory as it becomes a more complex, interesting, and potentially useful Theory (with a capital T). At some point, the results of such experiments will suggest a much larger and more effective way of looking at the problem, and, one hopes, a new and even better potential theory will be suggested to supersede the first. The process then goes through another iteration, and another.

The first step in testing the early version of Postformal Thought theory was to find out in a broader sense exactly what the respondents were thinking when they provided answers to the standard structured logical problems I presented. If my hunch was correct, if they were thinking some kinds of logical thoughts other than Piagetian formal operational logic, I needed to know what those thoughts were about. I needed to content-analyze those thoughts, or to probe them until they made sense, if that was possible. At the same time, since what we articulate in a response seems partly a function of what we see as socially acceptable and as "intelligent," I needed to know what respondents of various ages *thought* was intelligent behavior for mature adults to display.

Next, if I could discover and make sense of some intelligent or logical thing respondents actually were doing (other than or in addition to formal operational logic), could there be some standard way to describe the subcomponents of that logic? What were the steps or operations that they needed to master to make it work? Was there a pattern to the steps or subcomponents? Would they match the skills people previously said they thought represented the intelligence of maturity? Were the steps (or pattern, or operations, or reality) constructed like those steps (patterns, operations, reality) created by the thinking of the new physics? Were they qualitatively different from the prior stage, formal operations to some reasonable degree, granting the overlap of operations and stages that virtually always occurs in stage theories?

Then, if the data still supported the Theory of Postformal Thought at this point, I wanted to see what correlated with the existence of this complex thought. For example, did age relate to this complex thinking? Was this thinking somehow gender- or class-specific, perhaps due to some biological variable or life-experience variable? Did it relate to having a good IQ or a good memory, or to some other cognitive skill such as rapid-learning ability? Perhaps it was influenced by good health, either emotional or physical. What factors were correlated with postformal thought?

If there were correlational relations between postformal thought and some factors, the next step would be to try to experimentally induce or inhibit this thinking ability. A certain type of physical or emotional context or environment could be created to perform this experiment. For example, if I were to observe casually that a positive mood seemed to be correlated with occurrence of postformal thought, I might experimentally manipulate the moods of respondents (perhaps give them gifts to make them happy?) to allow them to enjoy more complex thinking (if my hypothesis were supported).

If the experimental and other research results were positive, my next step would be application of Postformal Thought to problem situations in real life that would be ameliorated if the participants could think in more complex ways. For example, we all know it takes a great deal of training or experience or both to "put yourself in other people's shoes" the way an expert teacher, negotiator, or clinician must. If we see a link between such expertise and the presence of postformal thought, we could try to teach new teachers or clinicians or negotiators how to think postformally. We could try to teach individuals living as intimate partners to think in more complex ways such as these to help them achieve more joy together. We could see how postformal thought might also relate to the life of the spirit, and whether it enhances the ability to balance across all these domains of life. So the studies began.

TWO DECADES OF THE STUDY OF POSTFORMAL COMPLEX THOUGHT

Following the aforementioned steps that always occur as a scientist builds a theory, I applied the steps to this problem that interested me. I did some of the work outlined in the previous section. I was gratified to see that my original questions seemed worth pursuing and led to useful, increasingly refined answers. The papers, articles, chapters, and books that resulted from this exploration are listed under my name in the references section. In every case, except for the Chap and Sinnott (1977–1978) reference, *all* the respondents in my studies were community-dwelling individuals, not institutionalized persons. As you will see later, numerous colleagues and students also took part in these efforts.

This research program took place in several different locations. My dissertation work applying and extending Piaget's theory to mature and older adults was done with the Psychology Department at the Catholic University of America. It was followed by exploratory work on the thinking of mature problem solvers in real-life and abstract situations, done with the School of Social Service at Catholic University and supported by grants from the Administration on Aging and the National Institute on Drug Abuse.

Research on sex role development in mature adults (complex role development being another everyday example of potentially postformal thinking) was conducted at the University of Maryland College Park, through the Center on Aging located there, supported by the National Institute on Aging (NIA). All projects after this date also were supported by Towson State University through assigned time, sabbaticals, leave, and grants.

Some of the work was accomplished through a postdoctoral award from the U.S. Public Health Service that permitted me to work with David Arenberg and others at the Gerontology Research Center of the NIA, housed at and cooperating with Johns Hopkins Bayview Hospitals (formerly Baltimore City Hospitals, later named Francis Scott Key Medical Center). The Gerontology Research Center maintained the Baltimore Longitudinal Study of Aging, and use of this sample permitted me to test individuals between the ages of 18 and 97 and to correlate their scores on my test to other factors in their physical, mental, and emotional performance on various measures.

Work done directly at Towson State University examined the postformal thought of mature primary and secondary teachers as well as the thinking of college professors. Undergraduate students were tested, too. We examined the postformal thought of middle-aged couples, both married and unmarried ones, as they solved problems together. Family members who were making health care decisions about an acutely ill family member allowed us to examine their thinking processes. Since certain occupations seemed to demand the expert use of multiple realities, I focused on postformal thought in selected professions. Psychotherapists, especially those working with multiple personality disorders, were tested and seemed to show this sort of postformal thought, as did expert research administrators and expert teachers who were willing to be interviewed. Along the way, we examined how artificial-intelligence-like models of postformal thought processes might look, using various case studies from the NIA and Towson State. Theories of cognitive problem solving from a *non*developmental point of view (a separate research approach from that of the cognitive–developmental point of view, as will be seen later) were used to analyze steps in the cognitive process of solving ill-structured problems such as postformal problems. An agenda for the study of all potential applications suggested by the research (e.g., teaching, couples conflicts, clinician training, family dynamics) and for other applications, such as the study of spiritual development and creativity, was created. *Multi*person cognition became the counterpoint to each study or application of individual thought processes, since postformal thought seems to involve consensual realities.

All these parts of this scientific adventure supplied the raw material for understanding a part of what was occurring in the complex thinking of mature adults. But perhaps the most exciting or useful part was still to come. That part of the work involved noticing relations or phenomena of the next order of magnitude and the next level of complexity, which began slowly to lead to a more inclusive theory than ever before. Postformal Thought gradually came to be seen to be the cognitive underpinning for understanding how to balance the complexities of our many identity realities so that we can consciously try to live in balance as adults. Humans, as a conscious, thinking, feeling species that survives a long lifetime, try to have identities that connect us to others, to the larger universe, and to our spirits, so as to infuse life with meaning. This means we must structure complex realities about our somewhat conflicting motives and identities and truths in order to feel really satisfied. Study and research about this larger overarching level of Postformal Thought Theory is my most recent focus of study.

PURPOSE OF THIS BOOK

This book is written to introduce interested readers to my Theory of Postformal Thought. It is a scholarly summary of my theory and the research supporting it, but it also outlines some practical, everyday uses of the theory. I discuss how thinking changes in quality as we move from adolescence into midlife and aging years. The logic and approach children and teens take to understanding their world is not sufficient for the tasks of adulthood. Adult logic—more than teen logic—is moved by a desire for deep connections and meaning, by an awareness of the interrelationships around us, and by the shortness of life. Adult logic has a relativistic, self-referential quality. Adults create a shared reality with others, and the most conscious adults seem to know they are creating it!

We humans struggle to balance the demands of mind, heart, body, spirit, and community. Adult life is often seen as a struggle to find meaning in spite of loss and suffering. The theme of the struggle to find existential meaning in life and to develop an adult logic of living in balance is a theme found in literature, philosophy, and spiritual writings as well as in psychology. This book outlines that logic from a cognitive developmental point of view.

In this book, I will first show the gaps in current theory of mature adult cognitive development, then outline the operations of Postformal Thought and discuss how this thinking may develop. I will describe the research base and theoretical studies associated with it. We will explore some applications of the theory to the world of mature adults, and discuss some interventions that might help adults learn to be wise in this way. Next, we will look at the "big picture," thinking about how Postformal Thought might apply to topics and problems such as ecology and ecopsychology, the reengineering of institutions, spiritual development, creativity, and emotional maturity. We will consider the passionate commitment to choices about reality that humans make, in the face of knowledge that our understanding of our existence is plagued by some sort of necessary subjectivity that prevents us from jumping out of our own minds.

The third part of the book reflects three additional important purposes. This part contains a discussion of how we create balance in our lives through the mechanism of postformal thought. It also contains an outline of the prerequisites for our being able to teach Postformal Thought in our learning institutions.

Our last topic will be a list of some suggestions for the next 20 years of research in this area. Overall, then, the purpose of the book is to give readers the tools to understand and use the Theory of Postformal Thought to enrich life and work.

PART I

THE THEORY

Description and Development of Complex Postformal Thought

CHAPTER 2

Limits of Traditional Approaches for Understanding Adult Logical Development

Consciousness is not reducible to neural events. The meaning of the message will never be found in the chemistry of the ink.

ROGER SPERRY

In this chapter, I will try to summarize some of the limits of current approaches that in some way describe or address the development of thought and logic in adulthood and old age. I regret that I will not be able to give a thorough overview of specific theories themselves, or even of general types of theories; space does not permit my doing them justice. My main goal in this chapter is to describe the *critical* gaps in the approaches that exist in order to suggest ways to fill those gaps. My second goal is to give theoretical reasons for the need to create and explore a new theory, namely, my Theory of Postformal Thought.

The limits of theories of adult thought stem from several different problems. First, the field of adult development and aging has evolved in such a way that there is a dichotomy between developmental studies and "aging" cognition studies. (Note that studies with respondents older than 20 have usually been conceptualized as "aging" studies, reflecting the American bias that, cognitively speaking, it is all downhill after the 20s.) Developmental studies represent the study of processes that are connected to one's place in the life span and processes that change over time. Younger persons are usually studied.

The latter, cognitive "aging" studies, usually focus on losses the over-30 person experiences while processing information. We lack adult cognitive developmental studies to understand mature cognition in its fullness and cognitive *growth* over later life periods.

Second, there is a tendency to ignore processes in mature adults who are in the middle of life. We need more cognitive developmental studies of midlife individuals.

Third, definitions of intelligence are more limited than they need to be, being based originally on items that predicted performance in school. We need definitions of intelligence specifically tailored to mature adults.

Fourth, Piagetian theory stops at adolescent development with formal operations. We need to explore the Piagetian sort of logical operations that might be found in maturity.

Fifth, studies of adult development tend to focus on pathology. They tend to separate issues such as adaptation, *shared* cognition, spirituality, and psychosocial stages from intrapersonal cognitive issues, thereby fragmenting human experience. We need to focus more on the nonpathological multifaceted, social, thinking person.

Sixth, the idea that adult individuals (to some degree) construct their own identities and realities has been raised only recently. We need to explore these accomplishments in light of (or linked with) cognitive functioning.

Seventh, we tend to overlook any cognitive skills that might be needed for success at various stages of mature development or that are stimulated by those stages. We need to make a point of looking at individuals' cognitive responses in the context of the developmental needs of respondents *at that stage* of their lives.

Eighth, we do very little to explore psychological analogues of new physics theory, general systems theory, complexity theory, or self-regulating systems theories, all of which are powerful conceptual frameworks, if nothing else. Some have compared overlooking these theories and their associated methods with doing statistics on a calculator when a computer is available. We can incorporate the key concepts and some methods of these advanced fields.

Finally, we ignore the *need for meaning* and *being true to one's spirit* that adults tell us motivate their major activities. We can make meaning and intention more prominent in our thinking. These gaps and the consequent need for a new theory to better address nonfragmented adult development will be discussed in sections of this chapter.

EVOLUTION OF THE FIELD

Studies of Mature Thought Usually Have Not Been Developmental

The quality of thinking and logic in mature adults is not often studied by developmentalists looking at processes over the complexities of the life span. Postformal Thought would help to remedy this neglect.

Developmentalists tend to study changes over time in the living organism as an adaptive system, one that coexists with other adaptive systems in a context. The subject of this book, Postformal Thought, is based on a developmental perspective toward cognitive change in adulthood and aging, and includes different, synthesis-based questions that differentiate it from other approaches in subtle ways. First, this developmental approach includes emphases on both laboratory and naturalistic studies. The developmental approach also complements psychometric and information-processing approaches to intelligence and cognition by opening studies to elements of emotion, life-stage tasks, and personal meaning. Thus, the developmental approach leads us across the boundaries of the "objective" and the "subjective," the experimental and the phenomenological, the clinical and the research domains.

We can approach our topic of mature adult logical development differently if we use a developmental approach in its current, modern sense. Without a modern developmental emphasis, we have been accustomed to asking questions about "average," "above average," and "below average" performance, about comparing performance among a wide assortment of persons (nomothetic studies). We have been accustomed to labeling kinds of thinking or factors of thinking, and to discovering kinds of settings or processes that raise performance to some desired norm or presumed underlying competence *at one point in time.* In other words, we have been following a particularly American sort of approach in which one tries to find out what is normal and (perhaps) "level the field" to get those other-than-normal individuals closer to (or above!) the norm. The value stated as "We're all created equal" is sometimes transformed into "We should all be the same in every way." This metamorphosis in turn translates to a research exercise comparing the logic of older and younger persons and trying to get the older to match the performance of the younger ones. Of course, the developmental approach sometimes serves that important value too, addressing questions such as "How do individuals achieve higher levels of intelligence (by some definition) as they mature?"

But beyond such comparisons of average scores, the developmental approach can be used to ask very different sorts of additional questions. The different questions favor study of individual differences, elements in the adaptive style of a real organism in a real context, elements of personal meaning and choice, elements of process and interactions of intelligence or action over time, and elements that define the parameters or limits of expert or unusually skilled performance. This side of the developmental approach feels less comfortable for most of us as scientists, since it threatens the nomothetic, positivistic, and mechanistic view of the world in which we are trained.

It also may feel dangerous to us, as participants in a democracy, to talk about basic differences, since such talk sometimes leads (politically) to discrimination in favor of or against certain persons with particular traits. But an emphasis on the developmental approach toward individual differences often feels very important to the study of human behavior, both to us and to those who make use of our studies. It seems missing, somehow, in other types of nondevelopmental studies.

As many scientists reach their own mature years, this individual-differences approach seems to them to be in line with their experience of human existence. It does offer bridges among the experiences of life expressed by science, by medicine, and by the humanities. And this side of the developmental approach even is grounded in the exploratory strategies of "hard" sciences such as quantum physics, evolutionary biology, chaos and complexity theory, and other theories of open systems. Thus, such idiographic inquiries may provide a useful alternative view of phenomena of interest to us now within adult cognitive development.

One analogy for combining the individualistic and the normative studies of adult cognitive development may be that of experiencing both the melody *and* the chords in a musical composition. The melody is analogous to idiographic, individual pattern-over-time studies; the chords, to nomothetic, look-at-norms (at a single time) studies.

INTELLECTUAL ANCESTORS AND COLLEAGUES OF POSTFORMAL THOUGHT

Figure 2.1 is an attempt to graphically illustrate the overlap of life-span cognitive *development* studies with other historically important approaches to the study of cognitive changes in adulthood and

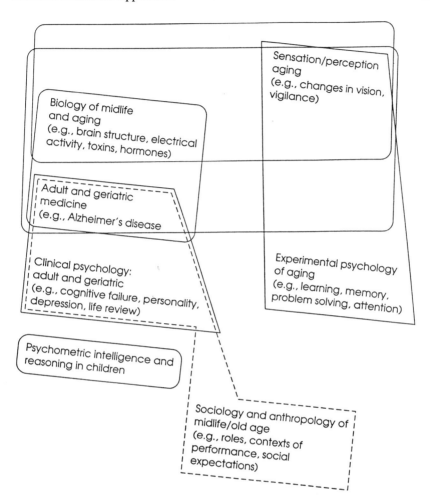

Figure 2.1. Traditions That Influence the Study of Cognitive Development in Middle and Old Age: Historical Overlap. (*Source:* Sinnott, 1996b. Reproduced with the permission of the McGraw-Hill Companies.)

aging. The other approaches sometimes overlap with each other, too, as shown by the figure. Recently, scientists in each of these areas have begun to explore questions in the other areas, using the preferred methods and tests of their particular areas. Thus, if I want to reflect today's reality, not historical reality, I might overlap *all* areas in the figure.

Table 2.1. Philosophical Models That Influence the Study of Adult and Old Age Cognition, with Some Results for Doing Science

Model	Results
Logical positivism	Polarities; categories and labels
Mechanism	Experimental study of cause and effect; linearity of assumptions; quantitative bias; reductionism
Systems theory	Multifactorial approaches; holism; nonlinearity; process emphasis; interactions expected; study of chaos and complexity
Humanism	Phenomenological studies; qualitative bias; focus on integration, wisdom, spirituality; added variables of communal ties, personal meaning
Developmental theory	Emphasis on process-over-time; emphasis on adaptivity; incorporation of models above; links to biological life span; links to other species and ecosystem; individual differences

I have included Figure 2.1 to give an idea of why developmental approaches such as Postformal Thought give fresh insights into adult cognitive changes. Notice that in the past, the field of adult cognition has rested on strong pillars of those sciences that can be described as reductionistic in nature, oriented to pathology, focused on a norm of young adult performance in Western middle-class cultures, and not oriented to change over time or process.

Table 2.1 summarizes some philosophical and scientific models of reality that influence the study of cognition in middle and old age in all of these fields. The kinds of demands generated by the models and worldviews at left in this table (which underlie the traditions listed in Figure 2.1) lead to the research goals, questions, and activities at right. For example, positivism (at left in Table 2.1), an underlying world-view of earlier biological inquiries connected with cognitive aging (Figure 2.1), leads to a labeling effort, a categorization, and a search for polarities (at right in Table 2.1). Adding the developmental model of reality adds to the range of outcome goals, questions, and activities in adult cognitive studies.

UNIQUENESS OF MIDDLE AGE AND OLD AGE

For the most part, prior investigations have been done by younger investigators who usually studied children, young adults, or, if they were interested in life-span studies, the very old. Notice that all these populations may safely be defined as "other" by the adult or middle-aged researcher. Of necessity, these investigators based hypotheses and theories on their own views of the world (as younger persons) and on the tools and paradigms they created for testing younger persons. But while all middle-aged and old adults have experienced being young, healthy young adults can only imagine the experience of being middle-aged and old. (If this seems an unimportant concern, imagine your elementary school-age or teenage child devising a test of *your* intelligence or cognitive ability, based on what they think is intelligent. How would you perform?) There is plenty of room for truly developmental questions of adult cognitive characteristics, questions added from the developmental perspective of adaptive mature adults.

Studies of postformal thought are also partly descended from the traditions of biology and the study of development of reasoning in children, via Piagetian studies. Based as postformal studies are on Piagetian inquiries into the development of adaptive intelligence in children, they lead postformal theorists to ask this question: "What is *adaptive* intelligence like, qualitatively, specifically in adulthood and old age?" They ask: "What (if anything) do the middle adult and the old adult do to know reality adaptively that is different at this stage of life from what went on before?" Since the emphasis in Piaget's original theory was on adaptive biology, epistemology, and child development, Piaget and early Piagetians spent their time examining qualities of reasoning, in children and adolescents, culminating in a list of qualitatively different stages: the sensorimotor stage, the preoperational transition period, the concrete operational stage, and the formal operational stage. It was clear when one heard Piaget speak that this focus on reasoning and young persons was meant to be a *first* step (you have to start somewhere . . .), and that stages were meant to show the order in which styles of thinking developed. Of course, the next thing that happened was the imposition of a different model for interpreting what Piaget was doing, with subsequent attempts to give age norms for development of each stage. The final state of Piagetian theory formation was the attack against straw men: Investigators tried to discredit statements that were never even a part of Piaget's theory, namely: "Everything important happens in childhood," "All behavior is based on reasoning," and "Age norms exist for an 'average' general development of reason."

Later, when I describe *post*formal thought, I will discuss it as an answer to Piaget's original, basic question: What is adaptive intelligence like at different points in development? Those who do research on the stage(s) after formal operations (i.e., *post*formal thought) usually do address their topic in the spirit of Piaget's original question. Their tentative answer is that many mature adults do demonstrate a different quality of adaptive intelligence than do most children or most adolescents.

NEW PHYSICS, CHAOS, AND OTHER COMPLEX MODELS

An interesting intellectual ancestor of postformal studies is the study of relativity theory and quantum physics, with their associated general systems, chaos, and complexity theory approaches. The most recent advance in this set of complex models is a theory of self-regulating systems. To describe physical reality in these newer ways, one needs to frame reality adaptively in ways more complex than formal operations, or learning theory, or psychometric intelligence, or information processing. The intelligence used by modern physicists to understand the new physics requires additional intellectual operations that seem to give us clues about how mature adults discover different ways to frame the reality of their lives.

Table 2.2 is a summary of some key aspects of the Theory of Postformal Thought. Listed in the table are key concepts shared between Postformal Theory and some other cognitive–psychological approaches. The table also summarizes and clarifies the genesis of the theory and the utility of postformal thought for the knower. It describes several other characteristics of the theory.

Table 2.2. Summary of Key Characteristics of the Theory of Postformal Thought

Links to:
  Piaget: postformal operations stage
  Riegel: beyond dialectical logic
  Information processing: expressed in larger problem space; expanded use of
    monitors and access devices; slippage of processing levels
  Problem solving: problem seen as ill-structured; no available heuristic; use of many
    logics; use of noncognitive states to reach new cognitive responses
  Philosophy: colored by existential, interactionist, humanistic views; postmodern
    structuralist perspective
  Clinical psychology: systems perspective, humanistic focus
  Philosophy of science: Kuhnian view of process; phenomenological and
    experimental approaches combined; a new physics reality
  Social development: social interactions being the genesis of this stage as interacting
    persons realize that they co-create reality
  Wisdom: realization of the limits of personal knowing
  Consciousness: awareness of the self-reference of truth at this stage
Genesis
  Social interactions: contradictions among formal logical systems of the knower
Purpose
  To adapt to the world by going beyond local consciousness to co-construct reality
Theoretical "kin"
  General systems, chaos, complexity theories; dialectical operations; wisdom; new
    physics and biology
Level of thought
  Metasystemic, holistic
Advantages of this concept
  Broad explanatory power; testability; many applications

Source: Sinnott (1989d). By permission of Greenwood Publishing Group, Inc., Westport, CT.

CHAPTER 3

What Characterizes
Postformal Thought?

For every perceivable phenomenon, devise at least six expla-
nations that indeed explain this phenomenon. There are
probably 60, but if you devise six this will sensitize you to the
complexity of the universe, the variability of perception. It
will prevent you from fixing on the first plausible explanation
as the Truth.
                    PAULA UNDERWOOD (NATIVE AMERICAN TRADITION)

This chapter describes a model of adult postformal cognitive operations that extends the thinking of Piaget to describe some intellectual
developments that may be unique to mature adults. Postformal operations as described here permit the adult thinker who continues his
or her logical development to operate adaptively in a world of relative choices. They also permit the thinker to overcome the fragmentation and isolation inherent in trying to know the emotional, interpersonal, and spiritual aspects of the world through abstract, formal
logic alone.
    My first purpose in this chapter is to describe the dynamics of
understanding or interpreting either relations among people or physical relationships that change constantly as a function of being known.
I want to provide a mechanism to explain how people adapt intellectually to the demands of everyday adult life, and to suggest how
shared relativistic thinking operations might influence individuals in
groups. I hope to describe a thinking state that relates contradictory
systems of formal operations to permit practical choice among those
systems. And I want to begin a discussion of those thinking operations
in terms of relations like those that underlie relativity theory and
quantum physics. All these elements of the discussion in this chapter

23

will be amplified in chapters to follow. These goals are not as incompatible as they may initially seem.

WHAT MAKES POSTFORMAL THINKING
OPERATIONS UNIQUE?

Postformal thought is made up of post*formal* thinking operations. According to Piagetian theory (Piaget & Inhelder, 1969), the developing person passes through the following stages of cognitive growth in an invariant order: sensorimotor, preoperational, concrete operational, and formal operational. An individual grows cognitively by assimilating a new piece of information to existing thinking operations and, if it does not fit, shaping the thinking operations until the fit is better. Thus, the thinking of the person and the reality that is known are, in a sense, both constantly changing and adapting to each other. With physical realities, *what is known about them* is adapted to the knower's structures; with social realities, their *very nature* can change by virtue of their being assimilated to the knower's reality or thinking structure.

Formal thinking was described by Inhelder and Piaget (1958) as the most sophisticated stage of Piaget's theory of cognitive epistemology. A person who can use formal operational thought can think abstractly (can think about thinking) and can use hypothetical–deductive reasoning as a scientist would. Postformal thought, by definition, goes beyond formal operations to the next step in the hierarchy of sophistication of thinking operations by which individuals come to know the world outside themselves.

The essence of postformal thought is the ability to order several systems of formal operations, or systems of truth. Doing so requires a degree of necessary subjectivity to make a commitment to one logical truth system and to act within that one system. It is relativistic in the sense that several truth systems do exist describing the reality of the same event, and they appear to be logically equivalent. The relativistic underpinning of postformal thought was studied and found later in postformal research tradition by Yan in an excellent series of research projects (Yan, 1995; Yan & Arlin, 1995). It is also non-relativistic in that the knower ultimately does make a serious commitment to one truth system only. That truth system then goes on to become true for the knower, since the knower's committed action makes it so. The knower finally sees that, as Bronowski (1974) realized, all knowing involves a region of uncertainty in which, somewhere, truth lies. All knowledge and all logic are incomplete; knowing is partly a matter of choice.

For example, the knower may be aware that both Euclidean and non-Euclidean geometries exist and that each has contradictory things to say about parallel lines. In Euclidean geometry parallel lines never come together; in non-Euclidean geometry, parallel lines eventually converge. These are two logically contradictory truth systems that are logically consistent within themselves and logically equivalent to one another. A mathematician bent on knowing reality must decide at a given point which system he or she intends to use, and must make a commitment to that system, working within it, knowing all along that the other system is equally valid, though perhaps not equally valid in this particular context. The selected geometry system then does become the mathematician's true description of the world. This is postformal thinking in action.

Looking at another example, relativistic, self-referential organization of several formal operations systems may also be seen. An attorney is trying to decide whether to defend a very young child accused of sexually assaulting another child. There is no conclusive physical evidence, and no witnesses were present. Both children are adamant in their stories, and both have been known to distort the truth to some degree when they were angry with each other. The attorney must make a commitment to a course of action and follow through on it as though that logical system were true. The attorney knows that, if she acts, that logical system may become true due to her actions, and will then become legal "truth" in court.

Formal operations presume logical consistency within a single logical system. Within that single system, the implications of the system are absolute. Postformal operations presume somewhat necessarily subjective selection among logically contradictory formal operational systems, each of which is internally consistent and absolute.

As is true for other Piagetian thinking operations systems, a knower who is capable of using postformal thought skips in and out of that type of thinking. Postformal thought is not always the best way to process a certain experience; it may be that sensorimotor thought (or some other stage of thought) is most adaptive on a given day. Perhaps a thinker with higher-order thinking skills is being confronted with a new situation for which she or he has no thinking structures to abstract from and no logical systems to choose among, not even sensorimotor logic.

For example, a grandparent of mine had never learned to drive, although she was a very intelligent woman. When presented with the chance to learn to drive, the first thing she did was to read about it, trying to use formal thought. Although she knew, after her reading, about "defensive driving" and other concepts such as the logic of the automotive engine, these "higher-level" skills did not help much when she first tried to engage the clutch and drive away smoothly. In fact, this particular grandmother was so shocked by her first-time, terrible, actual driving performance, compared to her excellent book understanding, that she panicked and let the car roll out of control until it came to a stop against a huge rock. Learning the sensorimotor skill of getting that stick shift car out on the road was "lower-level" thinking, but was the most adaptive kind of thinking for that situation. Using the right level of thought for the occasion may be one thing that people learn as they become postformal.

POSTFORMAL THOUGHT: A SPECIAL FORM OF INTELLIGENCE

What characterizes the adaptive power of postformal thought? Why is it helpful to an adult? How must an adult structure thinking, over and above the operations of the formal operational thinking of adolescents, to be in touch with reality and survive? The question here is not about specific facts the knower must know; rather, it is about general "higher-level" intellectual operations, or processes, that the knower must master to make sense of life and to make life work in situations that go beyond the demands of lower-level thinking.

Judging from their statements and from observation and task analyses, one key thing competent mature adults seem to need is the ability to choose one logical model (i.e., one formal operational structure) of the many possible logical models to impose on a given reality so that they can make decisions and get on with life. They also need to know that they are making necessarily (partly) subjective decisions about reality when they do this.

For example, you may be considering how to interpret some information you have read concerning adult cognitive abilities, so you open a textbook. In it, you find several models, each of which is an internally consistent logical system and has some merit (i.e., may be "true"). To actually interpret the information you have in hand, you have to choose a reality (a model) you want to adopt, for now. When you select the reality (model) you want to impose, you can go on to talk about the interpretation of your data. But you *know* that no outside authority or logic could have told you which model is "true"; you had to select one, act as though it were true, and go on with life or the experiment. This can be postformal operations at work in your life.

As another example, consider this situation: You know your parents are coming to town tomorrow. You realize from past experience that you and your parents have had good and bad times together during various visits over the years. You can meet them expecting the best or the worst to happen—and you *know* the nature of their visit is partly up to you. If you expect the worst, conversations probably will lead to confrontations, and it probably will be a bad visit; if you expect the best, your welcome will be more likely to lead to happier events. You will help decide the "truth" of your interaction with your parents—and you *know* this is how it usually works.

Notice that in these two examples, it certainly was important to know *content* about the subject. But something more was required, namely, the *general operational* rule that, when confronted with many "logics" about the "truth" of an event, or a relationship, one needs to select one and act as though it is true in order to go on with life. There is a kind of necessary subjectivity that must be used.

Knowing the general process rule and letting it filter your reality, consciously choosing the formal operations logical system you will impose and living it out as "true," are the essence of postformal operations. These two elements are often referred to as *necessary subjectivity* and *ordering formal operations*. The two elements are different from the kind of reasoning implicated in the last of Piaget's list of stages (i.e., formal operational logic) and are therefore considered key descriptors of a *post*formal "stage."[1] Since *post*formal thinking organizes formal thinking, giving a higher-order logic to formal operations below it, it is also post*formal*. I am emphasizing the logically distinctive elements here to highlight how postformal thought is a more complex Piagetian operation than formal thought. I am not emphasizing (yet) the social components that help it develop, the life-span developmental tasks that it seems to serve, the emotional life it seems to regulate, or the interpersonal tasks it seems to facilitate or that facilitate it. I am not yet emphasizing the context of thought. But these are all integral parts of postformal operations.

Postformal Thought includes cognitive epistemology (or the knowing of reality) and life-span development. Cognitive development is theorized to be accompanied by increases in social–cognitive experience and skills and by social interaction that leads to even

---

[1]The word "stage" is in quotes here to indicate that investigators argue over the qualities that make up a true stage (e.g., see Kramer, 1983).

greater cognitive development. During cognitive development, the ideas of others challenge the reality of the knower. Postformal Piagetian Thought is one theory that describes this development (Sinnott, 1984b, 1989a–c, 1990, 1991a–c, 1994b).

Such cognitive approaches go beyond traditional information-processing approaches. Postformal thought is a complex way of adaptively solving problems, one that develops with social experience, usually not before mature adulthood. It allows a person to solve problems even in situations in which conflicted formal operational belief systems and priorities overlap. In postformal thought, the solver faces multiple conflicting ideas about "what is true." The solver realizes that it is not possible to "get outside the mind" to find out which "truth" is "TRUE," but then realizes that the truth system picked as true will *become* true, especially in relation to other people, as the solver lives it to a conclusion.

RELATION TO THINKING
IN THE NEW PHYSICS

Piaget's analysis of formal operational thought provides sufficient structure to describe scientific thought up to and including the operations of Newtonian physics. It is insufficient, though, to describe the thought of physicists such as Einstein and those who came after him. Here we are faced with a quandary: How could Einstein think like that? How can contemporary physicists think as they do? And if contemporary physicists *can* think in such a complex way, the rest of us (or at least some of the rest of us) must also have the ability. What, if anything, is such a way of thinking good for in our normal lives?

Table 3.1 presents some Newtonian concepts or relationships in the natural world contrasted with the *post*-Newtonian idea about the same sorts of relationships. While we will talk more about this comparison in Chapter 5, just note for the time being that these are two very different but logically equivalent ways of thinking about the world and the realities around us.

To "know" a reality like this post-Newtonian physics one seems to mean that we must step very far away from an adaptive epistemological system based on *abstractions* from actions (i.e., a formal operational system) so that we can personally experience the actions themselves, at least at the level of the imagination. Piaget's basic ground for adaptive cognitive epistemology, after all, was taking action on objects, having experience with them.

Table 3.1. Newtonian and Post-Newtonian Concepts of Physical Relationships

Newtonian	Post-Newtonian
Space is Euclidian.	Space is non-Euclidian, except locally.
Time and space are absolute.	Time and space are relative and better conceptualized as a space–time interval.
Space is uniform in nature.	Space is composed of lesser and greater resistances.
Events are located topologically on a flat surface.	Events are located topologically on the surface of a sphere.
Undisturbed movement is on a straight line.	Undisturbed movement is on a geodesic, that is, by the laziest route.
Events are continuous.	Events are discontinuous.
No region of events exists that cannot be known.	Unknowable regions of events exist.
Observed events are stable.	Observed events are in motion, which must be taken into account in the observation.
Formation of scientific postulates is based on inductive or deductive reasoning.	Formation of scientific postulates also includes tolerance of contradictions inherent in the abstractions, due to the limits of human knowing or, possibly, of the human brain.
Causality is deterministic.	Causality is probabilistic, except in limited space–time cases.
Cause is antecedent to and contiguous with effect.	Cause is antecedent to and contiguous with effect only in limiting, local cases. When events are grouped about a center, that center constitutes a cause.
Egocentrism is replaced by objectivism in science.	Egocentric subjectivism and scientific objectivism are followed by taking ego into account in all scientific analyses.
Concepts in natural law conform to verbal polarized conventions of reality.	Concepts in natural law may appear contradictory in terms of verbal conventions.
The universe is uniform and locatable in linear time.	The universe is nonuniform, either because it is expanding irregularly or because it is continually being created and negated.

Source: Sinnott (1981). By permission of S. Karger AG, Basel, Switzerland.

Luckily, we also can experience directly and easily the kinds of "new physics" actions that are the grounding of postformal thought. We experience them when we have social or interpersonal relationships of any kind. The reason, as we will explore in more detail later, is that mature and functional interpersonal relations tend by their very nature to be post-Newtonian reality events. If they are viewed with a

Table 3.2. Interpersonal Relations in Formal Logical and Postformal Logical Thought

Formal logical thought

- There is only *one* way to structure our relationship to reflect its reality.
- Our relationship exists "out there" in reality.
- Our relationship involves only us, now.
- Since the relationship has *one* reality, there is no need for me to "match levels of thinking" with my partner to communicate.
- We can know the essence of each other.
- Role is more important than process.

Postformal logical thought

- Our relationship is logical within a set of "givens" that we choose to utilize.
- Our relationship is based on both our past relations to each other and our relations to other significant persons.
- Relating means "knowing where you are coming from" and interacting on that level.
- Relating means never completely knowing *you* because in knowing you I am necessarily subjectively co-creating you.
- Relationships are always "in process"; they cannot be described in a settled way until they end.

Source: Sinnott (1984a).

formal logic only (not postformally) they quickly tend to become fragile and very problematic. Table 3.2 provides a quick comparison of formal operational and postformal styles of interpersonal relations.

SEEING PROBLEMS (AND LIFE) AS ILL-STRUCTURED PROBLEMS

Postformal thought and postformal problem solving seem like perfect tools for working with what Churchman (1971) called *ill-structured* problems, whether such problems occur in formal logical problem solving or in encounters with everyday life. We often are faced with situations that seem to demand that we use logic but that have unclear goals. For example, in a work situation, we may have to choose between working toward maximizing productivity or working toward maximizing creativity. We might have to choose between creating the most logically elegant solution or the most practical solution. Such ill-structured problems have unclear goals, and no one optimum path toward the goal, and demand Kantian (or dialectical) inquiry systems. They seem to be more common in human experience than well-structured problems are. Well-structured problems have single solutions, optimal solution paths, and structured goals, and demand Lockean inquiry systems. We see relatively few such problems in life, but they are the norm in laboratory studies, in which problems are mostly defined and do not simply arise.

The study of the solving of ill-structured problems shows some age-related styles that have interesting implications for our thinking about postformal thought and development in midlife as described by Erikson (1982) and Schaie (1977–1978). Age-related styles seem consistent with potential strategic compensatory mechanisms for cognitive deficits at various levels of age and experience. We will discuss this in more detail in Chapter 9.

We *do* often solve ill-structured problems. The question is, how? We might assume that many of the processes used to solve well-structured problems (the kind often studied in laboratory studies) are used at some point. These processes are in the growing literature on problem solving, problem-solving models, and language comprehension. But investigators studying *ill*-structured everyday problems, such as understanding the point of discourse (Shank, Collins, Davis, Johnson, Lytinen, & Reiser, 1982) or planning a day's activities (Hayes-Roth & Hayes Roth, 1979), describe *additional* processes.

Even investigators who are using abstract logical (not everyday) problems of some kind often report processes that are beyond the purely cognitive (Schoenfeld, 1983). Additional processes, such as emotion, seem necessary to a more complete model of problem solving that can address both well-structured and ill-structured problems. When we examine actual problem-solving transcripts, there are too many steps that appear to be unexplained by traditional cognitive models. Postformal theory helps to explain additional processes going on during logical, everyday, or existential problem solving.

POSTFORMAL THOUGHT AND LEARNING

When we ask adults themselves how they learn and what they learn in mature adulthood and old age, we psychologists are dealt a blow to our egos. For the most part, adults ignore psychologists' theories. Instead, they say such things as these:

"I learned what was important in life."
"I learned how to make some practical things happen."
"I learned how to love and relax."

"I learned how to get along with people better."
"I learned there is more than one right way to do things."
And how did they learn? They give answers such as these:
"By having a family."
"By nearly failing at my job."

Is there a place for this kind of learning in the theory of postformal thought?

Learning is typically defined in undergraduate psychology textbooks as the acquisition of information and skills through experience or practice. Remembering (or "information retrieval") is an experimental operational definition of having learned something. Although traditional learning theory did not emphasize concepts of development, let us hypothesize for purposes of exploration that learning and postformal thought development could coexist within the same theoretical framework.

A relationship between learning and development might seem reasonable if we use a computer-programming analogy. In this analogy, both learning and development at first would seem data-driven. They represent a state of little order and a small database, so that data must be "loaded in" before any program to analyze the data can function. A pattern must be created from the first data in order to load further data most effectively. This state, early in developmental time, would have high potential and little order, in general systems theory terms. It would be very fact-oriented, data-driven, and concrete.

Later, a balance may be achieved between data-driven processing and order-driven processing. The latter "top-down" form of processing allows the initial structure to determine which available data will be taken in next.

We will see in Chapter 4 that certain types of learning seem to be needed before postformal thought can occur. For example, the thinker must learn that there really are multiple "true" views of reality. We will discuss, too, how possessing the skills of postformal thought can help a learner in a new field bridge conflicting "truths." For postformal learners, on a conscious or unconscious level, all learning becomes inherently social learning. Since any learned element can be used in either a postformal or a non-postformal way, the same learned facts can be building blocks for different types of realities, just as a book can be wildly different things—for example, the source of personal transformation or a paperweight.

Finally, postformal thinkers and non-postformal thinkers in the same situation learn different things. Let us say that an intimate couple is having, so to speak, a "postformal learning day," that is, experiencing a period of time when they are ready and able to think post-formally. If they are experiencing a conflict with each other on that day, they may learn to relate to each other in a new way that they co-created. But the same couple, on a "non-postformal learning day," in a very similar conflict, may only try to reinforce their prior negative beliefs about each other.

Thus, the joint influence of postformal thought and learning would seem to have widely divergent, significant consequences for individuals and, by extension, for groups and nations.

POSTFORMAL THOUGHT AS WISDOM

We can see a tendency for adult development models in traditional developmental theories to include "wisdom," more sophisticated interpersonal skills, concern for the group (over and above the self), deepening spirituality, and the ability to deal with paradoxes whether they are within the self, among persons, or in life itself. Troll (1985) and other textbook authors have reviewed major theories of adult development. These theories all hypothesize that mature adults have a tendency to tie things together, to give overall meaning to emotions and events, to find overall purpose in their feelings, lives, and deaths. Adult development, including postformal development, seems to mean increasing maturity, by all the definitions of maturity set out by Whitbourne and Weinstock (1979). The goal of later development seems to be to tie the individual's life to the group and to anchor both in a meaningful story that makes the struggle of existence worthwhile.

CHARACTERISTICS OF
POSTFORMAL THOUGHT

The main characteristics of postformal cognitive operations (Sinnott, 1984b) are: (1) self-reference and (2) the ordering of formal operations. Self-reference is a general term for the ideas inherent in the new physics (Wolf, 1981) and alluded to by Hofstadter (1979) using the terms *self-referential games, jumping out of the system,* and *strange loops.* The essential notion of self-reference is that we can never be completely free of the built-in limits of our system of knowing and that *we come to know* that this very fact is true. This means that we somewhat routinely can take into account, in our decisions about truth, the fact that all knowledge has a subjective component and therefore is necessarily incomplete. Thus, *any* logic we use is self-referential logic. Yet we must *act* despite being trapped in partial subjectivity. We make a decision about rules of the game (nature of truth), then act on the basis of those rules. Once we come to realize what we are doing, we then can consciously use such self-referential thought.

The second characteristic of postformal operations is the ordering of Piagetian formal operations. The higher-level postformal system of self-referential truth decisions gives order to lower-level formal truth and logic systems. One of these logic systems is somewhat subjectively chosen and imposed on data as "true." For example, Perry (1975) describes *advanced* college students as "deciding" a certain ethical system is "true," while knowing full well that there is no absolute way of deciding the truth of an ethical system.

This is also the logic of the "new" physics (relativity theory and quantum mechanics) (Sinnott, 1981). New physics is the next step beyond Newtonian physics and is built on the logic of self-reference. It is reasonable that the development of logical processes themselves would follow that same progression (i.e., Newtonian logic, then new physics logic) to increasing complexity. You have already seen in Table 3.1 some characteristics that separate new physics thinking from earlier forms.

A new type of cognitive coordination occurs at the postformal level. Another kind of coordination of perspectives also occurs on an *emotional* level, taking place over developmental time (Labouvie-Vief, 1987). This coordination parallels the cognitive one and is probably engaged in a circular interaction with it. Theorists expect that postformal thought is adaptive in a social situation with emotional and social components because it is hypothesized that postformal thought eases communication, reduces information overload, and permits greater flexibility and creativity of thought (Sinnott, 1984b). The postformal thinker knows that she or he is helping create the eventual *truth* of a social interaction by being a participant in it and choosing to hold a certain view of its truth.

Postformal thought has an impact on one's view of self, the world, other persons, change over time, and our connections with one another over time (Sinnott, 1981, 1984b, 1989b, 1991a–c). Tables 3.2 (presented above), 3.3, and 3.4 show how formal versus postformal thought leads to differing views of interpersonal reality (Table 3.2), what is prerequisite to thinking postformally (Table 3.3), and how postformal thought is activated and results of its use (Table 3.4).

Table 3.3. Prerequisites for the Shift from Formal to Postformal Thought

Ability to structure inherently logical formal systems.
Acceptance of the validity of more than one logical system pertaining to a given event.
Commitment to one set of a priori beliefs of many possible sets.
Awareness that the concept of causal linearity is erroneous when reality is multicausal.
Awareness that the same manipulation of the same variable can have varying effects due to temporal and environmental contexts.
Understanding that contradiction, subjectivity, and choice are inherent in all logical, objective observations.
Taking into account that contradictory multiple causes and solutions can be equally "correct" in real life, within certain limits.
Awareness that an outcome state is inseparable from an outcome process-leading-to-state.

Source: Sinnott (1984a).

THINKING OPERATIONS INVOLVED IN POSTFORMAL THOUGHT

In order to give a richer description of postformal thinking, it is important to look more closely at the details of this sort of thinking. The examination of operations that together make up the stage will make it easier for us to operationalize the concept so as to run studies and experiments related to postformal thought.

The operations described in Table 3.5 were taken from responses during open-ended dialogues—responses made by individuals who seemed to exemplify the wise, complex, generative, mature adult. These adults happened to cross my path while I was busy with other projects, but they caught my attention as adaptive and interesting people who not only survived the onslaughts of adulthood, but also actually thrived there in that developmental period. I wondered in particular what aspect of their cognition made them so good at life.

When I looked at the articulated thoughts of these adaptive people, I sensed that they had a special way of describing processes of solving problems, problems in both the narrower sense of structured logical problems and problems in the broader sense of difficult situations encountered in the course of a life (or a day!). I began to categorize the ways these people interacted with, constructed, and knew reality as they thought about it. That set of categories coalesced around the 11 key operations listed in Table 3.5.

These operations were the main ones, although others were present. The operations reflected some of the key thought patterns that distinguish the new physics from Newtonian physics. They also over-

Table 3.4. Activation of Postformal Thought and Results of Its Use

Three steps (1–3) might be involved in utilizing postformal thought once the potential for their use exists; four steps (4–7) might result from their use. Steps 1–4 are data-based; steps 5–7 are hypothetical.

Activation

1. Lack of fit occurs between formal operations and reality, as all data cannot be accounted for. A formal-operational respondent would notice the discrepancy but be willing to force the data into the given system.
2. Search for a better fit leads to test of new systems built by shifting either a prioris, logics, parameters, transforms, metrics, and so on. Fit may then be perfect, but is unlikely to be.
3. Realization occurs that fit may be arbitrary, at least for the present, and that system choice must necessarily be subjective for now. Subjective choice of best-fit system occurs.

Results

4. The individual reasons that if *this* choice of logical systems is necessarily partly subjective, perhaps other choices of logical systems are, too. The individual reevaluates other formal systems already in use.
5. Several persons together judge the "best-fit" system in a case in which no system completely fits a reality that involves them all and is seen somewhat differently by each. Group explorations concerning system choice lead to a consensus on the formal system to utilize in a given case. Necessary subjectivity leads to a collective cognition.
6. Shared invariants (e.g., agreed-upon metrics, logics, a prioris, parameters) persist beyond an individual or a group. Such shared referents may become the dominant philosophy or culture or belief if the necessary subjectivity of the choice is forgotten. If the fit with data still is not perfect, alternative logically competing systems are explored.
7. The expenditure of energy involved probably precludes frequent collective post-formal choices. However, individual searches for best-fit systems go on. Social change may result. Success, defined as construction of a formal system that fits with reality data in a given area, would most likely lower the use of postformal operations in that area. There is no limit to the use of postformal operations in interpersonal areas that are inherently constantly being co-created.

Source: Sinnott (1984a).

lapped nicely with some variables in the cognitive-problem-solving literature. It seemed possible to map their points of impact in the problem-solving process if I used tools such as the thinking aloud approach from cognitive studies and artificial intelligence (AI) models from the computer-based AI literature (e.g., see Ericsson & Simon, 1984; Newell & Simon, 1972).

A list of the key thinking steps or operations upon reality that appear to be present in postformal thought are in Table 3.5. The table

Table 3.5. Postformal Complex Thinking Operations

1. *Metatheory shift:* The shift between major ways of conceptualizing the demands of a problem, for example, the shift between seeing a problem as an abstract versus a practical problem. This is a major, paradigm-level, philosophical or epistemological shift.
2. *Problem definition:* Compared to operation 1, a relatively low-level labeling of the problem.
3. *Process–product shift:* Developing *both* a general process that would fit most problems like this but that provides no concrete answer to this particular problem *and* a particular answer to this very problem.
4. *Parameter setting:* Naming key variables that are limits to the solution to be created.
5. *Pragmatism:* Being able to select one of several created solutions as "best."
6. *Multiple solutions:* Being able to create more than one "correct" solution.
7. *Multiple goals:* Giving several points, each of which, when arrived at, would mean the problem is "solved."
8. *Multiple methods:* Giving several ways to reach the same solution.
9. *Multiple causality:* Considering several causes operating in the problem.
10. *Paradox:* Statements that indicate that the solver sees inherent contradiction in reality.
11. *Self-referential thought:* Statement of respondent's awareness of being the only ultimate judge of the appropriateness of a chosen logic, a logic which is then used to create a preferred solution.

Source: Sinnott (1991b). By permission of Greenwood Publishing Group, Inc., Westport, CT.

also describes major criteria for declaring that the operation is present in respondents' transcripts and narratives or in their answers to structured interviews, questionnaires, and computerized problem-solving tests. It is possible to consider respondents to be postformal thinkers even if they lack some operations in their answers. The more operations they show, however, the more certain the analyst is that they truly have attained postformal thought. Like so many other psychological qualities, postformal cognitive ability seems to be analogue rather than digital in quality.

It has proved useful to score some of the operations as being simply present or absent; others seemed to call for a count to be made of the times the operation appeared. This dual approach is based on practical concerns: Certain operations seem to occur once, at most, in response to a given problem or issue, while others occur often within one given issue or problem. For the latter, frequency of occurrence can be used in further analyses related to creativity, productivity, divergent thinking, and postformal thought. Within the list of operations, the following have generally been scored as simply present or absent: metatheory shift, process–product shift, pragmatism, paradox, and self-referential thought. The rest are scored for frequency, producing ratio-scale data, which can be reduced to nominal data as needed.

Rationale for the Operations

Metatheory shift indicates that the respondent is able to think in at least two logic systems because the respondent has shifted between an idealized and a practical interpretation of the problem and solved within those constraints. This shifting is important for postformal thought because one essential element of such thought is the ability to order several formal logical operational systems.

Problem definition is a second way to get at the respondent's ability to move within those two or more formal operational systems. If the respondent overtly labels the problem to be one of a class of logical problems (as is required to receive a point for this operation), the respondent is, by definition, excluding classes of problems to which the problem does not belong. The respondent is therefore ordering more than one system. Problem definitions are counted because the more there are, the better the assurance that logics are truly being shifted.

Process–product shift occurs when the respondent indicates that a problem is solved with either a *process* that is a logical system that would work in many cases like this problem case or a *product* that is a concrete solution, for example, a correct numerical answer. Again, two logical systems are coordinated in the respondent's thinking.

Parameter setting involves the respondent's limiting or organizing the problem space. This ability relates to postformal thought, since defining the space of the problem opens or limits the logical structure(s) of the problem. Again, to define the problem presumes that it could be otherwise defined, potentially having a different logic. Here, the number of defining acts becomes somewhat relevant. If the respondent gives only one parameter of the problem, he or she is less likely to be holding at least two logics about the problem.

Pragmatism, defined as being able to select one of several solutions as "better," is included in the operations set because the postformal thinker needs to be able to choose a single logic among more than one logic and make a commitment to go forward with that logic, as opposed to one of the other logics in play.

Multiple solutions is another of the counted operations. It is included because if one problem is posed but several solutions that are considered correct are generated, experience and probes of answers have led to the conclusion that more than one logic exists.

This finding suggests postformal thought. *Multiple goals, multiple methods,* and *multiple causality* are counted operations having the same rationale as multiple solutions.

Paradox is a device in literature and humor that takes advantage of the intellect's ability to find the weird aspect of the overlap of two logics. It therefore indicates the presence of ability to order logical systems. Paradox is not generated as frequently in structured and abstract testing situations as in everyday sorts of testing situations. The interesting people I noticed at first, when I was starting this series of studies, used paradox spontaneously as they spoke casually, and used it often.

Self-referential thought is the articulation of the respondent's awareness that he or she must be the ultimate judge of the logic to commit to. At this point, the respondent is conscious of using postformal thought.

Examples of the Operations

Table 3.6 contains a partial interview transcript from a professional in his 40s who was responding to structured problems. Some of the structured problems have been left in the transcript verbatim so that you can see examples of them. We will refer to this transcript at other times in this book to illustrate various concepts.

Statement III.16 is an example of *metatheory shift.* The speaker is shifting between relational logic and abstract logic.

A *problem definition* example includes statements I.11 and I.12. The speaker defines the problem as one of worker utilization.

Process–product shift is exemplified in statements V.10 (process) and V.5 and 6 (product). The speaker sees the "answer" as an ongoing general way to proceed and also as naming a specific concrete way to organize these specific people.

Parameter setting can be found in statements I.22 and 23 and V.15 and in many other places in this transcript. The respondent is expanding or contracting the possible elements to be considered in solution of the problem.

Pragmatism appears in the final choice seen in statements III.18–22. Here, the problem solver reviews other solutions and makes a commitment to keep one as the best of the lot.

Finding *multiple solutions* seemed easy for this respondent. Statements I.7, 15, 16, 19, 22, and 23 contain some solutions to this single problem.

Table 3.6. Protocol of Middle-Aged Respondent

I. *Magazine Workers:* You are supervising the assembly of a magazine that comes out monthly. Several workers are putting pages in order; others are binding the pages. The binders finish 20 magazines every half-hour. Those putting pages in order, however, finish 40 in two hours. Some of your workers are idle part of the time. Equal numbers of workers are performing each task, and there are more than enough supplies in each area. All of the workers can handle both jobs. What can you do to keep all of them equally busy?

1. Am I supposed to be saying anything as I go through the problem or read the problem?
2. OK. The first thing that hits me, I'm an editor of a journal, and so the workers, I bind pages, the whole bit. So, that's what pops in mind.
3. What I think I'm thinking right now is uh-oh . . . I don't typically do well with these type of problems.
4. *(chuckles)* You know, this reminds me of the type of problem where you have six workers producing *x* number of . . .
5. *(mumbles)* OK, I'm to attempt to solve the problem and talk as I go.
6. OK. I'm going to read back over this one more time.
7. I would, since the instructions aren't here pointing otherwise, I would assume that it would be OK to ah . . . this says that all workers can handle jobs. So, as there's a backlog, simply move employees over.
8. So, OK, the binders are finishing 20 magazines every half-hour, which means that they can basically finish 80 per two-hour period, whereas the, ah, the putting pagers *(chuckles)* finish 40 per two hours. So those binders would be idle.
9. As long as they can handle both jobs, I would move them over. The thing that I was hit with, which I think is fairly characteristic of me, is starting out by saying I'm never going to be able to do this.
10. And then just sitting down and start trying to generate some ideas, what is the essence of the problem.
11. As far as I would see it, it would be utilization of person-hours.
12. If I am truly on target with that being the essence of the problem, then it's a matter of . . . better utilization of person hours.
13. I think I kept the same idea on that.
14. I didn't generate too many different variations of it.
15. Yeah, sure, there are other solutions. Hire more people to put the pages together, so that you can actually match the amount produced by binders with the amount produced by the, ah, orderers or the putting pagers together.
16. Another possibility would be to, of course, slow down the actual work pace for the binders. They're the ones that're overproducing compared to the ones putting the pages together. To simply have them slow down and pace themselves a little bit, a little differently. The idea is to keep, to make sure that they are not idle. You want to keep them equally busy. But that doesn't necessarily eliminate the possibility of variation and time.
17. I don't know the problem is solved. I'm just offering a solution.
18. I don't know what you're going for. It is solved to my satisfaction.

Table 3.6. (*Continued*)

---

19. I have accomplished what is stated here, what can be done to keep all the workers equally busy. My first solution was to take some of the binders and have them also do the pages; that would satisfy this criterion.
20. Sure, it's possible to have some other criteria.
21. Being in a clinical field, I would also be concerned about how happy they are and the type of work they're doing.
22. So, there are some other solutions. "You want to keep them equally busy" does not necessarily say "equally busy doing this work."
23. So you could have them doing additional work. You could even have a recreation area for them that would keep them busy and happy. *(laughs)* I don't know if too many places are going to do it, but . . .
24. I'm sure I did operate by rules. I'm not sure how to actually itemize them. The first rule was to correctly read the elements of the problem.
25. Try to come to some conclusion on what the major elements are, what is not essential.
26. My first thought was that the binders and the people who put the pages together couldn't do the same work. And then I recall, yeah, that they can.
27. So, successfully identify the elements of the problem . . . what I would perceive to be the outcome of the problem, and then go through a logical process of trying to match elements with solutions.
28. My gut-level reaction would be (going back to what I said) that verge of panic. And then realizing, well, you can't do that, so let's go on and get down to it.
29. No, I haven't had open-ended [experience with problems like this]. Most of what I have had to do is in connection with SAT, GRE, where you're supposed to come up with *the* answer. *(chuckles)* Now maybe that's true here, too. I don't know, but from the elements of the problem and whatever is presumed to be the outcome, it is not a fixed answer.

II. *Camping:* You have six children who love to go camping. You have patience enough to take two children, but no more, with you on each trip. Each child wants a chance to camp with each of the brothers and sisters during the summer. How many trips would be necessary to give each child a chance to camp with every brother and sister if you take only two children a trip? How do you know?

1. Now this is more like what I'm used to. *(laughs)*
2. Interestingly enough, I don't feel that sinking feeling that I did on the first one.
3. OK. Two at a time *(mumbles).* It says I have patience enough to take two children, but no more, on each trip. Each child wants a chance to camp with each of the other brothers and sisters, try to give each child a chance to camp with every brother and sister *(mumbles).*
4. Oh, and ooh, ooh *(excitement)* it says, "How do you know?" *(laughs).*
5. OK, my approach to it would be much along the lines of the typical math problem, but I would try to work it out logically.
6. You have six children, taken two apiece and you want to match each one. So, it would be a matter of using a logic.
7. How do I know it would be through logic? That's interesting. I immediately jumped to the assumption that I was going to come up with a number. I read this twice and did not bother reading this last one.

(*continued*)

Table 3.6. (*Continued*)

8. Yeah, I read this twice. I may have read the last line . . . it just simply did not register because I had already locked in on the fact that it was going to be a math problem and I've got to come up with a number.
9. The criterion that I'm using right now is to try to examine the process by which I would have solved the problem. Now, I'm not sure whether that's what you're asking or not.
10. The criterion that I would have used if I would have continued to treat it as a math problem would have been what I would have perceived to be the correct answer. I would have simply sat down, worked it out on paper, but that's not the criterion I'm using now to say yes, I am finished with this problem.
11. I started to approach it with the same thing: a sequence of logic.
12. Then . . . I began to look at what would be involved in using logic, perhaps metalogic.
13. Well, my approach was very clear until I realized that I was off base. It was like da, da, the restored light bulb going. *(laughs)*
14. The biggest assumption was that it was a problem in mathematics that I would need to solve logically, which was incorrect.
15. My next assumption would have been that I must approach it . . . using metalogic.
16. If it were math, I would have gone ahead and worked it out. I am very poor in mathematics, so I would have gone the long route. We have six people and I would simply match them. *(chuckles)*

III. *Family Power Dynamics:* A family consisting of a father in his forties and a 15-year-old child live in the suburbs. They learn that a 70-year-old grandmother (the father's mother) will need to live with them due to her failing health. Right now, the family members have the following "power relationship": The father runs the house and the child follows his rules (father dominant; child dominated). The grandmother has made it clear that when she comes, she may not want anyone, including the father, telling her what to do. If the grandmother moves in, what are *all* the possible "power relationships" that might develop among pairs of individuals in the household? (The possible power relationships are: (1) dominant–dominated; (2) equal–equal.)

1. I would see this as a math problem. Well, again, math problem, problem in logic.
2. What you need to do is simply work out the combinations, the possible power relationships.
3. Ah . . . wait a minute . . . it does say "may not."
4. The problem is to work out the different power relationships and you have three people.
5. I thought I may have misread something for a minute, ah . . . I had remembered reading that the grandmother had made it clear she did not want anyone to tell her what to do.
6. Now I look back and it says "*may* not want."
7. So, that makes a better statement possible.
8. Do I work it out?
9. [Subject writes *D, d,* or *e* after each person's name.] *(pause)* You know, maybe there is another possibility but I'm honestly not seeing it. I would say three.

(*continued*)

Table 3.6. (*Continued*)

---

10. Oh no, wait a minute, that wouldn't be true either. I was going to say matching father with son, father with grandmother, so . . . but you can also flip-flop them because the father could take a dominated role as well as a dominant role.

11. So, six combinations.

12. It's getting more complicated.

13. No, it's more than six. You have three possibilities here. Dominant, dominated, and equal. And you have son . . . (*mumbles*).

14. No two people could have the same interaction.

15. Yes, they could.

16. I'm trying to figure out whether I could eliminate anything, and this goes beyond simply a problem in logic to the definition of relationships, for example. You could not have two people who were dominated in a relationship of two if you look at it from a psychological point of view or a rational point of view. You could have two people who were dominant.

17. So, you have some nice combinations there. (*laughs*)

18. Ah (*pause*), oh, wait a minute.

19. The prob . . . the problem specifies that the possible power relationships are (1) dominant and dominated and (2) equal and equal. So you have only two possibilities. Forget the six, forget the more than six . . . (*chuckles*).

20. What are all the possible power relationships that might develop among pairs? And it says the possible power relationships are dominant and dominated and equal and equal, so you only have two.

21. Is this a trick problem? (*laughs*)

22. Yeah, I will stop there. It's interesting how often I must conceptualize this as being right or wrong. Like it's built into the system.

23. Whether it's solved is going to have to depend on which way I choose to interpret this.

24. If math, by going ahead and working out the possible combinations. I would do that by eliminating anything to do with the ability to interact. So, I've got three possibilities and three people. So I've got, ah, x number of combinations.

25. If I look at it strictly as a relationship problem, I'm going to have to eliminate some of those possibilities.

26. Well, no, I wouldn't either. Both people could be playing a dominated or attempting to play a dominating role.

27. And the problem was almost from a logical/analytic point of view. Then I immediately slipped more over and began to think along the lines of quote, unquote intuitive. Ah, more concerned with relationship qualities than, ah, quantities.

28. Apparently, in all three problems my first approach was to treat it as a problem in logic.

29. I will pat myself on the back and say that at least I was able to back up every once in awhile.

30. The confusion that I generated for myself came out of trying to match a preconceived idea of how I should approach it . . . with the elements that were here.

31. I came up with a way of looking at it and tried to match the elements of the problem to that perception. And then tried to shake it down to see which one would be the best possible fit.

Table 3.6. *(Continued)*

---

32. My gut-level feeling after stumbling over this, first reaction was "How could you be so stupid? There's the statement there telling you what it was" *(chuckles)*. The second thing was "Wait a minute, is that statement really saying what I think it's saying?" *(laughs)*
33. All of a sudden I've got myself wrapped up. And that's why I said, "No, I'm going to stick with this." *(laughs)*
34. It was more blind determination than thinking I really have a good answer here.

IV. *Vitamin C:* Six foods are listed below. All six are good sources of Vitamin C. Your doctor has asked you to eat two *different* foods that are good sources of Vitamin C every day. (1) How many different pairs of foods might you eat when you make *all possible pairs* of the six foods? In other words, how many possible pairs are there? (2) In each pair you make, how many portions of each food must you eat to get at least two units of Vitamin C from that pair?

1. OK, do I write on here? [Writes 5, 4, 3, 2, 1, . . . 15.]
2. OK, so far I have not treated section 2 at all, so I segmented the problem.
3. I am now making the assumption that 2 will follow from 1 and not invalidate it.
4. So, I went ahead and came up with an answer for part 1. It says how many different pairs of foods might you eat to make all possible pairs of the six foods?
5. Wait a minute. *(chuckles)* How many different pairs of foods might you eat when . . . *(mumbles)* yeah, all possible, OK.
6. In other words, how many possible pairs are there? *(mumbles)*
7. It was incorrect.
8. It's just what I mean by being poor in mathematics. I cannot, to save my life, remember how to do this doggone thing.
9. I'm going to say 121.
10. I don't think that is correct.
11. I was setting it up so that I could match possible pairs, so if you take one orange, you'll have five combinations of matching. 'Cause that was my first number.
12. Then eliminating orange, since it has been matched with each one of them.
13. Then I go on to grapefruit.
14. And then you have, ah, four possibilities . . .
15. Ah, 20, 60 *(mumbles)*, it's 121, yeah, 121.
16. What I did the first time was to add it.
17. Now wait, I've got five pairs *(mumbles)* . . . it is an addition.
18. It's a good thing I went into clinical than to this. *(chuckles)*
19. I'm going to go ahead and say it's 15.
20. I honestly cannot or am not sure. Again, I'm trying to use logic here.
21. It would be nice and neat if I just could remember the formula for doing this.
22. So, I got, first of all I have five pairs of combinations. And I have another four pairs, so there would be no reason in multiplying those at all, so 15.
23. This is weird. *(laughs)* I see I'm going to have to do more thinking about this one.
24. How many portions of each food must you eat *(pause)* . . . with each pair? How many foods must you eat to get *(mumbles)* . . . it does say at least . . . *(pause)*.
25. It would be *one* with the exception of pairings with the grapes, which would require two.

Table 3.6. (*Continued*)

26. You can't have it there and not eat it? I'm not getting that from the problem" I'm imposing that on the problem. *(chuckles)*
27. Grapefruit, which is two units, would take care of the problem in and of itself. So if it is paired with anything else, with the exception of the grapes, you would be over two.
28. But it says "at least two," which means to me that you can go over the limit.
29. So, the only problem would be when you would have to pair with 20 grapes, which would require 2 units of grapes or 2 portions of the grapes in order to get the 2 units, with the exception of grapefruit, and then you do not.
30. I pretty much stuck with the way I originally saw the problem.
31. You don't have to necessarily treat it as a problem in mathematics, using those terms interchangeably here today for some strange reason, but it was a problem in logic again.
32. As I saw it, the question being asked in number 1 was to come up with all possible pairs, implying the quantity.
33. So, I set about trying to generate a number.
34. The second part is interesting. I just realized I didn't try to generate a number there.
35. It's interesting, because on the first part I had to actually make it concrete for myself to do it.
36. And I had switched it, the first time I saw it as a simple matter of adding these up, then I said no, that couldn't be right, then I multiplied them and realized well, oh, my God, you're generating all kinds of things there, none of which have to do with the problem, so I went back to the addition again.
37. I was trying to link it back to some vague remembrance of a formula for generating all possible pairs.
38. Well, actually it would seem like, it says how many, so it would seem like the second part would call for a number.
39. It's interesting I didn't approach it that way, though.
40. I simply tried to look at, and immediately jumped to the two unusual units . . . the two units for the grapefruit and the half unit for the grapes, and concentrated on those rather then actually going in and saying OK, now, I have an orange and tomato juice that would be one unit each, so that would meet the requirement.
41. So, I would need one portion of orange, one portion of tomato juice.
42. You could approach it a couple different ways every time.
43. One would be to make it concrete and map it out. I've got one orange and one tomato juice, so I have two units there. So I only need one portion of each, then an orange with cabbage, then an orange with the greens . . .
44. What I actually did was then to focus on "the grapefruit matched with anything takes care of it." But the grapes matched with anything but the grapefruit would require two units.
45. As I recall what actually struck me, when I looked at that second part and then glanced down to here, was "I really don't want to sit here to work this out." *(chuckles)* So I took the easy way out. I just didn't want to sit and write them out, so I looked at the two unusual aspects of it.

(*continued*)

Table 3.6. (*Continued*)

V. *Bedrooms:* A family consisting of a mother in her forties, a father in his forties, a 10-year-old girl, a 12-year-old girl, and a 15-year-old boy live in a small two-bedroom house in Detroit. One of the bedrooms is large and well-decorated, and has a single bed; the other bedroom also has a single bed. This summer, the family learns that a grandfather who lives alone in a one-bedroom apartment two blocks away can no longer live alone. He might move in with the family. What are all the possible ways that the six persons can use the two bedrooms in the house?

1. *(laughs)* I see this as being more of a problem of generation of ideas rather than . . .
2. It says what are all the possible ways six persons can use the two bedrooms in the house.
3. OK, you have two beds, each of them single, yeah, two bedrooms each with a single bed in it.
4. So, unless you're going to pile them three deep, then I don't really need to worry about that [using the beds] at all.
5. One of the things we can do is not have him move in.
6. We can take one of the single beds out, have all three girls have pads on the floor, put the father out on the front porch, I mean there are all kinds of different possibilities here, ah, in the use of bedrooms, so I'm going more the generating ideas on how two bedrooms might be used.
7. It would not be a problem in logic.
8. It wouldn't necessarily eliminate logic, but it's more of a problem of creativity. What kinds of things can we do?
9. You know, we can burn one of the bedrooms and eliminate . . . you know *(chuckles)*.
10. Well, I think the answer would be for me to generate as many ideas as I could about the possible uses for the bedroom.
11. *(laughs)* Unless you specifically ask me to do that, I'm going to just leave that as my answer.
12. You could turn it into a problem in logic. I just did not take a look at it from that particular perspective . . .
13. You can, and it is possible to, put two people on a bed, even a single bed, they're going to be crowded, but you still get them all in there.
14. Another possibility is to have the one person on a single bed, two people on each side; they rotate each night. So, then you've got a constant movement.
15. The basic thing was to eliminate how to match, because I'm dealing with a single bed, two single beds and six people.
16. You dealt with a pair as your basic element. Here the type of structure existing with the last problem does not exist, at least as I am seeing it.
17. I just jumped immediately to the idea that it was going to generate possible . . .
18. It's interesting, because with all the others, I seemed to approach it first as a problem in logic. And then that second step was to look at it from a different angle. This time I actually reversed that process. I don't know whether that's because I looked at all the others the other way.

VI. *ABC:* Six letters of the 26 letters of the alphabet appear below. Imagine that you're making pairs of the letters, writing down all the possible ways of putting two

Table 3.6. (*Continued*)

---

different letters together. How many pairs will you have when you make all possible pairs of the six letters? Remember, although any letter will appear several times in *different* pairs, the same letter should not appear twice in the same pair.

1. My first reaction on reading this is, it looks very similar to one of the others. So, I'm going to read back now to see if that is true.
2. It's interesting. I'm beginning to look at this as, "OK, these aren't straightforward. What is it that I'm supposed to be looking for?"
3. *(mumbles)* . . . pairs of letters, OK, that sounds all right. *(laughs)* Pairs of the letters, write down all the possible ways . . . *(chuckles)*.
4. Can I, I can go back, can't I? *(excitedly)* I'll go ahead and do this one first.
5. I'm curious now as to the wording on that other problem.
6. It just occurred to me what was said here was "writing down all the possible ways of putting two different letters together." How many pairs? It's interesting . . . and again I'm approaching this from another point of view, not logic at all. In other words, I'm looking at different angles of it. "How many pairs will you have when you make all possible pairs?" Now these two sentences actually, to me, imply two different things.
7. "Remember, although any letter will appear several times in different pairs, the same letter should not appear twice in the same pair." Oh yeah, I see that one is fairly straightforward. But now I can interpret this a couple different ways.
8. I can have A and B, that would be a pair.
9. I don't know if I can do this or not. *(laughs)*
10. So if I did all possible ways, I'd have to turn it all different angles, etc., etc., etc. [He is rotating the paired letters, each time a few degrees farther right, on paper.]
11. So, you know you have an infinite number of different combinations.
12. Ah, how many pairs will you have when you make all possible pairs? Now that to me is a different statement.
13. "How many different pairs will you have when you make all possible pairs of the six letters?" It goes back to being a similar problem to what I did here [Vitamin C].
14. What I wanted to check was to see how that was stated here.
15. So, I actually have two possible ways of reacting to this. I could take it very literally and say, OK, by "ways" you mean what is stated here in the second sentence [which implied rotation to the subject], and that's the one I'm going to go by.
16. Or I can choose to look at it as actual ways, and this is, ah, simply an additional statement or contradictory statement rather than a qualifying statement.
17. I'm going to choose the other route and say you have a number of possibilities here.
18. I keep saying logic versus intuitive. That's not true. There is a logic to all of this.
19. You literally end up with an infinite number of ways of putting two letters together to make a pair, 'cause a pair could be anything.
20. And then, after I get all possible combinations for an A, B, then I have the A, C, the A, D, etc.
21. So, as I said, I'm going to end up literally with an infinite number of possibilities because we even break this down into millimeter movements.

(*continued*)

Table 3.6. (*Continued*)

---

22. The choice has to be coming from my set, which has somehow changed.
23. The set was originally one of trying to break everything down into its logical components. If it was a sequence, then what are the logical sequential steps?
24. And somehow or another, I shifted gears.
25. I think it was because after hitting the first couple, it began to register as more of a test in creativity.
26. I'm trying to superimpose my assumptions about the project itself on the task being given to me.
27. Which may or may not actually be true, and that's, I think that shows up very clearly here. If I'm allowing that assumption to influence the way I look at this, I come out putting the emphasis on this particular thing.
28. And if I don't allow my assumption to enter into the picture, then I'm going to have to go with the other statement.
29. If I stay long enough . . . I might even come up with another one [assumption]. *(laughs).* . . .
30. Actually, what you're doing is taping my imagination.

Source: Sinnott (1989d). By permission of Greenwood Publishing Group, Inc., Westport, CT.

Multiple goals are also apparent in the transcript from problem I. Notice that, as so often happens, there are fewer goals than solutions. Statements I.12, 16, and 21–23 represent some goals for the respondent.

Multiple methods are also seen in this transcript. To reach the goal of "keeping them equally busy," the respondent comes up with several ways to do so, including statements I.19 and 22 and 23.

An example of an awareness of *multiple causality* is in statement V.18, in which the respondent examines the several demands and events leading up to his work on this problem. Notice that the thinking aloud method gives evidence of certain important considerations that enter into the respondent's problem-solving solving process that would never be seen in a more structured test.

Paradox is exemplified outright in statements III.18–21 and more subtly in statement VI.30. This respondent frequently comments on the paradox of his performance as a problem solver.

Self-referential thought can be found in statements VI.15–18. The speaker realizes that *he* must choose the logic on which a final answer to this problem, and others, will rest.

MEASURES OF POSTFORMAL THOUGHT

Appendix A has information on the measures that have been developed so far. We have created a standardized interview form; a thinking aloud form, with and without probe questions; a paper-and-pencil form specific to selected job contexts; and a computerized version. All of these versions are useful in obtaining information on a respondent's use of postformal operations. All forms but the paper-and-pencil form (which asks directly about the use of operations at work) use 6 to 12 problems that are based on formal combinatorial and proportionality reasoning in various contexts. The various forms are reliable and have face validity, predictive validity, and construct validity. Transcripts can be reliably coded using the scoring methods outlined above. Postformal thinking operations reliably appear in the thought of adults in every subsample tested to date.

SCORING CRITERIA FOR POSTFORMAL OPERATIONS

The scoring criteria for postformal operations, in some detail, are in Appendix A. I am grateful to Merrie Standish for working with me on a more "user-friendly" articulation of these scoring and coding guidelines as she worked on her thesis studying mental and physical activity and postformal thought in older adults (Standish, personal communication, 1997). Further comments and suggestions by readers are always welcome. I will be happy to consult with researchers using these scoring and coding guidelines or to give workshops on coding.

Now that we have seen examples of the operations of postformal thought, let us turn to a consideration of how this thought might develop.

CHAPTER 4

Development of Postformal Thought

Relationships are the crucible of the transformative process.

MARILYN FERGUSON

SOCIAL IMPETUS
FOR THE DEVELOPMENT
OF POSTFORMAL THOUGHT

Relationships are behaviors in which some shared truths are essential. Shared truth is shared between or among individuals in a family, couple, or society, individuals who each initially have their own views of what is true. Those truths are merged to form a couple's outlook, or even, as Ferguson (1980) puts it, a "cultural trance." Relationships are therefore likely to be fertile grounds for the initial logical conflicts that could nurture development of postformal thought. Two or more human knowers each bring their personal truths with them into a relationship. To have an interaction, they must somehow make those truths match in order to communicate. This necessity presents a possibility for them to enlarge their truth to accommodate to the truth of another in order to communicate well. When marriage partners, for example, each try to see the other's point of view, they may be trying to expand their logics to see reality through another's logical reality frame. If the framing were complex enough, the intelligence they would be using when they succeed at this task would be postformal.

Creating a shared reality is something friends or partners do all the time, together concomitantly nurturing their postformal thought development. Whether they develop common dreams about the future, common descriptions of the personality of someone they both know, or common values to share with fellow Democrats or Republicans, shared co-created truth is part of the interpersonal reality that makes interpersonal relations interesting and emotionally meaningful. In midlife and old age, many of the tasks of that life period are social and interpersonal, and cognitive processes must serve these ends too. I argue (Sinnott, 1994a) that creativity in midlife and old age takes on specific cognitive qualities (i.e., those of postformal thought) that are adaptive in everyday life because they regulate intellectual and emotional stimulation from events or people. Such regulation seems to be an important task of midlife and old age. This complex cognition is a bridge between affect and cognition and between one person and other persons. It is a way to make the demands and practical concerns of adult life meaningful. The products of this mature thought may be better reflections than the young person's thought, well-formed products of the union of emotion and cognition, of heart and mind. Midlife issues may be the key issues that motivate creative postformal thinking about the shifting nature of socially constructed reality in everyday cognitive events. For example, as baby boom generation members age, movies, TV shows, conferences, and songs all pick up their growing interest in generativity and integrity.

This complex postformal cognition can be described using research data and can be manipulated experimentally. Its style changes during the adult life span, at least so far as we can determine from the only set of studies, cross-sectional studies, that have been performed so far.

HEALING THE SPLIT BETWEEN "PARTS" OF HUMAN DEVELOPMENT

One of the small miracles of the ideas we have been discussing is that by using them we can take major steps to integrate the artificially separate "parts" of human behavior and development so that adult functioning can begin to make sense as a whole again. This integration can be immensely important for many applied areas of psychology.

Turn for a moment to a phenomenological realization: Many of us who are adults (more or less) do not perceive a split between mind and the social and emotional factors in everyday life, but we see such a split in research and in theory. To some extent, of course, it is necessary to be analytical and, to that end, to pare down research questions to be manageably small. But what an exciting challenge it is to start to bring the parts back together again in developmental and cognitive research instead of relinquishing the task of integration entirely to fields such as clinical psychology.

One main point around which this current potential synthesis revolves is that adult cognition can be construed as cognition in which the organism is adaptive on *all* levels of its functioning, that this adaptiveness involves cognition, emotion, and interpersonal relations, and that by interacting with important others in whom we have emotional investments, we can grow cognitively in mature years. One special domain we are considering in order to analyze that adaptivity, then, is the social–interpersonal domain.

But studies of greater complexity demand that we make clear what level of analysis we are using at any point. We also need to make clear in complex developmental questions whether we are addressing the *content* of that development or the *process* by which it occurs. Do we want to answer current-state questions, or dynamic, change-over-time questions, or questions about philosophical and epistemological implications? Are we speaking about truth on a microscopic or a macroscopic level? In analytical studies of lesser complexity, answers to such questions are often taken for granted. But we need to analyze these many aspects of our questions in order to effectively create the whole picture or synthesis about cognitive adaptivity. Thus arises another paradox: We must be analytical about our paradigms and methods to achieve our goal of being synthetic, "big picture" thinkers. The balance between polarities, in this case between analysis and synthesis, must still be maintained.

It may take use of a general systems theory approach or a new physics approach, at least at the level of metaphor, to deal with these questions. There may be some sort of general law operating here: At an early level of a research question, one separates things; at a later level, one joins things in a synthesis; at an even later level, one shifts realities among the levels of a system so that one is always creating and destroying analyses and syntheses simultaneously, seeing this adaptive reality as the wave and the particle.

Many facts that at first seem to contradict each other can all be true simultaneously from a new physics systems perspective, and so can they also in dealing with interpersonal relations and postformal thought. As we will see in Chapter 5, human interpersonal relations are much like the actions of willful planets with intersecting gravitational fields. As living systems interface with each other over time, they truly *are* determined by their initial states or qualities and they truly *are* created anew in relationship. These "contradictions" are simultaneously true from a general systems viewpoint. Living systems truly *are* determined by their experience or personal additive history and *also* by their place in history (i.e., by their developmental space–time coordinates). The contradictions of their pulling as they pass each other do change them, but they change in a chaotically ordered way.

Now, if those living interacting systems we just mentioned also are aware, have intentions and interpretations—in other words, if they are intelligent—then imagine their power to create, intentionally, as part of this process. They might come to see that the truth of their social interactions is partly based on what they know and feel. Their own personal interactions with each other might teach them the nature of the cognitive and physical laws around them. We and they might learn through interpersonal experiences about the nature of known truth, about thought processes, about the nature of the mind's filters, and about postformal thought.

ADULT TASKS: IDENTITY FORMATION, GENERATIVITY, AND INTEGRITY

In thinking about this whole developmental question further, let us examine one or two typical tasks of midlife and old age that are present in more than one culture and that are addressed in adult development theories, particularly Erikson's theory. We will see that these tasks are interpersonal and have the feeling of a systems theory.

At the entry point of midlife, perhaps around the age of 30, the younger adult must make a choice of a way to go, of a life to choose, in industrial cultures of multiple possibilities (Levinson, 1978; Perry, 1975). Even as that person sees the relativity of many truths, he or she must make a passionate commitment to live out only some of these choices or truths (Frankl, 1963; Perry, 1975; Polanyi, 1971). Doing so constitutes identity formation. That choice also involves relinquishing several illusions including (Gould, 1978) that there is only one correct way to proceed in life and that one's parents have the knowledge of that single way.

Erikson (1950) also describes the tasks of the midlife and old individual as developing generativity and integrity, that is, mentoring and caring for others, creating either children or contributions that will outlast the self or both, and finding a sense of the satisfying completeness of one's life story and one's place in the overall story of life. Again, the sense of existential meaning is in relations with others and the creation of a personal truth.

Many authors speak of midlife as a time to deepen commitment and to choose deliberately what one's life will mean (e.g., Frankl, 1963; Havighurst, 1953; Yalom, 1980). One must choose when (and why!) to deploy one's resources, newly aware of their limits. This choice of meaning, if it is truly adaptive, also incorporates one's emotional side, allowing for conscious orchestration of one's emotional and cognitive life leading both to emotional self-regulation (Labouvie-Vief, 1982, 1987) and (we hope) to maturity and wisdom, in due course (Chinen, 1992).

The midlife adult begins to see a bigger picture that involves time and persons existing before and after him or her. As Riegel (1975) suggests, discord or disharmony, whether from other people, a rapidly shortening lifetime, or the pressure of multiple social roles, demands a new adaptive stance. Jung (1930/1971) speaks of midlife as a point at which there is a new incorporation of the unknown sides of the personality into the conscious self.

These midlife tasks involve bridging realities, entering the reality of another person, and developing complex concepts of the self, of success, of personal continuity. By this time in life, the person has gathered the skills and the experience to make this potential midlife leap in thinking structures. Spurred by everyday social encounters, fresh from the everyday problem-solving tasks of creating a marriage, a long-term friendship, a parent–child relationship, an organization, a social role, a self, the adaptive midlife adult is primed to make new realities. Like the developing child in Piagetian theory, the midlife adult seems to use assimilation and accommodation to become skilled in new ways of filtering life with a new postformal logic that combines subjectivity and objectivity.

CAN THEORIES OF ADULT INTELLECTUAL DEVELOPMENT BE SOCIAL?

Traditional studies have described typical intellectual development in adulthood and old age as part of the continuum of intellectual development in childhood and adolescence. The traditional assumption has been that one of the following will be true: (1) Adults' and younger persons' intellectual abilities do not differ in characteristics, but adults decline in performance. (2) Adults' and younger persons' intellectual abilities do not differ in characteristics, and adults maintain performance. (3) Adults' and younger persons' intellectual abilities do not differ in characteristics, but adults perform better than younger persons. This traditional assumption seems to obtain whether the research domains include intelligence tests, problem-solving tests, or performance on Piagetian tasks, the three main types of intelligence tests traditionally given to adults. Within these traditions, which have been reviewed extensively in mainstream psychology, all three positions have received some support, depending on the type of design, the contexts of tasks, and the ages sampled. Decline is reported most frequently. An exception can be found in literature on wisdom, but wisdom studies will not be discussed here, since such wisdom has a special research operational definition that is expected from only a relatively few exceptional adults.

The impression a reader obtains from these traditional studies is that investigators have focused on the second half of each of the three assumption statements (i.e., that the performance of adults either decreases, stays the same, or increases) and more or less ignored the identical first halves (i.e., that the abilities of mature adults and younger adults are qualitatively the same and have similar characteristics). By contrast, in popular literature, more time is spent discussing the special intelligence that comes with the experiences of adulthood with its responsibilities and changes in perspective. The fruits of such experience would hardly be tapped fully by traditional tests, which were designed, after all, either for children or for very young adults. From the comments of some mature test takers (e.g., in Sinnott & Guttmann, 1978a,b), the traditional tasks are viewed as either "senility tests" or boring infringements on adults' time. How might adult intellectual abilities be appropriately tested if investigators truly believed that significant intellectual development leads to qualitative differences in thought in adulthood? What if tasks were developed using success in adult life, rather than success in school, as a criterion?

A small number of investigators who first began considering these questions included Piaget (1972), Riegel (1973), Clayton (1975), Sinnott (1975), Arlin (1975), and Schaie (1977–1978). Piaget suggested that adults be tested using forms of his tasks contexted in the everyday activities of the test taker to measure true ability, but did not clearly postulate that the type of ability the test taker had might be a qualitatively different structure. Yet Piaget's essential position, that intelligence is an adaptive function, should be equally true for adults and children, leading to the hypothesis that adult intelligence is qualitatively different from that of children. Arlin and Riegel began to think of the nature of adult intelligence as problem finding, based on Riegel's dialectical model. We have found evidence that the cognitive and behavioral synthesis of developmental dimension conflicts discussed by Riegel, which is adaptive for adults in that it lets them make life decisions, may be a form of intelligence unique to adulthood (Sinnott & Guttmann, 1978a,b). In one report that was never significantly expanded or clarified, Clayton described the general qualities of mature intelligence as qualities of Erikson's last developmental task, achieving integrity through contradictive cognition. Schaie suggested that abilities be measured by means of selected Wechsler Adult Intelligence Scale (WAIS)-type skills conforming to the needs and demands of the tasks of life periods, at least those typical for Western industrial society. For example, measures in the "responsible stage" would relate to building a family and might test using definitions and analogies about that task. And my own approach, as evident in this book, names the uniquely adult intellectual quality as *postformal thought.* These were the first pioneers in theorizing about the unique qualities of adult intelligence.

Adults themselves feel that they can define the nature of intelligent behavior in adulthood. They suggest that it is different from intelligence in youth. As part of an ongoing study, I asked adults in early adulthood (20s and 30s), middle adulthood (40s and 50s), and mature adulthood (60s and older) to respond to open-ended questions concerning the intellectual skills needed by persons at various times in life. I also asked about the behaviors that would be considered intelligent at those stages. Virtually every respondent to date has mentioned interpersonal skills as important at every stage in adulthood, irrespective of the respondent's age, gender, or level of education. "Intelligence" at every age virtually always included the ability to understand and deal with the complexities of interpersonal events, again irrespective of the respondents' levels of education, gender, or age. Respondents also frequently mentioned skills and behaviors related to adaptation to changing life events and to coping with change. These preliminary suggestions about the nature of adaptive adult intelligence, made by mature adults, would suggest that we turn away from traditional models to a social and cognitive approach that incorporates aspects of adaptive interpersonal skills.

STAGES AND DYNAMICS OF
DEVELOPMENT OF INTERPERSONAL
COGNITION PROCESSES

Development from sensorimotor operations to postformal operations is easiest to understand in the context of interpersonal relations structures, a knowledge area high in necessary subjectivity. It may be easier to understand postformal thought in the area of interpersonal relations if the earlier stages of thought are outlined. I will be emphasizing stages in the understanding of interpersonal relations processes, stages based initially on Piaget's notions of cognitive development.

Stages are not meant to emphasize permanent levels. They are hierarchical only at acquisition. The dynamics described here are as important as the stages, which are categories of points frozen in time. Descriptions of hierarchical levels of understanding of interpersonal relations are presented in Table 4.1 and are explained in the following

Table 4.1. Examples of Interpersonal Cognition Stages, at Various Levels of Temporarily Equilibrated Interpretive Complexity

Level I

Sensorimotor—based on needs, gut reactions; nonmutuality:
• Parent sees child as gratifier of needs, or too demanding.
• Intimate partners think they can not live without each other.

Level II

Preoperational—ego-deformed; single roles; nonmutuality:
• Child seen as extension of parent and parent's identity.
• Intimates expect that they will always agree.

Level III

Concrete operational—relations can be hierarchically classified; mutuality:
• Child views parent as parent/scientist, and as former child.
• Intimates see each other as able to have separate, noncouple lives.

Level IV

Formal operational—logical systems of relations:
• Child seen as assuming a work role with logical implications for his or her future way of living.
• Intimates predict any future "argument" behavior on the logical basis of the one coherent personality they now see in the other.

Level V

Postformal—contradictory formal logics, ordered by choice and "living out" of one logic:
• Child seen as potentially good or bad student, the outcome partly determined by parents' chosen view and subsequent actions cocreating one or the other (good or bad student) systems.
• Intimate partners' recognizing that if they choose to relate within the logical system that says the other will likely be unfaithful, they help bring about that unfaithful behavior.

Source: Sinnott (1984a).

discussion. Table 4.2 contains examples of stage levels of understanding of interpersonal relations by each of two persons who don't know each other very well as they go through the process of communicating with one another at a party. The communication is heard on each of their current levels of processing, and they respond in accord with that level. The communications are diagrammed in Figure 4.1.

Each thinker is an adult who potentially develops from level to level, as in Table 4.1. Each is challenged by the stance of the other to see the reality of their relationship in a way different from his or her own cognitive structure. If a person assimilates an event to a structure that does not match the event, there is the chance for the person to "grow" by accommodating the structure to the event and modifying it. New information is first taken in and interpreted, or assimilated, and then joined with other information and structures in a balanced way to reach equilibrium.

But, of course, interpersonal events are *created* by the individuals in them who are living them and knowing them; they never "hold still" for very long as objective reality. Thus, while each of the two speakers may or may not change structures due to this conversation, each has many chances to do so. Conflict between aspects of the experience and aspects of the knower's structures would be the impetus for change in the structure and subsequent changes in the mode of knowing future perceptions of the same event ("structural development"). Each has a chance to see that reality is partly a co-construction

Table 4.2. Strangers Communicating: Dialogue Content

Person 1 (who actually thinks on Level V): "I'm beat! I was up all night with the baby!"

Person 2 (who actually, so far, thinks on Level IV; reasons, with formal logic, that the career of "traditional mother of baby" does not imply an interest in career talk, responds in that logic): "I won't bore you with the details of my research project. I envy people like you who can go to the tennis courts during the day."

Person 1 (hearing with a Level V filter, and realizing Person 2 is trapped in the formal logic): "Actually, lots of my colleagues have kids and careers. We never have time to see those tennis courts. Go ahead, do tell me about your research. Are you a psychologist, too?"

Person 2 (challenged logically; can't decide whether to respond within work or family logical chit-chat system; moving toward Level V due to this challenge): "I'll bet your research is about children, right?"

Person 1 (staying Level V and trying to bring Person 2 to her level): "Actually, my research is about witness reliability. Have you ever noticed that people often 'see' an event turn out the way they logically expect it must?"

Person 2: "Just like I 'had to' see you as totally child-focused because you're a mom. Sorry!"

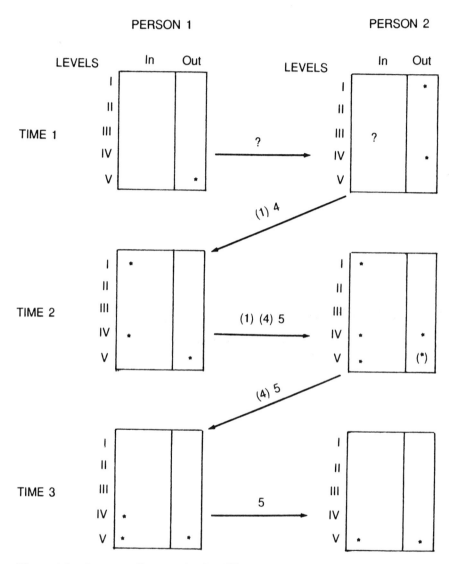

Figure 4.1.   Strangers Communicating (Changes in Each Knower and in the Interpersonal Event Due to Conflict Generated by the Multiple Filter System).

between something external and the self who knows it. Behavior based on a structure that only imperfectly mirrors a social reality might lead to changes in the social reality itself. Thus, in this cognitive (and real) dialogue, both social reality and the knower would change from encounter to encounter.

Stages

How can we describe the stages of complexity of thinking about interpersonal relations? Look again at Table 4.1. Sensorimotor thought is defined by Piaget as understanding at the level of basic needs and gut-level reactions without inclusion of a full-fledged symbol system. To extrapolate to social understanding, interpersonal relations at the sensorimotor level might include the parent and child related around the child's need for food, or the parent's need for food. In the first case, the parent may talk to the child about what the child wants to eat, and then offer that food; in the second case, the parent may ask the child to bring cookies to the TV room for the parent to eat. The relationship understood at the level of basic needs might also be true for two adults relating and understanding each other as providers of sex.

Preoperational thought is defined by Piaget as understanding at a level at which relationships can be symbolized, but are deformed by egocentric distortion of the symbols. The egocentrism is not used consciously. For example, at this level, a child or a parent can understand each other only in the role the other currently has. The child knows the parent as a parent, but cannot know the parent as a former child; the preoperational parent knows the child as a dependent, but cannot see the child as a future professional. Two adults knowing each other from a preoperational perspective are limited to their own experience of each other's roles. This sometimes seems to happen when a doctor and a patient meet at a party and begin to act as though they were still in the consulting room.

At the concrete operational level, where knowing is defined by Piaget as occurring in terms of classes of relations and relations between relations, interpersonal relations are known in the form of relational hierarchies. The child might be able to understand the parent as both a truck driver and a parent, seeing both as subcategories of "middle class." The parent may know the child as both a "B" student and a member of the school patrol, both subsumed under "elementary school student." The two adults at the party in the previous paragraph, rising to the occasion and beginning to think in concrete operations, might know each other now as the overriding category of "middle-aged neighbors" who are together "doctor and patient" and both "parents of kids at Springbrook High School."

At Piaget's formal operations stage of thinking, systems of relations, physical or interpersonal, are structured in binary logical form, and hypothetical–deductive reasoning, like that used by experimental scientists, can be used to logically analyze the system. Here, the parent may understand that within a middle class setting, only certain relations are logically possible with someone who is considered a child, and that some other relations will not be possible until the logical system of "middle class family" is discarded for some other logical system. If the child is formal operational, the child may also understand the same. For example, in the standard, middle class family logical system, a teen does not typically give an able parent a new car because the parent has neglected to get one but needs it for work; the parent does not require sex from the child; the child does not run the household or demand that the family move (and get his or her way!). Our formal operational logic says that within this logical system, it would not be logical for any of these things to happen. Between two adults, the logic of their mutual legal relations and obligations is codified in laws. Within that formal legal logical system, one adult may be liable for damage to the other adult's car after an accident; within a different logical system ("common sense"), no one may be held liable since the accident happened on a foggy, suddenly icy day.

At the postformal level, not included in Piagetian theory, a physical or interpersonal relationship might be interpreted as part of any number of equally logical formal systems, systems that may contradict each other but still be true within their own logical frameworks. Formal systems of logical relations are subsumed and ordered by the overarching postformal understanding that choosing the reality of the day, so to speak, is necessary before we continue to interact in a shared reality. A parent's response to a disobedient child will depend on that parent's child-rearing logical system. Two adults' views and behavior about the breakup of a marriage will be based on the logic of the philosophy of life (and marriage) they hold.

Dynamics

One important characteristic of the ideas presented here is that any social or interpersonal behavior can be filtered or encoded in terms of any level of thought. An event can be assimilated at any level of knowing. But at each increasingly sophisticated level of knowing, more complex aspects of the event can be organized and handled by the knower. As Tinbergen (1974) notes, this flexibility in assimilating information can be adaptive. For example, it is useful for an adult to match the thinking structure of a child to whom the adult wants to relate.

Incongruity between the knower's interpretation of the relation and the actual complexity of the communicated relation leads gradually to changes in the knower's structures of thought. This is similar to the case in Piagetian theory in which a child's chemical experiments lead to development of formal operations, or in which a baby's sensorimotor experiments in grabbing lead to a reliable sensorimotor grasping scheme. The next behavior based on the original interpersonal event is different because of the knower's altered thinking about the event. Both the event and the knower's structures determine how the event is interpreted. This result will determine the next resulting interpersonal event, which in turn will determine the complexity of the next encoded event.

It is expected that three dialogues will have taken place: The first will have taken place within the first knower's structures. The second will have taken place within the second knower's structures. The third will have taken place between the structures of the first and second knowers. In the case of interpersonal known events among more than two knowers, the number of dialogues can be expanded accordingly. Participants will have changed, if all goes well, as a function of past organismic states and current experiences. Figure 4.1 describes the dialogue in Table 4.2, reflecting changes in understanding. In the figure, IN refers to the level at which the person is trying to assimilate what is happening, and OUT refers to the level at which the person speaks. The numbers on the arrows refer to the level of the attempted match to the perceived level of the other speaker. In the figure, person #1 starts out at a more advanced level than person #2 but tries to match #2's level-as-perceived. In the process of the dialogue, #2 advanced to a better understanding, having been stimulated by the interpretational conflict.

There are two possible sources of change in the individual knower's thinking level. Both sources stem from conflict. First, conflict can exist between the potentially applicable structures the person brings to the interpersonal event and the group consensus or extrinsic reality held about the event. The second possible source of conflict is the high probability that any social relational knowledge is at some point in conflict with some other perceived social relational knowledge. This second source of conflict would come from the necessary subjectivity of social reality, which is in contrast to that of physical reality, which only sometimes includes subjectivity. Each interaction would numerically increase the chance for conflict and growth in structures.

PRELIMINARY EMPIRICAL TEST

If interpersonal cognition develops through interpersonal interactions and thereby leads to structural growth, two-person dialogues, focusing on interpersonal relations, should contain evidence of this process. For example:

- Adults should interpret others' statements in light of their prevailing levels of interpretation.
- Mature adults should demonstrate some high-level elements in their statements.
- Speakers utilizing different levels of statements should be perceived to be "in conflict with each other" if they do not become more similar in levels over time.
- Pairs of individuals continuing relationships should be expected to converge at a common level of social–cognitive discourse.

A preliminary exploration was conducted to see whether these expectations would hold true. Content analyses were performed on two-person dialogues recorded from selected dramas, including a movie *(Tom Jones)*, three soap operas *(Doctors, Search for Tomorrow, For Richer, For Poorer)*, and a situation comedy *(All in the Family)*. These dramas were selected because they were rich in interpersonal dialogues, were not fantasies, cartoons, or science fiction, and were on television during the week of the project. From two audiorecorded hours of this material, 25 two-person dialogues of various lengths (start of dialogue on topic to end of dialogue on topic) focusing on the understanding of interpersonal relations were found and analyzed. Dialogues were defined as verbal interchange between two persons responding to each other's statements with other statements.

Each statement (or group of statements until the speaker changed again) was scored as defined in Table 4.1 in terms of the social–cognitive level it represented. A speaker's highest level over-

all was also recorded. The following are examples of various statements and their level scores:

Level I: "Come back to me, John, I need you desperately!"
Level II: "You're my son, and no matter how old you are you'll do
as I tell you."
Level III: "I've been working so hard I think I put Joe in second
place in my life."
Level IV: "You cannot disgrace your family by marrying a bastard.
It's unthinkable! You are of noble birth!"
Level V: "I know I should put him out in the street because of his
base birth, but Vicar, as a Christian I should show him charity
and kindness."

Overall, statements ranged from Level I to Level V. Of 29 adult
speakers, 21 made statements indicating a Level V awareness of the
postformal nature of social relational knowledge. Most of the time,
however, they made statements at lower levels. Very few conversations (only 3 of 25) were held entirely at one level of understanding,
and these were brief exchanges. Of the 8 persons who never made a
Level V statement, 7 were young adults or teens; only 2 young adults
of 9 made a Level V statement.

In an attempt to see whether each speaker would interpret the
statements of the other from his or her own level, the first and second
statements of speakers were examined. Since the recordings were of
dialogues and the speakers therefore alternated in speaking, one person's second statement was in response to something the other person
had said. The result was a bell-curve distribution, with 52% of speakers maintaining the same level in their second statement, 15% moving
up one level, 15% moving down one level, and the remaining 18%
divided at the extremes of more-than-one-level change. From the
beginning to the end of the dialogue, 39% of the pairs moved on the
average one level closer together in understanding, 39% remained at
the same comparative distance from one another, and 21% moved one
level further from each other. During the course of their dialogues,
however, members of pairs were often as much as four levels apart.
Pairs having ongoing relationships in the drama itself ended their dialogues as close in understanding as they started, or closer, but this was
not generally true for other pairs not in ongoing relationships.

The levels of four older and four younger characters of both gen-
ders who appeared in several dialogues were examined to determine
whether the mature adult characters gave evidence of structuring

Table 4.3. Levels of Comments in Four Dramatic Dialogues

	Percentage of comments				
Speaker	I	II	III	IV	V
Younger women					
First	32	—	37	21	10
Second	25	—	75	—	—
Older women					
First	—	—	47	40	13
Second	14	—	36	24	24
Younger men					
First	50	—	37.5	12.5	—
Second	50	40	—	—	10
Older men					
First	3	36	14	21	21
Second	25	8	25	34	8

social cognitions on a higher level than the younger ones did. The results are presented in Table 4.3. The statement levels of the four younger individuals contrast with those of the four older individuals. In general, as the table shows, lower-level statements predominate with younger characters and higher-level statements with older ones.

The data reported in Table 4.3 represent only a pretest of the concepts we have just discussed. They lead to the preliminary conclusion, however, that complex postformal understanding of the structure of social relations may exist and may develop through conflict. This preliminary evidence suggests that knowers themselves co-create the social environment with others. A long-term association between persons may be related to structure convergence or synthesis.

SHARED COGNITION AND CULTURE

I have made the point that postformal thought is developed through interaction with other knowers—in other words, through social interactions, co-created by people in those interactions. People acting together and reflecting upon their interactions gradually mold a somewhat consistent view of reality, including the reality of their interactions.

Individuals co-create cultures. The culture in question may be one of the small cultures of the family or the workplace or one of the larger cultures that we might label, for example, "American culture,"

"New Age culture," or "the culture of poverty." These cultures, small or large, come with shared values, beliefs, and statements about people and roles. We will discuss cultures further in Part III, where we will examine the effect of postformal thinking on the creation and the persistence of various roles and cultural influences. Here, at this point, we will think for a moment about the role of culture in the *individual's* development of postformal thought.

We each dialogue with individuals and reflect on our relations with them. We know those relations, and we try to understand them at some cognitive level. Our interactions aid the growth of the sophistication of our understanding, spurring us, through social–cognitive conflict, toward developing sophisticated postformal thought.

For a moment, mentally substitute "the culture" (whichever culture it is) for one of the individuals in the dialogue. Now the dialogue is between the person and the culture, which itself is co-created by many knowers. The person communicates, or acts; the culture communicates or acts in response. Each operates at the cognitive levels it has available; each accommodates its knowledge structures to discrepancies between the two levels or defends against such accommodation. In this way, the dialogue continues and the structures of both are modified. Cultures, therefore, simply through epistemological conflicts engaged in with each of us, also have the potential to help us grow toward postformal thought as individuals. If we fail to engage in a dialogue with the culture and are consequently overwhelmed by it, we simply "learn" to fake its dominant-way-of-knowing behaviors without enlarging our structures.

Those who know reality in the same style as the dominant group in a culture knows reality feel a solid sense of belonging. Everyone sees eye to eye, cognitively speaking. But these individuals enjoy fewer chances for cognitive growth toward postformal thought. That growth relies on epistemological conflicts. In such a cohesive social reality, the only conflicts about shared social realities will occur with individuals.

Further, many postformal individuals gathered in a culture jointly can create a "postformal culture" in which are embodied ways of operating and "knowing" that tend to be postformal. Conversely, of course, a culture co-created by many *non*-postformal members will be *non*-postformal more of the time. An individual's dominant level of cognitive functioning will therefore not necessarily lessen the amount of conflict experienced in dealing with cultures, with one exception. If a person operates at the postformal level, that person can sidestep conflict *if he or she chooses to do so* by using her or his postformal knowing skills to meet the culture at its own level. We will see more about how postformal thought helps a person to cope with both interpersonal conflict and information overload in the chapters of Part III, especially Chapter 16.

SOME DATA: DEVELOPMENT OF INDIVIDUALS AS A GROUP DEVELOPS

I made a preliminary test of several of these assumptions by analyzing the course of individual and group (cultural) cognitive development. I used written accounts of the short-term evolution of isolated small groups. Several purportedly nonfictional accounts of this type exist, for example, Solzhenitsyn's (1973) *The Gulag Archipelago* and Read's (1974) original *Alive: The Story of the Andes Survivors*. The latter was chosen for this report, since that group was more thoroughly isolated for a longer period of time. (Readers who have seen the cinematic version of this event should note that the screenplay was highly fictionalized and bears no great resemblance to the book. The analyses to follow do not make use of the screenplay version.) We will refer to this analysis again in Chapter 6 when we discuss cultures as living systems. Here, our emphasis is on the individual's cognitive development, although the theory itself maintains that the individual's complex cognitive development cannot happen apart from the group.

Here are the assumptions we will examine: The cognitive level of a group should depend on the collective cognitive levels of its participants. The cognitive levels of participants should tend to (or at least appear to) converge over time if the group is a functional one. Individual members of the group would be expected to interact with one another at several levels of cognitive development. Individuals would be challenged to grow cognitively by disparity among the several individuals' cognitive levels. Individuals would be expected to create their own "social reality" as the group evolves.

The dialogues and interpersonal behaviors reported by Read centered on the experiences of a group of 45 Uruguayan air travelers who crashed in the peaks of the Andes mountains in winter and were officially given up for dead. Ten weeks later, 2 of the survivors walked out of the mountains and found help for the 14 others still alive. The story had its spectacular elements: Not only was the scenery awe inspiring, the cold deadly, some individuals heroic, and the government less than enthusiastic about a search, but also there was cannibalism. It was that last factor that occasioned repeated interviews with everyone involved very soon after the event, which makes the detailed, corroborated information useful for our purposes.

The portion of the analyses presented here focuses on the state of the group at the time of the crash and one month later, as expressed in the dialogues and in the reports of the interpersonal behaviors of the 19 who survived for an entire one-month period. It employs the stages or levels of interpersonal relations operations described above.

On the day of the crash, the survivors formed three basic groups, identified as family clusters, friend clusters, or isolated individuals. Except for the few families or friends, relationships were very superficial and infrequent. In the first few moments after the crash, virtually every survivor seemed to be interpreting the statements of others on Level I (see Table 4.1). This created a hysterical, demanding social situation with rapidly escalating conflicts, since they were all making demands on each other and no one had the capability to fulfill those demanding roles. Soon, those individuals who before the crash generally related at Levels III, IV, or V were able to engage in a dialogue with the others who also related at those levels until a temporary Level III consensus was reached. Dialogue could then go forward at that common level. Consequently, some degree of interpersonal calm was restored.

Those who generally related at Levels III and IV at the time of the crash based their understanding on role hierarchies that might well have been valid for the precrash social system in Uruguay, but were inadequate for dealing with the severe situation on the snow-covered peaks of the Andes. Those persons who most frequently related at Level I generally interpreted the dialogues and behaviors of everyone else in the group at Level I also. Level IIIs often "talked down" to Level Is, meeting them at their lower cognitive level until Level I persons grew to exhibit (or, in self-defense, feigned) some more complex understanding of the interpersonal event. In this way, a Level III harmony was achieved.

One month later, the group appeared to have restructured its society. A reasonably well ordered, logical social system had appeared, one at variance, certainly, with the ordered, logical, highly valued social system of the group's precrash experience, but radically improved from the immediate postcrash chaos. Individuals had had frequent and intense interactions with one another during the preceding month on the mountain. One tightly clustered subgroup characterized by a flexible Level V approach had appeared. Members of this group could respond on any level, depending both on the circumstances of the moment and on the level of the person with whom they were communicating. These individuals were either leaders or extremely well liked by all, despite their earlier status as strangers. Many persons had reacted to intense interactions by raising their dominant social–cognitive level several steps, some achieving Level V. The most effective leaders were those who appeared to use their Level V skills to coordinate the system of roles from the precrash society with the disparate system of roles in the postcrash survivor society.

A second subgroup typically responded on Level I or II, although they might temporarily feign a higher level when socially coerced. While past friendships, skills, or philosophical and ethical systems kept the first subgroup interacting with the second, the second was perceived as an infantile burden. The lower-level subgroup frequently tried to interact with others to fill its needs, though attempts were often futile. The first group frequently interacted harmoniously within itself. Members of the second group seldom did, since their interactions, based on structures of social relations embedded in needs, were less mutually satisfying. Cross-group interaction took place when members of the first subgroup were flexible enough to interact at the second group's lower level. Such interaction, however, demanded extra effort on the part of the higher-level persons and therefore was seldom attempted for its own sake. The members of the higher-level subgroup therefore experienced more stimuli for restructuring than did the members of the lower-level group.

This very brief description gives some idea of the potential utility of shared cognitions for the individual. The individual is stimulated to grow to the postformal level and can see that the postformal level is adaptive. My earlier stated assumptions were supported by these events.

The group's adoption of shared parameters of thought seems to lead quickly to a group behavior and a group belief system that persists more or less on its own. In other words, it can lead to a culture or a social system. It becomes easy later to ignore the chaotic dialogic give and take that leads to the social consensus about reality. Children and adults operating on lower social–cognitive levels often are shocked when it first occurs to them (perhaps as they develop Level IV thought) that the shared realities of their culture are somewhat arbitrary. This step toward individual postformal development may be connected with emotional issues in the context of small-group experiences (Stevens-Long & Trujillo, 1995). When it becomes apparent to enough individuals that the shared assumption system is not adaptive

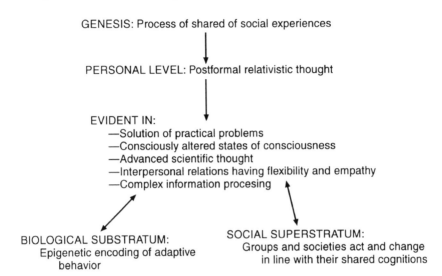

Figure 4.2. Postformal Thought: Genesis, Effects, and Behavioral Evidence.

in some ways, social change or the exploration of alternative competing formal systems occurs, and a new postformal synthesis can begin.

This concludes our initial description of operations and development of postformal thought. Figure 4.2 displays a summary of some of the ideas in Part I of this book, summarizing the genesis and effects of and the behavioral evidence for postformal thought. All these will be amplified in later chapters.

CHAPTER 5

New Physics Models Underlying Postformal Thought

We must care for the truth in front of us more than consistency.

MOHANDAS K. GANDHI

As I described in Chapter 3, new physics is one of the intellectual antecedents of postformal thought. New physics thinking is the kind of logical thinking structure that complex postformal thinkers—like my wise relatives and Einstein—have always had at their disposal in various forms. The purpose of this chapter is to review some important original ideas basic to the new physics as it was first articulated, that is, to relativity theory and quantum physics. Of course, physics has evolved immensely since the origins of the new physics. But my purpose is to show how useful even the basic new physics ideas are as metatheories for life-span development, especially for cognitive life-span development. Other post-Newtonian physics paradigms, especially general systems theory, chaos theory, complexity theories of self-regulating systems, and postmodern thought, will be discussed in Chapters 6 and 7. All these paradigms reflect elements of basic postformal thought and provide ways to study such thought.

Far from being frightening or difficult, new physics ideas are extremely practical when they are applied. These advanced models are being considered in realms as different as spirituality and organization management, and some forms of many of the ideas are apparent in Native American and other indigenous traditions. After all, those concepts must be understandable to us at some level if they can keep us, metaphorically speaking, cognitively dancing in balance on the orbiting, rotating planet of our reality! These ideas are integral to the universe that is our home. Historically, we have been accustomed to thinking that our home consists of one room, the layout of which is defined by "old" Newtonian physics. New physics simply opens the door to the rest of the rooms and provides us with the floor plan of our entire home. Like so many moving adventures, once we get accustomed to the new living space, we cannot imagine living without it. We move into the postformal larger-reality home and think of it as our natural habitat. We become like the child who reaches teen years and can no longer think within the limits of a 6-year-old mind.

The purpose of this chapter is to review some of these basic original new physics concepts to see how they might be used as metaphors to help us understand life-span cognitive development including postformal thought. New and old physics give us two different ways to describe the apparent same physical reality. Postformal thought permits us to cognitively process both realities at the same time, a cognitive structure that is useful for adaptive life-span development. Historically, cognitive developmental theory appears to be changing in ways analogous to the progress of theory in the physical sciences. The discussion that follows points out ways in which new physics thinking might enrich the understanding of life-span development and epistemology. The challenge of seeing the contrasting reality of new and old physics truths, old or new lenses on the world, might even challenge us to further develop our own postformal thought.

The purpose of this chapter is not to expound the new physics in detail, but to focus on a framework for developmental analysis. New physics thinking might carry the label "physics," but it is not the property of any particular science or individual any more than "Aristotelian" thought is the sole property of Aristotle. The fact that physicists have organized and articulated some structured relations within a body of theory at this historical point does make it simpler for adventurous psychologists and other interested thinkers to explore interesting applications and possibilities within those relations.

Life-span developmentalists have several important reasons for making this exploration. As complexity grows in descriptions of development, there is increasing desire for a paradigm that will give a broader picture of the causes of behavior. Some of us investigators are searching for a model of the complex, realistic thought characteristic of mature adults living in a changing world. Others are curious about the logical thinking employed by outstanding scientists and philosophers. Many are looking for a paradigm of social interaction or for a way of combining several useful but seemingly contradictory ways of viewing behavior or other reality. Perhaps new physics thinking can serve these needs and enlarge our perspectives as it did those of physicists not so long ago.

New physics thought is not a newly invented style of thinking peculiar to physics. It cannot be the purpose of this chapter to review the history of scientific thought, but even a cursory examination of that history suggests that large movements forward in understanding take place periodically, when contradictory systems are restructured. T. Kuhn (1962), in describing scientific revolutions, describes the shift from the prerevolutionary to the postrevolutionary structures in ways that suggest that an application of new physics metaphors occurs when paradigms shift.

Since they are more inclusive, probabilistic, and complex, new physics ideas are difficult to articulate in a verbal system dominated by more rigid functional relations. New physics ideas would be expected to occur later in the history of any systematic idea development than the simpler and more readily demonstrated earlier ideas. This chronology would be expected in psychology, philosophy, education, sociology, and physics, not because the others copy natural sciences, but despite the independence of these fields. Advances in a science, whatever the science, take place in a particular historical period and are influenced by the overall tone, the predominant thought patterns, and the cultural rules about reality current during that period (T. Kuhn, 1962; Riegel, 1977). If past history is any guide, new physics ideas will increase in any period as a function of the number of scientists dissatisfied with any paradigm, the developmental history of the science itself, and the capability of individual scientists to think in such inclusive and probabilistic ways. In sciences or in individuals, new physics thinking seems to occur because it is adaptive.

While many fields of science are not examining the new, complex relations, physics is. The new physics ideas provide a handy launching pad for developmental psychologists and others who would like to examine available metatheories to enlarge outgrown paradigms or to study the epistemological function of such thought.

BACKGROUND

To understand the background and concepts of new physics thought is the first step in its utilization. Interested readers may want to peruse physics textbooks, tap into the huge array of technical books and articles, read edited compilations of ideas, or scan the very reader-friendly work of writers such as Capra (1975), Wolf (1981), and Zukav (1979).

Let us look first at the old physics, Newtonian pre-Einsteinian physics. Classical mechanics had developed as an outgrowth of everyday physical experience with the environment. This experience was first summarized in intuitive and anthropomorphic generalizations, and then in abstract laws. New physics has been developed over a period of years in response to contradictions found while working with the theories of classical mechanics (Russell, 1969). The space of classical mechanics is Euclidian; all transformations in space are describable by Cartesian fixed coordinates and consist of either rotations or translations. Time is an absolute concept, and the calculus, presuming continuity of matter and space, is an adequate mathematical tool.

Because of the inability of the scientific observer to become sufficiently objective, measuring standards that appeared to be rigid and absolute were later proved not to be so. To use Einstein's famous example, it was as though the observer were on a speeding train but unaware of its movement. After carefully measuring and describing the environment and relations of objects observed while sitting in a seat on the train and looking out the window, the observer would have a certain amount of data. Some of the data would prove shockingly incorrect if the train were to come to a full stop and the observer were suddenly able to take into account the consequences of motion biases. None of the observer's measures would have been wrong for the observer's specific time and place conditions; they simply would not have been the entire picture of reality. What the observer had seen would be real data carefully controlled by scientific methodology, but colored by the fact that measurement was done with a changing measure, not a fixed one (Einstein, 1961).

The scientific or cognitive world of the pre-Einsteinian is like that of the traveler who is still unaware of the train's motion. As we will see later, developing minds are brought to awareness of their own "motion bias" by interpersonal interactions. The event that brought the awareness of motion bias to the scientist was work in electromagnetism. As a result of discoveries in that field, phenomena that are at variance with Newtonian physics were discovered. Newton held, for example, that only the distance between two objects determined the strength of forces they exerted upon one another. This view was contradicted by Oersted, who demonstrated that relative motion is also important in determining object interaction, and by Maxwell, who demonstrated the importance of field effects in the strength of forces between bodies. Attempts to deal with these contradictions led to the new mathematical tools of vector analysis and tensor analysis, to Einstein's elaborations on relativity theory, and to quantum mechanics. Contradictions led to a new physics.

Postulates

The postulates of relativity theory in new physics are simple to express but difficult to conceptualize. Observers fail to recognize that their standards of measurement of events are *not* truly rigid (i.e., consistent or absolute) *unless* they deal with small-scale, isolated, limiting-case events. The *first postulate of relativity* is valid only for such limiting cases: If, relative to K, K' is a uniformly moving system of coordinates devoid of rotations, K and K' share the same natural laws (Einstein, 1961). In other words, when two persons are both on the train, their scientific, objective findings are in agreement. The problem, as might be expected, comes when K and K' are not uniformly moving systems of coordinates devoid of rotation, that is, when both observers are not on the same train. When one goes beyond the somewhat reductionistic small-scale descriptions of nature, not every observer can be on the train.

The *second postulate, or the special theory of relativity,* was formulated in response to this type of problem and contradiction in data. In the second postulate, certain formerly rigid concepts such as time and space are made dependent on the motion (or nonmotion) of the reference body. The Lorentz transform (Einstein, 1961) was developed as a mathematical tool for moving from one system of positional coordinates to another, to allow for the effect of shifting vantage points. According to this postulate, general laws of nature may still be deduced from such idiosyncratic experiences, *if* their coordinate systems are related by the Lorentz transform. In other words, if the space–time position on the train can be related to the space–time on the road, a general law that applies to both locations can be determined.

The *third postulate, or the general theory of relativity,* was formulated to replace Newton's theory of gravity—which would be impossible under this new set of assumptions—with an explanation consistent with the new set of assumptions. The inseparable space–time dimension of one body was coordinated with the dimension of nearness-to-another-body. The result was that a graphic description of space–time took on a curvature. In other words, when two bodies approach one another, the closer they get, the more their paths in space–time deviate from a straight line. The closer a moving train spirals up a mountain approaching the top of a mountain, the slower its movement and the more circular its path. The mathematics of moving a vector such as the train from place to place without changing its size or orientation (i.e., the mathematics of "parallel transport") was developed to deal with movement in space–time across a curved surface. Assuming that objects travel the most efficient route from point to point, this new tool allows one to describe space–time movement despite the gravitational field. It therefore allows transformation of coordinate systems even when such transforms are multidimensional and continuous. The general theory of relativity demands that a natural law be applicable to multidimensional, continuous transforms of coordinate systems if it is to be a *general* law (Einstein, 1961).

Pre-Einsteinian theories include laws of nature that appear to be general, but are in fact general only under certain specific reductionistic space–time conditions. Einstein's laws of nature include Newton's as special cases.

Assumptions

Many assumptions characterize old physics and differ from those in new physics. We have already taken a brief look at some of these assumptions in Chapter 3; now let us examine them in more detail (see Table 3.1, p. 29). Note that both sets of assumptions have been verified with experimental evidence, so both contradictory sets of assumptions are true. Newtonian physics assumptions have been found to be true in small-scale, everyday systems, except for minor inconsistencies; new physics assumptions are true for the general case and include the others as special limiting conditions.

Space. The nature of space differs between the two sets of assumptions (Kaufman, 1973). Space can be described as Euclidean when the measuring standard is at rest, the limiting case. Space must be described as non-Euclidean in the general case. In the former situation, the shortest distance between two points is a straight line; in the latter, it is a geodesic (i.e., a curved path describing the shortest distance between two points on a curved surface). Aristotelian logic appears challenged by the destabilization of concepts such as space and time and by the allowance of logical contradiction in terms of limiting-case postulates versus general-case postulates.

Continuity. An assumption under Newtonian physics and the calculus that it utilized is the continuity of phenomena—time, place, events—that are assumed to be isolated, measured against rigid standards, and ordered in an unchanging manner. Under the new set of assumptions, phenomena are continuous only in the limiting case, but discontinuous in general (Robertson & Noonan, 1968).

The absolute nature of time and space in the Pre-Einstein perspective is replaced by the space–time interval (Einstein, 1961). The interval allows the effect of time on space, or of space on time, to be taken into account when locating an event or reasoning about it. As events approach the speed of light, time slows down. An event that is simultaneous with another event (in one view) also precedes that event (in a second view) and is subsequent to it (in a third view). On the other hand, if the time element is variously measured, the position of the event in space may assume several contradictory sets of coordinates for the same event.

The conceptualization of the uniformity of space also changes (Russell, 1969). In the former metatheory, space is uniform throughout; in the latter, space appears filled with hills and valleys that offer greater and lesser resistances to moving bodies. These gravitational fields, that is, the hills encountered, slow the moving body and make its path more circular, allowing it to approach but never attain the center of the field.

Movement. Two observers can never reach valid conclusions about the same event if they fail to take their own movement into account (Brillouin, 1970). What the two observers see at a given time would be determined by their motion relative to one another and to the event. Using the train example, if one person on the road and a second on the moving train see a star, the reality of their physical relation to the star can be ascertained only after the effects of the motion of the earth, the motion of the train, and the motion of the star are taken into account. The formulation of a scientific hypothesis—that is, an epistemology or a knowing of the relations between oneself and the star—is incomplete if it does not develop beyond pre-Einsteinian notions. In other words, if one attempts to know the star in terms of physical experience in Newtonian physics terms, one will lack a complete understanding of the star in a larger sense. The lesser knowledge may be sufficient for some situations, but not for all. An additional abstraction from abstractions must be made, one that permits egocentrism in a sophisticated sense in which one always takes one's biases into account. Both the small-scale principles of physical relations, which are useful every day, and the general-scale multiple-vantage-points principles of physical relations, which are the more inclusive assessment, must coexist in thinking, contradictory as they seem to be, to know reality in all its forms and to adapt to different situations. Postformal thought gives us the cognitive framework for doing so.

Causality. Conceptions of causality are broadened in new physics thought (Toulmin, 1970). The deterministic causality of Newtonian physics is enlarged by the deterministic probabilistic causality of quantum mechanics (Heisenberg, 1958; Schlick, 1970). Simple Newtonian deterministic physical causality would pertain in limited situations and would assume contiguity (i.e., cause and effect necessarily in contact). A new physics definition of causality, in contrast, could be "a timeless relation of dependency between two events" or "a center around which events (i.e., effects) are grouped." The relatedness of two specific events in a limited, fixed space–time can be predicted on a simple, deterministic basis, but the general relatedness of two events can be predicted only on a complex, probabilistic basis. The implications of this difference for the scientific method have been vast. While the new student of science may still look for simple experimental "cause and effect relations," the advanced investigator is now more likely to focus on chaos and complexity theory, self-organizing systems, and the implicate order as he or she thinks about causes.

Causality is determinable within a relativistic system, but the limits bounding those determinants are much wider than they are in simpler systems. Ideas of nonlocal causation and the paradox of Schrödinger's cat certainly intrigue us. Relativistic thinking seems more ecologically valid for explaining effects and causes in a naturalistic setting where many variables are in constant interplay. Looking at the Newtonian microuniverse of the developing fetus, for example, one chemical change does determine a specific limiting-case reaction. More important, though, is the overall general new physics reaction of the fetus, which is determined not only by the chemical, but probabilistically also by the prevailing fetal milieu and history. The chemical, in the general case, is simply the center of a complex but predictable response. Later writers examine such concepts as "nonlocal causality" in physics in general (e.g., Bohm, 1980), as well as in biology (e.g., Sheldrake, 1981; 1989; 1990) and medicine (e.g., Dossey, 1982, 1989).

Subjectivity and Linguistic Transform Systems. The concept of egocentrism comes full circle through transition from the prescientific ego-boundedness of the child, through supposed objectivity of the young adult, to the new physics notion that the data and the observer are in an ongoing necessary interaction. In the third stage, the person who attempts to be decentered and objective learns that subjectivity must be made part of the measure of the phenomenon itself, and that objective reality is better defined as the sum of observational invariants, even though each of those invariants is known to be necessarily partly subjective (Born, 1962, 1964).

But there is a catch. The logic and laws of nature have been formulated within verbal conventions that make it difficult to understand this new physics objectivity in a nonpolarized way. For example, present tense declarative verbal statements fit Aristotelian logic, but would not fit new physics general-case ideas well (Freedle, 1977). The "either A or non-A" forms in language usage are also basically old physics, making expressions of new physics ideas (e.g., "both A and non-A") seem contradictory. No wonder mathematicians and lovers sometimes avoid words.

Large-Scale Developments. Perhaps one of the most interesting issues integral to this thought transition in physics has concerned the nature of the universe and its development over time (Kaufman, 1973). Newtonian physics thought conceptualizes the universe as uniform and existing in a stable state. This was philosophically consistent with early views of human nature and creation (Russell, 1969). In new physics terms, the universe has proved to be nonuniform, with some portions more densely filled with matter and others more nearly empty space. These fuller and emptier portions of the universe are in motion relative to one another. The new physics view can accommodate three views of the universe: (1) The universe is continuously expanding and becoming less dense. (2) The universe is continuously creating and destroying itself. (3) Parallel universes exist.

A new physics pattern of relations among elements in the universe, applied to individual development or to social interactions, suggests that development might be either continuous differentiation or an alternating process of pattern creation and destruction. Perhaps readers can envision others. Using relations in the new physics universe as an analogue, development would not likely be the attainment of any long-term steady, unchanging mature state among individuals or within individuals.

APPLICATIONS TO LIFE-SPAN DEVELOPMENTAL PSYCHOLOGY

Can some parallels and analogies be constructed between old physics or new physics concepts and concepts in life-span developmental psychology? Do we see evidence of one or the other physics or both, indicating a time of transition? Psychology seems to be struggling with the situation in which we know many facts but relatively few general laws. Simultaneous reliable measurements of the same event are producing different and contradictory interpretations when viewed from the small-scale and the large-scale perspectives. Measures fail to yield deterministic results in ecologically valid situations. We are increasingly interested in multivariate relations that have nonlinear forms. This frame of mind suggests that we are in a transition state or a paradigm shift in psychology.

Several relationships studied by life-span developmentalists are analogous to relationships in the physical sciences. Listed in Table 5.1 are several concepts in life-span development studies, as described using Newtonian physics positions and new physics positions as metaphors. Only some of the new physics positions on the developmental concepts have been researched so far.

Postulate Applications

In model terms, early work in life-span development seems to have been concerned with clarification of the first postulate of relativity described above. Investigators have been expected to choose a limiting-case perspective and stay with it. Choice of several paradigms or referents has been considered evidence of logical inconsistency, as indeed was true of Aristotelian logical views of logical consistency. For example, the organism had to be considered either active or passive, not both, in Aristotelean terms. Within classical mechanics, analogously, a great deal of effort was once spent to describe light definitively as either a wave or a particle only to conclude that light really was both.

Studies in psychology examining cross-cultural differences, longitudinal versus cross-sectional studies, and demands for contexted personality and intelligence measures suggest that psychology is becoming aware of the second postulate and its analogues for human behavior and noting how both the subject and the observer are in motion. When time and space are viewed as discrete, the organism seems to change as a function of either time (age alone, the maturational perspective) or space (experience alone, the behaviorist perspective). If, instead of engaging in acrimonious debates, disputants could view the organism as moving across space–time intervals during its development, many contradictions could be resolved.

Table 5.1. Life-Span Developmental Concepts Analogous to Newtonian and New Physics Concepts

Developmental parameter	Newtonian	New physics
Impact of experience	Experience is additive.	Experience is additive in local events only; generally, experience has differential effects.
Impact of age and experience on development	Age and experience have separate effects.	Need dialectical analysis of age/experience dimensions.
Social development	Interpersonal space can be operationalized and treated in terms of a ratio-like scale.	Interpersonal space is made up of lesser and greater resistances that nonuniformly speed or slow interpersonal development.
Perception	Relations can be portrayed adequately on a two-dimensional surface.	Relations are more accurately portrayed on a Thomian surface.
Developmental change	Development is a straight-line function.	Development follows a geodesic.
Person perception	How one categorizes others should be logical in Aristotelian terms.	Categories of person perception reflect interplay between the constantly changing and contradictory other and self.
Stage concepts	Person attains a stable stage or manifests a stable personality trait.	Person is in a moving state; stable stages or traits are artificial abstractions.
Measurement tools	Completely objective measures of development can be created.	Adequate measures can be devised only when measures are considered necessarily subjective and this subjectivity is taken into account in interpretations.
Models of development	If models work only sometimes, or contradict each other, they are fatally flawed.	Contradictory models that describe behavior only in limiting cases may be related by transforms to provide general models of development.
Causality	Determinism is the underlying model.	Determinism applies in local cases; otherwise, prediction can be based on statistical probability.

(*continued*)

Table 5.1. (*Continued*)

Developmental parameter	Newtonian	New physics
Egocentrism	Decentration is the end state of ego development.	Egocentrism and decentration are followed by "taking the ego into account in all cases."
Logic	Aristotelian logic, expressed in verbal symbol systems, is an adequate model.	Non-Aristotelian logic is necessary, as is use of a mathematical symbol system.
Nature of development	Development is uniform, tending to a final steady state.	Development is continuous, with equilibrations and losses and gains constantly changing the person.

Source: Sinnott (1981). By permission of S. Karger AG, Basil, Switzerland.

The simple transformations of time and space that apply to the limited case of the old physics are replaced by the complex new physics transforms that describe "relative position in developmental space–time of interacting individuals and environmental factors." This tedious polarized language can be replaced by a formula or a graphic that better conveys the larger new physics picture. Picture two grids with elastic dimensions, the dimensions being influenced by past and present relations with one another. At any moment, the relation of one grid to another can be calculated. That relationship, rather than their comparative ages or the simple distance between them, is the most useful thing one could know to predict how (or whether) the grids will be alike, how much they will gravitate toward one another or repel each other, or how alike they will be in relations to other variables or grids. Using these concepts, one can explore the effects of the developmental histories and environments of social individuals on their individual growth and behavior.

For example, it may be true for infants that age (time) is isolatable as a determinant of much of neurological development. It may be true for 7-year-olds that experience (an analogue of space) with the written word is an isolatable determinant of reading proficiency. But a "space–time (experience–age) interval" seems to be more useful in describing the larger developments (motions) such as social development and adult development. The position of a developing individual seems to be most adequately conceptualized as an age–experience point in motion, a point that can be described as vector-like and potentially analyzed as such. The coordinated systems of two developing individuals at any point might be considered as though individuals are located on grids of differing proportions, grids that can be related only by transforms. Only in small-scale cases (i.e., those that take place within a short time or within a limited space) can the positional data for one individual be directly related to the positional data for the other, because under those circumstances both occupy the same grid ("are on the same moving train").

In view of these ideas, whatever measuring standard is used in life-span development can be a rigid standard only on the small-scale basis. One's past scores are a rigid standard measuring the same thing each time only if very little time or experience has passed; one would not have the same testing device in hand after a 20-year span of personal experience has altered the meaning of that device for the test taker. Attempts to make measuring devices rigid frequently make them meaningless or ecologically invalid.

As Riegel (1977) noted, even though the life span represents an ongoing time sequence, researchers persist in viewing it in frozen or rigid segments. Perhaps some psychologists freeze these segments of experience because they communicate and think in polarized language. Yet those segments of the life span are fluid because they are in constant motion, and what they are today is not what they will be tomorrow. We observers are moving through our own life spans, and what we measure against today (i.e., the meaning we give symbols today) is not what we will measure against tomorrow. Riegel stressed the importance of looking at contradictions in frozen segments over time, because those contradictions certainly are one measure of space–time. The task remains to find a manner of transforming the sets of space–time coordinates so that each set is understandable in terms of the other when both are undergoing constant change due to both their development and their interaction. The transforms needed may ultimately resemble Fourier transforms, and the task of communicating this information may ultimately resemble that of psychoneuroimmunological communication.

The third postulate appears especially applicable to the behavioral sciences, since those sciences study not only the development of a single individual in a physical world, but also the development of an individual who is interacting with other developing individuals. In an attempt to "stop the moving train," so to speak, and to make measures rigidly stable, the effect of developing individuals on each other is often put aside. Besides raising questions about the ecological validity of the resulting findings, the compartmentalization of all social development into a few studies seems to have largely isolated such studies from what could be useful cognitive and intraindividual developmental analysis (D. Kuhn, 1978).

Developmentalists are fortunate when they become aware that the Newtonian-model separation between the social and the individual spheres of influence is simply an arbitrary device used by one paradigm. In Newtonian physics, the effect of a moving body on another moving body was isolated and examined as a separate physical phenomenon (gravity), since Newtonians did not know that this separation was an artificial one. Developmentalists behave like Newtonians when they overlook relationships between developments on adjacent bodies or ignore psychological nearness of developing entities. This earlier paradigm weakness may have been a major impediment to moving from specific to general laws of development.

How might developing individuals mutually affect one another in terms of analogues of the third postulate? In relativistic terms, they might change the shape and the dimensions of each others' developmental space–time and affect the direction of each others' movement. Development may fairly be visualized as a straight-line function in a small-scale event, but it is not fair to so visualize them over the life course. We notice that the direction and speed of life-span development is often changed by encounters with persons and events that the individual later perceives as important. The first others encountered have stronger deflecting action than later ones, just as two planets caught in each other's gravitational fields remain influenced by that first encounter, unless changes within either or both of the planets themselves or the passing of a stronger third body are the occasion for changing relationships. The interaction with developing others encountered during one's own development probably describes, in natural science terms, a geodesic. One continually approaches, circles, and is repelled by the other, but one has been permanently deflected and is constantly affected by the other's nearness. The impact is also mutual. Interpersonal space during development can then be described as a hilly surface with each individual at the top of a hill and all the hills in motion through space–time. As each gets nearer to knowing or influencing the other, resistance increases, so that a slowing circular motion carries the approaching ones around each other. If one were on the surface of one of those hills, one body actually making giant circles around another would seem to be moving straight ahead in the plane of their mutual orbit; local small-scale events appear nonrelativistic and separable into individual developments and social developments.

The new physics view of social interaction has implications for understanding social development, emotional growth, peer pressure effects, group dynamics, and dynamics of successful therapy, to name a few. In considering, for example, whether a person will succumb to peer pressure to cheat, a researcher can predict cheating on the basis of such variables as the need to conform, past history of tax evasion, and moral code. If the researcher is using a new physics metatheory, the researcher would be less interested in specific factors predicting cheating and more interested in the cheating as one point in the person's movement through developmental space–time, a part of encounters with other developing persons sharing that domain. A particular person may appear to conform to pressure, but be, from a larger perspective, actually within the gravitational pull of a significant relationship that carries important shared meaning transforms that equate cheating with independence or some other positive trait. The most important benefit of this analysis is not that it allows one to predict cheating more accurately, but that it enables one to understand the complex course of development.

POSTMODERN THOUGHT AND OTHER PRACTICAL CONSEQUENCES OF NEW PHYSICS MODELS

Postmodern thought, also known as postpositivist and post-Enlightenment thought, seems to flow from new physics realizations. The postmodern perspective challenges positivist assumptions that reason can provide us with a truly objective view of truth and that science is neutral in terms of the lenses through which it views reality. Postmodernists also question the existence of a stable and coherent "self," a self that possesses a language that truly captures objective reality. Within postmodernism are social constructionism and deconstruction views. The former states that the knowledge we have of something is a constructed representation, not a replica, of reality. Deconstructionists (or poststructuralists) see language as a social construct for representing—and at the same time necessarily distorting—reality. These views help reframe questions along new physics lines in many of the humanities and social sciences.

We have outlined just a very few of the concepts in the new physics that have tremendous potential for models of life-span development. Additional extremely important ideas might be explored, ideas such as Bohm's (1980) concept of implicate and explicate order, superstring theory, antimatter, and unified field theories. Some additional topics will be addressed in the chapters on general systems theory (Chapter 6) and chaos and complexity theories (Chapter 7), since at this level of discussion topics in the new sciences begin to overlap. But staying within the few key concepts we have explored so far, those from the early part of the history of the new physics, what are the practical implications of several of those concepts for life-span developmental psychology?

In the small-scale study, nothing would change except the awareness that the laws obtained through analyses that are reductionistic (in the sense of Newtonian-level physics) apply only to small-scale situations, not to the general picture of development. Description of general laws, in contrast, would begin by viewing all measures to some degree as projectives. All events would be considered in terms of their meaning to the individuals who participate in them, and the consensus among individuals concerning meaning would constitute the invariant of the events, the portion perceivable by *all* participants, whether they are, metaphorically speaking, "on" or "off" a given train. No stages of development would be sought in describing general laws, and age alone would not be meaningful. The major objects of inquiry would be the direction, the rate, and the quality of developmental change. The vectors of two developing individuals would be related by means of appropriate transforms, and interpersonal studies would be based on "nearness-of-the-other" effects. Direction, rate, and quality of developmental change would be symbolically translatable from individual to individual; direction, rate, quality, and nearness would characterize groups of interacting individuals, and would also be symbolically translatable. The time dimension would become a part of the symbol; other persons and society would also be part of the symbol, not just factors to be controlled. Results would be visualizable on other than flat two-dimensional surfaces. The subject and object of experimental relationships would be inseparable, as would intrapersonal and social dimensions of any event. Rate, quality, and direction of development would be continuous in the individual until the termination of the group. Events would be neither indeterminate nor determinable from *single* causes; instead, the limits of possible determinates would be enlarged.

The practical consequences of exploring this metatheory, then, would include, but not be limited to, the following:

• Continuation of studies describing stages and age effects, with awareness that they are valid only for the limited-case situation.

- Graphic or mathematical descriptions of the developmental life course that include integration of biological, social, historical, interpersonal, and other psychological events, with development of new research strategies and tools.
- Deeper understanding of the effects of social experience, especially early social experience.
- Resolution of conflicts among many models.
- Understanding of conflicts among individuals.
- Techniques for describing social development across the life span in a cognitive and interpersonal context, and for describing the development of social groups.
- Better understanding of what is shared in verbal communication, how it can be shared, and the nature and limits of the verbal transform system.
- New approaches to the nature and experience of adult development.
- Growth in studies focused on postformal thought and the epistemology of new physics thought, including the relation of use of postformal thought to adaptation.

The last point mentioned, the growth of studies focused on postformal thought and on the epistemology of new physics thought, including the relation of use of postformal thought to adaptation, is one of great importance. As Cassirer (1923, 1950, 1956) writes, there is a sort of spiritual community between physics and epistemology that has been continuing a fruitful dialogue during the ongoing formulation of relativity and quantum theories. We are seeing in this book how this spiritual community may bear fruit in the understanding of human behavior and development, especially the cognitive and interpersonal development linked to postformal thought and wisdom.

In the next chapter, we will explore a subdiscipline allied to the new physics, namely, general systems theory. It extends the paradigm developed in this chapter and provides further grounding for the Theory of Postformal Thought.

CHAPTER 6

General Systems Theory Underlies Postformal Thought

The universe, far from being a desert of inert particles, is a theater of increasingly complex organization, a stage for development in which the human has a definite place without any upper limit to . . . evolution.

ARTHUR YOUNG

The second newer model or set of theories that underlies my Theory of Postformal Thought is general systems theory—or, as we can affectionately call it, GST. Developed hand in hand with the new physics and biology, GST is useful for students of adult development and especially adult cognitive development. It offers ways to think about complex system interactions—interactions not only among supposedly inert physical systems (the focus of physics) but also among *living* systems. Thus, we are about to journey a step further in complexity than we did in the previous chapter. One additional step further in complexity will be made in Chapter 7, when we explore chaos and self-organizing systems.

There are two reasons we are discussing these views of the world at all in this particular book. First, since these views are the precursors or underpinnings of the Theory of Postformal Thought, knowing more about them should help you, the reader, understand and evaluate the Theory of Postformal Thought. Second, scientists, philosophers, and humanists are turning more and more often to worldviews such as these to describe how 20th-century humans construct their world and give their lives meaning. Yet many well-educated professional adults have not had the chance to become acquainted with one or the other of these views. In the course of this chapter, I hope to share with you the principles of GST that are in my view the most important. In later chapters, we will apply these principles as we apply Postformal Theory to problems of adult development.

WHAT IS GENERAL SYSTEMS THEORY?

GST is an *amusing* theory. The physicist Wigner, in a lecture, once said that theories can be either "interesting" or "amusing." An interesting theory may have merit, but often such theories are quickly forgotten; an amusing theory is a theory that makes one *think* and play with the possibilities. GST is an amusing theory.

GST, as I shall use the term here, is an attempt to unify science by finding structures and processes common to many entities. Of greatest interest are entities that are complex organizations that have boundaries, have some continuity over time, and are able to change in orderly ways over time. Such entities may be called *living systems* (Miller, 1978), whether they are cells or societies or some other type of entity. GST included among its earlier theorists such luminaries as Norbert Weiner (1961) and Ludwig von Bertalanfy (1968). Today, it is expressed in the language of quantum physics, chemistry, the many family systems approaches in clinical psychology, game theory (von Neumann & Morgenstern, 1947), biofeedback, sociology (LockLand, 1973), and many other disciplines (Mahoney, 1991). The growth of interest in systems views is due in part to the growth of knowledge that prods us to go beyond single-variable studies to complex expressions of relationship and process. We also have new ways to analyze such complex systems data, and when tools exist, uses for them are created. Of course, that statement itself is a systems theory interpretation of these events over time.

What are some of the *core themes* of GST? The first is the concept of a *system*, that is, a network of related components and processes that work as a whole. *Linkage* and *interaction* are key themes, because whatever influences one part or process influences all of the parts and processes—that is, it influences the entire system. Systems coordinate their activities by means of *feedback*, either from within or from without. Feedback from within leads to homeostasis or equilibrium within; feedback from without leads to balance between two or more systems. *Equilibrium* is a balance between or among system parts. Given a state of disequilibrium, there will be an energy flow from one part to another. Any number of systems can have common mechanisms *(isomorphic processes)* for doing some task. For example, getting energy from one point to another may occur by means of chemical transmission or glucose metabolism or by moving commuters via subways in a "city system." Because systems do interact and trade things such as energy, GST recognizes that scientists need to make deliberate decisions to specify system limits or parameters and levels of description. We have not always done this in the past. Thus, there is an awareness of the observer's input on the "reality" observed, an emphasis reminiscent of the new physics. For example, if I draw living system boundaries at the person level, I may correctly say that a middle-aged woman's depression is due to poor coping strategies; if I draw the boundaries at the societal living system level, I may argue with equal correctness that the depression is caused by social stigmatization of women's aging. I would be correct in both cases but would investigate different things.

Systems theory examines multiple causal variables, or at least considers that they may be present, and focuses most on the processes used to go from one state to another. This focus makes GST a "natural" for developmental psychologists—of whom I am one—who are interested in the multidetermined processes behind changes over time as much as in the states of persons at various time points. GST as a worldview is interested in both the melody and the chords of any life song.

What are some system *functions* that are commonly present in all systems? First, a system that may be defined as "living" (in the broad sense used before) operates so as to *maintain some continuity over time,* some structured wholeness, even while continuing, if appropriate, to grow. Second, systems function to *contain and transfer energy and information* from one point to another, within themselves or between themselves and other systems. All systems have some means of *boundary creation* and maintenance, as well as means of *interaction with other systems.* This property implies that the boundary must be permeable, to some extent, but not so permeable that the system will merge with other systems. Other systems functions are to *control processes, run circular processes,* and *give feedback.* The overall goal is to provide optimum input for continuity and growth, while avoiding pathological abnormalities and *maintaining flexibility.*

CHANGE PROCESSES IN GENERAL SYSTEMS THEORY

Systems do change over time. How does this happen? The only way systems can change over time is if some entropy or disorder is present. If this requirement is counterintuitive, consider for a moment what would happen if no disorder were present and all elements were structured into some form: There would be no space available and no raw material to use to make new forms. For example, if a child used all available blocks to make a toy city (i.e., all the blocks were "ordered"), some disorder would have to be introduced (e.g., knock down or move buildings and push the blocks into a pile on the side) to provide materials and make room for the building of the next orderly structure (perhaps a large house). If my mind is made up about an issue, I must introduce doubt before a change of mind is possible. Thus, disorder (entropy) is not only the catastrophic final state predicted by the Second Law of Thermodynamics but also the beneficial means to a flexible reordering and growth to a larger order. Figure 6.1 illustrates this further.

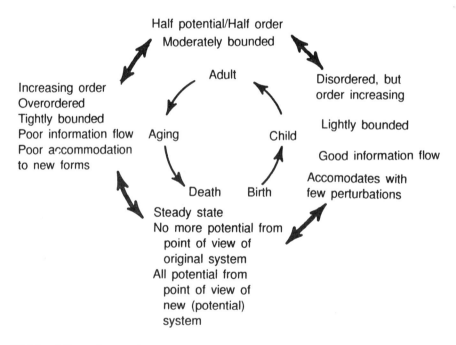

Which of these is true is determined by perspective of observer/system *and* level of observation.

Figure 6.1. Life Span of a Living System: Balancing Potential and Order. (*Source:* Sinnott, 1989c. Reprinted with permission of Cambridge University Press.)

When systems change over time, they usually move from complete disorder or potential through increasing order and bounding to a relative balance between order and potential, a state that may last most of the system's "lifetime." As systems "die," they move toward rigidity, which is a state of very low potential and overwhelming order. All the system's decisions have been made already, so to speak; all its choices are over. The overly ordered, overly structured rigid state admits no change and will be shattered by any input from outside. An analogy is what happens to a rigid crystal goblet that breaks under high-frequency vibrations, whereas the even thinner skin on the hand holding it does not. Prigogene (1980) notes that it is always possible to create a better structure by shattering a rigid state. From that shattering and the availability it creates will come a more flexible, more complex form. This means the death of the old system, or its reemergence in very altered form.

Imagine a situation in which two systems (e.g., societies), come up against each other and try to influence each other; that is, each intrudes on the other's boundaries. If the first system is *not* too rigid and too ordered, the influence and energy of the second will have an impact and alter the first. The reciprocal will also be true. But if the first system is rigid, the second will not influence it easily. It will have to try harder, if it can. Let's say the intruder system does try harder still. If it cannot influence the rigid first system subtly, the more violent influence it may resort to may result in a complete shattering of the first system. The first system did not "go with the flow," "co-opt the opposition," or "make a deal." For a rigid system in which compromise is out of the question, every fight with a worthy opponent is a fight to the death. What a high price to pay for necessary and ordinary adaptations!

The gentler dynamic—mutual influence of semiordered systems—occurs during political dialogues, or pretrial legal negotiations, or among the crash survivors in the Andes that we met in Chapter 4. The second, more catastrophic dynamic—destruction of an old overly rigid system—occurs during revolutions or court trials. Some other dynamics of change over time in a number of very different systems are given in Tables 6.1, 6.2, and 6.3.

The first column in Table 6.1 describes six (generic system) steps that typically occur over time in any "living" system. Examples of their presence are given for a physical system, a couple or dyad system, a family system, a social system, and a sex roles system to show how common and widespread is the evidence for such dynamics over time.

Table 6.1. Patterns of Living-System Change over Time in Six Types of Systems

"Generic" system	Physical system	Couple system	Family system	Social system	Sex roles system
1. Symbiotic undifferentiated	High entropy, low order	Honeymoon	Parent–infant relations	Subculture within group	Undifferentiated
2. Differentiation	Boundary, structures	Power struggle	Parent–adolescent	Emergence of group	Masculine/feminine Permanently M, F
3. Temporary hemeostasis	Stability	Stability	Adolescent given power	New group is now a force	
4. Dynamic homeostasis	Flexible balance of structure and openness to new information	Commitment to the paradox of the "other"	Equal relations, parent and child as peers	Organizational structure recognizes group	Androgyny, role transcendence
5. Reproduction	Spinoff of daughter systems	Co-creation of the relationship and the world	Grandparenthood	New subgroups rise	Transcendence of roles
6. Decay/death	Rigid boundaries, no information flow, any perturbation can lead to disaster	Divorce, widowhood	Family ties end	Organization goes bankrupt	Idiosyncratic fragments of roles are rigidly adhered to

Source: Sinnott (1989d). By permission of Greenwood Publishing Group, Inc., Westport, CT.

Table 6.2. Rules of System Change

1. All systems change, except those near death. *Change* itself is a sign of life, even if specific changes are pathological.
2. Patterns of change are predictable in the long run, based on the state of the system, the state of adjacent systems, and principles of emergence. Patterns of change are predictable in the short run (i.e., locally) based on analyses of local causes.
3. Change in any one system will influence nearby systems. Whether this leads to useful or maladaptive changes in those other systems depends on their states.
4. Boundary rigidity in the face of information or energy flow means death. Being completely unbounded means the dissolution of the system. Systems strive for continuity.
5. Interaction with a new system that is powerful can efficiently and effectively reorient a system that has had its relations with earlier powerful systems distorted.

Source: Sinnott (1993c).

Table 6.2 outlines the characteristics of systems that influence whether or not the potential changes over time in Table 6.1 can actually occur in any given case.

Table 6.3 relates those characteristics to the challenge of personal change, suggesting that change is a necessary, challenging, natural opportunity that need not be dangerous or overly stressful. Intentional personal change, such as may be sought in psychotherapy, simply uses these ordinary change processes more efficiently.

System change over time therefore demands a significant degree of entropy. But systems resist disorder on any large scale, and change means the temporary elimination of much order. The resistance to disorder in the psychological system is evident in the sometimes painful

Table 6.3. System Characteristics That Influence Change

1. The system *must* permit information to enter and provide flexibility with bounded control.
2. Systems resist disorder.
3. Change means temporary increase in disorder.
4. Systems monitor and control the amount of disorder.
5. Surviving systems contain the seed of their own change and are programmed to get to the next higher level of order (e.g., puberty is inherent in an infant).
6. Surviving systems balance potentials and activated processes.
7. Surviving systems fit many contexts.
8. Surviving systems are programmed to interfere with each other.
9. *Non*surviving systems have the same parts as surviving systems, but have different processes.

Source: Sinnott (1993c).

reorganizations during personal change, for example, change during psychotherapy or during crises. Any system tries to monitor and control the extent of disorder, but hopes not to need to resist absolutely, because that would take too much energy. Surviving systems balance their potentials and actualizations, have boundaries but are not closed entirely, try to fit many contexts flexibly, and attempt to interface with other systems without being engulfed or engulfing. Nonsurviving systems may have the same structures (e.g., a boundary), but may have different processes (e.g., *rigidity* in a boundary) that are less adaptive.

AN EXAMPLE: GENERAL SYSTEMS THEORY APPROACH TO "MEMORY"

Next-Generation Psychological Research

Systems theory provides a way for us to make sense of a new generation of psychological research. It also permits us to ask better questions. In doing research on memory aging, for example, we have allowed more information to enter our system and perturb it. We have seen that many factors including perception of events, attention, salience of events, context, the vantage point of the rememberer, and many more influence our aging memories. We have seen that change in memory over time involves compensatory mechanisms that help maintain homeostasis in the individual and between the individual and his or her intimates. How do we as researchers deal with this complexity? A scientific worldview in which causality is linearly dependent on single variables does not do it justice. Simply adopting a multivariate perspective is not adequate, either, because such a view often leaves us casting about in the choice of variables to explore. Adoption of GST gives us more options regarding ways to talk about process and structure, suggesting dynamics and even levels of study that would be relevant. GST lets us reorder our perturbed system on a more complex level, rather than make our boundaries more rigid in order to ward off the new information.

GST gives access to a new physics worldview (see Chapter 5) in which subject and object are necessarily related, but in which the scientific method can still be employed, and must be. GST, used in its general way (i.e., not reduced to single or dual variable studies) demands postformal thought. To use GST, the human living system must therefore cognitively develop these complex intellectual functions that are adaptive.

What Is Memory in a GST Model?

Memory in GST is a storage and organizing function. It can be represented by several different structures, depending on the type of system (e.g., physical system, social system) in which it operates. Note that each of the system types can have a storage mechanism, the final goal of which is always to maintain dynamic equilibrium. In each of the systems, there is some structure for storage and some process for storage. The structure might be a short-term bioelectrical charge in a cell of the body; it might be a library in a social system; it might be a shape-recognition center in the brain. The same system function is served by many structures and processes.

But what is the purpose of memory in a system? One essential purpose is to preserve dynamic equilibrium or to bring it about again by compensations if it is not present or is being threatened. The storage must be storage of information and processes that tend to make peace, so to speak, between the elements within the system or between that system and another system. This means that memory must be able to adjust itself, and to readjust the organism, to events in the ongoing flow of life, and to do so in a way that will lead to real-world survival. Whatever process is involved, real-world survival of the system must be the outcome. What is remembered can be defined only in terms of the real-world success of the "living" system that *lives*. To the extent that a system has good storage of some element that pushes that system toward abnormality or death, or to the extent it has *non*storage of adaptive information, we can say that it has "memory problems." Systems with memory problems might be cells that store erroneous information in genes, leading to tumor production, or humans who are obsessed with memories from childhood, leading to maladaptive responses today. The memory problem might be forgetting digits when recall of digits is needed, or remembering digits when remembering faces or love songs is needed.

Memory-based processes both result from and determine interactions among systems. In other words, a human memory process is grown through, is displayed during, and determines the quality of interactions with other humans, helping maintain social dynamic equilibration.

Another essential purpose of memory in systems theory is to preserve the flexibility of the system. With the passage of time, a system becomes more rigid and ordered (negentropic). Storage includes storage of rules that permit modification of that order to some degree. It also includes basic processes for restructuring the self at points of growing energy and disorder. More information on these self-restructuring processes is to be found in Prigogene (1980) and Prigogene and Stengers (1984). Material can be stored and accessed when needed in more flexible or less flexible ways. When one system interfaces with another and storage/access is more flexible, the interfacing can go more smoothly. So, when studying memory, the function of flexible change and interfacing with other systems must be addressed. What are the contexts in which memory is shaped so that the end result is flexible storage and access? What are the storage systems that lead to greater flexibility in real-world handling of information? The fact that we do not know the answers to these questions (which are generated from GST) argues for a GST approach.

A third essential purpose for memory in systems theory is to control and limit information flow. Memory/storage categories and processes can limit the perceptual filter and thereby decrease the risks of overstimulation or understimulation. They can permit more or less information to be processed, changing, for example, the number of other systems with which one might be capable of interacting meaningfully. Because the purpose of the control of information flow in GST is optimization of multisystem functioning in the real world, the systems view may be the most useful one for study of adaptive functioning.

A final major purpose of memory or storage in GST relates to entropy (i.e., disorder). Memory serves to keep disorder at bay and to increase the structuredness or orderliness of the system. This function, over time, increases internal order and efficiency at the expense of external order; in other words, outside the system there is greater and greater entropy, while inside it there is greater order. If GST tells us that the function of memory is an ordering function, and that this happens over time, memory studies might tease out the nature of that order (with its concomitant survival value) and allow us to see the effects on one system of increasing the order in that system.

Blauberg, Sadovsky, and Yudin (1977) and Miller (1978) have suggested more control-, attention-, and survival-related questions generated by GST. A few such questions are: Storage capacities may differ between those using much versus little stored information to solve problems. Memory may improve if boundaries become more flexible. Storage may be handled differently by overloaded versus understimulated systems. Several kinds of human memories may be hypothesized based upon knowledge of several different human survival needs. Because humans are nested in social systems and hold physical systems within themselves, changes in physical or social system functioning may be associated with changes in human information storage systems. Storage processes of two systems in proximity to one another may influence each other across flexible boundaries; there may be certain optimal contexts in which very good storage systems become excellent. It may be possible to introduce more entropy in an overly structured storage system. Younger systems may have to compensate for less orderly (i.e., less structured) storage systems. Aging may not as strongly affect storage of survival-oriented information compared with less personally important information. My own research on prospective/ intentional memory aging and on memory for space in naturalistic versus abstract maze-like settings speaks to some of these questions, demonstrating that memory aging looks very different through the lenses of GST.

CONCLUSION

This chapter presented an overview of general systems theory (GST). It contained an example of how memory could be understood within that theory, and examples of fresh and far-reaching research questions that would be generated by this approach. GST is connected to our discussion of the new physics in Chapter 5, and provides a further way of thinking about adaptive human behavior. Postformal thought, the topic of this book, is an adult logic predicted in part by GST worldviews. Postformal thought would provide the kind of adult logic that would make GST logically understandable to a mature adult.

CHAPTER 7

Chaos, Complexity,
Self-Regulating Systems,
and Postformal Thought

*The laws of nature must be considered as possibilities that
are changing with the evolution of the system itself.*
ILYA PRIGOGENE

In Chapters 5 and 6, we examined two 20th-century worldviews that
relate to my theory of adult logical development, the Theory of Postformal Thought. Those worldviews are the original, basic ideas of the
new physics, and ideas of general systems theory (GST). Although
there are ancient and current cultural, philosophical, and spiritual
metaphors that bear some resemblance to these theories (e.g., J. Campbell, 1988; Capra, 1975; Underwood, 1993), in mainstream science,
both sets descended from physics. These two related ways of describing complex interactions over time are joined in this chapter by a
third set of concepts, namely, the ideas of chaos theory, complexity
theory, self-regulating systems, and new biology. These concepts also
arise from physics to some extent, but are grounded even more
strongly in computer science and biology. The theories in this chapter
share common bonds with each other and overlap with new physics
(Chapter 5) and GST (Chapter 6), yet each is distinct. All are relatively
unknown, except by scientists on the cutting edge of their disciplines.
All seem useful as worldviews or methods for the study of life-span
development, especially for the study of cognitive development. All
have helped form my thinking.

The processes described by new physics, GST, chaos, complexity,
self-regulating systems, and new biology can be deeply understood

103

only by the postformal logical thinker because they often violate the core linear logic of the formal operational hypothetical–deductive scientific thinker. This is one reason these new sciences seem hard to grasp and hard to teach in the average high school or college physics class. Granted, a student can repeat back axioms of a science even if he or she does not understand them, but that is not deep understanding. The individual with deep understanding can use the concepts to solve problems creatively. Something very much like postformal thought is necessary to deeply *understand* these new science ideas, provided, of course, the thinker has the chance to become familiar with the jargon. If some "postformal adult logic" had not already been described by those of us who are studying it, something like it would have to be invented to describe the thinking processes of the creators of these new science fields! They seem to be postformal thinkers. At an epistemological level, the postformal thinker can choose a way to know the complexities of the world. These complex choices seem to frame the world in some of the same ways that chaos theory and the other new sciences frame it.

I examined these new science ideas to see more of the logical thought processes that let humans think this advanced way, to get some feeling for the stage of cognitive development that follows formal thought, and to obtain a wider view of philosophies and world-views in which postformal thought and its co-created reality could fit comfortably.

WHAT IS CHAOS THEORY?

Chaos theory is a new mathematical model that has been used in the last two decades to describe phenomena as different as weather, the structure of coastlines, brain wave patterns, adult learning, normal or abnormal heartbeat patterns, family transitions, the behavior of the mentally ill, and much, much more (Alper, 1989; Cavanaugh, 1989; Cavanaugh & McGuire, 1994; Crutchfield, Farmer, Packard, & Shaw, 1986; Gleick, 1987; Gottman, 1991; Pool, 1989; Sinnott, 1990). General and more lengthy descriptions of chaos theory are available in Abraham (1985), Barton (1994), Devaney (1989), Gleick (1987), Goerner (1994), Levine and Fitzgerald (1992), and L. B. Smith and Thelan (1993). Chaos theory describes the orderly and flexible nature of apparent disorder. It mathematically describes complex systems with nonlinear equations. It describes commonalities of *processes* over time that would otherwise appear *dis*orderly if viewed at one time point.

Key Concepts

Chaos theory works with those dynamic systems in which the contents of the system and the processes of the system mutually influence each other. In such systems, the current state of the system is fed back to it before it makes another iteration or goes through another round of changes. The system then repeats its process, each time with updated information. Such systems tend to begin to appear stable over time.

But such systems are deterministic, as well as unpredictable, with only the appearance of stability. The behavior at each iteration is not predictable, but the limits built into the system confine it to predictable ways. Thus, there is a "hidden" order that also gradually emerges from beneath the disorder. Chaotic systems somewhat resemble the rambling pattern of footprints made by a curious dog on a very long leash; at first there seems to be no pattern, but soon, after enough walking, a pattern emerges. Part of that emergent pattern is centered on the leash and on what or whoever is holding it; that part is truly deterministic. Part of what emerges is specific to the next part of the dog's rambling walk; that part is unpredictable.

One striking feature of chaotic systems is the way in which they explain why a tiny disturbance or "perturbation" can lead to complete rescaling of the entire pattern of the system due to structural instability. This has been termed the *butterfly effect* (Lorenz, 1963, 1979) because weather forecasters using computer models have seen the "breeze" from a butterfly moving its wings (the idiosyncratic perturbation) eventually lead to a whole new direction of wind movement, even though the overall pattern of the actual wind was not changed by the creators of the computer model. Dynamic systems are generally structurally unstable, demonstrating these large impacts from small changes. It is possible, however, for them to be stable. We humans certainly prefer to think of things as structurally stable and therefore "find" stability even where little exists.

Another feature of chaotic systems is the way a seemingly random set of events, after many repetitive interactions, can coalesce around a point in an apparently orderly way. The impression is of a dominant feature of some sort, analogous to a dominant personality trait or the eye of a hurricane. This phenomenon is termed a *strange attractor* because the point appears to pull in the events around it.

It sometimes helps to think of chaos as organized disorder, as opposed to sheer randomness, or *dis*organized disorder. In orderly disorder, a flexible structure is hidden in events that only seem to be driven by change when examined in linear or one-time slices. The hidden order unfolds gradually to make itself known when the longer-term nonlinear pattern is observed. In true randomness, or *dis*orderly disorder, there is no hidden underlying structure. Without some chaotic flexibility, some orderly readiness to fluctuate built into the system, a system—especially one like the heart or brain—is too rigid to adapt and live. For example, a rigid heartbeat pattern (i.e., one with no chaos) cannot effectively and efficiently correct for a small per-turbing error such as a skipped beat, so a heart attack occurs. A rigid brain wave pattern cannot respond effectively to an intellectual chal-lenge, so poor performance results.

Chaotic disorder is nonrandom and has a kind of potential to cor-rect for errors by the use of the underlying, hidden corrective mecha-nism of the basic, deeper pattern. Chaos is an order enfolded into apparent disorder; it is the pattern in the hologram, akin to the *impli-cate order* described by Prigogene and Stengers (1984). Implicate order means that an orderly message is encoded within the surface and the apparent disorder, so that the implied message can be unfolded and read. Genetic material is another example of this implied message that is unpacked, decoded, and read by the organism as the organism develops from its first cells to its full hereditary potential. But the unfolding makes even a very minor element powerful enough to cre-ate major effects.

Chaos theory gives a rationale for synchronous effects, those apparently unrelated events that seem to mysteriously occur together. The synchronous systems demonstrate entrainment in which one sys-tem locks on to the mode and pattern of another nearby system. The minor event in one system can then move the other system with it.

Chaos models describe the mechanisms of abrupt or qualitative change in interesting ways. For example, a thinker can move from see-ing the world with Piagetian concrete logic to somewhat suddenly see-ing the world with formal logic (an "Aha!" reaction). When a thinker suddenly begins to see the world in Piagetian formal operational terms (after having theretofore framed the world in concrete operational terms), many kinds of behavior are affected.

Bifurcation models within chaos theory seem to describe this kind of sudden shift event. In a bifurcation model, possibilities (actu-ally possible equation solutions) at first emerge from one point, like branches on a young sapling tree. Later in the tree's progression through time, however, the newest branches seem to cluster around several source points, not just one, with young branches coming off two or three more major limbs, going in different directions. This shift from one group of possibilities to several groups of possibilities is analogous to the bifurcation. Before the new branching becomes clear, there seems to be a considerable chaos; after it becomes clear, there seems to be more complex order.

Another way to think about transition and bifurcation is to think about before-having-a-first-baby to postpartum family development. In this example, in the "before" state, life seems to have a stable set of family relations configurations. Then, fairly quickly, something happens, and after a period of greater disorder, several new configurations within the new three-person family branch off on their own tracks. Earlier, we had variations on a parent–parent relational theme; later, we have three possible centers of relations (the original parent–parent, and now, parent 1–child and parent 2–child as well). In the example of the birth of a first child, we know what the proximate cause was that got the system to transform. In some bifurcating systems, the push to transformation is not so well known.

Implications

What might such a theory as chaos imply about reality? First, it suggests that there is more than one sort of disorder. Useful, chaotic disorder provides fresh options and room to correct for past errors; useless disorder provides nothing that seems meaningful, now or later. For example, L.B. Smith and Thelen (1993) describe in chaotic system terms the very young child's learning to walk. Surprisingly, that learning is not a simple practice of muscle movements of a predetermined type. Instead, the child randomly (or so it seems) tries out various movements somewhat associated with walking, finally settling on the set that best allows efficient walking behavior to occur. In other words, the child uses randomness to create an individualized optimal pattern for a skill that was encoded in the human behavioral repertoire and is now emergent.

Second, chaos theory suggests and implies the immense importance of each element in the system for the final outcome of the system as well as for the individual. Remember that a perturbation caused by the fluttering wings of one butterfly, in addition to enabling the butterfly to fly, can alter the weather pattern. And in our own personal histories, we all remember those small chance remarks or experiences that led to major life changes. Chaos principles help validate our phenomenological experience.

Third, chaos theory suggests the importance of openness to innovation in providing natural sorts of corrective devices for complex events, especially those events in which outcomes and goals are not totally clear to us. In that kind of event, a good process is our only safeguard against a manipulation that could cause unimagined damage when it has unforeseen consequences for a dynamic system. For example, we now understand the dangers we face if we severely limit the types of food crops we cultivate. Hundreds of variations on any given food crop species have been lost when we selected for the single species with the highest yield. But in the event that a disease attacks that one species (as in the famous Irish potato famine of the last century), we would have lost the chance to recover because our process of dealing with multiple types of plant species was flawed.

What might chaos theory imply for life-span cognitive development? We might begin to conceptualize life-span cognitive development as a potentially chaotic system. If we do so, we would not expect to find many simple deterministic relationships. We would expect that some deterministic basic elements might be found, but that they will likely be the underlying, hidden order beneath the apparent disorder.

The system of life-span cognitive development may be a structurally unstable system, subject to the large effects of tiny perturbations. As Cavanaugh and McGuire (1994) note, though, the whole idea in developmental research is to show how states change over time in a variety of individualized ways. Using chaos concepts, we *can* predict types of relationships during periods of relative stability in the life span and *can* predict ranges of variability and points of transition to unstable structures. This approach may not satisfy our desires to predict deterministically from moment to moment, but it may be a more realistic goal and a prime opportunity to study complex individual differences.

Predicting factors that lead to bifurcations of systems—for example, predictions about the events that trigger a bifurcation between formal and postformal logical thought in a person—can be made and tested empirically. The new center of events in that case, that is, postformal logic as the advanced thinking process of an adult might then be described as a strange attractor.

Cavanaugh and McGuire (1994) suggest that chaos theory can help us frame and answer several questions about adult cognitive development. It would offer insights as to why there are just a few qualitatively unique levels of thinking. It could help explain why cognitive development shows a few "spurts" at certain times, but smooth progression most of the time. It could address the question of why it is so hard to maintain cognitive flexibility (i.e., moving easily among attractors so as to solve problems creatively). It could show how modes of thinking develop. Finally, it could resolve the persistent question of why cognitive training usually does not generalize.

A WORD ABOUT
SELF-ORGANIZING SYSTEMS

Self-organizing systems carry the ideas of chaotic nonlinear systems one step further by examining what happens when such systems reach conditions that are very far from their state of equilibrium. At that point, systems reorganize themselves in unpredictable ways that are sometimes so dramatic—even if they *are* just computer models—that the term *artificial life* has been used to describe them (Waldrop, 1992).

The Santa Fe Institute was created to explore phenomena related to self-organizing systems and has become a mecca for complexity theorists. Interested readers may wish to explore this field in several books, including books by Goldstein (1994), on organizational change; Kauffman (1993), on evolution; Kelly (1994) and Maturana and Varela (1988), on adaptive cognition; and Nicholis and Prigogene (1989) and Waldrop (1992), on complexity.

Key Concepts

We tend to think of collective behavior as simply the accumulation of individuals' behaviors, but it is more than that. Collective behavior tends to be nonlinear and tends toward self-organization. One molecule or one person (ignoring for the moment that persons are systems) may respond in a particular way to being pushed past its limits, while a collection of those molecules or persons will respond very differently and somewhat unpredictably. Self-organizing systems studies work with the unique properties of such collections. According to Goldstein (1994), self-organization has the following features when it occurs: System structure is radically reorganized, novel patterns emerge, random events are amplified and utilized, and a new coordination of parts is attained. These changes are not imposed on the system, but emerge from it. Collective systems do not simply resist change or face destruction, but have the potential to ride the change to create a different organization within. The changes are self-orchestrated, as this system reconfigures its own resources in the face of a far-from-equilibrium challenge.

Goldstein (1994) describes some characteristics of self-organization: A spontaneous and radical reorganizing occurs, equilibrium-seeking tendencies are interrupted, the system utilizes the disorganization as a chance for change within some limits, and unpredictable outcomes occur that leave the system more optimally organized.

Complexity theory goes beyond qualitative descriptions of the kind of systems it deals with, namely, complex *adaptive* systems, by making complexity a measurable quantity. Complex systems also have similar qualities in whatever context they occur.

Implications

The implications of this theory are simply too vast to be outlined yet. Imagine a unified theory of adaptive system change being applied to everything, and consider the consequent scope of possibilities. Few topics would be off limits! Possibilities include prediction of developmental trends in adulthood and aging as multiple adaptive systems interact over time.

The most important implication, however, is that the possibilities for *self-created* adaptive order seem beyond the scope of our imaginations. Yet we hold them in our hands. As Kauffman suggests (Waldrop, 1992), we help make the world we live in and have a part in its story. We are neither victims nor outsiders, but team members helping design it all. Our impact on the evolving systems in which we have a part is a permanently transformative one for ourselves and the other systems (Waldrop, 1992). This exegesis sounds like Victor Frankl (1968) and the existentialist psychologists speaking! It sounds like postformal thought, the cognitive part of our human creation of this adaptive story.

A WORD ABOUT NEW THEORIES
IN BIOLOGY

Proponents of versions of a new biology include Augros and Stanciu (1987), Kauffman (1993), Kelly (1994), McLean (1988), and Maturana and Varela (1988), among others. Their work draws from earlier evolutionary theory and research and adds the new experimental data of modern medicine, complexity theory, and biology to attempt to answer difficult biological questions. Some applied, clinical aspects of this field include mind–body medicine, such as psychoneuroim-munology. The new biologists frequently come to conclusions that give us new outlooks on traditional biological theories such as that of evolution. They also help us understand our own era, in which machines and cultures are very complex and autonomous and almost indistinguishable from living things (Kelly, 1994).

For example, one basic new biology argument is that rather than modeling aggression or conflict, biological systems model synergy and cooperation. One thing this means is that species do not fight for the same niche in an environment; they evolve to fit a "free" space so that they need not incur conflict with other species. In the same spirit, "higher," more evolutionarily recent brain centers (like the cortex and prefrontal cortex) are not seen by these theorists to be in conflict with "lower," evolutionarily older brain centers over control of behavior. Instead, the higher centers and lower centers seem to work as a team to create clever ways to reach instinctive and emotional goals that serve both individual and community. The human immune system in these sorts of theories is more than an army that attacks invaders. It is also like a communication net, operating to deal adaptively with any breaks in the wholeness of the body and mind and emotional connec-tions. In the new biology, individual components or parts are seen as self-organizing, self-regulating, and cooperating, not standing in oppo-sition to each other.

Thinkers within these new traditions expect a kind of biological Second Law of Thermodynamics to emerge soon. This law would be able to explain *emergence,* the process by which organisms communi-cate and cooperate and a newer more complex structure comes into being. It would explain, for example, how fish become schools and how ecosystems evolve so "naturally." It would explain how groups of individuals somehow transcend themselves and become something more, perhaps a community with shared values. To make such a change probably requires that the network of nodes and connections either make the connections stronger or put in new connections. It also seems to require that organisms balance order and disorder so that they operate on the "edge of chaos" (Waldrop, 1992). Notice how this thinking connects with the developing systems perspective in Chapter 6. Postformal thought can be said to be "thinking on the edge of chaos," as we will discuss further at a later point. It is part of Kauff-man's thinking that complex organisms go to the edge of chaos to solve complex problems. There at that edge, they seem to use postfor-mal thought.

Implications

The implications of this new-biology approach are quite profound. The cocreated reality that we discussed as a part of adaptive functioning in postformal thought is the essence of both self-
regulating systems and new-biology concepts. Although biological
entities are clearly individuals, they are also defined by their relations within the larger whole.

The yearning for community that we feel today certainly res-
onates with descriptions of the self-organizing whole with which individuals naturally "flock." In these new-biology theories, though, the
"whole" does not engulf its parts or even subsume the individual. On
the contrary, it desperately "needs" the individual's uniqueness to
reach their mutually created goals. The whole provides part of the
meaning of action for the individuals, and a large part of the motivation. Empty evolutionary niches quickly go out of ecological balance
because they have lost their meaning. Nothing communicates meaning
and shares purpose with them.

A painful example of the disastrous effects of loss of collective
meaning can be found within the human body, in the immune system.
The immune system forms a sort of communication net. When the
communication links with the whole are broken, the system turns on
the very body that sustains it, leading to autoimmune disorders. The
new biology provides us with one more way to conceptualize the
adaptive purpose of the interpersonal cognitive development we are
calling postformal thought. The quality of thinking in complex ways,
described in Chapters 3 and 4, might be necessary for a *conscious*
emergent order.

A FINAL THOUGHT ON PART I TOPICS

We have examined the need for a theory of adult logical development such as the Theory of Postformal Thought. We have looked at
the characteristics of that theory and have seen how it might develop.
We have examined several new science worldviews into which the
study of postformal adult logical development would comfortably fit.
Each of these new worldviews offers another way of thinking about a
cocreated process-oriented reality, such as that of postformal operations. Armed with these models and a clearer sense of direction, we
see that understanding of the world "out there" is very much a matter
of very complex choices that seem to have an emergent orderliness

about them. Now, perhaps, we are ready to ask more sophisticated questions about postformal adult logical development.

In Part II, we turn to an examination of some of the research done on postformal thought.

In Part III, we will explore the many applications of the theory and some ways that postformal thinking might be taught or facilitated.

In Part IV, we will draw all these threads together to help us reach the goal of understanding and balancing the needs of mind, heart, body, spirit, and other people, over a lifetime.

PART II

SOME RESEARCH TO SUPPORT THE THEORY

Studies of Complex Postformal Thought

CHAPTER 8

Initial Research: How Do Adults Use Logical Thought?

Like the unassembled pieces of a jigsaw puzzle, discoveries about our developmental possibilities are scattered across the intellectual landscape, isolated from one another in separate lines of inquiry.

MICHAEL MURPHY

WHY ARE THEY DOING SO BADLY?

My interest in the process of adult thinking on complex tasks started with my disappointment with adults' failures on what I thought of as comparatively simple Piagetian thinking tasks. When I was doing research on adult performance on Piagetian tasks as a graduate student, I encountered the small number of studies in which older adults had been tested with Piaget's concrete or formal operational test materials. I thought it a bit ironic that the mature adult investigators never seemed to test adults between the ages of 20 and 60, only children and people over 60, but it did not strike me as unusual at the time. After all, when we "rounded up the usual suspects" as volunteers for developmental research, mature adults were seldom invited. It seemed a step forward when a developmental study had any mature and older adult respondents, yet experimentalists often performed adult and old age studies.

I therefore took a closer look at this relatively scant developmental literature on mature and older adults' performance, and I began to get depressed. The results overall said "decline." The message seemed to be that "they get a little older and they've lost it," at least as far as Piagetian cognitive logical performance, even simple performance, went.

But as I mentioned earlier in the introduction to this book, I knew too many very competent *and* very old people to credit that picture of general decline at 60. Armed with the chutzpah of the young adult, I thought that perhaps *I* could do a better study. Although in retrospect I used too simple a design, I tested 34 respondents age 68 or older with fellow graduate students Janet Chap and Anne Dean. Since a number of prior researchers had interviewed or tested respondents from nursing homes—respondents who, after all, were probably not feeling very well—we tried to control for the health factor at least a little by testing both community and nursing home respondents. Since older respondents often have lower educational levels due to cohort differences, we thought it would help us understand the true abilities of our respondents if we controlled for education. Then we gave a variety of Piagetian tasks, not just one or two. When we finished testing, we found that respondents with more education who lived in the community did better on the tasks and that the tasks retained their structural coherence. But older adults still did not do very well. For example, only 11% passed the formal operations test, which at that time was thought to be mastered by most people in adolescence. Many of our respondents did not even pass concrete level tasks (Chap & Sinnott, 1977–1978).

For my dissertation research, I decided to tackle this problem again, using a different tactic. My respondents in the earlier study had made plenty of comments about the tasks in the study. They thought the tasks were "for children" and too abstract to be at all interesting to someone of mature years who had a full life. I had to admit I would have felt patronized and out of place, even at the age of 30, with tasks out of a physics book, kids' clay to work with, and young research assistants "testing" me. At that age, and enrolled in a doctoral psychology program, I felt a little wise and had been certified as "smart," but what I knew best was not reflected in tasks from a physics book or work with clay. I decided for my dissertation work to test middle-aged and older adults on everyday or naturalistic forms of Piagetian tasks (along with other tasks) and see whether that would bring out more of adults' logical skills.

The results of my dissertation research were both encouraging and disappointing (Sinnott, 1975). The structural relations of the logic used by older adults were equivalent to those of younger adults. But older respondents still performed more poorly, usually significantly so, than the middle-aged respondents did, whether the tasks were traditional or everyday, concrete operations or formal operations. To add to the puzzle, middle-aged respondents did not master the tasks either, as they should have according to theory. Apparently I was still not able to sufficiently capture what I thought was the experience and intelligence of my respondents, although creation of everyday tasks was helping.

During my postdoctoral studies, I pursued the possibility that nondevelopmental cognitive aging studies from the experimental and personality traditions would hold clues to what was happening in my studies. There existed a huge body of literature on information processing, intelligence, perception, human factors, attention, learning, problem solving, and personality, and I eagerly perused it. I had hoped that some area I had not yet mastered would hold a key to what was happening with my respondents. I read about interesting and complex processes and more "declines" (though studies were mainly cross-sectional, so researchers could not strictly say respondents declined from some specific earlier score).

But I was not persuaded by writers' explanations of what was going on or how declines like these could so often coexist with ordinary functioning in competent people somewhere between 18 and 97 years of age. To simply say that respondents went downhill cognitively due to "aging," but that it did not matter much in their lives, seemed illogical and a little empty as an explanation of basic cognitive processes. It sometimes seemed as silly as saying that they deteriorated due to "death" or that we should confine our research to variables that are *only* of academic interest.

I was also intrigued by interviewing my respondents after they were tested and by observing what my respondents actually did when they were not taking tests. One man in his 70s specialized in making clocks by hand for about 12 hours a day, almost daily. Although he could have routinized the task, he did not. He was adventurous and made all different sorts of timepieces to amuse himself. In hearing him talk about his clock making or the conduct of his clock business (or lots of other topics), I heard formal operational thought. Yet this man scored only 1 point in 4 on formal operational tasks. I asked him why he didn't answer in that (formal operational) way on the test, if he thought as he just said he did. He answered that he had thought about lots of things he could say in response to the formal problems during the test, but he decided that was not what he *should* say, so he didn't. Then, since it was now OK to do so, he proceeded to articulate a formal operational solution to the task. I was impressed.

Other studies in which I asked older adults about life decisions (Sinnott, 1980, 1981), resolutions of life conflicts (Guttmann et al., 1977; Sinnott & Guttmann, 1978a,b), and complex roles (Sinnott, 1977, 1981, 1986b) and gave them cognitive problems reinforced my belief not only that most of my competent adult respondents were keeping their cognitive abilities, but also that many were continuing to *grow* cognitively in an interesting way.

Finally, as a good developmentalist should have done from the start, I began to ask this question: "When respondents fail complex tasks, what clever, adaptive thing are they doing *instead* of passing?" The results of asking that new question appear in this book as my Theory of Postformal Thought, as applications of that theory, and as research described in this section of the book. My respondents were not "failing" at all. They were essentially ignoring the simplistic old tasks and mental processes and going *beyond* them to an exciting new place! That new place seemed to combine cognitive processes with emotion, intention, and the needs of the person as a whole.

Once I realized, by thinking through what respondents had told me, that they were actually using a different, more advanced logic, I began to test for it using the problems and the thinking operations already described in Chapter 3.

GOING BEYOND FORMAL OPERATIONS: TESTS IN THE BALTIMORE LONGITUDINAL STUDY OF AGING

How Can We See What They Are Really Doing?

Suspecting, now, that mature adult respondents might be using some sort of "post"-formal thought when they seemed to be performing poorly on cognitive tasks, I decided to see what they might be doing. I began a first round of testing with participants from the Baltimore Longitudinal Study of Aging (BLSA), starting in 1980 during my postdoctoral training. The BLSA was coordinated at the Gerontology Research Center, which is part of the National Institute on Aging, National Institutes of Health, so I was in good company for scientifically improving my ideas. The BLSA is a sample of volunteers who are an optimum aging population, for the most part. There are relatively few women or minorities, however, especially among the long-term longitudinal respondents, since these groups were excluded during the early years of the study. BLSA members are well educated and highly motivated, enjoy an above average socioeconomic status, and are willing to travel to come to the center for three days of testing every two years, conceivably from age 18 until death. The only compensation they receive for this effort is a free physical examination during their visit. Details of this sample are in Shock et al. (1985). Respondents receive many kinds of experimental tests during their stay, including physical and psychological tests and clinical assessments. For some types of data (e.g., blood pressure) and for some respondents, data were on file for a 30-year period of time at the time I tested.

In the first round of my BLSA testing, 79 respondents between the ages of 26 and 89, one third of whom were women, were interviewed. A modified clinical method was used in which standard problems were given, followed by probes to clarify responses. The focus of the interview was problem solving. Respondents were told before they began that any given problem they would be working on might have a single solution, more than one solution, or no solution at all. Six stimulus problems (which readers will recall reading in the transcript in Table 3.6) were presented in written form in random order along with the standard probe questions. The problems were designed to test both formal and postformal operations. They demanded combinatorial reasoning and understanding of proportionality. The contexts of the problems varied, ranging from totally abstract to more everyday and interpersonal situations with embedded abstract demands. Respondents were scored on most of the logical operations seen in Table 3.5, but not all (because some of the operations had not yet been "discovered" at this testing).

I was most interested in the results for three problems on this first round of study: the Bedrooms (BR) problem, the Magazine Workers (WK) problem, and the ABC problem. ABC and BR were both combinatorial problems with the same abstract demand but very different contexts. I expected that postformal thought would be more frequent in an interpersonal context. The logic of the WK problem relied on proportionality more than combinatorial reasoning, but took place in an interpersonal context, so it offered a potential contrast to the BR problem. In addition to the planned comparisons, I was willing to learn from the exploratory postformal data. Since I reasoned that postformal thought organizes systems of formal thought, I needed to see whether I could fairly argue that respondents had formal operations in their cognitive repertoire.

Results

Results have been described to some extent in a number of presentations, particularly at the earliest Adult Development Conferences originally held at Harvard University (Sinnott, 1981, 1985) and in several chapters (e.g., Sinnott, 1984a,b).

The first question of interest was whether respondents using this more everyday type of test succeed at formal operational logic tasks. The percentages of respondents passing formal operations demands of each problem are in Figure 8.1, by age and gender. The BR problem, which was the most "everyday" and had the most social or interpersonal demand characteristics, was the least likely of the three to be answered in formal operations terms. In contrast, the ABC problem, which demands the same combinatorial logic for respondents to get a formal operations passing score, led to the greatest proportion of respondents passing in formal operational terms, an average 86% of the men (the only significant gender difference in performance). Since part of my hypothesis was that mature respondents were not as bad at logical thought as they appeared to be on the surface, it helped me to know that context made a huge difference in performance on formal operational thinking, Piaget's difficult "last" stage of thinking. It also helped to know that virtually every respondent answered in a formal operational way on *at least one* of the problems. Poor formal operational performance on BR and WK also gave lots of room for me to explore what respondents were doing when they "failed" formal operational logical thought.

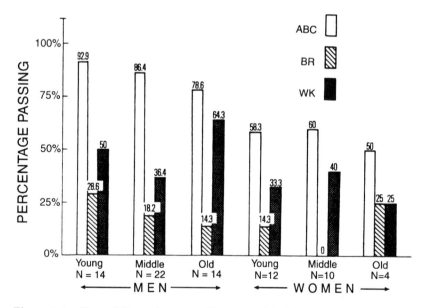

Figure 8.1. Formal Operations, as a Function of Problem Context, Age, and Sex.

If postformal thought as I was beginning to conceptualize it provided a coordination of several formal systems, I needed to see my respondents using more than one logical system. The easiest approach was to look for a "realistic" and an "abstract" version of a formal solution. Any respondent, then, could pass formal operations in the abstract way of Piaget, or by using the realistic formal logic, or by using both. Figure 8.2 shows the percentages passing using formal logic under the original (abstract) constraints only, under the realistic constraints only, or under both, by problem and age (gender differences were nonsignificant). Respondents apparently were "failing" formal operations on the BR problems because they were reifying the problem, being formal operational under realistic constraints. This provided part of the answer to the original question of "What are they doing?"

Ironically, the one problem most like the typical formal operations test, the problem that could *not* easily be read in a realistic way, the ABC problem, was the one that most adults found least important and least motivating. The average importance score given this problem was 2.55 of a possible 5.00. Ironically, the problems that respondents

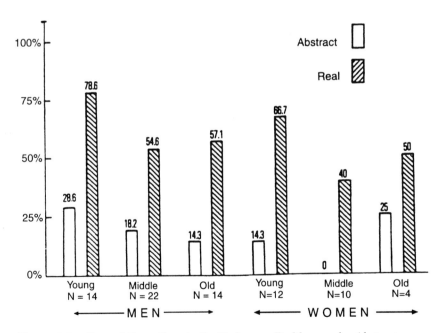

Figure 8.2. Formal Operations in the Bedrooms Problem under Abstract or Real Constraints.

found most important, scoring them around 4.15, were the ones on which they ignored the abstract formal operations demand and answered only in terms of realistic formal operational constraints. This practice would have made them look like failures at logical thought on prior tests. On any problem other than the ABC problem, these adults generally chose a *non*abstract solution as being "best" after generating a number of possible logical solutions. Here was another part of the answer to the puzzle: What respondents were doing was ordering several formal operational solutions and making a choice as to which one was right or "true." This was another factor that I began to look for as part of postformal thought.

Evidence for other operations that had been hypothesized to be part of postformal thought is in Table 8.1, by problem (age and gender differences were nonsignificant). Respondents were saying and doing what was consistent with their having what I was beginning to call *post*formal thought.

Discussion

The results of this first study indicated that it is possible for some adults to structure logical thinking at a stage more complex than that of formal operational thought. Some adults seemed to prefer this stage for solving problems involving more realistic scenarios. Interpersonal problems lent themselves to the production of postformal statements. Even subjects who did not solve problems in two clearly formal oper-

Table 8.1. Percentages of 79 Respondents Giving Evidence of Postformal Operations, by Problem

	Problem		
Operation	BR	WK	ABC
Metatheory shift	34.2%	21.5%	—
Problem definition	92.4%	49.4%	2.5%
Process–product shift	20.2%	59.5%	26.5%
Parameter setting	81.0%	45.6%	1.3%
Pragmatism	73.4%	63.3%	—
Multiple solutions	38.0%	11.4%	—
Multiple causality	31.6%	49.4%	—
Paradox	12.7%	—	—

Source: Sinnott (1984a).

ational ways still seemed to demonstrate sufficient capability for post-formal thought, since they showed some of the operations.

It is possible that many subjects who "failed" abstract formal thought tests did so because they were at a stage beyond formal operational thinking. They may have exercised their capacity for higher-level thinking to choose a pragmatic set of a priori rules. Respondents seemed aware, in many cases, that choosing a formal system to employ in one problem was necessarily subjective. Of course, some adults did strongly maintain that there is one and only one possible logical answer that is "right," responding on a formal or concrete level, but they constituted the minority in this study. In general, support was found for the hypothesis that evidence for postformal thought can be found in the thinking of ordinary adults.

But do postformal operations constitute a separate stage of qualitatively different thought development? By Neimark's (1975) criteria, they do. A higher level of abstraction is attained, since several formal systems are related in terms of a metric, such as the selection of an a priori and problem parameters. The elements of thought are now formal operational systems themselves, rather than lower-level abstractions. The structure of the relations within the stage is unique, since it includes necessary subjectivity and the incorporation of contradiction. That is, conscious choice is required among essentially equivalent systems that are mutually contradictory and that are based on a reality partly created by the knower.

The results of this study seemed to support the hypothesis that mature adults often seemed to fail tests of logical thought because they were using a more complex logic than we were asking for. The hypothesized postformal operations were beginning to appear.

At this point, it seemed important to test more respondents to see whether the findings of the original study would hold. A larger respondent base would let us see more operations and make more links between postformal thought and other aspects of respondents' cognitive and physical performance using data already gathered for the BLSA.

I also wanted to be certain that respondents were spontaneously generating this sort of thought, not simply responding to my clinical interview postformally. I had heard about a thinking out loud procedure and wanted to use it to record respondents' thought processes without the intrusion of any questions or statements from me.

Chapter 9 will summarize part of the next round of studies, studies that used a thinking out loud procedure.

Interview and Thinking Aloud Studies

A View of Process

Life is always changing one way or another through its adaptation to non-equilibrium conditions.

ILYA PRIGOGENE

All real living is meeting.

MARTIN BUBER

In the next round of studies, it seemed important to see whether testing additional respondents would give the same sort of results that occurred in the first round of testing. Even more important, the next several rounds of data collection could give us a view of the process adult respondents are using while they solve problems and, one hopes, use postformal thought.

FIRST OBJECTIVE: REPLICATION

Our research questions with the goal of replication were these: Is evidence for postformal thought reliable; that is, is it found again in larger samples? Are there age or problem-context effects in these larger samples?

The first objective was reached by testing more members of the Baltimore Longitudinal Study of Aging (BLSA), which was described in Chapter 8. The more refined version of the first research question was: Is there evidence for postformal self-referential thought in the problem solving of a life-span sample of adults? In all, 210 respondents from the BLSA were eventually tested using structured interviews in what came to be known as the standard administration [as opposed to the thinking aloud administration (Sinnott, 1985, 1991b)]. I was happy to see that the results were essentially the same as reported in Chapter 8, providing a replication of earlier work. Respondents often were solving the problems as though they could use the operations of postformal thought described in Table 3.5. The degree of use of the operations again depended on the context of the problem. The more interpersonal the problem context, the more postformal operations respondents produced. So once again, for example, the Bedrooms problem context was the occasion of more postformal operations than the ABC problem context.

One crucial operation emerged as a predictor of respondents' overall way of working with the problems: the number of solutions that respondents generated for problems. Later in this chapter when we discuss styles of problem solving shown by respondents, it will be clearer exactly how generation of solutions interacts with age and other variables to help define style. For now, see Table 9.1 to compare numbers of solutions generated across problems. From 26% to 85% of respondents used two or more solutions. The very abstract (comparatively speaking) ABC problem was the context for only a quarter of respondents using multiple solutions. The number of respondents who produced more than one solution increased dramatically when they were solving the Bedrooms problem, with its interpersonal context. On average, about 64% of respondents generated multiple solutions for a problem. Table 9.2 presents the most interesting age by problem context per-

Table 9.1. Evidence for Postformal Operations during Thinking Aloud and Standard Administration

Thinking aloud[a]	ABC	CAMP	BR	WK	VC	
Have formal operations	60%	57%	2%	30%	37%	
Use self-referential thought	10%	2%	27%	15%	7%	
State multiple goals	10%	12%	45%	15%	30%	
Standard administration	ABC	VC	WK	CAKE	BR	POW
One solution	68.4%	29.2%	28.3%	11.3%	20.8%	27.4%
More than one solution	25.9%	68.4%	65.4%	85.3%	75.5%	64.3%

[a]Before probe.
Source: Sinnott (1991b). By permission of Greenwood Publishing Group, Inc., Westport, CT. Problems: (BR) Bedrooms; (CAKE) Cake-Baking Interruption; (CAMP) Camping Trip Logistics; (POW) Family Power Dynamics; (VC) Vitamin C; (WK) Magazine Workers.

Table 9.2. Context Effects: Percentages of Age Subsamples Using Multiple Solutions for Magazine Workers, Bedrooms, and Family Power Dynamics Problems during Standard Administration

Age range	WK	BR	POW
One solution			
20s and 30s (N = 37)	40.5%	13.8%	16.2%
40s–60s (N = 109)	24.5%	18.2%	32.1%
70s and 80s (N = 52)	31.4%	32.7%	32.6%
More than one solution			
20s and 30s	59.4%	86.1%	83.7%
40s–60s	71.9%	81.7%	65.1%
70s and 80s	61.1%	63.6%	59.6%

Source: Sinnott (1991b). By permission of Greenwood Publishing Group, Inc., Westport, CT.

formance differences found during this testing among responses to the Bedrooms, Magazine Workers, and Family Power Dynamics problems.

From testing this larger number of respondents, we concluded that postformal operations could reliably be found and that problem context differences were predictably related to use of postformal thought operations. We were thus able to move forward and examine data related to the second objective.

SECOND OBJECTIVE: UNDERSTANDING THE THOUGHT PROCESS DURING POSTFORMAL THOUGHT

Thinking Aloud Approach

Artificial intelligence (AI) is the field that creates computer models that can imitate or at least model some types of human thought, for example, computers that can play chess. AI has given us a method of gathering and analyzing thinking aloud problem-solving protocols, which are the detailed descriptions of steps a person uses to solve a problem as articulated by the person while solving the problem. It has also given us a means of examining the flow of operations the person uses and speaks about during the solution of a problem. Computers can then copy the flow of operations to mimic that particular human thought process.

This set of tools is useful in research on postformal problem solving because it provides the means to "watch" respondents' logical thought processes while they exercise their problem-solving skills. It permits our knowing *whether* and *how* and *when* they might use any sort of logic, including postformal operations, or what they may be doing when they appear to "fail" our problem-solving tests. It permits us to see in detail the related behavior they use. The thinking aloud (TA) approach to the study of problem solving has been described and used by a number of researchers (for an extensive bibliography, see Ericsson and Simon, 1984). Giambra and Arenberg (1980) recommended its use in aging studies, in which it proved useful (e.g., Giambra, 1983; Rowe, 1984). Ericsson and Simon (1984) addressed all significant aspects of TA protocol analysis, including assumptions, instructions, coding, hypothesis testing, and impact of using the TA method on results obtained. In the studies reported in this chapter, the administration of the problems and the analyses of protocols were performed using the TA approach. The issues and solutions summarized by Ericsson and Simon were kept in mind.

TA approaches require minimal assumptions about the nature of processing, the chief one being that it occurs in an information-processing framework. Evidence suggests that instructions to think aloud do not significantly alter the sequence of cognitive processes. Verbal concurrent and retrospective reports provide a nearly complete record of the sequence of information needed during task performance, and verbally reported data seem as regular and valid as other types of data (Ericsson & Simon, 1984).

Several TA-derived research strategies were used over the course of the studies summarized in this chapter. The simplest involved presenting a written problem and asking respondents individually to keep talking about their thoughts as they worked on the problem. The respondents' comments were taped and transcribed. Another more complex version of the strategy involved the same request to think aloud; when the respondent finished, the experimenter then asked additional questions necessary to clarify comments made by the respondent while thinking aloud.

All thinking aloud respondents in this second version were told the following: "Think aloud as you work on the problems. Say whatever comes to mind, even if it doesn't seem important. When you've finished with the problem, I'll ask you about anything that seems unclear to me." The experimenter always stayed in the test room to hear what the respondent said and provide an audience for the respondents' ideas. Experimenters were not allowed to comment or dialogue. If the respondent stopped speaking, the experimenter asked "What are you thinking right now?" or said "Please remember to help us understand your thoughts by thinking *aloud*." Notice that by virtue of this simple prompt, both TA and occasionally very short-term retrospective data were gathered in this way.

Taped protocols were typed verbatim. A sample transcript was presented in Table 3.6 and may also be referred to as you read this chapter. Although it is customary in using this method to eliminate statements made by the respondent that seem to miss the problem's cognitive demands or that include the subject's analyses of his or her own processes, *all* the respondent's statements were included in each protocol in our studies. The statements were transcribed and were analyzed in the order in which they were made. The model of the respondent's process to be presented later in this chapter follows the real-time order of the respondent's statements and behaviors (e.g., a behavior might be the respondent's writing the letter pairs in the ABC problem on a sheet of paper).

Protocol statements were analyzed by rescoring them in several ways. They were first considered as episodes—for example, a working-forward path (overall) versus a working-backward path (Simon & Simon, 1978). They were next considered as processors—for example, processing a column of numbers (Newell & Simon, 1972). The entire protocol was considered as a unit at some levels of analysis; at other levels, a single statement was considered as one unit. This variation in treatment will become apparent during the following discussion of a protocol.

As a point of clarification, *goals, solutions,* and *essences* differ, so the several terms are necessary. Several solution processes may be used to reach the same goal, and several goals may serve one essential belief (essence) of the nature of the problem. One solution process may serve several goals, and one goal may serve several beliefs.

More about the Kinds of Problems Presented, from the Point of View of Cognitive Problem-Solving Literature

In the problem-solving literature, one sees discussion of ill-structured problems and well-structured problems and the effect of heuristic availability. These are interesting concepts that might also come into play in the study of postformal thought (see Chapter 3). Postformal thought might be most useful when the problem is ill-structured and when no heuristic is available for the solver to use.

Part of the "failure" of older adults who work on Piagetian-like logical problems may be ascribable to the experimenter's framing a problem as well-structured (in the traditional terms of problem-solving study), while the respondent frames it as ill-structured (in those same terms). Let us define some terms more clearly. A problem may be seen as either a puzzle or well-structured problem or an ill-structured or "wicked" problem. A well-structured problem has a structured goal, an optimal solution path, and a single solution for which an algorithm exists, and utilizes a Lockean inquiry system. An ill-structured problem, in contrast, has no unequivocal single solution and little certainty about the theoretical assumptions that fit the problem, and utilizes a Kantian or a dialectical inquiry system (Churchman, 1971). A respondent's perception of whether a problem is a puzzle or a less structured problem is part of his or her decision concerning goal clarity and whether it exists or not. Developmental differences in assumptions about the nature of reality influence the possibility that a person can consider a problem only as a one-goal puzzle (with goal clarity) or also as one that has potential for several goals (Toulmin, 1970). Problems seen as having several potential solutions are frequently dealt with by "satisficing" (i.e., choosing the "good enough" answer), rather than by maximizing strategies (Howard, 1983). The problems I use in postformal studies are hybrid problems, which can potentially be treated either or both of these ways by respondents. If a respondent truly answers in formal operational terms, he or she must be framing the problem as well-structured; if a respondent answers in postformal terms, he or she might be framing the problem as either well-structured or ill-structured. I hypothesized that since respondents' decisions about the nature of the problem use postformal thought, *both* making a decision about the nature of the problem *and* different styles of problem-solving processes should be related to presence or absence of postformal operations and postformal logic.

In two key articles related to these traditional problem-solving literature distinctions—articles that I found very useful—Sweller (Sweller, 1983; Sweller & Levine, 1982) discussed the impact of changes in goal specificity (goal clarity) on strategies employed on a problem. For problems *high* in goal specificity, means–end analysis was the strategy of choice. Little learning of general transferable solutions took place, and processing was more "top-down," that is, strategy-driven. For a problem *low* in goal specificity, hypothesis testing was the more usual strategy; learning was more likely to occur, history-cued (prior-learning-cued) rule induction was likely to take place, and "bottom-up" or data-driven processing was more likely. Concerning a heuristic or algorithm, the respondent might start out with one or develop one during the course of solving several problems. Greeno, Magone, and Chaiklin (1979) found respondents applying available rules or approaches without reference to stated goals. Available heuristics were used no matter what! Expectations for my study, expectations concerning the effects of goal clarity and heuristic availability on strategy, size of problem space, and other factors are in Table 9.3.

Table 9.3. Expected Relations of Perceived Goal Clarity and Availability of Heuristic to Some Dimensions of Strategy, Problem Space, Performance on Well-Structured Problems, and Skills Needed

Clarity of any one goal learned[a]	Heuristic/algorithm?	Probable strategy
1. Clear	Available	Use learned heuristic or algorithm. Performance on well-structured problems should be good if persons prefer this approach. Seeing problems this way is related to youth and good skills. Small problem space.
2. Clear	Unavailable	Use means–end analysis. Medium problem space. If performance on well-structured problems by solvers who prefer this strategy is poor, it is due to the time-consuming nature of the strategy to find a heuristic. Seeing problems this way is related to poor skills. Train for skills to improve performance.
3. Unclear	Available	Use learned heuristic/algorithm and assume that goal is "whatever is yielded by that process." Small problem space. If performance on well-structured problems by solvers who prefer this strategy is poor, error is probably due to "not having the concept"; performance may be rapid. Seeing problems this way may be related to aging-related decline. Train for flexibility to improve performance.

(continued)

Table 9.3. (*Continued*)

Clarity of any one goal learned[a]	Heuristic/algorithm?	Probable strategy
4. Unclear	Unavailable	Trail-and-error responding and search for positive feedback. *Or:* Decision about nature of problem; hypothesis testing for positive feedback from system to verify rules/goal; problem "solved" when an elected goal produces usable results within an accepted belief system. Very large problem space. Solvers capable of these strategies may make errors on well-structured problems because (a) they see more options than the task designer did and (b) they take too long. Seeing problems this way is related to maturity. Those who can reach a logical solution under these conditions can also do so under any of the other conditions in this table.

[a]May be examined in term. of subgoals or overall problem goal.
Source: Sinnott (1991b). By permission of Greenwood Publishing Group, Inc., Westport, CT.

Luckily for those of us studying postformal thought, the problems I used in such studies seem to be seen as ill-structured for the most part. Specific predictions based on Sweller's hypotheses are in Table 9.3. They relate problem-solving concepts to postformal thinking and indicate the conditions under which postformal thought is more or less likely to occur. Note that condition 4 in the table could stimulate the use of postformal thought operations.

Figures 9.1 and 9.2 and Table 9.4 display some of the traditional cognitive operations plus postformal operations demonstrated during everyday problem solving. Table 9.4 lists all potential operations shown by any of the respondents. The pattern of interrelations among these operations is in Figure 9.1. Figure 9.2 shows their dynamic interaction at one point in the solution of a problem, the point at which the respondent is ready to construct a new goal. Just one way the postformal thought operations play a part is at the monitor level (Figures 9.1 and 9.2). Note that many other components generally not studied in problem-solving studies also play a part. Emotions are one prominent example of such components.

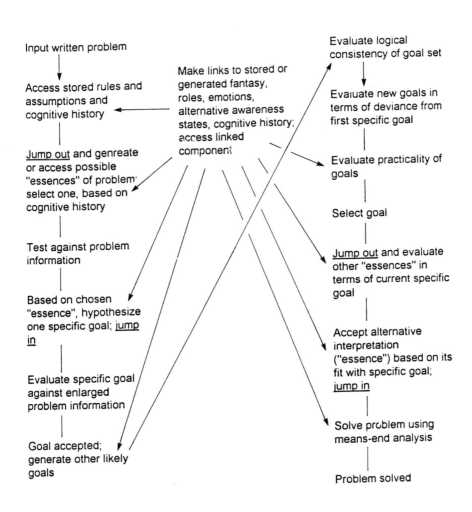

Model: Strange loops present, multiple goals and interpretations, no heuristic, use of intrusive components

Figure 9.1. Basic Components in the Solution of an Ill-Structured Problem. (*Source:* Sinnott, 1989b. By permission of Greenwood Publishing Group, Inc., Westport, CT.)

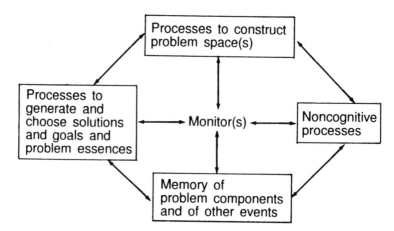

Figure 9.2. Model System State Early in the Problem. The system has achieved a "ready" state. (*Source:* Sinnott, 1989b. By permission of Greenwood Publishing Group, Inc., Westport, CT.)

The model in Figure 9.1, which displays basic components in the solution of an ill-structured problem, has five parts of special interest in regard to solution of these problems: (1) processes to construct problem space(s); (2) processes to choose and generate solutions; (3) monitors; (4) memories; and (5) noncognitive elements. While these five elements are most likely present in all problem-solving activities, they are emphasized as important in these studies because they were so prominent in thinking aloud protocols and are relatively ignored in the problem-solving literature.

Table 9.4. General Steps in the Everyday Problem-Solving Process

1. Decisions about the essence or nature of the problem
2. Generation of goals and metagoals
3. Evaluation processes
4. Testing for similarity
5. Processes to associate thought and feeling states
6. Processes to "slip" levels of processing during processing
7. Accessing processes
8. Solution processes such as means–end analyses, hypothesis testing, hill climbing to reach goals
9. Memory
10. Monitors
11. Input and output processes

Source: Sinnott (1989d). By permission of Greenwood Publishing Group, Inc., Westport, CT.
Note: In everyday problems seen as *well*-structured, omit steps 1, 2, and 6.

Processes to construct problem space are some of the most important processes to us in this series of postformal studies. Newell and Simon (1972) and others have discussed the set of processing rules and content items that make up the problem space in which the subject works out a solution. Problem space is often explicitly described by the investigator doing task analysis (Ericsson & Simon, 1984). Implied parameters of problem space that the task creator names usually demand relevance of that problem space element to the goal of the problem *as perceived by the task creator.* When we discuss problem solving within postformal thought, we begin to see problem space differently, namely, *as defined by the respondent.*

The construction of problem space seems to demand postformal thinking skills related to construction of reality. The task creator and the task taker may therefore construct the reality of the problem differently. If the task starts out with a predetermined problem space, the analysis of problem-solving processes must of necessity preclude some of the important steps about selection of problem space that appear in protocols. If all elements are considered, there may be multiple problem spaces available to the solver, who then accesses a desired number of them. This is similar to such operations of postformal thought (see Chapter 3) as the selection of a priori elements or parameter setting.

Accessing these problem spaces may occur through cognitive or noncognitive associations among problem spaces. Alternatively, thinking in postformal and new physics terms (see Chapter 5), access might be by means of a more complex mechanism, what Hofstadter (1979) calls a *strange loop.* A strange loop is defined as using processes *within* a given problem space and level of complexity to "jump out" and select a new space at a higher level, then to jump back in and continue lower-level processing within that new space. An example of a strange loop might be helpful. Imagine you are playing a game of checkers, but that you and your opponent are playing on several boards and with several sets of checkers. You play by normal checkers rules plus one additional rule: If a player makes a normal checker a king, that piece can be jumped from the board being played on to any of the other boards. The opponent must then join the player on that board, where they continue to play by standard checkers rules. Another way of describing a strange loop is "to use the rules of the cognitive game to change the rules of the cognitive game and then play by those rules." In playing a game of chess, for example, each person who captures a piece might be allowed to make up a new rule that both opponents must then follow. A political analogue might be that the constitutionally elected leader of a nation gets to rewrite the constitution that everyone abides by in the future.

The idea of a strange loop is a useful one because it not only explains some cognitive logical problem-solving behavior that is less than logical in appearance, but also seems to provide a mechanism for explaining some parts of postformal thought, new physics thinking, and other newer thought systems, albeit at a lower level of processing. The respondent in the protocol in Chapter 3 seemed to do this. He not only was aware that his choice of problem space was subjective, but also knew that it was necessarily so (see problem VI). This situation was one of truth uncertainty, in which one sees that truth cannot be known both completely and with certainty (Godel, 1962). At the very least, it called for jumping out of the process for a moment to decide what kind of logical game should be played after all.

There are many possible ways such "jumping" processes might be controlled. Schoenfeld (1983) pointed out ways that such control-level processes as belief systems influence intellectual performance. Solvers might express a belief system or metaprocessing constraints that arose from their experience with the problem and that also *changed* their experience with the problem. Alternatively, they might use what Kitchener (1983) called *epistemic cognition* or what D. Kuhn (1983) called *executive 2 strategies*. They may allow their attention to control their consciousness, which in turn controls their attention (Csikszentmihalyi, 1978). Perhaps they are operating as though one must construct the world and truth as one lives it, and then live by that construction as an existentialist such as Frankl (1963) or Yalom (1980) might suggest. They may synthesize across problem spaces, using intuition (Bastick, 1982). The cognitive developmental synthesis that includes that act is postformal thought.

The behavior of the respondent in the protocol in Chapter 3 seemed in accord with Polanyi's (1971) view that an expression of truth, in every case, involves some sort of passionate commitment to a choice of beliefs amid ultimate uncertainty. This commitment seemed to take the form of choice of problem space and slippage of levels by means of strange loops (see statements III.30–34). The knowingly arbitrary construction of problem space by the solver is a relatively unexplored dimension of the problem-solving process. Thus, adult postformal logical operations might potentially be studied in terms of ill-structured problems or information processing as "construction of problem space."

In-Depth Analysis of Three Thinking Aloud Protocols

Three respondents' thinking aloud products will be discussed at some length in this section. Altogether in this phase of the research, 50 respondents experienced the version of thinking aloud problem solving shown in the protocol reproduced in Table 3.6. (Additional studies tested many other samples and used the other versions of the thinking aloud methods described above.) The three respondents reported on here were selected because theirs were the first transcripts to be typed in the three age categories that were the focus of analysis. They represent three ages of adult problem solvers: younger adult (age 26), middle-aged adult (age 41), and older adult (age 69). As luck would have it, these respondents also portrayed what I have come to characterize as the *(young) data-driven style,* the *mature style,* and the *top-down (older/wiser) style.* (The older style is *not* to be confused with a dying system style; the former is adaptive while the latter is decompensating and maladaptive, near death.) All three respondents worked in professional or technical operations and were considered healthy, well-functioning adults. All three were white males due to the limitations of recruitment policies of the BLSA at that time.

To examine the processes that include postformal thought, we examined the first two problems the middle-aged respondent worked with and diagrammed his solutions (see Table 3.6 and Figure 9.3). A model was created. That model set of responses was hypothesized to exist in the remaining solutions of this respondent and in the solutions of other respondents. The model was supported for this respondent's other answers and for the answers of additional respondents. The model of the basic components of solutions to ill-structured problems is presented in summary form in Figure 9.2, in a form that represents a state within the problem-solving process. A list of the general steps of this "everyday" problem-solving process is in Table 9.4.

Diagrams of the middle-aged respondent's solution processes for three problems in his set appear in Figures 9.3, 9.4, and 9.5. Let us take a look at all the many logical and nonlogical things he was doing during problem solving.

His first problem (Figure 9.3) was ill-structured but not combinatorial. The respondent first read the written problem, clarified instructions, and immediately alluded to his personal history, experiences, and emotional reactions to this type of problem. He stopped those reactions and refocused his attention on the task, partly using repetitious behavior (i.e., rereading the problem). A pause occurred while

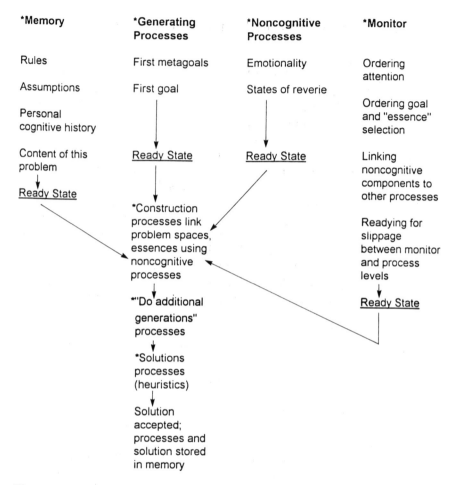

Figure 9.3. Process Steps for Respondent A: Magazine Workers Problem. (*Source:* Sinnott, 1989b. By permission of Greenwood Publishing Group, Inc., Westport, CT.)

his face demonstrated concentration. During this concentration [often a period of silence in TA reports, according to Ericsson and Simon (1984)], he sought clues to confirm his direction of responding, reviewed some information, and gave an answer. He verified the answer and looked relaxed during verbal play.

Some retrospective thinking focused on his conflict with himself over solving the problem at all, and also showed self-monitoring of personality and cognitive styles. He talked about his first step of generating ideas about the potential real purpose of the test, then decid-

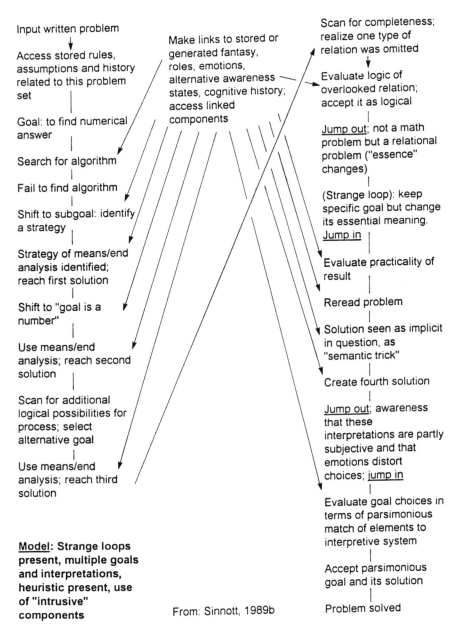

Figure 9.4.   Process Steps for Respondent A: Family Power Dynamics Problem. (*Source:* Sinnott, 1989b. By permission of Greenwood Publishing Group, Inc., Westport, CT.)

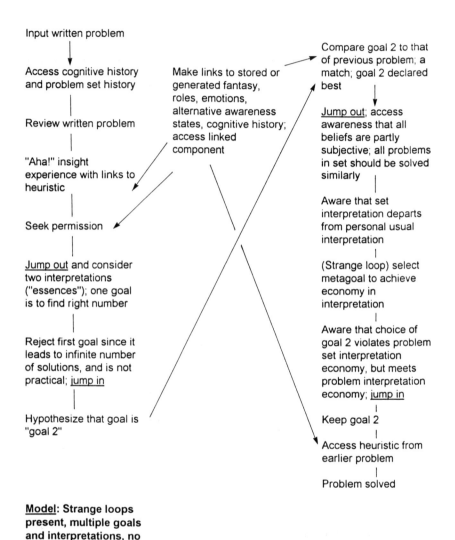

Input written problem

Access cognitive history
and problem set history

Review written problem

"Aha!" insight
experience with links to
heuristic

Seek permission

Jump out and consider
two interpretations
("essences"); one goal
is to find right number

Reject first goal since it
leads to infinite number
of solutions, and is not
practical; jump in

Hypothesize that goal is
"goal 2"

Make links to stored or
generated fantasy,
roles, emotions,
alternative awareness
states, cognitive history;
access linked
component

Compare goal 2 to that
of previous problem; a
match; goal 2 declared
best

Jump out; access
awareness that all
beliefs are partly
subjective; all problems
in set should be solved
similarly

Aware that set
interpretation departs
from personal usual
interpretation

(Strange loop) select
metagoal to achieve
economy in
interpretation

Aware that choice of
goal 2 violates problem
set interpretation
economy, but meets
problem interpretation
economy; jump in

Keep goal 2

Access heuristic from
earlier problem

Problem solved

Model: Strange loops
present, multiple goals
and interpretations, no
heuristic, use of
"intrusive"
components

Figure 9.5. Process Steps for Respondent A: ABC Problem. (*Source:* Sinnott, 1989b. By permission of Greenwood Publishing Group, Inc., Westport, CT.)

ing on an "official" purpose. He reviewed his next step of accepting a major essential purpose of "good utilization of employee resources," monitoring his consistency and ideational productivity. He was aware that other solutions would meet the same goal even if they were different from the essential purpose he selected. He viewed the adequacy of a solution as dependent on the intent of the audience, that is, the experimenter. He described his own process criterion and the ill-structured problem demands that permitted alternative interpretations and goal or essence choices. Some definitions of "what's possible" and "what's silly" further parameterized his choice of goal and solution. He monitored his use of rules; not *all* aspects of this solution were relevant. He recalled his emotional reaction and his need to focus to circumvent that.

These events, put into a time-ordered flow, are in Figure 9.3. The flow of two other solutions of his is illustrated in Figures 9.4 and 9.5 for comparison purposes.

From the respondent's own words, it appeared that he sometimes worked forward and sometimes backward. He worked out the essence of the problem, the goals, the criteria for selection of goals and solutions, the solutions themselves, and ways around difficult emotional and cognitive moments. Many of his statements deal with emotions, his past cognitive or emotional history, or his present roles in life. All these factors became part of the decisions about problem parameters or strategies for proceeding with the task. He seemed uncertain about the "real" goal (overall) and did not appear to have a usable heuristic. This would place him in Category 4 of Table 9.3. His responses were Category 4 for three other problems and Category 1 for two more. He did act, then, as predicted in Table 9.3.

Examples of Types of Processes Used by the Respondent

Processes to Construct Problem Space. Newell and Simon (1972) and others have discussed the set of processing rules and content items that make up the problem space in which the subject works out a solution. Problem space is often explicitly described by the investigator doing task analysis. Implied parameters of problem space usually demand relevance of the problem space element to the goal of the problem *as perceived by the task creator.* Therefore, when starting with a predetermined problem space, the analysis of the problem-solving process must of necessity preclude some of the processes we saw in the respondent's protocol. Therefore, if all elements are considered, problem space may be said to be larger for solutions to ill-structured problems, or it may be that there are multiple problem spaces available to the solver, who then accesses a desired number of spaces.

The respondent frequently bridged between problem spaces when working on the first problem. He sometimes found the essence of the problem by use of humor. He consciously noted that selection of a space to use was an arbitrary decision. He did the same on problem 2. Checking later problems to see whether the respondent continued to select a problem space clearly reveals that he did so. Even in his last problem, which was well-structured compared with the rest, it is evident that the respondent left what would be considered the usual focused problem space. Without considering his use of spaces, anyone scoring his response on the problem would have scored it "illogical."

After examining his digression, one must admit that he was very logical in his approach. He did not "fail" the logical problem, but simply worked in a larger space. He selected a space we might label a "rotational problem" and another we might label a "pairing-combinatorial problem" and moved within both to solve, finally, within one. He used the problem as a whole to determine the general nature of the *test* of which space to use more fully, and then to solve a version of the problem in that space accordingly. This complex shift is an example of the strange loop described earlier. Table 9.5 lists a number of ways respondents might find to "change the rules," based on their statements. Table 9.6 summarizes elements in the respondent's problem space.

Processes to Choose and Generate Solutions. The solutions to ill-structured problems also seemed to include processes to generate and select specific solutions. Clearly, construction of problem space, dis-

Table 9.5. Logically Derived Procedures Available to the Problem Solver Who Moves to "Change the Rules of the Game While It Is Being Played"

1. Unconsciously make the decision: "I had a feeling" (spoken in retrospect).
2. Consciously decide, based mainly on experience with this sort of problem: "This looks like the ABC problem I did first."
3. Consciously decide, based on examination of alternatives: "I had a feeling this was either a math problem or a people problem, and I decided it was a people problem."
4. Step 3, with supposition that this is a *logical, nonarbitrary* decision.
5. Step 3, with awareness that this is a necessarily *arbitrary* decision, outside the bounds of logic, that determines how logic is used in reaching the goal: "I'm going to treat this like a math problem, although there's no way to tell if it is. So I'll calculate the number of pairs according to a formula. . . ."

Source: Sinnott (1989b). By permission of Greenwood Publishing Group, Inc., Westport, CT.

Table 9.6. Summary of Elements/Representations/Operators Apparently Available in Respondent A's Problem Space: Magazine Workers Problem

1. Initial state
2. Goal state
3. Operators to perform chosen set of mathematical, move-related, or logical functions
4. Rules and assumptions that modify states and processes
5. Forms of individual's history, especially cognitive history, that modify processes and states
6. Emotional states
7. Operators to alter awareness, to monitor, and to alter levels of processing (e.g., metaoperators, epistemic operators)
8. Evaluation processes to test goal appropriateness, interpretation appropriateness
9. Subroutines to generate multiple goals and interpretations
10. Thoughts that seem task-unrelated but that are actually used in the problem
11. Operators to permit controlled slippage between levels of processing *during* processing

Source: Sinnott (1989b). By permission of Greenwood Publishing Group, Inc., Westport, CT.

cussed above, is involved in this set of activities. But the respondent, even after selection of larger problem spaces (or problem essences), spent some energy generating several goals and specific solutions. The essence of a problem must be selected; then the goal or goals must be selected; finally, a solution or solutions must be generated and selected. Sometimes a goal or solution is selected first, and then a new essence is chosen to conform to that chosen goal and solution.

The generation of possible goals and solutions is a creative exercise that could be said to take advantage of previous learning or unconscious processes. For our respondent, it seemed to be accomplished by bridges of associations or of task-unrelated thoughts or emotions. The larger the number of generated possible goals, the more the solver needs a mechanism for selection of the best goal or solution. One mechanism mentioned by our respondent was to select goals that were suitable to the decided-upon problem essence. Another was to select goals that he knew were reachable, or specific solution paths for which he had a heuristic available. He did this for the well-structured problem, too, which would make him appear to have failed it.

Monitors. Our respondent frequently monitored his own processes, shifts, choices, and style. He also monitored his emotional reactions. The monitoring process sometimes helped him stay on track and deal with his limitations, and also let him decide about the nature of the problem and the goal to choose. Sometimes monitoring distracted him from the goal and slowed the process. The monitor therefore controls more than the flow of the process through a restricted problem space; it links other problem spaces, regulates choice of problem essence, and maintains continuity. The monitor probably has numerous specialists to handle subtasks.

Memory. Memory was a predictable component, but the sort of memories evoked were less predictable. Much of the protocol dealt with memories of school performance, emotions, job-related factors, and other personal historical data. Memory as repository for elements of the solution while working on the problem was also important. Lack of memory did not seem to be a serious problem for this respondent, and the personal history elements were useful in making available alternative interpretations of problem essence and in offering heuristics.

Noncognitive Elements. The presence of emotional reactions was obvious in this subject's responses throughout the protocol. Emotions and task-unrelated thoughts often were the impetus for choice of goal or problem essence. They kept the solver going, motivating him to continue through the process even when he was temporarily stalled. This and the other four components are certainly apparent in the protocol, and might also appear more frequently in well-structured problem solving, if reports were not edited to remove this information. The reader might see later chapters for more on noncognitive processes.

Goal Clarity and Heuristic Availability. The predictions in Table 9.3 concerning goal clarity and heuristic availability were supported by the responses of our respondent. Responses of the other two (younger and older) respondents also supported our hypotheses. There were 15 clear instances in which a goal was considered and use of some heuristic was possible. Of the 15, 14 were associated with a strategy (on that portion of the problem) that was predictive of the solver's strategy on later problems in the set and on the well-structured problem at the end of the set.

The processes described here give a window on the problem-solving process of which postformal thought is a useful part. In the next chapter, we will examine some age-related differences in process. In Chapter 11, we will look at the relation between respondents' use of postformal operations and their use of other physical and cognitive factors. Experimental manipulations of the process will also be discussed.

CHAPTER 10

Age Differences in Processes

There is only one history of importance and it is the history of what you once believed in and the history of what you came to believe in.

KAY BOYLE

Since postformal thought is related to wisdom within my theory, I expected that mature adults generally would display more elements of it than younger adults would. I expected that in general, older adults would more often be "wiser" in postformal terms. With this expectation in mind, I began looking at age differences in postformal operations and in the related problem-solving processes in the information-processing traditions that were discussed in Chapter 9. This chapter describes some of the differences that were hypothesized and found. Differences that will be discussed include differences in the use of formal operations, in the use of postformal operations, in the use of steps to solution of potentially postformal problems and crucial errors during the solution process, and in the style of problem-solving steps as evident during thinking aloud problem solving. Age was also significantly correlated with several "noncognitive" factors such as use of emotion, factors that were elements in the problem-solving process. These noncognitive factors will be discussed in Chapter 11.

AGE AND USE OF FORMAL OPERATIONS

It was evident in all of my studies that young, mature, and older adults were not equivalent in their tendency to give a formal operational logical response to my problems. By that criterion, the three age groups appeared to be differentially logical. Age differences did not reach significance, however, in any study beyond the first. We can examine some of the trends in my studies, trends that are not consistent with prior research results of earlier developmental investigators. The reader may recall from Chapter 8 that in the initial study of my research program, one done with older adults dwelling in the community and in nursing homes (Chap & Sinnott, 1977–1978), only 11% of respondents demonstrated Piagetian formal operations when tested with a combinatorial reasoning problem. When this low rate was compared with the theoretical (not empirical) assumption of that time—since then disproven empirically—that most adolescents reach formal thought, the older adults looked unskilled.

My results from mature and older respondents from the first study testing respondents in the Baltimore Longitudinal Study of Aging (BLSA) (see Chapter 9 for more information) (Sinnott, 1984b) offered the first sign of more hope that adults were able to master Piagetian formal logical tests. Figure 8.1 displayed the percentages passing formal operations in that first BLSA study, as a function of both age and gender. The Bedrooms problem proved to be the most difficult, with only about 25% of the women and men passing it formally; the ABC problem (a variation of the one used in the 1977 study) was the easiest, with about half the women and 86% of the men passing it at a formal level. As the figure shows, the middle-aged generally outperformed the other groups on the abstract, formally structured ABC problem. Among male respondents, the young passed formal operations on the Bedrooms problem more than other age groups did; among the women, in contrast, the oldest group did best on the same problem. For the Magazine Workers problem, old men and middle-aged women did best. A look at Table 10.1, which displays the mean

Table 10.1. Mean Age of Respondents Formally Passing Various Numbers of Problems during Standard Administration

Performance	Mean age (years)
Fail all 6	60.40
Pass 1	63.22
Pass 2	57.89
Pass 3	57.18
Pass 4	56.23
Pass 5	54.62
Pass 6	50.00
Mean of sample	57.61

Source: Sinnott (1991b). By permission of Greenwood Publishing Group, Inc., Westport, CT.

ages of individuals formally passing 1, 2, 3, 4, 5, or all 6 problems, suggests that the mean ages of the more or less successful "passers" were equivalent. Virtually all of the respondents passed at least one of the six problems at the formal operational level. But as can be seen in Figure 8.1, there were still many failures. Were these respondents thinking in interesting ways when they appeared to fail to use formal logic on one or more of the problems?

AGE AND USE OF
POSTFORMAL OPERATIONS

It was interesting to realize that many of the respondents who "failed" in answering correctly in terms of abstract formal logic seemed formal operational in what they did do: They answered with realistic, not abstract, formal logic. In other words, they used formal logic processes but decided to change the problem content from abstract numbers to a more realistic situation. Consequently, they did not arrive at an abstract number as an answer and were judged to have failed by traditional criteria, but they had the mental operations of that formal logic and were using them very well. What led to "failure" was the postformal part of their process, which included a decision about which form of the formal logic, abstract or realistic, to use.

Figure 10.1 shows age-group and problem-context differences in the comparative use of formal operations under abstract versus realistic ways of framing a problem. On both of the problems in the figure, the older group was more likely (but not significantly so) to show formal thought in *both* the abstract *and* the realistic framing of the problem. In other words, the older group demonstrated a shift between logics and the ability to decide which logic to articulate and impose on the situation. They demonstrated *post*formal thought, in other words.

Looking at the respondents' use of individual postformal operations (see Table 3.5 for the operations), we see some complex age differences that again do not reach significance. Differences in the proportion of respondents who create two or more solutions (the multiple solutions operation) appear in Figure 10.2, by problem and age decade, for 80 respondents. The problem contexts occasioned differing patterns of multiple or single solutions, patterns that were significantly different from each other, but age itself did not lead to significant differences. The tendency, though, was for the middle-aged and young to produce more solutions than the old-old, who were in their 70s and 80s.

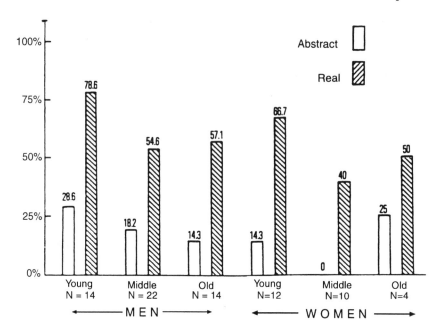

Figure 10.1.   Formal Operations under Abstract and Real Constraints.

Table 9.2 summarized some work with a larger sample of 198 respondents (Sinnott & Cavanaugh, 1991) and showed the percentages of age subsamples using the postformal operations of multiple solutions. These age differences were significant, but the effect size is small. Some few other significant, but small, age by postformal operations correlations included: the number of goals set on the Bedrooms problem ($r = 0.32$) (older produce more); use of self-referential thought on ABC ($r = -0.31$), Camping Trip Logistics ($r = -0.25$), Bedrooms ($r = -0.29$), and Magazine Workers ($r = -0.40$) (older consistently use it less); and number of solutions to Family Power Dynamics ($r = -0.14$), Bedrooms ($r = -0.15$), and Magazine Workers ($r = -0.12$) (older produce less). Overall, the age effects have been small.

Most likely, the age effects were overwhelmed by the large individual differences encountered in use of postformal operations. For example, look at Figure 10.3, which shows the variability in the quantity of adults' self-referential statements, with the age of each respondent shown. In the preceding paragraph, you read that some significant age by use of self-referential thought correlations were found. But which is more impressive, the correlations explaining less than 10%

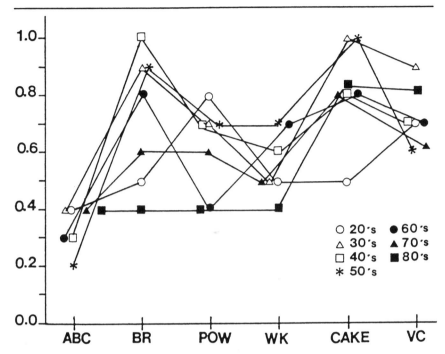

Figure 10.2. Proportion of Respondents with Two or More Solutions, by Problem and Age. Problem types: (BR) Bedrooms; (POW) Family Power Dynamics; (WK) Magazine Workers; (CAKE) Cake-Baking Interruption; (VC) Vitamin C.

of the variance or the huge individual differences within age groups? Individual differences seem to play a large role in postformal thought.

The hypothesis that age significantly influences expression of postformal operations so far had not been supported. But I wondered if perhaps some of the other age differences, those in problem-solving strategies, would be more impressive or more interesting, given my larger overall goal of understanding complex thought.

AGE AND USE OF STEPS TO SOLUTION AND MAKING OF CRUCIAL ERRORS

The next set of questions I wanted to answer about the relation between postformal thought and age made use of individual intensive analyses. Thinking aloud studies provided a wealth of data from each

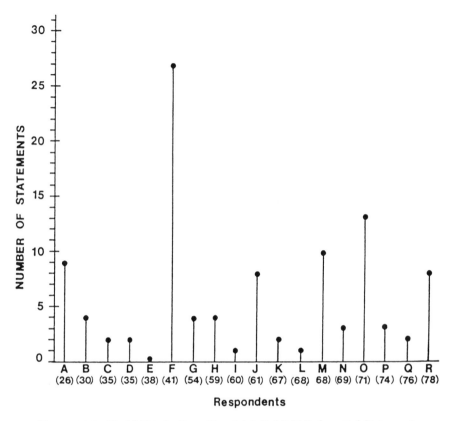

Figure 10.3. Variability in Quantity of Adults' Self-Referential Statements.

individual, data that spoke to each person's processes of thought. It was time to return to those transcripts mentioned in Chapter 9, especially to the three previously selected at random—one from a young adult (age 26), one from a middle-aged adult (age 41), and one from an older adult (age 69)—and examine their processes more completely. This individual-intensive case study sort of activity proved to be surprisingly useful in outlining three different types of processes or problem-solving strategies. It was useful in shedding light on the overall facilitators of postformal thought and the overall uses for it in cognition (e.g., Sinnott, 1989a,b; Sinnott & Cavanaugh, 1991).

In this discussion of the three sample transcripts, we are going to compare the processes of problem solving used as respondents address the Family Power Dynamics problem, processes expressed in three transcripts summarized in Figure 9.4 (Chapter 9) (middle-aged), Figure 10.4 (young adult), and Figure 10.5 (older adult).

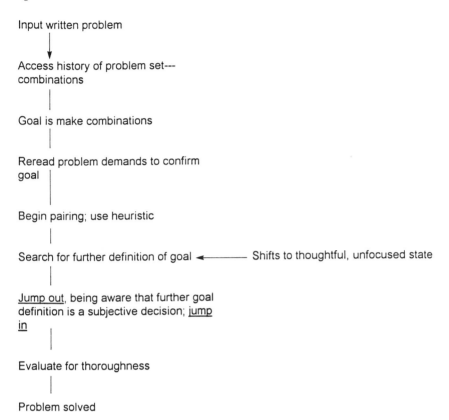

Input written problem

Access history of problem set---
combinations

Goal is make combinations

Reread problem demands to confirm
goal

Begin pairing; use heuristic

Search for further definition of goal ◄——— Shifts to thoughtful, unfocused state

Jump out, being aware that further goal
definition is a subjective decision; jump
in

Evaluate for thoroughness

Problem solved

Model: **Strange loops absent; single
goal and interpretation; heuristic
available; little use of "intrusive"
components**

Figure 10.4. Process Steps for Young Respondent: Family Power Dynamics Problem. (*Source:* Sinnott, 1989b. By permission of Greenwood Publishing Group, Inc., Westport, CT.)

First let me summarize differences in a general way. Postformal thought and its operations were key in the processes of the three respondents and were used or not used in very different ways, leading to different problem-solving styles. The responses of the young adult subject had a straightforward analytical quality and occupied a relatively small problem space compared to those of the middle-aged respondent we encountered in Chapter 9. This younger respondent avoided multiple goals, unrelated thought, and emotion compared to the middle-aged respondent. The responses of the older adult were

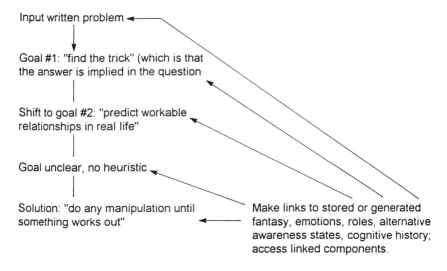

Model: No strange loops, multiple
goals, no heuristic, use of "intrusive"
components

Figure 10.5. Process Steps for Older Respondent: Family Power Dynamics
Problem. (*Source:* Sinnott, 1989b. By permission of Greenwood Publishing Group,
Inc., Westport, CT.)

very different from the other two, in that this respondent described
goals that were the creation of a general process, not the creation of a
product (i.e., a set, concrete answer such as the number 15). The older
respondent used task-unrelated thoughts and emotional processes to
do this.

The contrasting worldviews and truth systems of these three problem solvers were also interesting. The middle-aged respondent
seemed to live in a world of many truths and options, all of which
could be effectively monitored and shifted. This respondent saw the
objective world as partly created by the knower, and could synthesize
and analytically test propositions about reality. The young respondent's world was more analytical and focused, with less complicated
truths and single specific answers. In the older respondent's world,
"good process" constituted truth. The right answer was a right process
or template. The content of the problem helped determine the process.
The good-process truth for this older respondent was very much in
touch with everyday social reality. The three contrasting worldviews,
then, were truth as relative fact, truth as simple fact, and truth as good

process. These worldviews correspond in an interesting way to aspects of the three inquiring systems described by Wood (1983) and Churchman (1971).

Next, let us examine the effect of age and problem context on the three respondents' use of specific steps to solution of problems, the 12 steps described in Chapter 9. Table 10.2 indicates which of these steps were present, by respondent and problem. Generally, the older and younger respondents did not make use of as many operations as the middle-aged respondent did (17 omissions for the older and 18 for the younger, versus two and a possible trial for the middle-aged). Those two respondents were prone to omit the postformal-like step of "slipping levels" and "evaluating the choice of goals." The younger respondent was prone to omit processes focused on noncognitive elements and selection/evaluation. The middle-aged respondent had the largest number of solutions, goals, and problem essence statements. These profiles suggest an age difference in ideational productivity, association, and flexibility in responding to ill-structured problems. These differences also are in accord with my general sense of the response quality for hundreds of respondents I have interviewed over the years.

The steps to solution give us a clue to some differences in crucial errors that also square with my overall interview experiences and often relate to age. Table 10.3 summarizes age differences in success, crucial errors, number of solutions, goals, and problem essence statements, by problem. On the basis of earlier experience, I hypothesized that the middle-aged and older respondents would make errors (and therefore not "pass" formal operations) by having too large a problem space on ABC (the well-structured problem); they did so. I also hypothesized that they would also have too large a problem space to "pass" on the other problems; often this was true.

The middle-aged respondent, with too large a problem space to "succeed" on abstract problems, and with a capacity to shift attention, had the greatest number of solutions, goals, and essences, and most often slipped levels; the young, with little productivity and very focused attention, succeeded well in the abstract, but only in the abstract.

If success were redefined as "finding a solution, by some criterion, when the problem is *not* seen as *abstract* combinatorial or propositional," the young respondent would be a dismal failure and the middle-aged would shine. This may be an important consideration in a world where many practical and political problems can be framed either as abstract and well-structured *or* as practical and ill-structured.

Table 10.2. Effect of Age and Problem Type on Steps to Solution

Steps[a]	Middle-aged						Old						Young					
	POW	BR	ABC	WK	VC	CAMP	POW	BR	ABC	WK	VC	CAMP	POW	BR	ABC	WK	VC	CAMP
1. Input	X	X	X	X	X	X	X	X	X	X	X	X	X	X	X	X	X	X
2. Monitor	X	X	X	X	X	X	X	0	0	X	X	0	X	X	0	X	X	0
3. Remember	X	X	X	X	X	X	X	X	X	X	X	X	X	X	X	X	X	X
4. Create essence	X	X	X	X	X	X	X	X	X	X	X	X	X	X	X	X	X	X
5. Create goals	X	X	X	X	X	X	X	X	X	X	X	X	X	X	X	X	X	X
6. Generate solutions	X	X	X	X	X	X	X	X	X	X	X	X	X	X	X	X	X	X
7. Slip levels	X	0	X	X	—	0	0	0	0	X	0	0	0	0	0	0	0	0
8. Noncognitive processes	X	X	X	X	X	X	X	X	X	X	X	X	0	X	X	0	X	0
9. Select	X	X	X	X	X	X	X	0	0	X	0	0	X	X	0	0	X	0
10. Evaluate	X	X	X	X	X	X	0	0	0	X	0	0	X	0	0	0	X	0
11. Move to goal	X	X	X	X	X	X	X	X	X	X	X	X	X	X	X	X	X	X
12. Output	X	X	X	X	X	X	X	X	X	X	X	X	X	X	X	X	X	X

[a]Derived from the middle-aged respondent's responses to the Family Power Dynamics problem (see Figure 9.4). *Source:* Sinnott (1989b). Key: (X) present; (0) not present; (—) questionable.

Table 10.3.   Age Differences in Success, Crucial Errors, Number of Solutions, Number of Goals, and Number of Essences for Each Respondent, by Problem

Age	Pass/ Fail	Errors	Solutions	Goals	Essences
		Family Power Dynamics			
Young	Pass	None	Two	Two	One
Middle	Fail	Adoption of large problem space	Four	Four	Two
Old	Fail	Adoption of large problem space; poor input	Two	Two	Two
		ABC			
Young	Pass	None	One	One	One
Middle	Fail	Adoption of large problem space	Two	Two	Two
Old	Fail	Adoption of large problem space	One	Two	Two
		Bedrooms			
Young	Fail	Erroneous heuristic	One	Two	Two
Middle	Fail	Adoption of large problem space	Six	One	One
Old	Fail	Adoption of large problem space; no heuristic	Two	One	One
		Magazine Workers			
Young	Pass	None	Two	One	One
Middle	Fail	Adoption of large problem space	Four	Four	Two
Old	Fail	Goal was equal to a process	One	Two	Two
		Vitamin C			
Young	Pass	None	Two	One	One
Middle	Pass	None	Two	One	One
Old	Fail	No heuristic	Two	One	One
		Camp Trip Logistics			
Young	Pass	None	One	One	One
Middle	Fail	Adoption of large problem space	One	Two	Two
Old	Fail	No heuristic	Five	One	One

Source: Sinnott (1989d). By permission of Greenwood Publishing Group, Inc., Westport, CT.

The older respondent had the unfortunate experience of having too large a problem space and a poor grasp of problem information with the absence of a heuristic. Without the last two drawbacks, which could be related to memory problems and the cascade of effects that accompanies them, the older respondent might have done better than the young or even the middle-aged. The solutions finally produced by the old respondent also were equivalent to very general processes and therefore were potentially very useful in a wide variety of situations.

This model and these analyses suggest the central controlling role that postformal operations, belief systems, intentionality, and creativity may have in problem solving. Polanyi (1971) says that in every act of knowing there is a passionate contribution of the knower. We might substitute *problem solver* for *knower*. Even science, the most objective form of problem solving, involves a personal commitment to a theory or hypothesis. These self-referential personal commitments might take the form of beliefs or judgments about what I am calling problem *essence*. They may be part of the regulatory process that defines problem space and focuses attention, allowing for modifications in the structure of the rules *during* the process done *by* the rules. They may therefore serve the same function that recombinations of DNA serve: introducing variety and range into the process. The same could be true for the function of those noncognitive variables seen in the summarized transcripts: They might provide the bridges between problem spaces that effectively enlarge problem space. These two mechanisms—bridging and recombination—introduce variety into an active system. The system is bounded or limited or given parameters by other processes, such as memory or heuristics. These complementary processes are, then, both enlarging and narrowing, and together, and only together, provide the maximum number of useful options to the solver during complex ill-structured problem solving.

From a systems theory point of view, any problem-solving system must encompass enough disorganization (openness, entropy) to meet adaptational demands over a lifetime plus sufficient organization to maintain continuity. Theories of complexity might say that the optimal problem solver operated at the edge of complexity and chaos. The cycle shown earlier in Figure 6.1 outlines the shifting balance between that openness and continuity over a lifetime. Only systems that have means to handle these fuzzy sets in interpretation of situations will be able to be innovative in somewhat new situations while still making sense of those new situations.

AGE DIFFERENCES IN STYLE: COMPENSATORY STRATEGIES

Four age-related styles of problem solving were found in the analyses described above and in other sets of responses not reported here due to space considerations. They were not rigidly bound to calendar age. The four styles appear to be consistent with potential strategic compensatory mechanisms for cognitive deficits at various levels of experience, and consistent with tasks of psychosocial development. They appear to be especially consistent with the psychosocial demands of life periods as described by Erikson (1982) and Schaie (1977–1978). An older style seems to be built on younger ones and presumes skills of lower stages, but any style in the repertoire might be made manifest on a given occasion. The highest stage need not be displayed. If one *can* use the top-down style described below, one is likely to also be able to use the mixed and data-driven styles described below. If one is postformal, one can use other lower levels of cognitive styles, by definition.

The *youthful* style seemed best for data gathering, learning, and data-driven processing. In that style, attention was focused and narrow; memory content was readily available. Past experience, monitoring, and products of unconscious processes were not important to the solution. There was a tendency to view the problem in abstract, noncontextual terms. This style, of course, could be the most useful one for the concrete-thinking inexperienced solver who has relatively few structures of knowledge available. The young solver may compensate for lack of structures, monitoring skills, and experience by staying close to the data and marching in a linear way toward solution. There is little postformal thought in this youthful style.

The *mature* style seemed best for data gathering and optimal organizing of information experienced *in context.* Both top-down and data-driven processing were found much of the time. Attention varied from focused to diffused; memory contents were richer and were available. Monitoring and unconscious processes were important to the solution. This strategy could be the most useful one for the executive, generative, responsible, mature adult active in the world of work and family. The mature thinker seemed to compensate for the high difficulty level of his or her environment full of ill-structured problems by strategically utilizing large problem spaces, syntheses, postformal thought, and monitoring-related decisions.

The *older* (but *not* "declining" or "dying" [see Chapter 6]) style seemed best for thinking at a deliberate pace. It allowed rapid, low-energy-demand solutions arrived at by an experienced solver with many available structures of knowledge. It was top-down in style, with little attention to data, probably because of poorer memory capacities. Attention was diffuse, possibly due to limited arousal capabilities. This style, then, seemed to compensate for low memory

and energy and for extensive (perhaps too extensive) data and structures. A solution was seen as "finding the best process or heuristic
that would be useful for several cases," and other possible steps in the
process such as "reaching a concrete solution for this specific case"
were minimized. While this style was useful and far enough in touch
with the reality of the problem context that the processes that were the
solution did make sense, it was less useful than a mature style that
permitted a *choice* of a process *and* carried it through to concrete
completion.

One can imagine that a respondent with even less energy, one in
true decline, might simply impose some well-known heuristic
quickly, top-down, whether or not the heuristic really fit the problem
well. Such an idiosyncratic style, if found in more extreme forms in
declining or unmotivated respondents, is better labeled a *decline*
style. Such a decline style compensates, though somewhat inade-
quately, for the deficient system seen in very old and ill problem
solvers or in those with limited capacities who are, however, experienced enough to have some structures to impose. Note that these compensatory mechanisms—cognitive operations themselves being one
general form of compensatory mechanism—help to guarantee that the
person system and the social system interact without overwhelming
each other or overly harming the delicate homeostasis within each.

Note, too, that the use or absence of postformal operations is different for each of the different styles. It is integrated into the overall
adaptive thought strategy.

Now that we have summarized the explorations of age differences in postformal thought and its allied processes, we can state one
main conclusion. Age, per se, is not the dominant predictor of the
quantity or presence of postformal complex thinking, at least given
that a respondent has reached a postadolescent state. But postformal
thought does seem to serve the goals of some life periods better than
others. Its presence or absence seems part of the adaptive style of
responses at several life periods. If age is not the key variable, might
some others be?

The next chapter summarizes studies of other variables that I
thought might have an impact on the use of postformal thought by my
respondents.

CHAPTER 11

Emotion, Intention, Health, Goal Clarity, and Other Factors in Postformal Thought

We look around and perceive that . . . every object is related to every other object . . . not only spatially but temporally. . . . As a fact of pure experience, there is not space without time, no time without space; they are interpenetrating.

D. T. SUZUKI

Space exists only in relation to our particularizing consciousness.

ASHVAGHOSHA

Age was not the perfect predictor of postformal thought. It was time, then, to examine some other factors that might reasonably be related to use of postformal thought and to try some experimental manipulations of the use of postformal operations. This chapter examines a few of the more interesting correlational, experimental, and case study results of this further work. Several research questions are addressed in this chapter. First, do physical health variables such as health or other cognitive variables such as memory and vocabulary relate to postformal operations? Second, how do traditional problem-solving variables such as goal clarity and heuristic availability relate to postformal thought during problem solving? Third, how do manipulations of problem context, use of probe questions, emotion, intention, and mind wandering relate to postformal problem-solving performance? Each will be addressed in turn.

161

PHYSICAL HEALTH, MEMORY, WECHSLER ADULT INTELLIGENCE SCALE VOCABULARY, AND POSTFORMAL THOUGHT

Physical Health

One interesting way to address the first part of this question is to correlate blood pressure (as one operationalization of health) with postformal thought data. Blood pressure is an easy variable to measure and can be related to a number of age-related physical decline processes. My pool of respondents in the Baltimore Longitudinal Study of Aging (BLSA) had had pressures routinely taken and recorded, sometimes for many years, so *changes* in pressure over time, 12 years' time, could also be examined. Several problem-solving variables in addition to the postformal operations listed in Table 3.5 were used, including passing at the formal logical level, and the perceived

Table 11.1. Simple Correlations between Blood Pressure and Problem Solving

Measure	r
Systolic pressure level (N = 54)	
Time to complete ABC	0.37
Passing WK	−0.22
Systolic change (12 years) (N = 15)	
Time to complete WK	0.45
Passing VC	0.46
Diastolic pressure level (N = 54)	
Time to complete BR	−0.29
Importance of:	
ABC	0.26
BR	0.27
POW	0.32
Diastolic change (12 years) (N = 54)	
Time to complete BR	−0.45
Passing:	
BR	−0.28
POW	−0.28
Importance of:	
WK	0.36
BR	0.29

Source: Sinnott (1991b). By permission of Greenwood Publishing Group, Inc., Westport, CT.

importance of the problem (scored on a 5-point scale, with 5 being most important).

It was expected that elevated blood pressure would be positively related to time spent solving a problem (due to the intervening variables of health and stress) and to perceived problem importance (due to stress and cognitive dissonance), and negatively related to performance on the postformal operations. But for most of the variables, there was no significant relationship between blood pressure and performance. Table 11.1 summarizes the relationships that proved to be significant. Even when the results were significant, the relationships were not always as hypothesized. Still, there were more significant relations than would have occurred by chance, which implies that future thinking and work need to be done to understand this complex relationship. When multiple regression analysis was used and age effects were statistically removed, only two relationships remained significant, a chance rate of occurrence. It was concluded that there was no evident relation in this life-span sample between systolic or diastolic blood pressure or pressure change over 12 years and postformal performance other than the relationship that depended on age as an underlying variable. Other operational definitions of health may lead to different results, however, in light of earlier research such as studies of nursing home residents versus community residents.

Memory

Four types of memory tests that were given to BLSA volunteers can be used to illustrate some relations between memory and postformal operations during problem solving. It was expected that memory skills would make it easier for respondents to be postformal thinkers and access the larger problem space that was hypothesized to accompany postformal thought. The first memory test was a naturalistic memory test (Sinnott, 1986a). This untimed test included two sets of 13 paper-and-pencil items that required recognition or recall of events of some of the test experiences during BLSA testing. Respondents spent about 20 minutes alone in a test room during their testing visit (Time 1) answering either Form A or Form B, randomly chosen. A second test session (Time 2) was conducted 7–10 days later using both forms. Each time, the naturalistic test yielded a total score and scale scores for recall, recognition, prospective memory, retrospective memory for action taken, and retrospective memory for trivial details.

A second type of naturalistic memory measure was for metamemory, in which respondents evaluated their own memory abilities.
These items asked for the respondents to rate their general memory
ability and their memory ability compared to that of others their age
and to give a rating of recent memory changes.

The third type of memory test was a laboratory test (Sinnott,
1991a). It included a test of immediate free recall consisting of a
demand to produce as many nouns as possible from a learned list, a
delayed free recall of that list a few tasks later, and a delayed recognition test in which respondents had to judge whether a word had been
in the original list or not.

The fourth memory test was the Benton Visual Retention Test
(BVRT) of memory for geometric figures (Benton, 1963). A respondent
looks at a figure for 10 seconds and then reproduces it from memory.
Errors are counted to obtain a score.

Table 11.2 summarizes some of the most interesting relations
between the memory tests and postformal operations during problem
solving. Notice that the more ill-structured and realistic the problem
was, the more success on that problem was related to memory at Time 1.
Memory was connected with speed of solving, the number of solutions produced, and how important a respondent rated the problem to
be. Action memory was the subscale most strongly related to postfor-

**Table 11.2. Summary of Significant Results: Correlations between Problem
Solving and Memory**

---

1. The more illustrated the problem, the more it related to everyday memory.
2. Memory was most often related to importance, time to solve, and number of
   solutions.
3. Number of solutions was positively related to memory performance, most often for
   BR and VC, least often for ABC and CAKE.
4. Time to solve was positively related to memory especially for WK, least for ABC
   and VC.
5. The strongest relations were at Time 1.
6. Metamemory related positively to problem solving on the few occasions when
   relations were found.
7. Action memory was the scale most positively related to problem solving.
8. The worse the everyday memory, and the better the lab memory, the more important
   solving problems was judged to be, especially for illustrated problems.
9. Total (delayed) word recall (lab task) related positively to number of solutions for
   VC and POW.
10. WAIS vocabulary and BVRT performance related positively to solving logically and
    creatively.

Source: Sinnott (1991b). By permission of Greenwood Publishing Group, Inc., Westport, CT. Significance: 0.01 level, standard administration.

mal problem solving. Metamemory related positively to problem solving using postformal operations, as did visual memory.

How can we interpret these results? It seems consistent with these results to say that memory abilities help a respondent to deal with a large problem space and make a complex, creative multiple-solution thought order within it. Perhaps to shift reality frames requires a better-functioning memory to hold the fragments of solutions. As usual, more research is needed to truly understand what is happening here.

WAIS Vocaulary

The WAIS vocabulary subtest is part of the Wechsler Adult Intelligence Scale (Wechsler, 1955) and involves defining 40 words. It measures memory for the meaning of words. Respondents can score from 0 to 2 points for each word. This vocabulary subtest is one of the most stable intelligence scales; individuals maintain their scores far into old age until death or severe disease takes its toll. I expected that this verbal, general knowledge sort of test would have little relation to the process of postformal thinking or to formal or postformal logic.

Again, there was a surprise. WAIS vocabulary was significantly related to solving logically and to creation of many solutions. I considered the possibility that respondents may seem to be postformal because they say more and have longer transcripts, so that the correlation rests on an intervening variable of verbosity. But some respondents say a great deal and never express postformal thought, while others say little and are evaluated as postformal thinkers. An underlying variable, however could be memory. Postformal logic may also be another very stable ability that is maintained throughout life once it is acquired. There are many other possible explanations that might be tested in future research.

RELATIONS AMONG GOAL CLARITY, HEURISTIC AVAILABILITY, AND POSTFORMAL THOUGHT

In earlier chapters, I discussed the relationships one might find among goal clarity, heuristic availability (in various combinations), and problem-solving variables of the postformal sort, my focus of interest. Table 9.3 summarized these hypotheses on the basis of the thinking of Sweller (1983) and Sweller and Levine (1982). The idea was to begin to understand how traditional models of problem solving and postformal logic might fit together. How might postformal thought be adaptive in problem solving as it is studied in the language of other cognitive traditions?

The reader might keep in mind that in real-life problem situations, goal clarity and heuristic availability are analogue constructions, not digital constructions. Goals are more or less clear; heuristics are more or less available. Here, I have artificially dichotomized them for purposes of preliminary experimental tests. In retrospect, this strategy was dangerous, since it is not clear, for example, where on the continuum of clarity individuals cross the line between what for them is a "clear" goal and what for them is a "not clear" goal. Due to practical constraints, however, I compromised in my solution to this metaproblem and decided on the temporary use of the simplistic dichotomy.

Two hypotheses from Table 9.3 were selected for the first tests of overall relations based on this research question. The data from standard administration respondents (a sample balanced for age) were used.

Hypothesis 1. If a respondent has an available heuristic (i.e., a clear algorithm or method of moving toward a particular goal) and used it to successfully move toward a clear goal, the respondent will use *that* heuristic for every problem at hand that can be construed to be remotely similar; that is, he or she will give *all* the problems clear goals. This tests one prediction for situation 1 in Table 9.3.

One way of addressing this question was to see whether respondents did see the problems as similar to one another, and then to see whether they used the same heuristic to work out each of them. From the taped thinking aloud interviews, we saw that the great majority of respondents saw a pattern of similarity in the problems, namely, that four of six were combinatorial problems. Those respondents who got more abstract, well-structured combinatorial problems (like ABC) first had virtually only one way to reach a solution and to reach the only goal, namely, combinatorial abstract logic. If they passed the problem, they used the logic. Consequently, the operationalization of the independent variable for situation 1 in the table (condition 1 of the independent variable: "clear goal, available heuristic") was "Formally passed ABC when given first" or "Formally passed VC [the next most structured problem] first." Performance of "ABC first, pass" versus "ABC first, fail" groups on the other problems was compared using Age × Group status ANOVAs. "ABC first, pass" groups were significantly more likely to pass VC later, but no other results were significant. In contrasting "VC first, pass" groups with "VC first, fail" groups on performance on later problems, the "VC first, pass" respondents proved more likely to pass Bedrooms and Family Power Dynamics.

Results were interpreted to mean that the hypothesis was supported to some minimal extent. Seeing ABC or VC, given first, as "clear goal, available heuristic" problems led to the solving of other problems (except Bedrooms) using the same heuristic, narrowing problem space (Newell & Simon, 1972). A single abstract approach became the dominant problem-solving style, and there were few postformal operations and (by definition) a small problem space. How quickly we seem to "get into a rut" even in a set of only six problems. What a tribute this is to our cognitive efficiency. Of course, complex postformal processing is not often seen under these circumstances.

Parenthetically, it quickly became clear that those who received a more naturalistic (ill-structured) problem first (by randomized partial counterbalancing) focused on the *practical* aspects and the *uniqueness* of the situation in subsequent problems. This supported the hypothesis in a general way. Since everyday adult life presents a learning experience that teaches us to expect ill-structured naturalistic problems, it does not seem surprising that mature adults want to interpret even abstract, laboratory, school-like problems in naturalistic ways. In summary, then, there is some limited evidence that strategies predicted for situation 1 in Table 9.3 were found in these respondents' transcripts.

Hypothesis 2. If a respondent can use an abstract combinatorial logic on the BR problem (the most ill-structured one) presented first in the set of six problems, then he or she can use that strategy on all the other (less ill-structured) problems. This hypothesis tests the last strategy prediction for situation 4 in Table 9.3. A series of Age × Pass BR status ANOVAs did not support this hypothesis. As noted above, almost all respondents who got BR first, even those who chose to use abstract combinatorial logic to solve it, tended to focus on the uniqueness of the subsequent problem situations. Their doing so did not lend itself to the consistent use of formal combinatorial logic, whatever the respondent *could* have done. Probe questions might demonstrate that respondents *could* use such logic if requested to do so. If they *could* indeed do so, it would support the "very large problem space" prediction for situation 4 in Table 9.3.

In this section, I have summarized some tests of the many predictions one can make about the effects of goal clarity and heuristic availability on strategy and use of postformal operations. My goal was to begin an attempt to link traditional problem-solving studies with postformal thought studies. Goal clarity and heuristic availability, the first variables chosen, had very limited effects on strategy and use of post-formal thought. It was becoming apparent that studies at the microlevel had so far failed to capture the dynamics of the postformal thought phenomenon. Further research will still be useful here. But it seemed that greater gains might come from examining affects of a different type of variables, as seen in the next section.

PROBLEM CONTEXT, PROBE QUESTIONS, AND OTHER SOCIAL FACTORS IN POSTFORMAL THOUGHT

What I have loosely termed social factors seem important to post-formal thought. The social context seems to be the impetus for experiencing, and needing, postformal thought. Social factors in adult and old age development spur the growth of postformal thought. As a researcher, I wanted to examine some of the ways social factors might operate to stimulate or impede postformal cognition, but I wanted to do so within an experimental context as well as in case studies, descriptive work, and phenomenological studies. Varying problem content (i.e., *problem-solving context in the problem presented to the respondent*) to alter the degree of social factors in the problem itself was one way to approach this experimental task, one I used from the start. A second possibility was to have individuals solve the problems alone, or in groups, in which the cognitive operational level of the members would work in a dynamic way, but this difficult strategy would have to wait for additional resources and time. A third way to operationalize "social factors" might be to let the individuals solve the problems and then give them "feedback" from other problem solvers, some of which feedback would challenge their original logic and answers. This approach was accomplished by using controlled probe statements and questions, but only after respondents had solved the problem on their own. The use of the two practical approaches (i.e., context and probes) is described below.

Problem Context

Throughout the series of studies of postformal problem solving, at least six problems, varying in context, were given to each respondent. They all tested combinatorial and proportional formal logic, but the contexts of the problems ranged from very well-structured to ill-structured, from abstract to naturalistic. I hypothesized that for any respondent, the ill-structured problems would occasion postformal thought more often than the well-structured ones would.

From the very first study, this hypothesis was supported. You may have noticed the context effects in earlier chapters. They occurred again in the thinking aloud studies as well. The more naturalistic the problem context, the less the respondents passed formally and the more they used *post*formal operations such as multiple goals, multiple methods, and multiple solutions. Problem context also influenced the degree to which emotion, mind wandering, personal history with the problem, self-evaluation, and representational style differences (i.e., verbal, visual, or kinesthetic representations) frequently (up to 84% of respondents) and differentially became part of the process of problem solving, as illustrated in Table 11.3. This influence was supported by the later very interesting findings of Luszcz and Orr (1990), who compared the styles of thinking described in the book *Women's Ways of Knowing* (Belenky, Clinchy, Goldberger, & Tarule, 1986) to use of postformal thought and found it influenced by the nuanced problem context and to be related to the epistemological stance of "constructed knowing." We concluded that manipulation of problem context was one of the key variables for the presence or absence of articulated postformal thought.

Probe Questions

In my thinking aloud administration of logical problems, three of the six problems were followed by structured probe statements. The probes were ways to simulate some social factors in the expression of postformal thinking. The probes were designed to make more explicit demands for postformal thought by the following means:

- *Asking for* several goals, several ways of conceptualizing the problem.
- *Offering* formal operational and nonformal operational solutions based on smaller and larger problem spaces and asking respondents to judge the truth and logical correctness of each solution.
- *Demonstrating* the possibility of postformal statements by creating some in order to prime respondents to create some of their own.
- Getting respondents to *reflect* on their thinking processes.

Table 11.3. Significant Correlations among Some "Noncognitive" Data and Problem-Solving Variables

General description of use of noncognitive processes

Incorporation of mind wandering into solutions: 50–75% of respondents
Use of personal history: 38–68% of respondents
Use of emotional responses: 16–63% of respondents
Use of evaluative judgments: 42–84% of respondents
Respondents used both verbal and visual representational systems.
Problems judged "interesting" led to fewer postformal self-referential statements.
"Emotional" and "attention-grabbing" problems were not solved with formal logic.

Passing using formal logic

Correlations between use of emotion on some problem and use of formal logic on some problem ranged from –0.32 to 0.63.
Only for CAMP did emotion on CAMP correlate significantly with formal logic on CAMP: –0.32.
Correlations between mind wandering on some problem and use of formal logic on any problem ranged from –0.32 to 0.53.
Mind wandering and formal logic were never correlated on the same problem.
The correlations between use of personal history on any problem and using formal logic on that problem were generally negative and ranged from –0.49 to 0.36. Within the problems of ABC, WK, and BR, these correlations were –0.34, –0.36, and 0.36, respectively.

Correlations between degree of experience with the problem and using formal logic ranged from –0.48 to 0.34 and were generally negative.
The only correlation between experience and formal logic on any one problem occurred for the WK problem: –0.43.

Correlations between self-evaluation and formal logic ranged from 0.35 to 0.78 and were all positive.
The BR problem was the only one for which self-evaluation predicted use of formal logic: 0.43.

Correlations between representational style (i.e., verbal, visual, or kinesthetic) on any problem and using formal logic on any problem ranged from –0.67 to 0.44.
There were no problems on which representational style and formal logic were related within the same problem.

Number of goals

Use of emotion correlated with the number of goals respondents named, ranging from 0.62 to 0.32.
Looking within single problems, we found a correlation of 0.62 on CAMP.

Correlations between mind wandering and number of goals ranged from –0.32 to –0.39.
The correlation for VC was –0.39.

Table 11.3. (*Continued*)

Correlation between personal history and goals ranged from 0.40 to 0.61.
There were no significant correlations within any given problem.
The correlations between experience with the problem and goals ranged from −0.33 to 0.55.
There were no significant correlations within any given problem.

There was only one correlation between self-evaluation and goals, namely, between ABC evaluative statements and number of goals on VC, 0.37.

The correlations between representational style and goals ranged from 0.57 to −0.39. On any given problem, the two variables were correlated 0.36 (visual representational system, on the BR problem), 0.33 and 0.34 for the verbal style and goals on VC and WK, respectively, and 0.36 for the kinesthetic style on ABC.

Number of methods

Only ABC, POW, and BR were analyzed for number of methods.
The correlations between emotion and methods ranged from 0.54 to −0.40.
Only BR showed a correlation within that problem: 0.54.

Correlations between mind wandering and goals ranged from −0.42 to 0.38.
No correlations occurred within a given problem.

Correlations between personal history and methods were two, each 0.43.
In one case, the correlation was within BR (0.43).

The correlations between experience with the problem and methods ranged from −0.45 to 0.55.
There were no significant correlations within any one problem.

The correlations between self-evaluation and methods were three with the same value: 0.34.
For the POW problem, the 0.34 correlation was found within the problem.

The correlations between representational style and number of methods ranged from −0.43 to 0.54.
For ABC, visual style related to methods: −0.33. For BR, visual style related to methods: 0.51. For BR, verbal style related to methods: 0.37. For ABC, kinesthetic style related to methods: 0.41.

Source: Sinnott (1991b). By permission of Greenwood Publishing Group, Inc., Westport, CT.

Answers to any one problem could be scored either before the probe intervention or after it when the respondent had been given more input and had responded to that feedback.

Multivariate ANOVAs for three different types of problems with varying social content demonstrated that postformal thought in general was significantly more likely to be stated out loud after the probes were given. For the ABC problem, with little social content, effects were much smaller than they were for Bedrooms or Family Power Dynamics, which had a more social content. Table 11.4 presents some results of using probe questions. Probes increased the rate of postformal operations for all of the problems to the point where 85% of respondents expressed an operation after the probe. When respondents were faced, during the probe, with the logic of another respondent that was different from their own on the more interpersonal-context Bedrooms and Family Power Dynamics problems, about a third agreed that both their logic and that of the other were true and logical. Self-referential logical statements increased on all three problems, even the very abstract ABC problem.

I concluded that probes were valuable in bringing out latent or unspoken postformal operations because they simulated the sharing of alternate realities about the problem that would occur naturally in ordinary interpersonal (social) exchanges. It also appears that for some reason, respondents are censoring their problem-solving statements until such thought is expressly requested. My tentative hypothesis about that result is that adult respondents have been socialized to be practical and efficient and to eliminate discussion of all the nuances of their thought because such a discussion would take too much of the listener's time.

Table 11.4. Evidence for the Utility of Probing for Postformal Operations: Thinking Aloud Data

	Percentage		
Measure	ABC	BR	POW
Passing (formally)			
Before probe	60	2	30
After probe	77	20	52
Multiple methods			
Before probe	20	27	30
After probe	82	62	55
Self-referential statements			
Before probe	10	27	17
After probe	67	80	85

Source: Sinnott (1991b). By permission of Greenwood Publishing Group, Inc., Westport, CT.

An Experiment on the Effects of Manipulation of Emotion, Intuition, and Motivation

We wanted to see whether manipulating certain parameters of experience, parameters suggested in the literature of a wide variety of subdisciplines, would influence the frequency of postformal operations. In conducting an experiment to this end, respondents were given one of four kinds of experiences in addition to the general task of thinking aloud and solving the problems: (1) Positive mood was induced in some past studies by giving a small gift (Isen & Shalker, 1982), and we attempted to do the same by giving the respondent a candy bar; (2) we attempted to enhance motivation by directly urging respondents to create as many good solutions as possible; (3) we attempted to induce a more relaxed, "no big deal" attitude by telling respondents to feel free to let their minds wander so that they might access intuition more easily; and (4) a control group was given no special instructions. These comments were made in a conversational style before the task. We reasoned that in a test situation, people might need a little permission to loosen up and be themselves, and that the manipulations might be increased to stronger versions as time went on, at some point having intense effects.

Even these minimal manipulations had some significant effects on some elements of the problem-solving process for certain problems, as demonstrated by ANCOVA analyses controlling for age. Five effects reached significance and six effects were marginal, as Table 11.5 reveals. Generally, the BR, POW, and WK problems were the most likely to be influenced. The processes most likely to be influenced were passing formally, number of goals, and number of methods used, although use of self-referential thought statement was also influenced. For the first three of the processes just mentioned, giving candy led to better scores, and encouraging more production led to poorer scores. Paradoxically, the mind-wandering permission led to respondents' making more self-referential thought statements, but did not lead to more mind wandering or intuitive rumination.

The fact that these minimal manipulations had any effect at all was surprising. The effect of positive mood was similar to that found by Isen and Shalker. It makes intuitive sense that focusing attention (even focusing attention on mind wandering or productivity) could create tension and possibly hamper performance—like being told: "Quick! Relax!" This suggests that the greatest number of solutions might be produced by those who are kept happy and instructed to relax and do nothing for a few moments, allowing them to relax.

Table 11.5. Summary of Significant and Marginal ANCOVAs after Manipulation of Mood, Productivity, and Mind Wandering (Age Covaried)

Variables	ANCOVA means			
	Mood	Control	Productivity	Mind wandering
Significant				
Number of methods: BR				
$F(3,34) = 3.822, p = 0.01$	1.78	1.27	1.11	1.20
First solution logical? BR	1.29	1.00	1.63	1.56
(1 = no, 2 = yes)				
$F(3,29) = 3.862, p = 0.01$				
Number of goals: VC	1.56	1.45	1.00	1.10
$F(3,35) = 2.886, p = 0.04$				
Refer to personal history:				
ABC	1.11	0.45	1.33	0.20
$F(3,34) = 2.740, p = 0.05$				
Marginal				
Pass formally: WK	1.56	1.27	1.00	1.40
$F(3,34) = 2.529, p = 0.07$				
Pass formally: POW	1.50	1.27	1.00	1.40
$F(3,34) = 2.616, p = 0.06$				
Number of goals: WK	1.00	1.45	1.10	1.10
$F(3,35) = 2.342, p = 0.09$				
Number of methods: POW	1.22	0.82	0.44	1.00
$F(3,34) = 2.246, p = 0.10$				
Self-referential thoughts:				
POW	0.11	0.00	0.20	0.50
$F(3,35) = 2.325, p = 0.09$				
Emotional expressions: POW	0.67	1.73	0.67	0.30
$F(3,34) = 2.426, p = 0.08$				

Source: Sinnott (1991b). By permission of Greenwood Publishing Group, Inc., Westport, CT.

Focusing attention on producing a great deal apparently led the respondents to somewhat futilely reach back into their personal histories, perhaps for ideas. Complex postformal thought might be like creativity in that it flourishes in an environment that makes few demands but offers rewards for quiet reflection. The outcome of this particular experiment was to suggest that small manipulations of emotional state by means of problem instructions may free or freeze our respondents' abilities to demonstrate the postformal operations they can use. There may be a lesson here for our work with undergraduate students and others.

Chapter 12 describes the styles of some attempts to dig deeper into the processes that lead to expression or nonexpression of postformal thought. The chapter describes a sample case study that includes a real-life event in which the respondent used postformal thought effectively. The chapter also describes the research strategy of finding subsamples whose members are likely to need access to postformal operations and then testing them to see both *whether* they use the operations and *how* they use the operations.

CHAPTER 12

Digging Deeper

A Case Study and Suggestions
for Studying Special Subsamples

The road is better than the inn.
MIGUEL DE CERVANTES

Once a general process is discovered in psychology or in any other science, and once that process can be defined, discussed in theoretical terms, and reliably found, the next step is to study the parameters of the occurrence of that process. In Chapter 11, we saw summaries of some attempts to carry out this next step with general populations. In this chapter, we will see attempts to dig deeper into the processes and their parameters using case studies.

This chapter describes how single case studies can be used to get a better understanding of the types of occasions when individuals who have access to postformal thought make use of such thought, as well as of the purposes for which they use it. This chapter also briefly describes how we can study selected subsamples of respondents who seem especially likely to need postformal thinking to succeed in their work or family lives. We can confirm that these special subsamples do use postformal thinking and find out more about how they make use of these thinking operations in a given context. Our ultimate goals remain to understand both the phenomenon itself and the factors that cause it to be more or less likely in adults so that postformal thought might be used by more adults more often.

A CASE STUDY OF
POSTFORMAL THOUGHT

This case study applies ideas about the nature and parameters of postformal thought to the thinking processes of individuals in a family faced with the very difficult real-life problem of deciding what to do to help a close relative experiencing a first-time acute paranoid psychotic episode. After presenting the case, we will examine the value of the case study method so that we might illustrate three things: the complex problem-solving process in an emotion-laden domain of family and clinical issues, the part emotional and interpersonal factors can play in the postformal process, and how the presence or absence of postformal skills is associated with family members' views of the event, the problem, and themselves, as well as with the outcome for the patient. This analysis is not meant to be a clinical assessment of the patient or his family or to predict treatment outcomes except as these things relate to the logical cognitive functioning of postformal thought.

The case described here is a real one, but the names and identifying features related to this event have been altered sufficiently to preserve the anonymity of the individuals involved. Events have been described by a key participant who has given the author permission to retell the story here. The story was obtained through extensive interviews in person and by telephone and from notes and diary entries during and after the event. The informant reviewed and approved the information and analysis presented here.

The hypotheses were that postformal thought is personally and socially adaptive, can be modeled in a useful way in a case study, and involves noncognitive and interpersonal elements. Events associated with this case also suggest hypotheses about clinical ramification of postformal thought—hypotheses that can be tested empirically. For example, we might hypothesize, on the basis of what we see in this case, that individuals who can use postformal thought are more likely to show a different style of pathology from those who do not have access to postformal thought.

The Story

One peaceful afternoon, the main informant, "Jane," received a telephone call from her father, who lived hundreds of miles away. According to her father, her brother, "John", who lived in the father's city, had been behaving very strangely. John was accusing family members of trying to get rid of him, making him sick, and plotting against him. Others were against him too, trying to control him. The situation was at a crisis point.

This was very upsetting news for Jane, for more than one reason. It was the first she had heard of this problem, as communication was not a strong skill in her family. Two weeks earlier, it had appeared that John, for the first time, was taking responsibility for his life. Only the previous week, John had been examining familial relationships and trying to piece together family motives. John had wanted to see Jane very much. Also, Jane and John always had been very close, although she was nearly a decade older than he. They were each other's emotionally closest relatives. For the better part of 30 years, John had experienced problems with drugs, alcohol, and dependence on his father, but had never experienced a psychotic break.

John's life seemed always to get worse. As a teen, John had been intensely hurt by his parents' destructive divorce, and he later had been a troubled participant in his father's second marriage, whereas Jane and an older brother had distanced themselves. Over and over again, John would be involved in some problem and his father would try to "handle" the situation, while his mother complained about them both and his stepmother complained about John. Jane felt lucky to have escaped the family situation, but she felt helpless. She grieved over her brother's and family's pain.

Jane had planned a short visit with her father in a few days to keep family ties intact and to take her children to see their grandfather. She had hoped for a peaceful visit, but that hope was rapidly fading with the phone call. Instead of feeling peaceful, she was going into the eye of a hurricane. Nevertheless, Jane had always thought of herself as the "invulnerable child" of the family (Garmezy, 1976) who could cope and love in spite of all difficulties. Now it seemed time to take that role again. With children in tow, she headed for the airport, unsure of the reality of the situation or of her brother's actual state.

Upon her arrival, she found that her father had already hospitalized John and was in a state of great anxiety himself. John's behavior had frightened their father seriously when John had sought refuge at the father's house, although John had not threatened others or himself. Since John refused the medication prescribed by a "renowned" psychiatrist, the father, acting on the psychiatrist's advice, was certain that commitment was the only solution. John valued his freedom and was angry with his father's unilateral decision to hospitalize him and to commit him involuntarily. Even worse, John would be under the control of a private psychiatrist who John felt was not listening to him or sympathetic to him. John had seen this psychiatrist several years before, but had refused treatment from him at that time and had felt antagonistic toward him.

John's stepmother was glad he was out of the house.

John's mother was distancing herself from the problem.

The father pleaded with Jane to avoid John, the hospital, and the whole problem, and to pretend to her children that nothing was happening, so they could "have a good time."

Jane was too upset about her brother to pretend that everything was normal, and intended to communicate with John unless the doctors specifically disapproved. When they told her they had no objection, she drove at once to the hospital to visit and to find out some facts, determined to offer love and support to John.

When she arrived, she found that John was refusing to take the prescribed antipsychotic medication because he "needed to keep his mind clear." Clarity was needed, John said, because their father (with the famous private psychiatrist) had chosen to involuntarily commit him for a longer period. As a prelude to that action, the police were due to arrive momentarily to transfer John to a locked ward at a private hospital. John's agitation was increasing. No one paid any attention to what he said! Why wouldn't anyone listen? Even his family seemed to be plotting against him! Jane listened and talked and tried to describe John's options to him. She told him she loved him and that he could count on her support. They discussed their "crazy family," and John became more calm and rational. Hours passed, and the police, who they had feared would arrive at any moment, did not appear.

When night came, the staff made it known that a family member needed to stay overnight with John to ensure that he would not leave the psychiatric ward. Jane said she would stay because she could see no other options. She made the 40-minute drive to her father's house, comforted her children and her father, argued against involuntary commitment with her father, and drove back to the hospital. She urged John to take his medication to avoid commitment. John agreed to do so, but was concerned he would not have a "clear" head to defend himself at the court hearing in the morning. Jane talked to him about the pros and cons of strategies for the hearing. That night, she explored her own terrifying issues about her childhood, as she waited with John at the hospital, wondered how and in what ways she might be able to affect the commitment hearing in the morning, and tried to sleep.

In the morning, she prompted her brother to tell the judge he would take the medication, convinced her brother to agree to actually do so, and negotiated with her father to delay the commitment proceedings. At the hearing, however, none of these things went as planned, and John was involuntarily committed.

Jane spent the next three days trying to understand when (and if) a second commitment extension hearing was to be held, trying to find a new psychiatrist, talking with John's current and prospective psychiatrist and therapists, and talking with John. She was unsure which of John's stories were true and of the extent of his paranoia. She feared that involuntary commitment would destroy John's remaining threads of trust and self-esteem, but she also feared that her father could not cope with John if he were to be released. She was looking for an ethical and practical solution to John's situation in the midst of continually shifting demands and expectations from both her brother and her father. She was concerned for her children, for their anxiety in the middle of this chaos and the lack of time she was spending with them. During this time, she sustained herself through journal writing, meditation, and the support of a couple of close friends.

John finally took the medication, established a relationship with a therapist, and seemed better, but no one would call off the second commitment hearing.

Everyone else in the family seemed worse—more changeable, angry, and confused. Her father and stepmother were frightened by the idea that if John were released he would want to stay with them.

John lapsed into paranoia as the commitment hearing was on, then off, and then on again, regardless of how he behaved. It appeared that Jane was unable to comfort John, find another doctor acceptable to their father, penetrate the legal system, or shift her father's perspective from involuntary commitment to voluntary commitment. She grew depressed. Everyone grew more confused and less able to cope. In this highly charged atmosphere, it was hard to say whose reality was "real" and whose goals merited attention.

Finally, the second hearing took place, and John was involuntarily committed. John's father now opposed the psychiatrist he originally picked, and John then chose this very psychiatrist, the one he had originally rejected. No one in the family really thought of the commitment as necessary or useful, although they seemed to think there was no other alternative.

As more time passed, John continued contact with Jane and broke contact with the father. He was soon able to discontinue medication and enter a halfway house. Exhausted, Jane returned home with her children and a new awareness of her family of origin. The mother and stepmother seemed unchanged, but the father shed some illusions and began to communicate with Jane in new ways. John, however, remained convinced that he was and always had been fine, the father decided to blame the psychiatrist for all the chaos, and, as things calmed down a little and they needed her less, no one bothered to keep in touch with Jane.

Analyses

Illustrating Processes in Family Problem Solving. Figure 12.1 summarizes the processes that appeared to be used by the key informant (Jane). Symbols in the figure denote the use of selected problem-solving elements (see prior chapters) and postformal operations from Table 3.5. Table 12.1 contains samples from Jane's notes and journal entries. The decision process was a complex, multistage one, and postformal thought was present.

Analysis of the case study bore much fruit. From the descriptive information drawn from this case study and summarized in the figure, several of the following relations can be hypothesized and later tested in larger populations. Emotional and interpersonal factors are clearly part of the process. The solution of real life, ill-structured interpersonal problems clearly can be modeled in terms of postformal operations. The procedure of solving can be described with elements from information-processing traditions. Postformal thought can be seen to be essentially a subroutine that can prevent an infinite cognitive loop from stopping the problem-solving process. Finally, we can see the effects of using and not using postformal operations in a crisis situation.

The situation in which many thinkers cocreate a problem and a solution is the kind most likely to either lead to infinite loops or be solved using postformal thought. In such a conflict, there are separate realities for each thinker that can truly be resolved only by using postformal skills.

Social Factors in Solution of the Problem. Sources of social factors encountered in this case include role-related factors, current interpersonal relationship factors, belief systems, and factors based on a past history of interpersonal relations. These factors are like those found in the earlier studies summarized in previous chapters. Each of these social factors delivered information to the key informant. Each

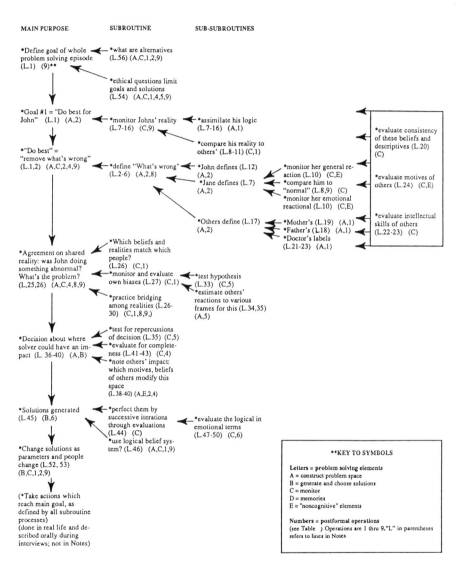

Figure 12.1.   Summary of Processes Used by Key Informant, Based on Her Notes Alone.

Table 12.1. Sample Notes and Journal Entries of Key Informant

Sample notes

Line Number
1. Goal—to do the best thing for John
2. 1. Define what is wrong with John:
3.   immediate
4.   long-term
5. Who is defining—value system
6. Criteria for defining
7. a. I define:
8.   I spent time with John watch his behavior judge how it
9.   varies from *his* "normal" behavior and "normal" behavior
10.   I pay attention to gut reaction, my emotions, how I react
11.   to him and what I am feeling
12. b. John defines:
13.   How to distinguish whether what he says happened or not.
14.   Work from known facts, gray area, obviously false.
15.   What causes him to think these things—his logical leap
16.   within his framework
17. c. Others define:
18.   Father—his behavior, words
19.   Mother—motivation, ability to be objectively defined
20.   Are descriptions consistent?
21. Doctor—labels—analysis (question basis—dependent upon
22. amount of information available, reliability, his ability
23. to distinguish what happened from imagined)
24. Motivation involved
25. What has happened?
26. What is whose reality?
27. Motivation and biases involved
28. (including my own)
29. How can questions be presented to obtain answers?
30. (verbally rehearse)
31. Need understanding of emotional involvement
32. of each player and myself.
33. Test hypothesis.
34. Test for probable reaction.
35. Weighing possible repercussions could result from decision.
36. Analysis of what I could probably, possibly affect—focus
37. there
38. dependent on others' decision strategies
39. emotional involvement
40. motivation
41. Scan for missing elements
42. missing repercussions
43. unexpected consequences

Table 12.1. (*Continued*)

Sample notes

44. Talking, feedback—testing
45. helps formulate solutions until they feel good
46. Logic weighed against emotional
47. Even if most logical solution monitor against emotions if
48. uncomfortable
49. try to examine why
50. understand
51. reevaluate
52. Continually changing solutions as actions, people
53. emotions, circumstances change
54. Larger ethical question—under what circumstances is
55. it ethical to commit a person?
56. What are the alternatives (ideally and realistically)?

Journal entries

Sample entry I

Committed, such a strange term
   Devoted, focused, determined
   locked away
   My heart aches
   As he struggles
The butterfly with glistening wet wings
   newly formed
   Beats them frantically
   Against walled cocoon
   Desperate to break through
   one hole
   Glimmer of light
   Knowing deep down
   There must be a world out there
   Beat harder
   Torn wings
   beat and frayed
   drop off
   wild eyed staring
   Entombed
As I fly and soar
   together
in love and peace and joy
   Will John make it?

Sample entry II

Tightrope juggling act
Two children lost in feelings of anxiety, worry, guilt, despair confusion, fear

(*continued*)

Table 12.1. (*Continued*)

Journal entries
Father balanced between control and total loss of all even self
Stepmother removed, defensive but there
Doctor of power, ego trip
And is he to be trusted with my brother's life
When any other alternative may break my father
Superwoman
All things to all people
John, how to reach him through his reality while being honest and
maintaining trust
Mother—what does she think now
Already blaming John for my honesty
Video of kids
An intimacy of love and sharing
That once existed
Now gone

Source: Sinnott (1991c). By permission of Greenwood Publishing Group, Inc., Westport, CT.

is a product of—and a creator of—perceptual filters. In the last two relationship factors, each acts to alter the path or trajectory of the key informant's decisions by adding a kind of "gravitational field" from others' decisions to the sum total of forces operating. The role-related factors seem to change the flow of problem solving via mechanisms of social learning; the interpersonal relations factors seem to change the flow of the problem solving of the key informant by setting up a dialogue between others' processes and hers; the belief systems seem to use both mechanisms. In any case, elements are introduced into her problem-solving process that have no well-defined counterparts in traditional artificial-intelligence literature, problem-solving literature, information-processing literature, or Piagetian theory. These elements appear only in clinical models, general systems theory models, postformal models, or new physics models.

How are some of the factors seen in the informant's notes? At what point did they seem to have an impact on the problem-solving process? Table 12.1 summarizes answers to these questions, though the listing is not exhaustive.

The social factors in this case were more often expressed as interactions in present time, or as belief systems, but role factors and history-of-interactions factors were also frequently present in the report. Social factors seemed to be connected with nine of the postformal operations examined at that time and with all the information-processing factors described above, and the key informant verbally expressed their influence on her thought. This suggests that our measures of problem-solving performance are frequently interlaced with social elements of which investigators do not seem conscious and that they do not measure or analyze directly as part of the *thinking* process.

The informant's awareness of the social factors, however, lets her shift among levels of reality while making her decisions. The impact of these "social" shifts during problem solving was evident at many points, but was especially important for the outcome early in the process. At that early point, the key informant left for her family hometown with her own definitions of the problem, which would have led to her fighting her father and the doctor to "save" her brother, whom she saw as being railroaded into a pathological role. Upon entering her brother's, her father's, and the doctor's versions of the reality of the problem through dialogue with them, she could see several new versions of the reality. Her brother was frightened, confused, and truly unable to live alone; her father had run out of emotional resources and was nearly incompetent from stress; the doctors were more flexible than they first appeared, and possibly were just as eager as she was for her brother to be released. These insights led to her shifting her problem-solving heuristic from a battle for rights to a balancing across the needs of many persons. In an ethical sense, she moved from a Kohlberg stance reflecting rights to a Gilligan stance reflecting consideration of the needs of all participants (Gilligan, 1982). The new heuristic resulting from the shift in reality seemed to lead to more positive results and new strategies to help her brother. Further, it fueled her sense of having to take care of everyone and everything to avoid catastrophic outcomes.

Social factors, as stimuli for a shift in realities, took up the majority of the key informant's decision-making process. Determining how she logically solved the problem while ignoring the interpersonal factors would leave us with very impoverished data, data that would fail to reflect her real decision process. Keeping *all* of the information displayed in her process allows us to begin an analysis of her various "logics" and to begin to see her postformal use of those elements to help solve the problem, as well as her use of them as data, feedback, or content.

This descriptive ideographic analysis suggests hypotheses for future experimental research. First, we could hypothesize that knowing that a person with whom one is emotionally close holds a disparate belief from one's own about the reality of a situation leads to a large problem space, hypothesis testing (as a problem-solving strategy), and postformal thought. Second, being in close relationship to others over time is more likely to lead to postformal thought during problem solving than is *not* being in a close relationship. Third, the individual who is able to resolve family crises and emerge as a leader is most likely a postformal thinker. Fourth, the more emotional and realistic the problem-solving scenario, the greater the extent to which social and interpersonal factors will be present in the problem-solving process.

Adaptive Postformal Thought. The third reason for analyzing this case is to reflect briefly on the utility of postformal thought for these family members as individuals and as a group and, conversely, on what difficulties seem to arise from the lack of such thought. Note, however, that while we hypothesize that postformal thought is adaptive, we must be fair and examine whether it seemed to have negative effects as well.

While in this case I have stressed the thinking process of the key informant, we could look at the processes of Jane, John, and the father, based on Jane's notes (which, of course, could not be independently verified in their totality, although they generally agreed with comments by other family members). Postformal thought appeared to be available in this context to Jane, but unavailable to John and the father. Postformal thought seemed adaptive for Jane in several ways, since it let her effectively operate in any one of several realities (those of her brother, her father, and the doctor), let her avoid being caught up in arguments over what "really" happened or who is "right" about the situation, and let her keep communication channels open among the participants, who did not share a common reality. It seemed to allow her to get the best treatment for her brother and to keep family bonds intact.

Lack of postformal thought, in contrast, seemed to hamper John and the father. John seemed to express a problem of family dynamics in a maladaptive, paranoid way because he could not move into the reality of his family or that of the larger society to attribute more benevolent motives to other people. For John, only *his* reality was "true." This is not to say that the lack of postformal thought leads to psychosis, but that without such thought, the person may manifest different psychotic symptoms or be more easily trapped in the psychotic reality.

The father struggled and expended considerable energy to maintain personal control over what he saw as chaos in the family because he could not enlarge his set of realities to include (in a meaningful way) the separate realities of other family members such as Jane or John. If someone's actions appeared to have no meaning, chaos would loom over them all, and would have to be controlled.

Both John and the father limited the overstimulation coming from others to a bearable level, but only by sacrificing information and seeing everything in black and white terms, thereby controlling stimulation in the way we discussed in Chapter 3.

Jane made overstimulation more bearable by jumping out of her own reality system to a larger system of which her reality as well as the reality of John and her father were parts. She viewed all these realities as true, for purposes of consideration, and chose one to operate in at a given time. Jane could then handle more stimulation and information, and could potentially reach a solution of greater utility. She also could respond in a more complex way to the differences, difficulties, and anger around her, seeing those things as reasonable responses within a different reality system, rather than as attacks. Jane enlarged problem space so that more strategies could be used to work out the family crisis to everyone's advantage.

We might assume that a therapist working effectively with this sort of family would be a postformal therapist. He or she would then have all necessary thinking tools to intervene at any of the steps in Figure 12.1 or to bring the whole process with its emotional components to awareness. The figure could also be used to teach conflict resolution skills by using it to show how alternate views of reality operate to influence decision paths.

It is possible to theorize that postformal problem-solving ability lets one enlarge one's identity and make it more flexible, and by doing so makes it easier for one to avoid some of the cognitive or behavioral pitfalls that show up as pathology. The idea of a concrete, unchanging identity, acting in defensive opposition to other concrete identities, might give way with further development to the idea of a flexible identity that is a sum total of one's (not necessarily consistent) ways of interacting with others and the world, and one's ways of transforming the self. The challenge of other persons may open the window to multiple views of truth *and* multiple views of the self, held together by consistent relational processes. The complex thinker is freer to live out more of his or her potential selves. When a potentially pathological response threatens such a thinker's adaptivity, a wider range of reactions can spring to life. The utility of this thought is limited, however, by the context in which the thinker can operate. The postformal thinker who is excited by the possible reality choices may be frustrated by more limited environments or people, unless saved by a spiritual/philosophical stance (one more reality shift [see later chapters]) that permits the thinker to learn from frustration and difficulty. Of course, the "incompletely postformal thinker" might bring a different pathology of unending relativism and inability to be, to choose, or to decide. The postformal thinker with significant psychopathology, too, might demonstrate a different style. For example, a sociopathic individual who is postformal might find it easier to adopt

Table 12.2. Social Problems in Problem Solving of Key Informant

Factors from Sample Notes in Table 12.1 (line number)	Point of impact in process
1. Goal is in service of others (1)	1. Goal setting; increase size of problem space
2. Value system of others defining: "What's wrong with John?" (5)	2. Set size of problem space; define goal, solution, metatheory, heuristics; parameter setting
3. Others' criteria for definition of what's wrong (12, 17)	3. Same as 2
4. Reaction of informant to John—object relations (10)	4. Problem definition; problem space
5. Accessing John's framework of logic (15)	5. Problem definition; parameter setting
6. Father as codefiner of problem (18)	6. Problem definition; parameter setting
7. Mother as codefiner (19)	7. Problem definition; parameter setting
8. Comparison of reality of several persons (19, 20)	8. Metatheory shift; monitor; self-referential thought
9. Doctor as definer of reality (21)	9. Metatheory shift; monitor; self-referential thought
10. Doctor/Mother as subject to distortion of reality due to own motives (19, 24)	10. Problem definition, problem space
11. Ownership of realities (26, 27)	11. Metatheory shift; self-referential thought
12. Information gathering to fit others' frames of reference (29, 31)	12. Monitor
13. Reactions of others that could influence quality of solution (34, 35)	13. Multiple causality; processes to choose solutions
14. Worth of heuristic dependent on others' cognition and decision processes (37–40)	14. Processes to choose solutions
15. Feedback from others to determine value of solution (44)	15. Processes to choose solutions
16. Fitting solutions to continuously changing input of others (51)	16. Self-referential thought
17. Overall ethics of personal freedom (53)	17. Monitor; self-referential thought

Source: Sinnott (1991c). By permission of Greenwood Publishing Group, Inc., Westport, CT.

the guise of the con man or woman; the enabling family member might have more complex ways to enable; the postformal multiple personality might be the "healed" multiple personality who can work with the discovered "selves" in a conscious way; the postformal paranoid might better imagine the intrapersonal plotting machinations of his or her tormentors; the postformal psychotherapy client might run rings around a psychotherapist!

Table 12.2 summarizes the social factors in the problem solving of the key informant, with their points of impact in her process. Table 12.3 summarizes the advantages of postformal thought suggested by this case analysis. We examined a single case (in the example in this chapter) to take a look at family-context postformal processes, to see the large role played by emotional and social factors, and to explore the practical and social effects of having access to this thought. Results of many case studies appear in summary form in ideas articulated in several chapters in this book. Cases have been used to generate hypotheses and to confirm ideas about the nature, genesis, and adaptivity of postformal thought. In the next section, we can explore briefly another research strategy, one exploring the thinking of "special" groups of respondents selected because they were likely to need postformal skills in their work or their lives.

STUDYING SPECIAL RESPONDENTS
LIKELY TO NEED POSTFORMAL THOUGHT

Another research strategy that is yielding dividends is that of targeting respondents whose job or life experiences seem to predispose them to develop postformal thought and test their postformal abilities. On the basis of ideas of postformal thought development, individuals who must coordinate multiple realities because it is part of their job to do so should be more likely to show postformal thought than those with different sorts of job experiences. The style of operations, the quality of the process itself, might be expected to vary from life context to life context as thinkers face differing sorts of challenges to any one reality. The postformal thought of two or more of these individuals talking and problem solving together—for example, the two members of a long-term intimate couple—might give us direct information about how realities are interpersonally cocreated. Exploring the quality of the operations used by any of these special respondents would help us obtain a fuller picture of the scope, diversity, use, and nuances of this complex adult thinking ability.

Table 12.3. Advantages of Postformal Thought in a Family Crisis

Ability to "speak in others' languages" or belief systems leading to better communication
Ability to argue within others' logics
A flexible view of what is possible for a family
More effective interventions by family members
Greater awareness of one's own biases
Ability to limit stimulation without limiting information flow
More creative problem solving
More flexible interpersonal relations
Ability to get perspective on family problems
Greater effectiveness in emotional situations
A more flexible view of who the other "is"
Ability to reach the best solution in view of all realities
Lower anxiety and lower need for control and defense

Some examples of explorations with these several target groups can be found in chapters still ·to come in this book, of which the next chapter is one. Results of these targeted studies have also informed the earlier chapters about the nature, purpose, and development of complex postformal thought.

Various combinations of measures may be given to the targeted response group. They might receive any one of the forms of the postformal problems, that is, thinking aloud, computerized, standard interview, plus other tasks suitable for the specific population. Other tasks or scales have included marital adjustment inventories, paper-and-pencil tests concerning use of postformal operations at work, interviews on how the respondent would solve selected teaching problems, grades in selected classes, videotapes of body language, completion of joint research projects, sex role inventories, and more. Tasks might be given prior to and after a certain event. All these methodological permutations serve the same goal, namely, obtaining a fuller picture of postformal thought.

In this chapter, I have spent a little time discussing the value of looking at case studies and doing research with specific targeted groups of postformal respondents. In this Part II of the book, I have focused on some of the research that has been done to "ground" the theory in data. In Part III, the Theory of Postformal Thought is applied, first to phenomena such as education, family relations, growth within the context of the workplace, conflict resolution, and more, and next to the "big picture"—more abstract topics such as spirituality, ecopsychology, and humanist and existential movements in psychology.

APPLICATIONS OF THE THEORY OF POSTFORMAL THOUGHT AT HOME AND IN THE "BIG PICTURE"

CHAPTER 13

Applications of the Theory of Postformal Thought to Education

At first the idea of creating new order by perturbation seems
outrageous, like shaking up a box of random words and pour-
ing out a sentence.

MARILYN FERGUSON

Maybe the world *is a hologram!*

KARL PRIBRAM

In what ways might we apply all this information about the Theory of Postformal Thought to the activity of education in its formal or informal, institutional or casual, primary or secondary or postsecondary forms? There are five areas to which Postformal Theory applies: its relation to the concept of "learning," the methods and philosophies by which teachers teach, how master teachers reason, the structure of learning institutions, and how adult learners learn (or fail to learn). The Theory of Postformal Thought applies to all these areas, since it describes one kind of person who might teach and a kind of institution in which teaching might take place. In Part IV, Chapter 21, we will examine educational interventions that facilitate the development of postformal thought both in students and in teachers in training.

Several books that have appeared recently contain material that speaks to the topic of this chapter and that uses the Theory of Postformal Thought. The reader might wish to examine the book on teacher change edited by Kahaney, Janangelo, and Perry (1993); Sinnott's (1994b) handbook of adult lifespan learning; the book on paradigm bridging edited by Sinnott and Cavanaugh (1991), especially the chapters by Johnson, Lee, and Tanon; and Sinnott and Johnson's

(1996) book on reinventing the university. These are just a few of the latest attempts to assess and improve the state of education in a historical period that demands great flexibility in dealing with major change and demands the processing of huge amounts of information. These demands of the current historical period might create sufficient motivation to seriously examine how we educate and what we expect others to learn. Postformal thinking provides a complex cognitive structure to think about teaching and learning in rapidly changing co-created realities. The theory suggests that the most important learning challenge we face is learning *how* to learn and think.

POSTFORMAL THOUGHT
AND "LEARNING"

In this section of the chapter, I will consider the relationship between the concepts of postformal thought and learning, which is typically defined as the process of acquisition of information or skills through practice or experience. The primary goal of education systems is to promote learning. If adults continue their cognitive development and attain postformal abilities, one would think they must be "learning" by some definition. If these adults start to think at a postformal level, they might very well "learn" in somewhat different ways on subsequent occasions. But since life-span developmentalists and learning theorists ignore each other's work, for the most part there is little dialogue about learning and postformal thought development. "Postformal" and "learning" studies are seldom joined, since they emerge from differing research philosophies and traditions. Roles for learning in postformal development and the effect of postformal development on learning are unclear from data, but six principles seem obvious from theory. They are outlined in Table 13.1 and described below.

Learning before Postformal Thought Can Occur: Hypothesized Relations

1. *Some processes and facts must be learned before postformal thought can be shown.* First, the theoretical position flowing from Piaget's original thinking suggests that formal operational thought must be present before postformal thought can be shown (Commons, Richards, & Armon, 1984; Sinnott, 1984b). Second, it seems necessary

Table 13.1. Six Relations between Learning and Postformal Thought: Implications for Theory, Research, and Applications

Learning necessary prior to postformal thought

PRINCIPLE 1

Basic processes such as memory and formal thought, and basic facts such as information about a certain context, must be learned prior to postformal thought.

Theory: Learning is integral to postformal thought. Use of postformal thought may be accelerated and stimulated by teaching prerequisite processes.

Research: Experimentally manipulate learned material to effect change in postformal thinking; for example, teach students to recognize ill-structured problems. Examine case studies of thinkers beginning to be postformal.

Applications: Conflict-resolution experts can teach postformal thought prerequisites to conflict participants to accelerate resolution of conflict. Teach parents to work in larger "problem spaces" to help solve parent–child conflicts.

PRINCIPLE 2

A thinker must learn that there can be multiple "true" views of reality.

Theory: Cognitive development studies begin to utilize quantum physics, chaos, complexity, and general systems theory change models to allow for multiple truths in cognitive change events, especially interpersonal events.

Research: Perform multiperson cognition experiments to determine conditions that best teach multiple realities. For example, does group (versus individual) problem solving more often lead to postformal solutions? Do expert (versus novice) therapists more often show acceptance of multiple realities?

Applications: Teach clients and university students how to take in and consider multiple views of reality.

Presence of postformal thought alters learning processes thereafter.

PRINCIPLE 3

Postformal thinkers help new learners bridge "conflicting" realities. Postformal thinkers learn that change in the only constant; therefore, they tend to learn processes in addition to content.

Theory: The understanding of *processes* and the awareness of *change and shifts* may be key areas for further theory development in developmental psychology.

Research: Study the ways in which cognitive development changes the understanding of process. What are steps in such an understanding? Study how individuals maintain a sense of self if they see reality as (in part) commitment to a truth cocreated with others and ever-changing.

Applications: Teach beginning therapists and new professors how to best present multiple views of reality. Teach international development workers how best to span the realities of life in economically developed countries and life in less-developed countries.

(*continued*)

Table 13.1. (*Continued*)

PRINCIPLE 4

For postformal thinkers, learning processes become inherently social.

Theory: The multiperson nature of thought can be added to most theories of cognitive development that lack such dimensions.

Research: Studies of dyadic problem solving can be conducted. Studies investigating the factors that influence postformal thinkers' learning processes can be done.

Applications: Cooperative learning and dialogic processes in learning settings may be useful to adult learners, who tend to be postformal.

PRINCIPLE 5

Any learned element can be used in postformal or non-postformal ways.

Theory: Theory can include elements thought to determine whether a given fact will be used postformally or formally.

Research: Study how persons of various ages and cognitive levels use the same facts to build formal and postformal systems.

Applications: Develop tests of "readiness for postformal thinking" to be used in corporate and other reorganizations.

PRINCIPLE 6

Postformal thinkers and non-postformal thinkers in the same situation learn different things.

Theory: Add cognitive development level to theories about effects of context.

Research: Experimentally analyze the determinants of use of formal versus postformal thought.

Applications: The elements of intragroup conflicts can be learned postformally, leading to conflict resolution.

Source: Sinnott (1994e). By permission of Greenwood Publishing Group, Inc., Westport, CT.

to learn that some problem solving involves the kind of problem that we might officially term "ill-structured" (Churchman, 1971), the goals and parameters of such problems being unclear. Third, it seems necessary to gather and learn relevant facts about the problem at hand and hold them in working memory or long-term memory long enough to see the larger complexity of the problem space (Sinnott, 1989a,d). These three sorts of learning seem to be the prerequisites for simply *moving* to a postformal worldview in any given context. This is some of the complex material on which the manipulations of postformal thought can begin.

Of course, even more primitive or basic processes must also be present. For example, if a thinker does not know anything about relationships and their possibilities or has been virtually devoid of personal encounters, he or she would have no "data" loaded in this area and would therefore be hard-pressed to think about relations in a complex way. The earlier Table 3.3 shows additional prerequisites for shifting from formal to postformal thought. Table 3.2, also presented earlier, shows the formal and postformal ways of knowing interpersonal relations and suggests the learning that must occur at a formal thinking level of functioning before postformal functioning can occur in that context.

My studies of problem solving reported in 1991 (see Chapter 11) demonstrate how individual thinkers learn from probe questions that problems can be seen in more than one formal way. This activity of responding to probe questions seems to help thinkers learn to be postformal. Similar activities will be discussed in Chapter 21, which discusses interventions to promote postformal thought. Using this probe-stimulated learning, individuals can go on to solve other problems in more than one formal way. In a similar way, a thinker can learn that problems can have more than one goal and go on to generalize that knowledge to other problems. In the case study of "John" (Chapter 12), who began to display psychotic symptoms, his sister could not think postformally about his condition until she learned about his behavior and thought, about her options, and about the formal logic being used by her father and the psychiatrist.

What does principle 1, stated above, mean for theory, research, and practical applications? Table 13.1 displays one implication for theory, for research, and for application for each of the six principles, including this one.

2. *A thinker must learn that there can be multiple "true" views of reality.* This principle means that more information about the complexity of a situation must be offered to the thinker. Perry (1975), for example, saw the university experience as a chance to make more complex multiple views of realities available for college students. Lee (1991) (see below) credits expert teachers with the ability to use this shift themselves and suggests that they teach it, in turn, to others. Some theorists credit intimate relationships with giving a participant in such a relationship several ways of looking at the reality of the world, courtesy of the feedback of the intimate partner (Basseches, 1984; Kramer, 1983; Sinnott, 1981, 1984b, 1991a,b), or the feedback of intimate others (Hogue, Bross, & Efran, 1994; Lee, 1994a,b; Meacham & Boyd, 1994; Phillips, Lipson, & Basseches, 1994), or even the feedback

of a mystical and spiritual nature (Sinnott, 1992, 1994a, 1996a; Wei-bust & Thomas, 1994). Therapeutic encounters or encounters related to personal growth seem to provide this possibility to clients as their views conflict with the views of a trusted therapist (Armstrong, 1991; Benack, 1984; Frankl, 1963; Maslow, 1968; C. Rogers, 1951; Yalom, 1980). Problem solvers learn to shift their realities to become more oriented to multiple realities, as we saw in the earlier research chapters.

Some theory, research, and an application related to principle 2 are shown in Table 13.1.

Postformal Thought Changes Learning Processes

3. *Postformal thinking helps learners bridge conflicting truths.* Expert teachers (who are labeled as such by their peers and schools), persons good at conflict resolution, international development project personnel who are successful at teaching behavioral change and empowering project participants (Johnson, 1991, 1994), and therapists working successfully with clients all seem to facilitate this bridging among conflicting truths. It almost seems to follow that postformal thinkers are more likely to integrate and understand the several sides of themselves and interact with others within that framework, teaching those others. Some theoretical work and some data do suggest that this is true (see Chinen, 1984; Koplowitz, 1984; Labouvie-Vief, 1982, 1984; Rogers, Sinnott, & Van Dusen, 1991).

As stated in Table 13.1, the principle that postformal thinkers learn all truths as though those truths were "definite maybe states" lets us become sensitized to how little traditional cognitive developmental studies inform us about how individuals come to know a *constantly shifting* change and how they process realities of life. We psychologists understand too little about how we learn process and change. We have too few theories about the knowing of social realities, which shift from moment to moment as they are cocreated by dyads or families or societies. In my own problem-solving studies described in earlier chapters, middle-aged and older respondents given logical problems tended to produce solutions that were actually generalizable *processes* that would bridge changing conditions from the reality of one problem to another. They had learned something new, namely, good processes. Perhaps, in Erikson's (1950) terms, they learned a general process of integration that could help them with the larger problem-solving experience of creating integrity in their life stories.

See Table 13.1 for theory, research, and applications related to principle 3.

4. *For postformal thinkers, learning processes become inherently social.* Once a postformal thinker knows his or her role in the creation of truth (that role being to choose a view of reality to commit to and work from), that thinker is aware of the role of others in also creating the "reality" around him or her. This social creation of reality is even true of the reality of the physical world. The postformal thinker wants to know which physics theory you have chosen, or even your choice of theory about clock time and being "on time", not to evaluate whether you are correct, but to move logically from your chosen theory to hers or his. While both positions on time, for example, grant the existence of "time" as a physical variable, each of two persons talking about time needs to know whether the concept of time emphasizes punctuality, social rules for dinner party guests being a half hour late, or space–time overlap in post-Newtonian physics. When you decide which formal logical system about time you are using, the conversation can proceed. The postformal thinker seems to cross over between cognition and emotion, learning with an empathy for the learned material and for others' positions on the learned material (Powell, 1984).

New social variables become important to learning when we realize the social component that exists in postformal thought. For example, in couples' problem solving, the adjustment of the dyad members to each other seems to relate to whether postformal thought or simpler thinking is displayed over a series of problems (D. Rogers et al., 1991).

Again, see Table 13.1.

5. *Any learned element can be used in postformal or non-postformal ways.* Postformal and non-postformal thinkers simply use the facts like building blocks in service to different cognitive purposes. Besides using learned elements in service to several different logics simultaneously, postformal thinkers probably can manipulate more learned facts at one time than non-postformal thinkers because those learned items can be combined in more inclusive logical hierarchies by postformal thinkers. This ability to juggle a multitude of facts may be a way for postformal thinkers to adaptively avoid overstimulation and unnecessary reductionism when faced with too much information. Stereotyping and simplistic positions, the last resort of the overloaded non-postformal thinker, can be avoided by the postformal thinker. Of course, the probability that the *same* learned fact can be used in both postformal and non-postformal logic suggests that communication problems might occur if both thinkers are not postformal.

If one thinker is postformal, he or she might create a bridge to the other's logic.

This communication challenge can be the basis for further research and for intervention strategies (see Table 13.1).

6. *Postformal thinkers and non-postformal thinkers in the same situation learn different things.* Conflicts among members of a group—be that group a family, a government, or an organization—are not pleasant experiences. But they sometimes teach us things about ourselves and others, at the level at which we are able to absorb or receive them. While experiencing these conflicts, people differing in readiness learn very different things from the same conflict because they have differing subjective cognitive experiences (Sinnott, 1991a, 1993c).

I recently experienced part of a protracted conflict between two members of an intimate couple, one of whom showed postformal thought in the relational context and the other of whom did not. The former partner ended this round of the conflict having learned more deeply the paradox that they were creating an unhappy marital history by always relating around the topic of their problems. The latter partner, in contrast, ended the round having "learned" that the first *still* would not acknowledge being the cause of their troubles. Studies of intimate-couple interaction are one application of principle implied in Table 13.1.

In this portion of the chapter, I have shared some thoughts on the relation between postformal thought and learning. I outline ways that certain learning is prerequisite to postformal thought and that having postformal thought changes learning. Next, let us take a look at the relationship between postformal thinking and how teachers, our official promoters of learning, teach.

HOW TEACHERS TEACH: TEACHING AS A DIALOGUE WITH REALITY

Teaching involves the induction of change. Our present historical time involves rapid, large-scale change. The Theory of Postformal Thought is precisely about the understanding of—the knowing of—a changing, dynamic reality that is cocreated by those who know it as they construct a chosen logic for it and frame the world in terms of its emergent structures. Teachers who embrace this dialogic quality of reality empower their students to live fully and adaptively and to more easily survive the changes in their own educational institutions.

From a postformal viewpoint, incompatible realities are not to be narrowed to one correct truth; each may have its own correct logic. Learning the truths of others can give us greater flexibility and teach us to use more tools in working with our construction of reality. The postformal teacher is a translator of realities and a guide to the construction of realities. These realities are not only cognitive or mental ones; they are at the same time emotional, spiritual, social, and interpersonal realities. The postformal teacher must teach appropriate choice (to the extent suitable for a given age group) and balance in life, along with the content of a given subject.

The line between the postformal teacher and a learner becomes a vague one. Because several truths are simultaneously valid, dialogue is more appropriate than lecture. After all, the postformal teacher knows that truth is partly a choice of vantage points around which we build our reality. This knowledge helps such a teacher help students take responsibility for their intellectual lives. Such awareness lets the teacher see a changing society as one shifting from one vantage point to another. This is a shift the teacher may join, go beyond, incorporate into a larger shift, and point out to learners. Meanwhile, such a teacher works with learners to be flexible and to see future shifts in truth as normal, necessary parts of life. Such learning is adaptive, not sabotaged by a rigid world view. The postformal teacher also facilitates creative chaos to allow the disorder that leaves room for a reordering of potential to occur.

The postformal teacher sees learners in relationship to others. They are both individuals and part of the larger whole. The part or individual will provide the means for life to go forward while the whole or community provides the larger meaning for the move. The postformal teacher therefore facilitates learning teams, learning communities, and learning organizations.

Table 13.2 lists some core principles of the new physics and general systems theory bases of postformal thought. The reader may recall that these principles underlie the postformal operations seen earlier in Table 3.5. Some of the principles especially call to mind selected postformal operations of thought, although all the principles *as a whole* underlie the whole of postformal theory. Table 13.2 also shows how each principle specifically leads postformal teachers to encourage more complex thought.

Principle 1 in Table 13.2 is that *change can occur only if there is potential.* In teacher behavior, this translates into opening up the meaning and possibility of things by, for example, asking questions that have no answers. Something as simple as asking "What is the

Table 13.2.   New Sciences as a Framework for Teaching

New science principle	Teaching impact
1. Change can occur only if the system includes *disorder, potential, unstructuredness*.	1. Teachers create disorder; challenge thought and rules; open questions that have no clear answers; reward students' adoption of alternative ways to think, be, and see the world around them; challenge interpretations.
2. Systems construct their own realities.	2. Students can construct class rules, goals, value systems.
3. An "entity" is not necessarily the result of a boundary; it is also a "consistent set of relations with others."	3. Teachers honor class members' identities as they try new consistent styles of relating to people, things, self, or knowledge.
4. Systems are synergistic.	4. Students explore knowledge cooperatively.
5. Systems that survive have "porous" boundaries.	5. Teachers offer positive and negative critiques of ideas.
6. Systems go through predictable life stages.	6. Students can be taught to honor their own stages of growth in thought, and those of younger and older students.
7. Rigid systems are dying.	7. "True believers" in any ideas are best banished from classroom positions of authority.
8. To change, systems need to interact with other systems.	8. Students can learn to use disagreements to grow.
9. Systems strive for continuity.	9. Co-opting an idea, theory, or practice is easier (and potentially more useful) than fighting it. Teach "giving alternative views a try."
10. Systems change on the basis of context.	10. Teachers need to consider their own contexts and their students', as to effects of those contexts on their growth.

Source: Sinnott (1994c). By permission of Greenwood Publishing Group, Inc., Westport, CT.

right way to study for a test?" can lead to a discussion during which it will be revealed that there are many right ways, many realities (the postformal operation of more than one a priori). Some of Paula Underwood's (1991) questions of this type are based on a Native American "rule of six," which demands that one find six equally plausible ways of explaining a given phenomenon. As the title of her 1991 stories *Who Speaks for Wolf?* suggests, a useful traditional Native American way to ask questions from these many different standpoints is to ask individuals to speak from the point of view of others in the greater community of living things, others who will feel the impact of whatever answer emerges. Underwood specifically applies these ideas to teacher training. In Underwood's tradition, however, one must ultimately choose some action (the postformal operation of pragmatism); this is not a relativistic infinite loop.

Core principle 2 is that *systems construct their reality with the outside world.* In teacher behavior, this might mean that students are given part of the power of constructing their own grade system (postformal operation of parameter setting). It might mean that students are asked to write a term paper in which the same situation is seen through the lenses of several different philosophical systems (Rabin, private communication, 1995).

Principle 3 in the table is that *one need not be defined by boundaries but may be defined by a set of relations to others.* The teacher might borrow again from Native American thought and construct a medicine wheel in which various community roles are represented by spokes in the wheel. For example, in a workshop attended by the author, participants took the roles of "those who create structure" and "those who destroy structure," "those who perfect a step in a dance" and "those who relate the steps to each other" (the postformal operation of process–product shift). Participants quickly learned how indispensable other viewpoints were and became adept at creating the degree of openness or structure that they could tolerate.

Principle 4 is that *systems are synergistic.* Teachers operating in a postformal mode can allow many diverse human systems to nourish each other in the learning situation. Writing projects in which each person writes alone about a common topic, then shares that piece with others, eventually lead to a leap forward in the quality of all papers and an awareness that all papers still remain unique. Principle 4 relates to principle 5, which states that *systems that survive have "porous" boundaries and can admit new information* (leading to a larger or smaller problem space [the operation of parameter setting]). The teacher's behavior is the best model for this.

Teachers can demonstrate principle 6, that *systems go through predictable life stages,* by pointing out developmental stages in the life of a class or group. For example, the reassurance that others initially feel anxiety about some subject and confusion over cooperative exercises, but later feel at ease, lets students feel safe enough to experiment with their thinking. The teacher can also talk about personal experiences, demonstrating that if he or she made it through anxiety like theirs, the students can stand the uncertainty of complex thinking too. A side benefit is that power is then more equal between teacher and learner, and so is responsibility.

Principle 7 is that *rigid systems are dying.* Ironically, one of the most striking ways for teachers to teach this principle is by being rigid themselves. The opposite stance leads to principle 8, that *teachers promote change by calling forth greater potential from others,* though it must be noted that *systems strive for continuity* (principle 9). The postformal teacher must support change and continuity by linking systems together.

Finally, principle 10 states that the teacher can show that *system change is sensitive to system context.* One of the most interesting ways to demonstrate this sensitivity is to give several groups the same problem to solve, but give them few guidelines. Groups quickly become aware that it is their particular mix of individual histories and skills that makes their product different from the other groups' products. As Stevens-Long and Trujillo (1995) have noted, membership in a small group sometimes spurs individual members toward postformal thinking.

Why Is It So Difficult to Change a Structured Learning Setting?

The principles outlined in this chapter predict some roadblocks to change in a traditional learning setting. A system must have unstructured space available if it is to change, but most traditional learning settings are nested in a strong bureaucracy and are run in a style that is more authoritarian than dialogic. Time is to be filled by directed activity, not left open to possibility. There is often a right and a wrong way to do things. Classrooms that do not seem rigidly ordered are considered to be poorly run. All these traditional attitudes and expectations militate against the nurturing of potential that is necessary for change to occur in a setting that enhances postformal thought.

Identity is a product of relations. Many teachers have only one type of relations with their students. In a single-relationship environment, opportunities for change are stillborn. Classroom environments are limited to just a few, which means that the change permitted by porous boundaries is foreclosed. Even the great diversity students might find if they were permitted to examine their own processes, reactions, group dynamics, and responses is usually off limits. The life stages of ongoing classroom groups are ignored.

Many structured classroom contexts forbid cooperative projects in which knowledge is really shared. This stricture means that there is no system–system interaction (as in principle 8), and significant change is less likely to occur. Since systems strive for continuity (principle 9), one way to derail change is to suggest that it will totally destroy an old order, along with whatever benefits the old order confers.

The key to creating learning situations that are open to change—both change inside classrooms and change in the larger culture—may be to arrange for them to be led by teachers who are open to change through dialogue. Persons who have experience as "change agents"—for example, returned Peace Corps volunteers—might contribute additional fresh postformal qualities to teaching.

Postformal Teachers' Problem Solving in the Classroom

Lee (1987, 1991, 1994a,b) has described the ways in which postformal teachers make decisions that can support a diversity of meanings by being willing to see the problems of teaching as ill-structured, "wicked" problems (Churchman, 1971). The postformal teacher is aware that knowledge cannot be objective and that a dialectic must take place. Situations with inherent contradiction, that is, dilemmas, must be separated from contradiction-free situations in which a choice can be made using formal operations. Postformal operations can be a framework for describing teachers' problem posing and problem solving.

HOW MASTER TEACHERS REASON: TEACHING AS LEARNING TO SURF REALITIES

The master teacher, that is, the excellent, experienced teacher who is judged by peers and supervisors to be a master problem solver in the context of education, is likely to be a postformal thinker, if my earlier reasoning is correct. He or she is also likely to be using postformal thought to teach others how to teach. Lee (1991) examined the thinking operations of master teachers and illustrated the usefulness of describing their thinking using the concepts and operations of postformal thought.

Lee's in-depth analysis in that study was based on one master teacher's problem identification and problem solving. The teacher was observed during classroom activity and interviewed afterward.

Audiotapes were used to record interviews and classroom dialogues. Determination of whether this teacher used postformal operations was made on the basis of analysis of this material. The teacher's practice itself, not standard tasks brought in from the laboratory, formed the basis of the analysis. The master teacher who participated in the 1991 study was a full professor in education policy, planning, and administration at a large university and had taught at the elementary and university levels for many years. The observations were made as she taught a course on curriculum theory at the graduate level. Those of her deliberations that met the criteria for postformal operations were noted. Two questions formed the basis of the study: Does the thinking of this teacher while teaching and reflecting on teaching demonstrate postformal problem solving? Is the Theory of Postformal Thought useful for analyzing master teachers' cognitive functioning in the area of their expertise?

The results of Lee's analysis supported the idea that master teachers make use of postformal skills in teaching and thinking about teaching. Excerpts from the teacher's commentary on the directions that curriculum should take in the future included all the postformal operations except for the operation of paradox. As Lee noted, in real-world classrooms, teachers must work with incompatible interpretations and with situations that demand action even when absolute solutions are not available. Postformal thought is useful in such situations. The individual intensive analysis of this teacher's thought and of the thinking of other master teachers interviewed by Lee (1987) shows that postformal operations are present in these master professionals. It also shows that the ability to use postformal operations helps them to work in this masterful way, whether they are teaching in a typical classroom or teaching newer teachers how to teach in a university setting.

When master teachers teach or define aspects of their teaching for less experienced teachers, they describe the shifting of realities and the balancing act that is analogous to keeping one's balance while standing on a surfboard atop a wave, with a strong wind blowing, surrounded by erratic fellow surfers and hell-bound for a beach with submerged rocks. Like Lee's master teachers, the master "hands-on" science elementary teachers I interviewed balanced their classroom activities and solved the everyday problem of "what to teach" in a postformal way. New teachers in training, however, in research under way, seldom appeared to express postformal thought during interviews that tested problem posing and problem solving (although they were not yet in a context in which they could address the question of "what to teach" that was answered by the expert teachers mentioned earlier). We therefore have some reason to believe that the master teacher gradually develops postformal thinking in the context of the teaching career. We also have reason to speculate that master teachers, while teaching future teachers, convey or stimulate the ability to think postformally as they teach and mentor the next generation of teachers. Perhaps this ability could be taught in a more deliberate and structured way, as suggested in later chapters on interventions.

POSTFORMAL THOUGHT AND THE STRUCTURE OF LEARNING INSTITUTIONS

Learning institutions are defined as culturally created organizations that are established specifically to promote the acquisition of greater knowledge among clients or users of that institution. The learning goals of various learning institutions may be narrow or broad; the goals of an art center or a preschool are likely to be more narrow than those of a university.

Consider a *first type of scenario:* The learning goals of an institution are narrow and do not include the development of complex thought per se. Under these circumstances, the only institutional support for postformal thinking that is required (beyond that which allows its own administrators to be better at keeping the institution alive at all!) is the support for the functioning of its master teachers. They will then serve the institutional goals by being better at their profession.

Consider, however, a *second type of scenario:* The learning goals of the institution may be broad enough to include the development of complex thought in its students. Then the institutional support required for postformal thinking is much more complex. The structure and the function and the demands of the institution itself can militate for or against development of postformal thought in its learners.

Further, consider a *third scenario:* The learning institution's clients may be *adult* learners, an age group in which many individuals most likely have already attained the ability to think postformally. Under these circumstances, a learning institution structure that fails to support postformal thinking is failing to support its own goals. It is trying to speak to adults about complex things in the limited cognitive language of children.

Considering the *first scenario,* it is my observation that most cultural institutions and organizations do not support the postformal complex thought of their staffs (see Chapter 15). Learning institutions usually do not support the postformal thought of their teachers—and perhaps even punish it. Considering that, in terms of general systems theory (Chapter 6), systems attempt to maintain continuity and minimize change, institutions do well to avoid the kind of employees who shift realities and have the power to *choose* which realities to cocreate together. The very concept of "cocreation" suggests that employees would take more power than most institutions want to relinquish! But the learning institution is less effective than it could be if it hampers the postformal thought of its potentially master-level teachers, who in turn are less effective in their teaching work for the university.

A learning institution might support the postformal thinking of its teachers in the teaching setting. Looking again at the "Teaching impact" column in Table 13.2, substitute the word *institutions* for the word *teachers* wherever it occurs; then substitute the word *teachers* for the word *students* wherever it occurs. For example, the first entry would then read:

> 1. *Institutions* create disorder; challenge thought and rules; open questions that have no clear answers; reward *teachers'* adoption of alternative ways to think, be, and see the world around them; challenge interpretations.

The learning institution has been "teaching" its staff, the teachers, without either party acknowledging what is going on. Changing the entries in Table 13.2 to reflect the fact that a university's administration teaches its employees just as a teacher teaches her or his students makes the dynamic more explicit. Recognition of this fact in real life would open the possibility for changes in support of postformal thinking in the context of any learning institution.

In regard to the *second scenario,* in which the institution intentionally supports postformal thought in its students, or the *third scenario,* in which students using the institution are all potentially postformal adult students, the functions and the structure of the institution *should* serve to stimulate complex postformal thought. The reality is that most institutions that declare that they specialize in teaching complex thinking—for example, the university—or that they specialize in adult learning—for example, on-the-job training in a workplace—ignore or avoid the teaching or learning of complex thought. The reader is invited to look at the chapters in the *Interdisciplinary Handbook of Adult Lifespan Learning* (Sinnott, 1994b) to see the range of adult learning institutions and how little they generally promote complex thought. Also, Chapter 14 in this volume deals specifically with reinventing the university.

Table 13.3 describes ten current problems for adult life-span learning organization structures and potential solutions that might lead those institutions to promote development of complex thought. In the future, we as a culture may want to maximize the potential of mature learners. To do so, we have to see them as general living systems growing cognitively to become postformal thinkers. The next section will discuss the problems and solutions in the table in more detail.

Table 13.3. Adult Higher Education: Ten Problems and Solutions

Problems	Solutions
1. Universities have not been structured to make use of the fact that adults come with their own motives, goals, developmental tasks, and experiences.	1. Capitalize on learners' individuality.
2. Competitive approaches to learning run counter to much of adult life experience.	2. Replace competition with cooperative team learning approaches.
3. Universities often separate personal and creative aspects of learning from logical analytical ones; this practice hurts adult students.	3. Overlap the creative–synthetic and the logical–analytical.
4. Current generations of adult learners are more visual and could make use of more video or other visual media.	4. Study visual learning processes. Use the strengths of both learning modalities when teaching adults.
5. Adult learning has mainly served economic goals.	5. Structure learning to serve both personal development and economic needs.
6. Learning for its own sake has been split from learning for practical purposes.	6. Notice the links between basic and applied, practical and esoteric learning, and foster both in each case.
7. Adults are taught as though they learn alone (like identity-creating adolescents), but they are more likely to be learning as social learners (like members of families and cultures).	7. Use dialogues among teacher and learners to reap the benefits of postformal thinking and multiple perspectives.
8. "Learning" too often means "memory" in the rote sense.	8. Think of adult learning as more complex than rote memory.
9. University authorities tell adult learners what to learn.	9. Let learners help generate the learning agenda.
10. Current structures of universities do not serve adult needs.	10. Restructure the university to meet current needs.

Source: Sinnott and Johnson (1996). By permission of Ablex Publishing Corporation.

STIMULATING POSTFORMAL THOUGHT
IN ADULT LEARNERS

The adult human learner is more than a mind. Numerous authors addressing the nature and contexts of adult life-span learning (Sinnott, 1994b) have noted that an adult learner is an emotional, biological, social, intentional creature, adaptively moving through time while structuring a bigger picture of reality that gives life meaning. As we have seen in an earlier chapter, this adult needs postformal thought to make sense of a complex situation and his or her place within it. Keeping in mind the desirability of adults' developing postformal thought, we will now discuss some problems (Table 13.3) with current adult learning institutions as well as some potential solutions that would enhance development of postformal thought.

1. *Adult learning institutions have not been structured to make use of the fact that adult learners come with their own motives, goals, developmental tasks, and experiences.* We have discarded the best "pluses" of adult learners, leaving only their deficits to consider. We have used the learning behavior of the younger person as the gold standard and have ignored postformal thinking. This single-vantage-point reality deprives us of an understanding of what is possible in human learning processes, which are part of the clues to human possibility. Learners' motives and intentions are often the strongest forces moving their performance; consciousness matters (Sperry, 1987).

2. *Competitive individualistic approaches run directly counter to the developmental goals of adults to be intimate and generative (Erikson, 1950) and to think postformally.* Adults often choose learning projects involving expertise, complex interpersonal coordination, and creation of lasting institutions and relationships—but we do not create learning institutions that foster these traits. Teaching methods, even at the university level, cater to the child mind, loading basic information given by an authority. Adult learners, however, even if they enter the learning situation with childlike knowledge of a field, do not come with a child's mind or a child's social skills and personal incentives.

3. *Learning institutions have separated the personal–creative aspect from the hierarchical–orderly aspect of learning; this split is especially damaging to mature learners, who are using or developing postformal thought.* Learning implies imposition of order and structure on an environment. Our scientific experimental paradigm has fostered objectivity. This approach disregards the other legitimate forms of knowledge based on other paradigms or nonexperimental methods,

forms such as phenomenology, synthetic (versus analytical) thought, case studies, and clinical or group dynamics studies. Fact-laden presentations run counter to the tendency of mature learners to be motivated by solving problems (especially those they have personally encountered) by putting pieces of the puzzling event together. Given the choice of learning discrete, abstract facts and learning problem-related facts, the mature adult selects the problem-related learning. For example, the research scientist may voraciously learn thousands of facts related to her current research interest, yet remain oblivious to the name of the scientist in another field working two doors down the hall.

4. *Adult learners seem more oriented to visual presentation of material such as video and less oriented to forms such as books.* A shift is occurring in the dominant representational styles of mature learners. Forms for teaching them have not effectively bridged the styles and kept pace. We are wasting an opportunity to enhance postformal skills by failing to encourage the shift in reality representation across both visual and verbal skills.

5. *Mature adult learning has been conceptualized mainly in terms of economic survival.* Harman and Hormann (1990), in their discussion of the meaning of work, suggest that education that simply prepares good workers and sustains their productivity may be futile in a time when meaningful work is not possible over a lifetime for everyone. Learning, they suggest, might better be oriented toward developing each person's full human postformal thinking potential. A sense of fragmentation afflicts many midlife adults when their learning is focused on preparation for work-related tasks but has no connection with their other life tasks or their own potential as persons. Most adults are also aware that their work roles will change more than once during their lifetimes.

6. *Learning for its own sake has been split from learning for practical purposes.* Adult learning in our culture and in most others is considered serious only when the outcome pertains to a critical work-related problem at hand. Other learning for its own sake is supposed to be done only by children and retirees who have no other work-related purpose. This polarization deprives mature adult learners of the chance to solve those critical problems they are engaged in in fresh ways. (Notice that children, adolescents, and retirees with broad exploratory learning are not permitted to apply it to any real, job-related problems. This taboo forces them to remain "impractical" and disempowers them.) Overall, investment in learning to meet *whatever*

challenge arises is sacrificed for a short-term, crisis-driven investment in learning. This error is analogous to corporations attempting to max- imize short-term profits by avoiding costly long-term investment in research and development. Such corporations find it hard to sustain high performance in changing markets. Educational institutions that serve adults have a similar problem with sustaining high, flexible per- formance.

7. *Mature adults are taught as though they must learn alone, com- peting against others (as though they were adolescents first creating identities) when they really learn best in a cooperative context (as though they are connected to others and generative members of fam- ily and culture).* The mature learner seeks not only differentiation (i.e., analyses) of concepts, but also syntheses of concepts. The mature learner might often do her or his best cognitive work in a cooperative learning enterprise with the stated aim of furthering the good of the group along with furthering her or his own good (Eisler & Loye, 1990; Vygotsky, 1962, 1978). Thinking and everyday postformal problem solving have an interpersonal dimension (Meacham & Emont, 1989; Resnick, Levine, & Teasley, 1991).

8. *"Learning" in institutions is too often equivalent to "memory" (in the most rote sense), rather than to postformal learning.* The mature adult generally wants learning to go beyond an exchange of facts to a deeper structuring of matters. When one is learning to solve problems, the cognitive processes involved in memory for details and incidental memory may be different from processes involved in learn- ing paths through a problem-solving space (Sinnott, 1986a; West & Sinnott, 1992). For example, many additional processes are involved in map learning (or "memory for maps") compared with learning (or memory) of strings of numbers (Lipman, 1991).

9. *Adult learners too often are told by some authority what they need to learn.* Sheer imposition of the task makes no use of the slowly developed wisdom and intrinsic motivation of adults. The self-motivated adult will tend to seek out knowledgeable authorities, allowing for input from both learner and authority (Freire, 1971; Kindervatter, 1983). Projects partly formed by the learners themselves offer the best of both worlds if the authority can tolerate the anxiety of waiting to be asked for his or her expertise.

10. *Current structures of universities do not serve mature adult needs or development of postformal thought.* Chapter 14 will address this topic more fully. Readers might also enjoy *Reinventing the Uni- versity: A Radical Proposal for a Problem Focused University* (Sinnott & Johnson, 1996).

In this chapter, we have explored a number of relations or potential relations between postformal thought and educational institutions. In the chapters that follow, we will apply ideas about postformal thought to the teaching of adult learners, with a special emphasis on the university. How might the university be reinvented to serve adult learners, especially by honoring or teaching them postformal thought?

CHAPTER 14

Reinventing the University to Foster and Serve Postformal Thinkers

The whole structure of our society does not correspond with the world-view of emerging scientific thought.

FRITJOF CAPRA

In this chapter, we will explore the changes needed in the university as a learning institution in light of our understanding of complex postformal thinking processes. Recently, Lynn Johnson and I have written extensively about the ideas you will see outlined here (Sinnott & Johnson, 1996). If postformal thought is a valuable characteristic of mature adult cognition, the university would be the ideal place to foster it and to use its special logic. Since the university as an institution is currently under attack from many constituencies (e.g., Anderson, 1992), and since it already is undergoing considerable reform, why not consider a broadly restructured model of the university at this point in history? This chapter's discussion includes a rationale for a new model of the university, a discussion of the several possible purposes of adult learning in a historical context (some in special advanced institutions such as the university), and a summary of a model of university structure that would serve the university and its mature adult learners in more useful and cognitively appropriate postformal ways.

217

WHY DO WE NEED A NEW MODEL
FOR THE UNIVERSITY?

As we discussed in Chapter 6, every institution in a living culture undergoes testing and adjustment as conditions around and within it change. Every living institution, like every species, has a range of flexibility of operations within which it might change and continue to survive. Whether we look at the form of the institution or at its function, we see it maintaining either form or function by accommodating to its new conditions and by assimilating the new events to its basic goal or form.

Universities reflect the consciousness of their times. As historical epochs change, the university is reformed to fit the patterns of the emerging culture. We are moving from a postmodern age to an age of chaos–complexity consciousness (Francis, 1992). At the same time, we are feeling that our universities have lost touch with their (particularly American) populist ideals, for which they are substituting elitist tendencies. The university, defined here as any institution of higher education, has always been the target of reformers (for examples, see Grant & Riesman, 1978). We seem to have had difficulty deciding whether the purpose of the university is the cognitive development (or the general development) of adults, moral education, preparation for professions, conveyance of broad cultural knowledge, or some other purpose. All these ends have been pursued by the university as an institution. Kerr (1964) chronicles the university's gradual change from a community of masters and students, to a cultivator of mind, to a cultivator of science and practical skills, to the "multiversity" with its many intellectual communities and needs. In the disastrous event that a living institution loses flexibility, it dies, so it is good that universities can be so flexible.

I will assume for the purposes of this argument that we can *all* agree on at least one sustained goal and purpose for the university over the years: *to enhance the growth of personal and public knowledge.*

Currently, there are several types of institutions of higher education that have had differing missions in regard to that general goal and that are criticized for differing shortcomings. The research university has carried the burden of generating knowledge and has been criticized for doing too little undergraduate teaching, public service, and career training (except for professional training). The comprehensive university has had the mission of teaching a wide spectrum of students, especially undergraduates, and preparing them for a broad spectrum of careers; it has been criticized for failing to perform enough research. The liberal arts college has been given the task of being a nurturing place for contemplation of great traditions and critical thinking, but it is criticized most for sheltering thinkers who do too little practical work in their ivory towers. Vocational training schools, sometimes considered part of higher education, are most criticized for focusing too much energy on vocational training. Community colleges, devoted to teaching entry-level college courses, are most criticized for being unfocused extensions of high school. All the levels of higher education are criticized for failing to teach their students to think well, and for "dumbing down" the curriculum rather than nurturing complex thought, critical thinking, wise thinking, or even analytical and synthetic thinking, not to mention sophisticated personal development. Current problems with adult learning institutions in general, including universities, were listed in Table 13.3 and discussed in Chapter 13.

Future Role of Universities in Adult Learning

Recent national and international events have demonstrated the rapid pace of change in the modern world. Learners must adapt to change, and so must universities. It is hard to adapt to what we cannot predict; it is even harder to adapt to change as a constant. Into this shifting reality comes the student of adult life-span development and learning, knowing that adults must learn in order to develop and adapt, personally. Sometimes complex learning occurs in formal settings, but advanced learning is frequently found in nonformal settings, too, as I described in some detail in my *Interdisciplinary Handbook of Adult Lifespan Learning* (Sinnott, 1994b). For example, advanced learning occurs in college continuing education programs (Harriger, 1994) as well as in the workplace (Demick & Miller, 1993; Froman, 1994), in general life experience (Merriam, 1994), in collaborative activities (Lee, 1994b), and even in psychotherapeutic settings (Hogue et al., 1994). What do we need to do to maximize adult learning for an unknown future? The learners and their cognitive styles are changing. The expectation that learning can or will stop after youth already has changed. For example, many politicians have been talking about the need for lifetime learning, integrating it with plans to promote a partnership of academia with government, industry, and labor (Clinton & Gore, 1993).

In the formal educational setting of the university, mature and older adult learners now are now enrolling in ever-greater numbers, along with more traditional students. Universities around the country are reporting rapidly increasing numbers (up to 47%) of students in their late twenties and far beyond. As Harriger (1994) reports, it is predicted that by the turn of the century, more than 50% of college students will be of nontraditional age, with a significant proportion over 35. Now that demographic and economic changes have given us a rapidly changing technological workplace, a new global economy, and a population that is largely middle-aged, the university has been asked to respond with changes designed to serve them. University programs are now expected to serve career change, postretirement stimulation, on-the-job retraining, and policy-related learning, in short intense bursts.

More and more thinkers are considering what skills may be useful for today's university students. Many of these new skills seem related to the skills of postformal thought, as we discussed earlier, although the language of the thinker may not initially be the language of cognitive or educational psychology. For example, Elias (1987) names five characteristics for education to develop in students: capacity for intimate communication, capacity to see patterns in relationships, commitment to ongoing social transformation; awareness of contexts for events, and capacity to use technology to serve alternative social visions. While this sounds like a broad menu of tasks, it is no broader than the spectrum of tasks that adults have historically been asked to learn, as we will see in the next section. And these are tasks that appear to be applications of postformal thinking to several applied domains (see Chapters 15 through 20). It is possible for the university to meet these changed demands by approaching its task as one of enhancing postformal thinking in its students.

ADULT LEARNING: PAST AND PRESENT

Without being an anthropologist or historian, but informed by 20 years of reading interdisciplinary and cross-cultural and historical works, as well as by personal experience, I have come to see some historical trends in adult learning. Several general purposes for teaching new bodies of information to mature adults have been described repeatedly. They suggest the scope of possible adult learning in the reinvented university and some factors that make it successful. In recent United States history, universities as we know them have served the youngest adults almost exclusively, and have performed only the third and fifth functions outlined below.

One primary type of adult learning involves integrating new ways to perform a necessary task or role that one is already performing. For example, a generation of workers learned to do jobs using computers. Workers learned to reorganize their workplaces. Prior to World War II, women were taught to stay at home and do "women's jobs"; during that war, they were taught to help the war effort by doing manufacturing jobs; after that war, they were taught to work at home again and have many babies. These types of learning involve the operations of postformal thought such as multiple goals, appreciation of paradox, and shifts in a prioris.

A second type of mature adult learning involves acquiring full membership in a tribe or group by learning the full complex wisdom of that group. Adults may learn the stories or rituals that are keys to the culture, allowing them to become keepers of the culture. Newly elected members of Congress may rise to prominent positions as they "learn the ropes" and who the key players are. Practitioners in a field (e.g., social work) learn to be experts, perhaps gaining a credential for their expertise (e.g., LCSW or a state license). In each case, the beginning level of skill is replaced by a more synthesized overarching level of expertise. The new level uses a postformal logic that allows the new expert to make a commitment to a single logical way of operating in that field, while that expert knows that any problem in that field could be seen within several competing logics.

A third type of adult learning involves obtaining a ticket or gaining entrée into a larger role. In the days of the Chinese empire, candidates for government positions learned to pass the writing examination (which included poetry and prose) as a ticket into desirable government jobs. Academics obtain PhDs to allow them to perform research that will be taken seriously, to teach at universities, and to get grants. The degrees are certificates of competence and permission even though the learning experiences (i.e., the course work) to obtain them may be virtually irrelevant to the actual job. Merely grasping the truth of that last sentence may require exercise of postformal thinking to appreciate the paradox inherent in thinking about advanced degrees in this way.

The fourth type of learning involves updating or retooling a skill that is still very useful. For example, professionals are urged to obtain continuing education credits to demonstrate that they are up-to-date in their disciplines. The purpose of these learning activities is a post-formal one: to see old things in new ways while also seeing, it is to be hoped, the value in the old way.

A fifth function of mature adult learning seems to be one of control: It teaches conformity and discipline. The learning may serve to strengthen bonds within the group or tribe and at the same time to weaken bonds with other groups. It may effectively limit access to certain rewards and privileges. For example, "re-education" of dissidents by Red Guards in China or the mandatory haranguing and brainwashing of American hostages in Lebanon led to the learning of conformity. Only those licensed as plumbers or admitted to tenure at universities can enjoy the rewards of those positions, which are obtained by conforming to the demands of the particular profession. This is education as social control.

Finally, mature adult learning may be used to serve personal development and increase understanding of the "big picture." The staff of the modern university evolved from the nobility, who pursued knowledge for its own sake and their own growth, with the freedom from economic concerns that we associate with jobs in academia. Noncredit college classes are popular for personal development reasons. These learning experiences are personal expressions of an individual's "growing edge." To broaden one's identity in this way may mean being postformal in regard to personal identity, or it may mean developing postformal thought itself, as do workshops or training programs in mysticism and transpersonal awareness.

We can conclude that the spectrum of possible adult learning experiences seems quite broad. Skills, philosophies, interpersonal behaviors, and worldviews are seen as learnable by mature adults. At least some mature adults are expected to learn the kinds of data-intense things that young persons learn, as well as the kinds of things that younger persons are *never* expected to learn, such as expertise in management skills, mystical skills, and sophisticated interpersonal and organizational relations. So far, however, there seems to be too little systematic consideration of any specific operations of thought that may be required for complex mature adult learning and the development of postformal thought to be most successful. We know only that we want that "cognitive complexity" to be an end product!

We might think about the pros and cons of expanding our societal repertoire of formalized adult learning possibilities, the cognitive operations needed for them, and the interventions by which we can get them to happen. The rapid changes going on in our world suggest that the more we as a society or as a species encourage learning by mature members, the greater will be our flexibility in the face of rapid change. An analogy for our species' current need to change and learn rapidly could be that current scourge, the human immunodeficiency virus (HIV), which causes acquired immunodeficiency syndrome (AIDS). Mutating at tremendous speed, learning new protein patterns,

HIV overruns and outflanks the body's attack mechanisms, and medicine's as well. The virus is a learner par excellence, shifting to other proteins' realities of pattern, winning the biological war by seeking to try every usable biological variation, in effect co-opting the opposition. We need to learn such flexibility in global and practical ways, many of which seem to demand postformal thought. The university needs to change in order to help us do so.

A NEW UNIVERSITY MODEL DESIGNED TO STIMULATE POSTFORMAL THOUGHT

What can the university do to transform itself? A complete description of detailed changes in structure, administration, community outreach, roles of professors, and other components of a university can be found in *Reinventing the University* (Sinnott and Johnson, 1996). A much shorter description can be offered in this section of the chapter. Some general changes are outlined in Table 14.1. Further descriptions of specific interventions with classes, usable in today's university setting, will be discussed in Chapter 21. Earlier, Chapter 13 discussed many ways in which educational practices could be modified in response to postformal operational thinking by teachers to promote postformal operational thinking by students.

Examine Table 14.1, which lists some general changes in the way universities see themselves that can help promote postformal thought. We see that, first, the university can acknowledge its complex role as the institution that does try to see the "big picture." This acknowledgment means it can reclaim the role of philosopher, "lover of wisdom," even when short-term profits and glory are at stake. In short, the uni-

Table 14.1. The Transformed University in the Next Century

1. Focuses on the "big picture," teaching synthesis and complex thought along with analysis.
2. Includes physical, intellectual, emotional, biological, interpersonal, cross-cultural, spiritual, developmental, political, and economic aspects of topics and learners.
3. Becomes an expert interpreter of complex truths and multiple realities.
4. Develops human resources in ways that had been relegated to family or community; nurtures the whole human spirit.
5. Creates problem-focused multicampus versions of itself, each devoted to solution of one significant human problem.

Source: Sinnott and Johnson (1996). By permission of Ablex Publishing Corporation.

versity can be true to itself, that self that makes it different from other institutions. It can be the seer that looks dispassionately at all sides, using postformal logic and promoting it in students. This demands a return to self-discipline and a higher ethic than pragmatism.

Second, the university can accept its mission as one serving what Ornstein (1991) speaks of as the many minds within the one mind. This demands postformal thinking. As it does so, it will acknowledge and serve the mature human, who is always changing and often reintegrating sides of self, who is emotional and spiritual and physical and social–interpersonal, as well as intellectual. It will serve the learner as a world citizen as well as the learner as a next-door neighbor.

Third, the university can become what H. Smith (1991) called an expert in "symbology." In the big picture reality, where truth can be seen from many valid perspectives in a postformal way, the university will take the role of displaying for the learners and for the culture what things can *possibly* mean. It will also look at the impact of meaning selections.

Fourth, the university can accept as its main role the development of human potential (Hutchins, 1968) by means of many activities, including the range of activities from development of technology to development of postformal thought. Thus, the university will not perpetuate the mind–body split, the mind–emotion split, the mind–society split, or the technology–person split. Perhaps in light of MacLean's (1990) triune brain theory, it will see these splits as reflecting a brain structure that evolution is leaving behind. The university will weave its fabric of learning in a long-term framework, rather than responding to the demands and needs of the moment. It will be aware that funding sources are fickle and that it is counterproductive to "prepare people for jobs" when no one is able to make even a good guess about where the world or the economy is headed.

Fifth, the university can restructure physically to help promote the more abstract changes. It would be reinvented as a problem-focused institution comprising many smaller universities physically dispersed over various sites (Sinnott & Johnson, 1996). Each of these umbrella institutions would be devoted to the solution of one major human problem, for example, "health" or "housing." The problem would be judged as a major one by the nation or the global community. This *problem focus* means that all study and research is cross-disciplinary, and every problem is considered in systems theory terms. Problems would therefore be considered from their constantly transforming intellectual, emotional, biological, interpersonal, cross-cultural, physical, spiritual, developmental, political, and economic perspectives. This task promotes the development of postformal thought. Course work at each of these universities would be oriented around the organizing human problem, but core courses on topics such as "means of communication" or "structure of organization" would be standard for all beginning students. Research, in its applied sense, would be focused on the university's chosen problem, although basic research by its very nature is more free-ranging. The campus of the university would be national or global (not a difficult feat, given modern communications technology), since instances of these problems exist worldwide. Research parks connected to each university might or might not be physically located near any single site, but would be affiliated because of their relation to the university's core problem focus. These research parks might contain institutions of many types, including industries making use of the expertise of a given campus. As an alternative, the research parks might market newly created ideas or services related to the problem focus of their university. They might also be demonstration sites for service delivery related to the problem.

This remodeling of the university does not mean that courses or activities without immediate practical benefit would be eliminated. On the contrary, the university problem focus would simply provide a ready theme for the work. For example, if the problem focus is housing, the university would support any activity, including teaching, basic research, philosophical discourse, artwork creation, and others, as it applies to the housing problem, as well as support services (e.g., introductory courses, administrative activities, student housing) connected to each of those activities. For example, works of art would be developed by specialists in fine arts for display in the demonstration geriatric housing complex located at each of the worldwide sites of this university, where they would be directly available to users of that housing and be integrated into on-site programs such as art therapy programs.

A university restructured along these lines would be flexible in a changing world, yet would retain the core of the university vision. Most important, it would enable, challenge, and make use of the cognitive development that is appropriate for mature learners, namely, postformal thought.

In the next chapter, we will examine another institution, the workplace, and interpersonal relationships within it. Our goal will be to look at the use of complex postformal thought in that context. We will see how use of postformal thought leads to creative conflict resolution and ultimately to adult development in the work context.

CHAPTER 15

Postformal Thought and Multiperson Groups

The Workplace

To find perfect composure in the midst of change is to find ourselves in nirvana.

SUZUKI ROSHI

Adult life involves participation in groups of individuals. In a group, thinking and complex problem solving occur as the products of several minds, not one alone. The several minds may belong to a group called the family, or to the two persons in an intimate couple, or to a work group. In every case, being part of a thinking group larger than the self creates cognitive and procedural dangers and challenges for the group as well as for the individual. The process of change may be predictable, but specific outcomes are not.

This chapter offers a panoramic view of the ways in which the theory of Postformal Thought enriches understanding of human behavior related to work. The basic argument of the first section of the chapter is that intragroup conflicts and complex postformal thought interweave with each other to bring about (if all goes well) both adult development and group development. Even if the conflicts are not of our making, we can consciously use them to further our own growth and, indirectly, the growth of others and of the organization itself. The second section considers the structure of the workplace, the reengineering of the workplace, and the organizational change that is so common today, and how these interact with postformal thought as an individual cognition or a shared cognition. The third section examines the thinking of expert administrators to see how they use postformal thinking on the job.

THE CHALLENGES OF
INTRAGROUP CONFLICT

The workplace is one of the contexts in which we must deal with one another's realities and learn to live with the frustrating differences among us in the way we see the truth of our situation. Postformal thinking seems to help with that task, but the task itself is a challenge. Despite Riegel's (1975) compelling argument that conflict is a necessary stimulus to growth, I know of very few persons who welcome it in real life. While therapists and conflict resolution experts make statements to the effect that partners who recognize and work with their conflicts as a couple usually feel closer to one another as the situation is resolved (e.g., Efron, Lukens, & Lukens, 1990; Paul & Paul, 1983), few of us want to have those great intimacy-enhancing experiences with the most important persons in our lives. If a teenager starts arguing and finding fault with everyone in the family (a prelude and rationalization for a necessary move toward independence), no one else in the family says, "OK, great, here comes one of those conflicts that are a path to personal and family development!" Not when the arguing and faultfinding are so frustrating and hurt so much. Even looking at groups that are less emotionally entangled than the family, there were no shouts of joy among Democratic party activists when the anti–Vietnam War movement challenged traditional party politics at the Chicago convention. Neither was there happiness among movement activists when we "won" but the movement was absorbed again into the larger political organizations. There was no special satisfaction at IBM when it was first challenged by the alternative worldview of Apple Computers and both identity and economic survival were at stake. It is terrifying to individuals and groups to realize that one's success at postformally bridging across multiperson multiple truths might come at the price of the reevaluation of one's own local cognitive reality. To be a "success" at bridging is to be like a seed that is destroyed as it produces the next plant and seed. Awareness of this painful truth creates the philosophical and mystical dilemmas that have troubled and challenged humans and their organizations throughout our history (e.g., J. Campbell, 1988; Frankl, 1963; Gandhi, 1951; Gould, 1978; Hugo, 1938; Maslow, 1968; Peters & Waterman, 1982).

When an intragroup conflict occurs in the workplace, there is a challenge to the status quo and a potential challenge to the realities about group truth that each person in the interaction holds. This process is like the one specified for the development of an individual's postformal thought in Chapter 4. It is consistent across numerous "living" systems, as was shown in Table 6.1. During this process, the several realities have a chance to dialogue, and if all goes well, a postformal sense of truth may emerge for the individual knowers or for the group.

Predictable Group Development and Conflict

What goes on when intragroup conflict occurs? We can suppose there is a challenge to the status quo, because of the normal developmental dynamics either at a single time or over time. We are especially interested in the cognitive dynamics here. To illustrate this process using a less threatening setting than the family or even the workplace, let us consider the evolution of any new society. Look back at Table 6.1 and Chapter 4. At first, a group or society more or less integrates all individuals or factions under its banner in a tribal way that suggests symbiosis and shared identity. For example, all the colonies were willing to some degree to be part of the new republic after the American Revolution ended; once upon a time, psychologists were all willing to be part of the new American Psychological Association (APA). As time passed, differentiation among the colonies and among psychologists continued to take place, and the differences began to show. The several colonies (states) evolved different philosophies and values; the psychologists formed specialty divisions, and clinicians and researchers fought with each other about the "proper" way for the organization to represent psychologists. Sometimes one faction or the other forced a vote that made them temporary winners, but soon the fighting would grow louder again. They no longer knew themselves to be part of one single tribe in the same cohesive way as was originally the case.

Both danger and opportunity can be found at this point in the process: The group may go on to organize itself cognitively and behaviorally at a higher level. It may disintegrate. A subgroup may break away. In other words, either all sides will find a complex way to give each other's truths mutual respect and accommodation, or they will mutually part company, or a splinter group will break away while the larger portion of the group remains together in the sense that its members know the same truth about their group identity. It seems that the American culture resolved its conflict (after a bloody Civil War) by creating that higher-level complex dynamic homeostasis (see Table 6.1); the APA has (so far) fragmented into two groups: the APA and the

American Psychological Society. The more rigid an organization is, the more likely it is to fragment like this in the face of intragroup conflict. But the IBM–Apple Computer detente shows how a rigid group can effectively lessen its rigidity by allying with a group that specializes in flexibility. In that example, we see the adaptive value of input from several realities if a postformal logic can deal with them.

A similar pattern of growth or nongrowth possibilities can be seen in both individual and group development over time when an individual who is very identified with a group (like that adolescent in our earlier example) begins to differentiate and challenge the group. The outcome here is similar, namely, one of the three mentioned above. But it takes cognitive complexity of the person or the organization to see the potential, achieve the change without losing identity, and go on to use the opportunity to develop.

When there is a difference or a mismatch in cognitive complexity, it may be a mismatch within a group, between groups, between a member and the rest of the group, or between a splinter faction from the original group and the original group itself. In any of these cases, a mismatch in realities or in the complexity of the realities can spur the growth of any participant in the conflict. For example, albeit oversimplifying a little, an organization can be seen as composed of "haves" (e.g., entrenched managers or workers) and "have nots" (e.g., new workers). The "haves" will be operating from a reality such that they will be seeking stability and equilibrium to maintain the gains they have and will structure their logical realities accordingly. They may find illogical and unacceptable the desire of the "have nots" to do riskier things (influenced by their "nothing to lose" reality).

In a situation like this in IBM a few years ago, the members who saw the work world as a "stable state reality" overpowered, but did not postformally incorporate or bridge to, the logic of the splinter group members who saw the work world with a different logic. But a shared organizational complex postformal logic was not created. As a consequence, the splinter group members left the IBM main group. Because it did not need to bridge logics postformally, the organization did not cognitively develop at that time in postformal ways. A few years later, however, the organization was failing to such a degree that it was forced to think of things differently. A new logical shared reality, developed since that time, now characterizes IBM, which finally bridged postformally to the different logic it had found illogical years before.

What happened to a particular company is not the most important thing for us to know, though. The most important principle to observe is that mismatch of developmental stages is a potential stimulus for both conflict and cognitive growth in the work group, organization, or person.

Positive and Negative Effects of Intragroup Conflict

There can be both positive and negative developmental results for the person or group from participating in intragroup conflicts of cognitive realities. This is a truism that can be observed daily. What is less often observed is *conscious* participation in intragroup conflicts with the intent to learn or grow from it.

Recall the line from Shakespeare's *Twelfth-Night:* "Some are born great, some become great, and some have greatness thrust upon them." One may take an analogous view of group members' differential propensity to tolerate clashes of logical realities. The first sort of person may have a seemingly mindless and unskilled predisposition to be in cognitive conflict or to create such conflict with others, whether due to biology, patterns of behavior, or other causes. Having in the group a member born to fight who starts fires by challenging the realities of others much of the time generally leads to destructive ends. The energy of others is spent restabilizing the shared reality of the group, an activity that seems prerequisite to the group's work being done.

Some, however, seem to have cognitive conflict thrust upon them, the second style. Group members trying to work with the aforementioned fire-starter may wonder why seemingly irrational arguments break out constantly. Forcing a conflict on unwilling group members usually leads to defensive moves rather than growth moves, and no one develops cognitively from closing down defensively.

There is the third possibility in the saying: those who *achieve* greatness. Its analogue, "those who achieve cognitive conflict," sounds undesirable at first until it is recast as "those who willingly experience inevitable intragroup cognitive conflict in order to learn." Neither employees of IBM nor the members of APA could wish away the cognitive conflicts that befell them, but they could observe their thoughts, truly listen to the other side, and perhaps modify their logics. The "achievement" in question here is the achievement of really experiencing the difficult moment with the intent to enlarge and make complex one's reality, if such action is warranted. One of my favorite metaphors for this state of willing awareness is that of the warrior of whom Don Juan speaks in Carlos Castaneda's books (e.g., Castaneda, 1971). The warrior goes through life with death right behind, death as a teacher, letting fear be replaced by a state of heightened awareness. The Eastern martial arts offer another metaphor: One welcomes the blow that makes contact because it can be a gift of awareness about one's vulnerabilities. In the crucible of the intragroup conflict of realities, one can refine and expand one's ideas and logics. Conscious welcoming of one's cognitive conflict experiences is therefore very different from just being in conflict. In the former, one is fearlessly looking for the opportunity to think postformally. Without the postformal thinking component, one member of the conflict is always labeled "wrong," one position dominates another, and a synthesis cannot occur. Without it, relations seem to calcify and become rituals, lacking diversity and flexibility. Without it, "change" means that someone loses.

The cocreated reality of postformal knowing lets us freely play with the options of creating a different kind of group interaction. We are given the power to rise above cognitive conflict by creating a synthesis that is more advanced and that gives us a bird's-eye view. The intragroup conflict might be changed to an intragroup opportunity. This is the polar opposite of one combatant in a workplace simply capitulating to another.

The methods in Table 15.1 are some that might help bring about postformal thought and, hence, higher-level resolution for a person or an organization experiencing a conflict. System characteristics that

Table 15.1. Methods for Transforming Intragroup Conflict Experiences into Personal Developmental Experiences

Purposely attempt to shift perspectives so that some other reality about the problem can be explored.

Consciously expect conflicts in the group, and make them constructive.

Consciously expect and accept intragroup conflict (at some level of intensity) as a routine experience.

Consciously see ourselves as "all in this together."

Posit that no one is to blame for this problem.

Assume that others act in the best way they know how (but that not all actions need be tolerated).

Address facts about a conflict, but don't assume that others see the same "facts."

Create a story around the conflict—and let the story show you the solution to the conflict.

Enlarge the problem space by redefining the problem or its parameters.

Shift the metatheory the group uses to form the problem.

Generate many "crazy" solutions to the conflict.

Shift from focusing on a concrete solution to focusing on finding a good *process* to cover many solutions like this.

Source: Sinnott (1993c). By permission of Lawrence Erlbaum Associates, Inc.

Table 15.2. Some Effects on Society, Organizations, and the Family of Nations of Members Consciously Using Conflict to Grow

Energy formerly used to hold polarized positions can be available to go toward the goal or observe the learning process.
Members will be less reactive, since they are not in a state of high (angry) tension.
Group solutions will be more numerous and more adaptive.
The group will get stronger.
Bullies can be contained without the situation escalating.
Social change will be possible with less pain and destruction.
There will be fewer group crises and more gradual changes.
Group focus will shift to "good process" rather than specific content solutions to a problem.
The politics of paradox will be used (e.g., we will learn to defeat our enemies by becoming a valuable resource to fill their needs).
We will create much more realistic solutions to cross-cultural problems.
Group identities will expand to be global ones.
Group depression, despair, and anguish will be replaced by group hope.
Members will cooperate better.
Chaotic transitions will be revealed as inherently orderly.
Members will feel less split between their emotions and their cognition and will feel more valued.
"Winning" by domination will be replaced by "winning" by mutual empowerment.
Opponents will honor each other.

Source: Sinnott (1993c). By permission of Lawrence Erlbaum Associates, Inc.

influence whether that postformal development can occur, whether the overall system is ready for a step forward, can be found in Table 6.2. If that system is ready to change, some rules for that system change process can be found in Table 6.3.

One can speculate that the work group or organization itself would also develop a postformal reality along with its members using such a reality if a critical mass of its members consciously used conflicts about realities in a postformal thinking style in order to learn (Harman & Hormann, 1990). Table 15.2 shows several changes that could be expected in such a case. The next section of this chapter focuses on today's organizational changes. Some of the most popular ones resemble the achievement of postformal thought by the living system of the organization.

ORGANIZATIONAL CHANGE

We are seeing a rapid restructuring of organizations in the United States. That restructuring is fueled by a difficult local and global economy, by technological advances, and by our ongoing philosophical debate about the value of individual workers and the nature of communities. In our pluralistic society, we are not likely to resolve in a completely satisfactory way debates about issues such as these. Yet the outcomes of such debates have very concrete effects on workers and organizations, not to mention on the economy as a whole.

Postformal thought may offer a cognitive tool for surviving as a worker or as an organization during debates over values and during organizational changes. It is also a means of understanding what is happening as employers all around us change the ground on which we build our work lives and our economic identity.

Recent Themes of Organizational Change

Numerous sources have discussed recent themes of change in the workplace (e.g., Chowla & Renesch, 1995; Davenport, 1993; Goldstein, 1994; Hammer & Champy, 1993; Harman & Hormann, 1990; Kinlaw, 1991; Ludeman, 1990; Scott & Meyer, 1994). I am indebted to Johnson's work (Sinnott & Johnson, 1996) for a most useful summary. We can locate central themes in these discussions.

One key theme is the push to redesign or reengineer workplaces to achieve greater efficiency and higher-quality performance. This is done by incremental changes, use of technology, and continuing built-in reevaluation of processes and goals. Some of these redesigns have specific names that have become popular buzzwords, for example, creating a "learning organization," "restructuring," "reengineering" a workplace, or achieving "TQM" (Total Quality Management). Key qualities of this changed workplace would include a flatter hierarchy of workers and managers, a change-friendly structure, collective responsibility, a sense of teamwork or of a work community, valuing of people (whether workers or customers), and general awareness of the big picture of the entire organization in context.

A second theme concerns the valuing of people, as opposed to seeing them as Adam Smith's (1796) replaceable parts who can serve only one purpose. This means that a "good" employee is redefined metaphorically and philosophically as something more like a full person who belongs to a community, rather than as a part of a machine or the one responsible for one single step in a process.

A third theme is the supposedly "inevitable" reduction in the workforce (due to technology and restructuring), with its equally inevitable residue of leftover workers who are eliminated from their teams and work communities. The value expressed in this theme philosophically contradicts the values of the first two themes. This value conflict is resolved to some extent when the ousted workers are either redefined by the culture as substandard in some way or consoled by the culture with the notion that the reduction is a general systems process that is random and inevitable and has nothing to do with them personally (although they, personally, turned out to be unneeded). This latter rationalization, with its "act of God" quality, does not include a notion of charity or concern for the (former) team member experiencing difficult times. The former work community member is expected to revert to his or her deep-seated "go it alone" tendencies and creatively fend for herself or himself in these hard times. Many workers seem to see through this one-way loyalty expectation, either consciously or unconsciously, and subtly sabotage the work "community," looking out for their own interests, making a preemptive strike against unemployment.

A fourth general theme—one that is universal in current change theories of all sorts—is that of sustainability. A sustainable structure, process, or change is one that has qualities that allow it to last over time despite a wide range of adverse circumstances. For example, farming is considered sustainable when it is done in such a way that the land and the people can renew themselves and continue the farming practice indefinitely. Starving the farmers or eating the seed corn does not lead to sustainable farming. Sustainable organizational change is change that allows the transformed organization to survive over time without going bankrupt or burning out workers, managers, and stockholders.

Many reforms make such high demands on time and energy that they cannot be sustained unless they take effect rapidly and become routine. For example, one organization in the Washington, DC, area used about half its workers' hours for several months in intense, politicized meetings to discuss reengineering their processes. During that time, the workers were made aware that they must keep up their usual work, too, or be at risk for being "excessed" when reforms were completed. At the same time, three times in one year, the organization physically moved and rebuilt these employees' office spaces to conform to several (apparently temporary) grand plans, so that the creative restructuring activities, and keeping up with the workload, and job angst had to go on amid boxes and carpenters hammering, with no end in sight. None of the resulting changes were sustained, and neither was the change process itself sustainable. As physics laws of dissipative structures would dictate, instead of reform, there was a general deterioration in every aspect of that work situation.

As this example illustrates, if structures and morale deteriorate enough, the deterioration itself may become sustainable, leading to the death of that living organizational system.

A final theme is that of organizational culture, defined as the sum total of the collectively perceived institutional realities (Sinnott & Johnson, 1996). The culture sets parameters on what is possible in terms of actions, thoughts, values, and processes. If the organization says that people are valued, but has a culture that conveys the message that employees are expected to work until they drop and are replaced, the reforms flowing from a TQM or a learning organization stance will go nowhere. The organization may harbor several conflicting realities that are poorly integrated, just as conflicted individuals often do (see Chapters 18 and 19).

Postformal Thought and Organizational Change

Workers and organizations as living systems can make use of postformal thought, especially in times of rapid change such as our own. Postformal thought is a way to structure an epistemological reality that contains several contradictory logics. Its very adaptivity is based on the fact that it can permit action in spite of such contradictory logics and cognitive overload. Given this adaptivity, we can assume that postformal workers are able to ride over changes and understand each other's contradictory logics better than workers without postformal thought. In people-serving occupations, postformal workers should be able to understand the realities of the customers they serve better than workers without postformal thought.

The organization can also have a postformal culture. If it does, it is able to envision the several ways it might "be" or operate as a unit. This makes ongoing reform easier and more likely to occur whether the current CEO is calling for a "learning organization" or not. Organizations that enjoy a postformal culture are more likely to be able to reinvent themselves as the need arises and emerge with a sustainable transformation. But if the organizational culture is not yet postformal while some of the workers have that cognitive skill, the skilled workers will keep their broader analyses of the situation very private so as not to frighten their defensive, more rigid management. Everyone will then "agree" for the record that there is only one way to do things, with clear bad guys and good guys. Restructuring will lurch from one version of the party line to a new version, with workers feeling cheated and betrayed. Postformal managers will find it helpful to quietly interpret the shifting realities for their workers, many of whom may see the necessary choice of realities but be unwilling to say so at first. It is necessary to develop a postformal organizational culture, and doing so depends partly on developing a critical mass of postformal thinkers in the organization, especially at decision-making levels.

The conflicting themes of valuing people on the work team or in the work community, but expecting a necessary reduction in the workforce, can more easily be bridged by postformal workers and organizations. Postformal thinkers can live in the gray areas of conflicting logical realities more easily. They also see clearly that the two logical realities *do* conflict. Because they operate in a large problem space, they empathically understand the concerns of fellow employees and the overall state of the world if large numbers of its workers become redundant. They will try harder to bridge between the realities while keeping the idea of community intact. In many ways, the work community of postformal workers operates on the ethical system described by Carol Gilligan (1982). That system builds ethics somewhat on rights and responsibilities, but also on the maintenance of fairness for the entire community, that is, persons with whom one has some bond or connection. The search for fair treatment in the face of change can lead to very creative and profitable ideas for using the skills of the "extra" workers who are found to be essential in a new way that benefits all.

Some new ideas being presented to organizations and individuals suggest exercises that can bring postformal thoughts about work into consciousness and action. Harman and Hormann (1990) called their book *Creative Work* because work in that sense is seen as adding to the fullness of life for workers, organizations, and society. Books such as *The Reinvention of Work* (Fox, 1994) carry that theme to the individual trying to develop several realities about what we commonly call employment, challenging the economic system and the capitalist form of it.

A complement to all these is a project and series of exercises that now operate internationally, the Narings Liv Project. The title of the project translates from Swedish to mean "Work/business as nourishment for life." The project moves forward through dialogue and collaborative inquiry, proposing questions such as these: What if work is for profit? For nourishment for life? What deeply held assumptions keep us bound to a profit view of business? Are they currently realistic? If the purpose of business were nourishment for life as opposed to profit and growth, what would be business's relation to education, the environment, other organizations, and who would hold a stake in it?

Such questions have been informing many discussion about restructuring in for-profit and not-for-profit organizations, for example, universities (Sinnott & Johnson, 1996). More information on the Narings Liv Project is presented in Appendix B.

Overall, the questions stimulated by these books and the project can advance the development of postformal ways to cope with organizational change.

The level of postformal thought of key decision makers in an organization can be used as a predictor of whether certain types of reorganizations will work at all or will be sustainable. Postformal employees can be a source of group evolution for organizations. Chapter 19 will discuss ways that reorganization consultants can predict the strategy that will work best, given the cognitive level of an organization and its key players.

In the last section of this chapter, we will see how some employees in management positions that demand people and abstract skills make use of postformal thought in their work. Administrators are one group of employees who can be expected to make good use of such thinking on the job, with or without organizational change challenges.

USE OF POSTFORMAL THOUGHT BY ADMINISTRATORS: SOME RESEARCH

On the basis of Postformal Theory and my understanding of the qualities needed by administrators who deal with customers, colleagues, and employees, I expected that postformal thinking would be very useful and necessary for them to do their jobs well. I expected that the form of postformal thought they would use would suit the context of the workplace.

The group of skilled administrators who were the first to be willing to answer my fairly long questions were expert research administrators, who help university faculty create, submit proposals for, and administer externally funded grants and contracts. Research administrators need the creative and practical abstract skills to deal with research ideas, proposals, government and university regulations, budgets, and the demands of funding sources. They also need to successfully interface with faculty, staff, outside agency personnel, and the university's administrative hierarchy. Often, these various demands of the job conflict with each other; each of these groups and tasks comes with its own particular logical reality. Expert research administrators are likely to have learned to bridge logical realities and select and commit to appropriate ones—in other words, to be postformal thinkers.

Details of this project (Johnson & Sinnott, 1996; Sinnott & Johnson, 1997) are summarized here. There were four purposes for exploring the thinking of this group. The first was to verify that they did use postformal thought at work. The second was to examine patterns in their thinking processes. The third was to look at their responses on the standard interview problems (see Chapter 3) compared with job-context problems, and on interviews compared with paper-and-pencil questions. An underlying fourth purpose of a different sort was to use some of their responses to begin to develop ways to facilitate others' use of postformal thought.

Respondents were 11 volunteers employed by major universities, considered experts at their fields, and recruited at a professional conference. The group was balanced by gender and included members ranging approximately from 30 to 50 years old. Respondents were interviewed individually using thinking aloud methods described in earlier chapters, responding to both standard and work-context problems. No probes were used. They also answered 10 paper-and-pencil questions about the likelihood of their thinking or behaving in certain ways on the job, ways linked to the cognitive operations that are part of postformal thought. They circled a number representing the likelihood that they would use the operation, then described in writing an example of their having used it at work. If the example had not fit the operation, the data would have been discarded, but this was never the case.

Respondents had scores on each operation for each interview problem. They each had scores for operations on the written responses. The qualitative answers in the examples they gave and in the interviews could be analyzed for thinking style. These research administrators demonstrated postformal operations in several ways. On the written questions, they acknowledged a strong likelihood of using each operation and followed up by showing examples that confirmed that they did use the operation on the job. The all-operations mean of the likelihood means was 5.20 on a 7-point scale on which 7 meant "used very frequently," indicating that they used many operations often. In the thinking aloud portion of the test, the vast majority used almost all of the operations in the work-context problem. For example, 100% used "metatheory shift," "problem definition," and "multiple methods." Only one respondent used "paradox" in this portion of the test, however, which squares with earlier studies and standard problems, but does not match questionnaire data from this group. Although respondents showed fewer postformal operations on the standard problems, and the operations count varied by problem, the respondents again showed postformal thinking, with up to 81% using a given operation. Overall, as in prior studies discussed in earlier chapters, the more familiar and interpersonal a problem context was, the more likely the respondent was to demonstrate postformal operations.

Concerning some qualitative aspects of the research administrators' responses, the work-related use of operations was highly and positively correlated with the standard problem use of the operations, although the small numbers prevent the correlations from reaching significance. Even the "worst" respondent showed some postformal operations. However, the two respondents with most frequent use of operations on the standard problems were very different in their scores on work-related problems, one being much higher than the other. Thus, we do still see individual variability. Since different problems elicited different types of operations, even if all were work-related, it may be wise to continue to give a variety of problems to ascertain whether a given individual is capable of a certain operation. Respondents may not have been consistent in demonstrating a given operation, but most respondents demonstrated use of each operation *somewhere* in the response.

Overall, these data support the hypotheses that research administrators do use postformal thought, especially in a work context, and that postformal thought is useful in the workplace. They support the idea that either written or interview data and either work-related questions or general questions tap into postformal operations. It would be interesting to give these respondents probe statements to follow up on their responses and dig deeper into their thinking, but time constraints on these busy and productive senior administrators have so far precluded our doing so. It was our impression that some respondents had automatized certain operations like "parameter setting," so much so that they neglected to write about them on the job-contexted questionnaire. Given their normal job demands to focus on *this* specific problem today, get right to the point, and *apply* a parameter (perhaps known to the university administration but relatively unintelligible to the faculty member dropping off a draft of a grant proposal today), certain operations like pragmatic choice, paradox, or process–product shift might be used routinely but go unnamed.

In the next chapter, we will examine how postformal thinking can have an impact in another multiperson context, the context of couples and families. Once again, multiple realities must be faced and actions must be taken. Perhaps thinking postformally can be of help.

CHAPTER 16

Postformal Thought in Multiperson Groups

Couples and Families

Do not believe that the battle of love is like other fights. Its arrows and blows are gifts and blessings.
FRANCISCO DE OSSUNA

Just as individuals in the workplace must coordinate multiple realities postformally at least some of the time, if they are to succeed in working together, individuals in intimate couples and in families must also do so. We do not have as much success coordinating family realities as we do coordinating work realities. We find it more difficult to bridge cognitive realities that are so emotionally important to us. Intimate relationships by definition involve intense interactions with emotions weaving through each interaction and often contributing heat to any light that cognition may shed. Framing actions of family members in one cognitive context rather than another has implications for daily encounters and decisions, far more so than anything that might happen on the job (unless the work group *is* "family"). For a couple or a family that remains together for a relatively long time, the entire enterprise is colored by the history of past cognition, emotion, and action.

   Styles of dealing with this intensity are defined by the emotional defense patterns, the shared cultural reality, the history, and the cognitive development of each person in the relationship. The presence or absence of postformal thinking can skew not only defense styles, but also responses to shared cultural reality and the history of that couple or family. Similarly, the emotionally based defense mechanisms, the shared culture, and the relationship history can distort the development or use of postformal thought by individuals or intimate groups at later points in history. Further, these patterns are taking shape within the psychodynamics of each individual, within the individual's ongoing dialogue between the ideal and real self-in-relationship, between members of the couple, in the couple as a unique living system in its own right, between any of these "selves" and society, *and* in the family as a living system.

Notice that even the relationship itself begins to take on a life of its own, going on with a history somewhat separate from the histories of the individuals within it. It is as though additional layers of complexity were overlaid on "triangular" theories of intimate relations such as Sternberg's (1986) or Marks's (1986) and on relational "stage" theories such as S. Campbell's (1980), such that each triangle of relationship features or each stage becomes four-dimensional and transforms over time! A look at Chapter 6 and at the several research and case study chapters earlier in this book (especially the section in Chapter 12 on the case of the paranoid schizophrenic brother) might serve as reminders about parts of some of these complex processes of intimate relations that already have been discussed in this book in the general context of postformal thought.

Researchers and therapists who discuss processes in couples and families usually tend to focus on only one or two of those several elements of the volatile intimacy mix, and then shape questions or therapeutic processes around that element. Sometimes the nature of the problem demands this reductionism; sometimes the therapist's skills are stronger in that area; sometimes there is simply not enough time. Ironically, when I focus on the element of postformal thought in this book, I employ a similar narrowing of vision, since I am looking most of all at a cognitive logical process rather than at some other sort of process. My plan, though, is to bring the discussion around full circle to show the interplay of *all* the forces as they are affected by and as they affect postformal thought.

In this chapter, we will start our discussion by examining the interplay and mutual causality of each of the aforementioned main relational elements (which interact with postformal thought): defense patterns, cultural reality, and relationship history. How might postformal thinking help couples and families make it through life? How might their relational life stimulate the development of postformal thought? We will examine how these connections relate to marital and family harmony and distress. What kind of therapeutic strategies might become more common if we acknowledge the place of postformal thinking? Then we will summarize a sample of some research on couple relations, a project initiated by Rogers (D. R. B. Rogers, 1992; D. R. B. Rogers et al., 1991) in which postformal thought is taken into account as a factor.

INTERPLAY OF POSTFORMAL THOUGHT AND OTHER ELEMENTS IN INTIMATE BEHAVIOR

The adaptive value of postformal thought is that it can help bridge logical realities so that partners in a relationship can reorder logically conflicting realities in more complex ways. This skill can let the knower(s) handle more information, live in a state of multiple realities that logically conflict, and become committed enough to a chosen reality to go forward and act, thereby reifying the chosen (potential) reality.

In an intimate relationship, individuals attempt to join together to have one life, to some degree. As the Apache wedding blessing says, "Now there is one life before you . . . [so] . . . enter into the time of your togetherness." For a couple, three "individuals" begin to exist: partner 1, partner 2, and the relationship, which begins to take on a life of its own. For a family, of course, there are even more "individuals" present, as family therapist Virginia Satir (1967) noted when she worked not only with the real humans in her office but also with the remembered aspects of other absent relatives with whom the real humans psychologically interacted. To have that one life together, to whatever extent they wish to have it together, individuals must effectively bridge their logics. Those logics might be *about* any number of things, some of which do not sound especially "logical," including concepts, roles, perceptions, physical presence, emotions, and shared history.

EFFECTS OF THE INDIVIDUAL'S COGNITIVE POSTFORMAL SKILLS ON INTIMATE RELATIONSHIPS

In some cases, the individual has access to a cognitive bridge across realities, but not a postformal one. After all, realities *are* bridged, though poorly, if one person in a relationship dominates another and the dominant one's reality becomes the other's as well. But this domination does not require a synthesis of logics, since one logic is simply discarded.

There is a variation on this theme. Two members of an intimate union, because of religious beliefs or personal emotional needs, also may drop their own logics to give preference to that of the new "individual," "the relationship," letting its role-related reality dominate both of their own individual ones. This, too, is a capitulation, not a postformal synthesis.

A converse scenario might find the logic of that third individual, "the relationship," dominated and discarded by the logic or logics of one or both partners.

In all these cases, one "individual" has lost part of the "self," most likely in order to maintain the relationship.

Members of the intimate partnership may find this winner/loser solution to conflicts large and small to be the best fit for them; they may not be capable of any higher-level solution, may not be motivated to find it, or may not be emotionally ready for one. But *postformal* thought is not involved in this sort of resolution. As Maslow (1968) might suggest, this less skilled move might simply be the best move they can think of right now to deal with their situation, even if it raises new problems (in relationship terms) down the line. Perhaps this less skilled behavior is so incorporated into their shared history that it would be a challenge to their relational identity for them to have a relationship without it. But it is not postformal thinking, and it is less adaptive overall than postformal thinking would be.

Predictable Couple Problems When One Logic Dominates

When one logic dominates the other, a chance for growth is lost. There also come to be emotional overtones that begin to color the relationship processes and relationship history. The partner or family member whose logic is dominated usually exacts a price, whether consciously or unconsciously, expecting a payback to allow the balance of power to return to the relationship. And less information can be taken in, integrated, and acted upon by an individual using one simpler logic (e.g., in Piagetian terms, concrete operational logic), as opposed to two logics or as opposed to a more complex single one such as postformal logic.

There are several predictable outcomes that are less than optimal when one logic dominates another. Lack of movement forward toward postformal thought slows the individual's growth. Having a single dominant logic begins or continues a story in the relationship history that is a story about winners and losers and simplistic cognitions about complex life events. It slows the individuals' movement toward understanding and learning how to work with the shared cultural reality [or the shared cultural trance, as Ferguson (1980) puts it]. It does prevent any challenges to whatever emotional defenses the individuals may have used in the past, but keeps the peace at a cost.

A special case is that of the intimate group being a family with minor children, none of whose members happen to use postformal thought. The predictable difficulties mentioned in the last section are multiplied in a situation with more individuals. It is harder for children to gradually learn a more skilled cognitive approach when there are no daily role models. It is harder for the children to grow up, create their own personal view of the world, and leave that family when power struggles centering on control of the family reality have been going on for so long in their own family history.

Benefits of Using a Complex Postformal Logic

Alternatively, the bridge across realities may be a postformal one. The incompatible several logical realities of the relationship then might be orchestrated more easily and orchestrated at a higher cognitive level to permit a more complex logic of the relationship to emerge. Postformal thinkers can adapt to the challenges of intimate relationships better than those without postformal thought because no one's logic needs to be discarded for the relationship to go on. For the postformal couple, power and control are not the same level of threat looming on the relational horizon as they are for individuals without postformal thought who must worry about cognitive survival in their relationships. For postformal intimates, shared history reflects the synthesis of cognitive lives rather than alternating dominance of one reality over another. Each logical difference or disagreement becomes another piece of evidence that the relationship remains a win–win situation for the participants. This enhances the value of the relationship and tends to stabilize it even further.

In the situation in which one individual in the relationship is the *only* postformal one, we see a different opportunity and challenge. Several resolutions are possible each time an interpersonal logical conflict occurs. Perhaps the less cognitively skilled individual(s) will use this chance to grow cognitively, with predictable benefits. From my point of view, this is the best outcome and one of the desirable cognitive outcomes of having intense intimate relationships.

Alternatively, perhaps the increasingly aggravated postformal individual will let emotions overtake him or her and will temporarily resolve the situation by regressing cognitively and acting out against or withdrawing from the other(s) in the situation. This course will lead to the previously mentioned predictable problems for couples using lower-level logics.

Perhaps the more cognitively skilled individual will decide to wait and hope that the other(s) will in time come around to a more skilled view of the situation. This situation is easier for that postformal person to tolerate, since the postformal individual sees the bigger picture and does not have to take the power struggle quite as seriously as other members of the intimate group. But predictable conflicts will still occur and growth may be stalled.

A special situation occurs when this intimate group is a family with minor children. The postformal parent has reason to believe that the children will develop further and possibly become postformal thinkers themselves. The postformal parent might consciously try to encourage the cognitive development of the children in the direction that the postformal parent has mastered. The mismatch in cognitive levels in this case will be a cause, not for frustration, but rather for challenge and hope for the future development of the children.

THE OTHER SIDE OF THE COIN: EFFECTS OF INTIMATE RELATIONSHIP FACTORS ON POSTFORMAL THOUGHT

The factors in ongoing intimate relationships that we have been discussing, mainly emotional defense mechanisms, shared relationship history, and shared cultural reality, potentially can *influence* the development and use of postformal thought, not just be influenced by it. For example, a person who is emotionally damaged and is responding to all situations out of need (Maslow, 1968) is less likely to take a risk in a relational situation and let go of her or his own cognitive verities long enough to be willing to bridge to someone else's realities. Even the postformal thinker would not be likely to use that level of logical thought in such an interpersonal contest in which she or he is emotionally needy or "one down." Just as negative emotions often dampen the higher-level creative spirit, emotional damage means that the individual will try to regain safety before meeting the higher-level needs of the relationship (other than those in which she or he is the nurtured one). Children in a relationship in which the parents are damaged emotionally, or children who themselves are emotionally damaged, will find it harder to learn postformal responses to family dynamics. Such families function at the lower levels of unproductive patterns on the Beavers Scale (Beavers & Hampson, 1990), for example, described so well by Scarf (1995) in her book on the intimate worlds of families. The life-and-death emotional struggles that occupy such families prevent those children from having the emotional space or energy to bridge realities.

Shared relationship history also is a strong force influencing postformal thinking. The habits of relating that individuals have developed in earlier years tend to perpetuate themselves over the lifetime. If those habits do not include postformal cognitive processes for relating at the time that a given relationship begins, and if many years are spent bridging the related individuals' realities in a non-postformal way, then it will be increasingly difficult for anyone (child or adult) in the relationship to move on to a postformal way of relating and thereby violate earlier habit.

An exception to this effect of habit is the family situation in which parents are postformal but young children are not. Postformal parents will likely find this cognitive discrepancy easier to bear than less cognitively skilled parents, though they will likely still be influenced by living in relationships in which they are always using a logical level that is beneath their own. One's tendency to permanently distort perceptions about an intimate's logical skills, based on the cognitive skills that intimate has shown during the history of our relationship with him or her, is very strong. We see just how strong when we see parents relating to their adult children as though those adults were *still* very young children. Parents must make significant efforts to overcome history, or at least to reconsider whether historical patterns need to be revised before using them to predict today's behavior. Intimates influenced by their history face an equally daunting task if they want to relate on a new (to them), more skilled, logical level.

Shared cultural reality, or social forces and roles, also influence the ways that postformal thinking can be used in intimate relationships. This is a domain in which social roles often interfere with the choice of possible processes of relating. The shared reality of the social roles "appropriate" for various intimate relationships must be a "lowest common denominator" reality that the vast majority in a society can achieve, or pretend to achieve. The shared social role reality for couples relations and family relations is often structured enough and at a low enough skill level that no bridging of conflicting logical realities is necessary at all. All that is necessary is to act out the appropriate roles in a convincing way and to make the socially appropriate comments about feelings connected to those roles. Tradition does save cognitive energy!

Notice that the first time in this discussion that we need to consider whether a couple or family is heterosexual or homosexual, legally married or not, childless or not, a May–December union, divorced or previously married, with or without stepchildren or other relatives, or characterized in any other particular way, is in the context of this "shared social cognition" element. Other than here in this paragraph, the processes discussed in this chapter apply to *all* of these differing roles and family configurations. Only the shared social cognition element discriminates among the various family configurations. Persons in all the various family configurations *can* use the same cognitive relational processes and can experience the same styles of relating.

A conflict may occur when the views of any knower, let's say "the couple," about the reality of their relationship come into conflict with the views of society about the same intimate relationship. This conflict might stimulate in the couple the growth of a postformal way of seeing their relationship and seeing the world. For example, it has not been many years since the existence of a childless marriage was considered an ongoing tragedy for everyone and, if intentional, a sign of problems in one's personality and maturity level. Imagine a couple who feel very happy in their relationship, even secretly happy to have evaded the encumbrance of children, coming face to face with this tragic and pathologized view of their "selfish" childless life together and their part in the "problem." Knowing that such a view does not square with their personal knowledge may be the impetus for them to realize postformal elements of knowing, perhaps for the first time. The motivation in this case is social.

When the reality of one person in the relationship clashes with another's view, the intensity of the bond is what motivates them to seek a resolution. The intensity is a push toward development of postformal thought, or perfection of it, since lower-level logics will leave the conflict unresolved. Since framing such a situation postformally can help keep blame and anger at bay, postformal skills are often welcome conflict resolution devices!

The recent past has been a time of social change, especially in regard to the forms of intimate relations. While the possibilities for intimate relation behavior in the human behavioral repertoire are inherently limited, certain of these possibilities are more fashionable than others at a given time. Living at a time of social change means that the individual and even the relationship is challenged to maneuver amid others' logical realities without becoming lost, all the while under shifting shared social reality pressures. Access to postformal thought makes it easier for the social change shift to occur while a person or a relationship maintains its identity.

POSTFORMAL THOUGHT, DISTRESS, AND HEALING IN INTIMATE RELATIONSHIPS

You may have gathered from the foregoing discussion that acknowledging the role of postformal thought in intimate ongoing relationships might lead to some new ways of conceptualizing couple and family distress and some new approaches to healing distressed relationships. Postformal thought may be an additional tool for keeping relationships from running into serious trouble when the inevitable difficult times occur—but it may also be the source of discord.

To look at the bad news first: attaining this more complex cognitive level might lead to trouble and discord in a relationship. Imagine the case of a couple, neither of whom was postformal when they first became a couple. Time and the events of life have passed, and one (but only one) member of the couple has developed the ability to think postformally. This development has led to their each seeing the world and their life together from very different vantage points on many occasions, living different cognitive lives within the boundaries of their life together. For a couple who desire a deep level of closeness, this becomes a challenging situation; they no longer speak the same language. Of course, differences of opinion, differences in ways of seeing the reality of the world, come to every couple, to some degree, at one time or another in their relationship, and their task as a couple is to grow through the difficulty and build a stronger union. In the case of a difference in the ability to understand at a postformal level, however, the couple have begun a time of profound and far-reaching differences in worldviews. The very nature of their usual realities is different much of the time; one sees it as concrete and existing "out there," while the other sees it as coconstructed and cocreated through commitment to its reality. Even more challenging, one of the partners (the postformal one) can visit the reality of the other (the nonpostformal one), but the other cannot yet return the visit. So when one develops but the other does not, discord in worldviews may provide a temporary challenge (or a permanent one).

A second piece of potential bad news related to postformal thought and relationships is the type of pathology that may intrude

when any unskilled behavior becomes unskilled in a much more complex, postformal way. For example, if a couple are temporarily
engaged in a power struggle with one another, they have access to a far
broader range of strategies if they are postformal, since weapons like
sarcastic remarks can be used at several levels of the argument! Chapter 19 has a discussion of psychopathology and postformal thought, to
which the reader is referred for a further discussion of these possibilities.

In spite of these negative possibilities, it has been my impression
that the positive features that postformal thought might bring to a relationship difficulty far outweigh the negative ones. In a time of conflict,
partners of a couple have to handle emotions and deal with their individual unskilled behaviors. If they can do so looking from an overarching logical vantage point that gives them the big picture, it is easier for them to gain perspective on their individual problems and
avoid blaming each other. They can weather the changes in the developing relationship better than members of a nonpostformal couple
who see the world in polarized terms.

Let us look at one practical area of life in intimate relations in
which postformal thought may make a difference: the roles related to
gender (sex roles, sex role stereotypes) and behavior related to those
masculine/feminine roles. I have written about this topic extensively,
and have included it in my research efforts, because gender roles and
the cocreation of social roles have been a central aspect of historically
recent social changes in the United States (e.g., Cavanaugh, Kramer,
Sinnott, Camp, & Markley, 1985; Sinnott, 1977, 1982, 1984a, 1986b,c;
1987, 1993b; Sinnott, Block, Grambs, Gaddy, & Davidson, 1980; Windle
& Sinnott, 1985). "Gender role" is a concept different from that of sexual identity, sexuality, or masculine/feminine behavior. Gender roles
may at various times be ambiguous, polarized into opposites, synthesized into an androgynous larger version, reversed, or transcended
entirely. The general age-related progression of gender role development is from polarizing masculine/feminine roles to transcending roles
entirely in favor of giving energy to other parts of identity. Gender-
related roles enter discussions of intimate relations because couples
tend to divide the work of living together, and gender has often been
used by society to define roles. So couples enter relationships, even
homosexual ones, with ideas of what proper socially dictated masculine and feminine behavior is. Sometimes identity is being challenged
when there is conflict over role-related behavior, making an apparently simple negotiation over something concrete like housework into
a complex, full-blown struggle over identity and worth.

If a couple are struggling about gender-role-related behavior, post-formal thought makes it easier to sort things out. A postformal partner can readily understand that if he or she gets beyond emotional or habitual reactions, the two of them can validly coconstruct their roles in any number of ways, as logical systems to which they commit them-selves and weave into their lives. That partner can also understand that a gender role and its related behavior are only a minor part of his or her constantly transforming identity and a poor index of personal worth. For the postformal partner(s), the negotiation then moves back to the domain of "What job do I want?," rather than remaining in the domain of identity and worth in terms such as "I'm a terrible person if you make more/less money than I do, and my identity is in danger."

In terms of doing therapy with a postformal couple or with the members of a couple of whom at least one is postformal, their levels of cognition can be a real asset or a real drawback. The couple who understand that they are cocreators of the reality of their relationship, to some degree, find it easier to open to possibilities and to change, in spite of history. They already feel that power and choice are partly in their hands, and that taking action is part of creating something new. They know that partners seldom have absolute characteristics that are unmodifiable. *Given the motivation* to reduce pain and create a better shared relationship, and that motivation is the crucial part, progress is made with comparative ease. If the motivation is to obstruct change, though, the postformal thinker can create more ways to avoid real con-sideration of issues than other clients, all things being equal. Defenses can be more sophisticated. Such defenses cut across several types of psychological problems, and Chapter 19 will offer further discussion of issues related to postformal thought and psychotherapy.

A STUDY OF COUPLE RELATIONS
AND POSTFORMAL THOUGHT

If the availability of postformal thought is related to the quality of intimate relations, we should be able to see an empirical connection between those two variables. Rogers (D. R. B. Rogers, 1991; D. R. B. Rogers et al., 1991) set out to investigate the joint cognition of two persons trying to solve the postformal problems together. These two persons might be longer-term married adults or strangers in a dyad, status which might influence status cognition. Rogers also wanted to examine marital adjustment and social behaviors evident during prob-lem solving. She expected that well-adjusted married dyads would demonstrate more postformal problem solving and more socially facilitative behaviors than poorly adjusted married dyads.

For this study, 40 heterosexual couples between the ages of 35 and 50 were recruited. They were mainly Caucasian, married for an average of 15 years, 75% for the first time, 25% having also had a long-term previous marriage; one or more of 41% had bachelor's, master's, or PhD degrees. After individuals were prescreened for intelligence, they were tested for marital adjustment using Spanier's (1976) Dyadic Adjustment Scale, a widely used self-report instrument that tests for, among other things, diadic cohesion, consensus, and satisfaction. The individuals were randomly assigned to work in one of the following contexts: well-adjusted couple, working as a couple; poorly adjusted couple, working as a couple; well-adjusted-couple individuals, working with someone not their spouse; and poorly adjusted-couple individuals, working with someone not their spouse. Then each "couple" (real or artificial) was videotaped solving the postformal logical problems. Tapes were scored according to the coding schemes of Pruitt and Rubin (1986) and Sillars (1986) to obtain counts of the social behavior factors of avoidance, competition/contention, accommodation/yielding, and cooperation/collaboration.

While there were no marital adjustment or dyadic context relations with using *formal* logical operations, there were such relations with using *postformal operations.* In all, 80% of the maritally well-adjusted dyads, both real couples and paired strangers, gave evidence of significantly more postformal thinking operations than did the poorly adjusted dyads. This was especially true for responses to the problems with an interpersonal element, just as was true in research reviewed in earlier chapters. Analyzing facilitative social behaviors from the videotape, Rogers once again found that ability to use formal operations did not relate to the social behaviors, while use of postformal operations did. For example, dyads without postformal thought demonstrated more contentious and competitive behaviors while problem solving. The social behaviors demonstrated by respondents during testing were also strongly related to marital adjustment. For example, well-adjusted respondents demonstrated fewer avoidance behaviors.

Rogers's results support the theory described earlier in this chapter. Postformal thinking and adjustment in intimate relationships are positively related. There seemed to be some generalized ability present that operated whether or not the spouses were working with each other or with strangers. It may have operated by means of facilitating positive types of social behaviors and interactions, as evidenced by the fact that postformal thinkers produced more cooperative and fewer avoidant behaviors. Postformal thinkers seemed to explore and create to a greater degree, tolerate others' ways of seeing reality, and ultimately be able to commit to one solution. When working with strangers, they also took more pains to communicate "where they were coming from" in their views of a problem's many realities. Rogers's work suggests that postformal thinking is useful in intimate relationships.

Postformal thought has appeared to be useful in connecting persons to others outside the self and useful for individual growth through relationships. In the next two chapters, I will discuss the place of postformal complex thinking skills in processes within the self, namely, creativity and spiritual development.

CHAPTER 17

Development and Yearning
Postformal Thought
and Spirituality

Just as mysticism is not a rejection of science but a transcendence of it, science is not a rejection of mysticism but a precursor of it.

HERB KOPLOWITZ

In this chapter, we will discuss four related ideas. First, I propose that spirituality (as opposed to religiousness), as it becomes conscious, makes use of the type of complex cognition that I have described in this book, a type known as postformal thought. Second, we examine how we might perform psychological research on spiritual development using the theory of postformal thought. Third, we examine the overlapping of the new physics, Eastern spirituality, and postformal thinking. Finally, I propose that being able to think postformally facilitates the individual's being able to live in balance, integrating mind, emotions, body, and spirit into the dance of living.

DOES SPIRITUALITY GROW WITH THE
AID OF POSTFORMAL THOUGHT?

Religiousness and spirituality are two separate things. To be religious is to observe the dictates and customs of a particular "church." To be spiritual, or to be a mystic, demands that we look with the eyes of a lover both on the world around us and on our fellow beings. Spirituality may demand that we consciously shift realities and "know" the lovableness of what we see at several levels, in order to love at least one aspect of it. Religiousness is different from spirituality; we can be religious using concrete or formal thought without making the postformal cognitive shifts that spirituality demands. I can observe the dictum to give alms simply because my church says to do so, without necessarily taking the ultimate spiritual leap of loving, identifying with, and empathizing with the dirty panhandler annoying me today. With maturity, adults often become both more religious and more spiritual. Adulthood encourages the awareness of death, and that awareness helps motivate both our obedience to religious customs and rules and our cognitive wrestling with the spiritual and mystical aspects of "de-identifying" with our mortal bodies.

Spirituality and spiritual knowing are important to humans, at least if we go by what they say and do in all cultures. But neither gets much attention in life-span studies, especially life-span studies of cognition (Sinnott, 1993c, 1994a). Yet we are thinking beings who do conceptualize the spiritual and the transcendent, who yearn for unitative states of being united with God or Universal Consciousness. When we think about spiritual things, we want our thoughts to make sense, to us and to others around us, as potentially *shared* cognition.

Also, we psychologists historically have found it very difficult to integrate our "psychologist" selves with our own spiritual, yearning selves, or with the spiritual, yearning selves of individual colleagues or clients. After all, we have been told in recent generations, it isn't rational or logical to talk about this sort of thing. We might lose our credentials as scientists if we did! But, in the meantime, we could secretly admire Meister Eckhard, or Buddha, or Mother Teresa, or Hillary of Bingen, or Christ.

But it may be time at this point in the history of our profession to try to make this elusive integration between psychological science and spirituality. We see all around us, for example in the integration of new physics with Eastern spirituality, that the old ways of describing reality are being reformulated and expanded because they are too limited to describe the current changes we see. Now we study the evolution of consciousness (e.g., Ornstein, 1991), but such a concept as consciousness was not even acknowledged in the psychology of the '60s.

The question of the nature of the logical operations connected to knowing the spiritual eventually arises. How can we even *think* about the ideas of spirituality, which violate the scientific logic of our formal operational minds? How can we make any kind of cognitive sense of the multiple realities of the new physics, much less of spirituality and mysticism? Spiritual ideas seem opposed to logic of any kind.

Millions of adults have been intrigued, however, by spiritual books such as Bach's (1977) *Illusions* or *The Celestine Prophecy* (Redfield, 1993) and its sequel (Redfield & Adrienne, 1996), even when they find little personal meaning in standard psychology. Some sorts of cognitive operations allow them to consider these questions

The purpose of this chapter is to suggest a way to make some integrations between our psychological science and our spiritual experiences by seeing them both as knowable in postformal operational terms. As psychologists and scientists, we may find it useful to understand the cognitive processes involved in complex, transcendent, spiritual knowing, as well as how such thinking becomes part of the skills and processes and experience of the normal, nonpathological, developing human. The concepts of postformal thought can help us do this. We also need to explore how ideas of transcendence, multiple realities, and "higher" meaning in life appear in our cognitive models. We can apply the model of postformal thought. Postformal thought can help us understand how we can know these experiences from a cognitive point of view, and can help us generate testable, even experimental, hypotheses about this knowing.

From our own experience and from descriptions by others, we know that individuals do this multiple-reality knowing in many contexts (see earlier chapters). Analyses of thinking that are done in terms of postformal thought specifically address the question of how two logically disparate frames for reality can coexist in a coordinated way in the human mind. How can a transcendent thinker such as Kübler-Ross (1969, 1991), in her latest work, see life as both "real" and "maya" (illusion) and still function? Postformal thinking may help explain how humans can function on a day-to-day, practical level while experiencing the conflicting basic logical frameworks that underlie spiritual knowing. Could postformal thought be among the logical processes that allow this transcending of multiple realities, and even of "self," and this achievement of a unitative state?

Jean Valjean, in *Les Miserables* (Hugo, 1938), asks who he *is*—convict, spiritually condemned man, pillar of the community, or one whose life has been purchased by God for a special role in doing good works. When he asks these questions, he must develop to a point where his "self" can bridge across those smaller selves within each of those contradictory logics to arrive at a larger self that is part of the unitative self. This sounds like an activity of postformal thought.

Madeline. L'Engle (1974), in her "children's" book *A Wind in the Door,* shows us a heroine who must shift her views of who and what she and others *are* (on the level of spirit) to prevent the physical death of her brother, and in doing so transforms the logic of self, life, and death from a concrete one to a transcendent one in which the unlovable is also lovable (in the sense of *agape*). The demand to do so helps her develop postformal thought.

Points of Interface

There are four potential points of interface between these two domains, points from which it would be easy to start our studies: the *form* of this logic; the *developmental process* to attain this thought; the connection between this sort of thought, its underlying logic, and *emotion* and *will;* and the multiperson, *cooperative cognition element.*

With respect to the *form* of this logic, the scientist can examine the information processing and the cognitive style of any thinker, including the thinker in a unitative state. The scientist can elaborate on the logical processes being used by that thinker (as Piaget elaborated on the processes of infants and scientists), whether that thinker be Blake or an adolescent, Saint Teresa or an Alzheimer's disease patient, Buckminster Fuller or an unknown gifted musician. Just as Sinetar (1986) used questionnaires and methods from organizational psychology to study the process of becoming self-actualized (Maslow, 1968), cognitive developmental psychologists can examine the memory, problem solving, and logic of the healthy, spiritually questing person. Tart (1983) explored the cognitive processes of individuals in many states of consciousness; we can explore the logic of mystics and spiritually questing persons in many settings.

The *developmental process* by which a person arrives at multireality logic skills is also ripe for study. Pearce (1973) has described developmental stages in which the first pass through the stages leads to *intra*psychic growth, while the second pass through the same stages leads to *transpersonal* psychological growth. That second pass through the stages is expected, Pearce says, in the middle and later years of adult life. But not every adult achieves this growth. What makes the difference?

A third way to approach the cognitive study of spiritual development is to tap the methods that incorporate *emotion* and *will* (or intention) into cognition. Emotional elements in processes such as problem solving are difficult to study, but some of us (e.g., Bastick, 1982; Isen & Shalker, 1982; D. R. B. Rogers et al., 1991; Sinnott, 1991b) have taken steps to incorporate these factors. Since spiritual experience is often felt to be an *emotional* knowing that *does* demand the use of intention and will, it is important to be able to incorporate such elements into studies. Emotional reactions might be one way to enlarge problem space to permit the development of an enlarged worldview such as postformal or spiritual thought.

The fourth set of studies may be similarly difficult, but also possible. Studies of *cooperative cognition* are fairly rare in standard cognitive experimental settings, in which variables can be controlled in ways that are not practical in real-life organizational or educational settings. Yet such studies are recommended (e.g., Meacham & Emont, 1989) and sometimes done (e.g., Laughlin, 1965; Laughlin & Bitz, 1975; D. R. B. Rogers et al., 1991). Studying multiperson cognition would help us understand spirituality in two ways. First, we could understand how the shared belief system challenges or facilitates cognitive growth. Second, unitative states are, in certain ways, shared cognitive states. These four areas—process, development, emotion and will, multiperson cognition—therefore offer a promise of research utility in our study of the cognitive aspects of spirituality.

A Necessary Skill

I propose that postformal thought is a necessary cognitive skill for deep, mature, spiritual development and that it can be found in the thinking of spiritually wise individuals, saints, and mystics. I propose that postformal thought is the form that logic takes in these mature thinkers and that it develops through the thinkers' relationships with others, with whatever ultimate reality or deity the thinker believes in, and with the universe. It includes the union of mind and emotion as well as a modified and expanded concept of self.

Postformal thought could allow the mature spiritual thinker to know that he or she is operating by two or more mutually contradictory but simultaneous logics in the course of experiencing higher awareness. Postformal thought could leave the thinker comfortable with that knowing and with the behavior that flows from that knowing. The spiritual seeker who (as the *Bhagavad Gita* has it) experiences all persons as Buddha, all places as Nirvana, and all sounds as Mantra is either totally out of touch with ordinary reality without a reality to replace it, or much *more* able to orchestrate the multiple ordinary and nonordinary states of consciousness described by Tart (1983) by virtue of improved cognitive abilities. What if the built-in human possibilities include a cognitive possibility of transcending the prison of our own cognition to enjoy a God's-eye view of it?

The spiritual yearnings that accompany generativity and integrity for many persons often sound like this postformal thought, as do the comments of sages, mystics, and saints. Underhill (1961) has written that the mystic lives in a world, unknown to most others, where she or he sees through the veil of imperfection to view creation with God's eyes. The mystic is lifted out of the self to a higher self in order to see everything and everyone as lovable. There is a sense of choice about whether one is to spend a certain hour or day in a place of limited (ordinary) understanding or in a place of the larger understanding. The shaman walks in the upper and lower worlds, as animal spirit and human spirit simultaneously. Don Genero (Castaneda, 1971) can choose to see in a unitative way, with the eyes of the sorcerer, or in the more ordinary way; he can violate physical laws or obey them. Spiritual seekers who are mystics say that they share in all of being while being one part of it. To sustain and understand these experiences takes the ability to coordinate multiple contradictory formal logical systems and to be able self-referentially to choose one to commit to at a given moment. This sounds like postformal thought.

SOME TESTABLE HYPOTHESES AND SOME DIFFICULTIES IN STUDYING THE RELATIONS BETWEEN POSTFORMAL THOUGHT AND SPIRITUALITY

Let me briefly describe four sample hypotheses with which we could test some relations between postformal cognition and higher-level spiritual development:

1. Individuals who report a unitative state of consciousness show postformal operations; those who do not report unitative states may or may not show postformal operations.
   One might sample university students, the public at large, religious leaders, older adults labeled "wise," or master transpersonal therapists (among others) to find individuals reporting experiences of unitative states. Members of some of these groups would be expected to report them more frequently than would members of other groups. The groups reporting such experiences would be tested for postformal thought.
   Conversely, one might hypothesize that postformal thinkers are more likely to have unitative states of consciousness than

are non-postformal thinkers. This direction of causality (i.e., the cognitive state causing the unitative state to be conscious and reportable) better reflects the direction in which events probably occur. It would probably be more fun, however, for the researcher to use the hypothesis variation stated first, since doing so would permit one to have conversations with groups of individuals expressly chosen for their interesting spiritual experiences!)

2. Those who report unitative states have highly efficient styles of processing large amounts of conflicting information and would function better in the face of that overload than those who do not report unitative states. I hypothesize that relation because of the underlying postformal thought components that organize disparate realities more effectively. Chapters 3 and 16 discuss these overload states.

3. Middle-aged and older persons, whose life tasks involve developing generativity and integrity, are more likely than younger persons to describe spiritual searches that link them with others and that operate to give a unity and meaning to their lives. They are even more likely to do so if they have access to postformal operations. The rationale for this hypothesis is that underlying postformal cognitive skills provide a similar form to personality development and to spiritual development, both of which serve the good or adaptation of the person.

4. Choice of the experience of life events, workshops involving self-development, or psychotherapy in which one challenges the meaning of one's life and the grounds of the self are likely to let a person make a transition to both postformal thought and spiritual development. The rationale for this hypothesis is that a challenge of serious magnitude is needed to motivate reorganizing complex cognitive structures with the concomitant ability to articulate the aspects of deeper spiritual development.

Following are several difficult aspects of all the studies just proposed above:

1. It is difficult to reach agreement on what constitutes spiritual development, unitative experiences, and other aspects of advanced spirituality. Concrete polarized language is a significant problem. It is necessary to craft operational definitions carefully.

2. If we are researching an "advanced" cognitive or spiritual state, relatively few persons will have experienced it. We will need large samples to find enough target respondents. Few will read the reports we generate about the phenomenon with enough understanding and interest. Few will want to review proposals or journal articles favorably, or generally support the effort.

3. Cognition, spirituality, and science have traditionally been split apart. Trying to find the bridges among them frightens both the complex thinkers who fear reductionism and the simpler orthodox thinkers who fear bad science.

4. Some argue that we should not even try to study these subjects scientifically because such studies are really attempts to advocate a particular religion or some single value system and are not about science.

These objections and difficulties, however, can be answered. Spirituality and spiritual yearnings cross cultures and religions and can be seen in some form in all human groups. Nothing at all is value-free; science in its traditional form has its own values and hidden or overt basic paradigms. Also, *all* behavior is open to scientific investigation, if science is the powerful tool we believe it is. Using several tools can give us measures of a phenomenon from several additional perspectives. There is general agreement between both traditional and nontraditional scientists that study of only selected facets of a phenomenon by either group is always expected to yield limited information, be it in the field of spirituality or particle physics. Thus, it appears that none of the difficulties mentioned above is sufficient to keep us from conducting some research on cognitive aspects of spiritual development—research that is innovative and "clean" from a traditional scientific perspective. What is left to prevent us from approaching the study of this phenomenon?

NEW PHYSICS, EASTERN SPIRITUALITY, AND POSTFORMAL THOUGHT

It has been more than 30 years since Western culture, as a whole, rediscovered Eastern spiritual systems and mediated that understanding through selected concepts of the new physics. These phenomena have in turn been linked culturally with an emerging sense of *global* community. An "end of the millennium" mind-set further energizes these current cultural transformations of meaning. Perhaps the children of both Depression and buttoned-down '50s parents reacted against the limits of their parents' world views and found common cause with the children of the '70s who reacted against the cynicism and closing options of the culture of their own birth era. In any case, we have seen what could be described as a "sudden" interest in "new" ways of conceptualizing all levels of realities and relationships-over-time in physical, psychological, and spiritual realms. The "new" paradigms, of course, are really one of the several basic philosophical stances vis-à-vis reality, recycled throughout human history, each time dressed in the current fashion and the necessary accessories appropriate to the historical context in which they emerge. In the field of psychology, this "new" paradigm found varieties of expression in the subfields of cognitive psychology (especially study of consciousness and intention); chaotic, evolving, and general systems models of behavior; humanist psychology; existential psychology; transpersonal psychology; and the psychology of mind–body interactions. Some sample titles of books from these categories can be found in Appendix C. Chapters 6, 7, and 8 also address aspects of these categories.

In this chapter, I am limited by space considerations to making very brief summary points about this major cultural and philosophical phenomenon that, fortunately, has been described much more adequately elsewhere. Interested readers might wish to feel the excitement of the unfolding historical event by reading such classics as *The Phenomenon of Man* (Teilhard de Chardin, 1959), *The Tao of Physics* (Capra, 1975), *The Dancing Wu Li Masters* (Zukav, 1979), and *The Aquarian Conspiracy* (Ferguson, 1980).

The key point relevant to this book is that the new physics, Eastern, transpersonal and other rediscovered spiritual traditions, and the emerging "new" paradigm itself all include a view of logical known reality that is like that described in the Theory of Postformal Thought. Postformal Thought can help us study how the human mind "knows" the "unknowable" (Sinnott, 1996a)! I am not trying to reduce each of these other fields to the reductionistic position that it is "only" Postformal Thought in disguise. Rather, it seems possible that the epistemology is similar for each. In other words, it seems possible that the intellectual operations by which the human mind *knows reality* in these fields are similar ones. It seems that the way Einstein knew or Capra knows the reality of physics and the reality of the spiritual realm reflects the self-referential awareness of *truth* in general possessed by the individual with access to postformal thought. The coconstructed truth to which we make a passionate commitment of our lives, which we come to and leave as we shift our realities, may be spoken of in different words than these by a Schrödinger or by a mystic, but the final epistemological result is the same. Each field seems to express a different side of the same reality of its own epistemology. Furthermore, since the *Tao Te Ching* (Mitchell, 1988) says that the tao that can be spoken of completely is not the true tao, why shouldn't each field express it differently?

LIVING IN BALANCE: MIND, EMOTIONS, AND BODY, WITH SPIRIT

I propose that access to postformal thought permits the individual to balance, to orchestrate the physical and mental elements of the self not only with each other but also with the element of spirituality. As we will discuss in Chapter 22, our "self" seems to be composed of a sort of collection of selves that we need to coordinate. We struggle to balance the often competing needs of our bodies, our minds, our emotions, and our spirits, each of which seems to "know" (in its own way) a separate and very logical reality about what it is experiencing.

For example, the body self may be very interested in having sex with an attractive person we met this summer, while our emotional self may feel love toward a long-term partner and guilt (in a complicated historical scenario involving relations with our parents) about even being aware of this attraction, much less acting on it. Meanwhile, the intellectual self may be thinking through the meaning of this attraction and how much we should say about it to our partner with the aim of being honest about trouble in our relationship but avoiding bad feelings that might hurt the long-term relationship. The spiritual self, in this example, may have an intuitive sense that we need to learn something, somehow, about the nature of universal love (what? how?)—though not necessarily sex—by means of interaction with this person.

In this example, each aspect of the self may offer a different vote about the behavior that should occur, and some of the behavioral votes may be contradictory. In fact, the human condition is as interesting as it is because these balancing dilemmas are so frequent. Yet some behavior must be chosen actively or passively by the human who wishes to survive. Denial of any aspect of our complex human agendas, refusing to honor that aspect's needs, leads to trouble down the road in the form of mental or physical or emotional or spiritual illness. Only when we can work out a balance among the needs of aspects of the self (as we will discuss more fully in Chapter 22, which is devoted entirely to this topic) can we make choices that maximize our ability to fulfill the needs of all aspects of the self.

We can hardly be expected to use our spiritual challenges and spiritual awareness as a chosen logic that overarches the several often-contradictory logical system demands of body logic, mind logic, and emotional logic if the postformal cognitive system has not yet developed. While the body and mind and emotional systems can to some degree "run on automatic" or instinct, spirit cannot be added to a coordinated conscious and mature balance honoring all of these aspects without the operations of postformal thinking. Postformal thought would seem to provide the conscious balance-including-spirit tools to make it possible to *creatively* reach this sophisticated, transpersonal balance for ourselves, or to reach it through awakening in an intimate relationship with a partner (Welwood, 1996).

In the next chapter, we will see how creativity is generally part of the postformal thought experience and how postformal thought influences creativity itself.

CHAPTER 18

Postformal Thought, Creativity, and Creating the "Self"

Sit down before fact like a little child, and be prepared to give up every preconceived notion, follow humbly wherever and to whatever abyss Nature leads, or you shall learn nothing.

T. H. HUXLEY

Can we maintain a clarity of vision that reveals to us our oneness in time and space with all else?

LARRY DOSSEY

The creative reaching out into novelty is a fundamental property of life.

FRITJOF CAPRA

Data show that postformal thinking is a tool with which adults can express creativity in everyday life as well a way to describe the process of adult creativity. Creative postformal thinking is expressed in many domains of life, as we saw in earlier chapters. Creativity in adulthood and old age, using the tools of postformal thought, can regulate the integration of intellectual and emotional stimulation from events or people, bridging affect and cognition and making the demands of adulthood bearable and meaningful.

In the next few pages, I will discuss the following topics: definitions of creativity, links between postformal thought and creativity, and creation or construction of the "self."

BROADER DEFINITIONS OF CREATIVITY

What kinds of creativity will we be addressing in this chapter? Although dictionary definitions of creativity are usually restricted to something like "intellectual inventiveness," practical and everyday definitions are broader. In practice, we seem to define creativity in dichotomous ways, polarized around seven issues:

1. *Process* focus versus *product* focus
2. *Art* (the emotional, the visual, the aural) versus *ideation* (verbal, cognitive)
3. *Uniqueness* or *originality* of products versus *abundance of high-quality work*
4. *Communication* (representation of the product to others) versus *private experience* for one's own growth
5. Quality as *judged by others* versus *quality as judged by the creator*
6. A *requirement for* the presence of *emotion and synthesis* versus *no need for emotion or synthesis*
7. Whether the creative impulse comes from the creator's *life pain* versus from the creator's *life's fullness and abundance*

All these aspects are reasonable ones, but only some are consciously addressed by a given researcher or scholar. Thus, it is hard to compare "creativity" in studies or life situations.

Some combinations of these dimensions seem "better" than others. For example, many parents have received very creative surprise "special" breakfasts for their birthdays—breakfasts made by young children who have used every pot and pan in the kitchen. These creations are full of emotion and color ("Look!! We made ketchup and jelly faces on the toast!"), are unique and communicate clearly ("The faces are all smiling at you!"). These creations are "creative," at least to their creators, and a synthesis—sort of—of all the meals the creators ever liked. Yet is such a breakfast as "good" a creation as the Mona Lisa? If the quality dimension of the creativity polar description is changed, to "quality as judged by *others*", the creativity of the breakfast easily disappears, even though the breakfast, unfortunately, does not. It is not surprising, then, that a definition of creativity is as hard to seize upon as the morning mist.

The links of creativity to the happiness and psychological development of the creator are also the subjects of many stories. The main question seems to be whether creativity is "good" or "bad" for an individual's psychological development. When we think of creativity, we sometimes imagine flamboyant mad artists and starving, rejected geniuses, but those who live creatively also seem to be among the happiest adults. These happy people cannot even commute to work without being amazed by the wild and wonderfully strange behavior of others on the highway or the subway, creatively seeing all parts of life's trip. The Buddhist saying has the enlightened soul creatively hearing all sounds as Mantra and seeing all places as Nirvana; saintly Christians creatively find the Kingdom of Heaven within and all around them. This type of joy seems like a reward that comes with optimal development.

For this chapter, I have chosen to view creativity in a limited number of its possible dimensions. I am most interested in the kind of everyday creativity that is part of *skilled* life-span development. I am focusing on the creative *process,* and the *joint presence of emotion, synthesis, and ideation.* My work on postformal thought explores how adults show the development of creative processes of thinking that synthesize knowledge and emotion and experience, that lead to a lot of high-quality behavior production work. I am very interested in how people use their logic when they create a wise and well-lived life. Postformal thought allows one to craft one's life consciously in creative ways.

This creativity involves others. It takes place in a real interpersonal context and in a real period of history, and has a real impact on people and society. A society values only selected forms of creativity. The creativity I want to discuss takes place in a context that helps shape it. Each individual develops his or her ability to be postformal and to be creative in order to be a more adaptive organism. He or she also, then, contributes to the adaptivity or the society or the family or the dyad within which he or she creates. For example, if I become capable of postformal thought and become more creative, my partner and I can more creatively cocreate our union (in the context of the 20th-century United States, where marriage takes many forms). The quality of the union, then, will reflect my partner's and my levels of developmental creativity (see Chapter 16). In another example, the degree of creativity with which my society attacks and solves problems of the environment partly reflects the postformal logical creativity of the society's members acting together.

Because creativity takes place in another context, that of a life over time, the age and experience of the creator would seem to make a difference in the quality of the creation. The younger or less experienced artist or author more often creates products that communicate raw emotion and less-refined ideas; the older or more experienced one more often produces the interpreted emotional expression and the integrated, synthesized idea. In general systems theory terms (see Chapter 6), the younger society creates structures and processes that are less politicized, less subtle, and less integrated than the older society. For example, the United States has gone through its early adolescent creative phase in which simple, idealistic, emotion-laden solutions were imposed on social problems by strong-willed, charismatic individuals. The newer thinker creates new but simple solutions ("Shoot the developers to save the earth") or new specific *products* to help the environment (e.g., the catalytic converter). Now the United States seems to be in its mature system phase, in which *process* solutions (e.g., a series of Earth Summits) are appreciated more than they were before.

The differences between values of "young" and "mature" creative societies can also be seen in the political realm and in science. The young society (which may be one reinventing itself) likes maverick, iconoclastic politicians and scientists who campaign for change or new paradigms (with that change being a simple or unspecified one) or who seem to be lone political or scientific geniuses who are not part of the club. The mature society also values the creativity of the ongoing problem-solving program to be put into place and the creativity of the brilliant scientific mentor and agenda setter.

Younger and mature societies often dismiss each other's creations as "uncreative." In the competitive younger society, one creative individual sometimes tears down what another creative individual creates; among mature creators, individual geniuses are sometimes dismissed as troublemakers. Ideally, an integration of the two can occur—*if* there is some critical mass of postformal thinkers.

The role of creative social organizations also reflects the creative life cycle of the society. For example, the role of the university in a young culture is to prepare clever individualists; the university's role in a mature society may be to produce good processes or good solutions in the sense that they integrate most persons' needs and most problem components as well as take into account the problem's history. My recent book with Lynn Johnson (Sinnott & Johnson, 1996) discusses how the university as an institution might reinvent itself, given all these factors.

In this chapter, I will focus on the ways in which postformal thought interacts with the *mature* creative process. I will also focus on the creative products of postformal thinkers.

LINKS BETWEEN POSTFORMAL THOUGHT AND CREATIVITY

Postformal thought is linked to creativity because it describes the process by which mature adults think creatively in logical domains.

Postformal thought also is linked to creative production by virtue of its production of *multiple views of reality* and its *multiple solutions, definitions, parameters, and methods* during problem solving. It is also linked to creativity in that it changes creative products from solely intellectual or solely emotional ones to products that combine subjective and objective understanding. Rathunde (1995) observes the same sorts of processes under the rubrics of wisdom, abiding interests, and self-regulation. Postformal creative production occurs in an experiential context that has a historical perspective, and with awareness of social consequences. We have seen in earlier chapters (and will see in later ones) how adults can express this postformal creativity in a number of content domains, for example, family life. Increased creativity of this sort can thus be said to be one of the potential *positive* cognitive developments in the mature phase of the life span. Since it is the *process* that is inherently creative in postformal thought, and the *process* that is productive, if a thinker has access to a postformal process, she or he has cognitive mechanisms that constitute a form of creativity. Whether the product of that process is generally considered valuable seems less important than that the knower has the means to generate more products until a valuable one is created. Postformal understanding itself tells us that both "reality" and "quality" are socially constructed realities that demand choice of one of the many solutions produced and at least temporary psychological commitment in ongoing time to that single reality.

Yet productivity alone is not enough for postformal creativity, since making a lot of something, even ideas, may not include the essential acts of postformal thinking, namely: (1) ordering logically disparate formal reality systems and (2) being self-referential. To be postformally creative, one would need to make many systems, and then be able to select one as "true," knowing that this choice is somewhat arbitrary and made in reference to one's chosen view of the world. Postformal creativity, then, may be likened to creating many romantic possibilities or relational systems by dating many persons and even falling in love with more than one, then consciously choosing to make a commitment to one person.

The developmental demand for organism adaptivity fuels this process. Being able to create multiple formal systems or views of reality seems adaptive because, with proliferating systems, the odds of finding the most useful one increase. This ability is adaptive, however, only if the thinker ultimately makes a contexted choice among solutions that are less than perfect, then goes on to do something in an interpersonal world. Production and choice are parts of the creative act, as is the "passionate commitment" that involves the heart and emotions. Even in logical creativity, intellectualization is not sufficient. And why should it be when developmental issues of adulthood are probably what prod the thinker to consider the shifting nature of socially constructed reality in everyday events?

Some 20 years of studies have related adults' practical creativity to their complex postformal thought and have described creative processes developed as part of postformal thought itself. The major results of my own research and scholarship as it relates to creativity are summarized in Table 18.1. Under each of the citations are listed a main finding or idea about creativity that can be found in the work or works cited, a description of a possible adaptive mechanism for regulation of adult life stimulation, one future study that would be useful, and one application of the findings. Data gathered from study of postformal operations (some described in earlier chapters) are consistent with the idea that creative processes and creative products are hallmarks of postformal thought.

REGULATION OF STIMULATION
OVERLOAD: NURTURING THE
UNFRAGMENTED SELF

Regulation

At each stage of life, the organism is confronted with multiple demands that must be met to sustain life. It is also confronted with demands specific to growth during its particular stage of life. For example, a 2-year-old child or any human adult must meet the demands of the body for food, drink, rest, and an emotional bond with another person. The 2-year-old also feels specific developmental-stage-related psychological and social demands for greater personal control and autonomy. Creativity at age 2 may lead to production of numerous clever ways to get one's way and to bond by subtly pleasing others so that one stands the best chance of having one's needs met.

Teens, of course, still have these basic needs, but they also have some stage-related needs that are different from those of the 2-year-old. The teen must construct a logic of his or her physical demands, school or work life, and love life to make sense of strong impulses and feelings. This logic must be consistent internally for the life to "work" and the teen to progress on into adulthood. The creative production of a consistent logic, that is, formal operations, is needed.

The mature adult is faced with similar demands for food, drink, and bonds with others, and is also faced with some additional stage-

Table 18.1. Summary of Theory and Data on Postformal Creativity from Sinnott's Main Studies: Proposed Mechanisms of Stimulation Regulation with Suggested Studies and Applications

One main point/finding	One possible mechanism for the organism's regulation of midlife/aging stimulation	One future study needed	One application
		Source: Sinnott (1984a,b)	
1a. Experimental study: Mature respondents give more than one paradigm for solving logical problems.	1a. Adaptive shifts in logics process more stimuli at low cost in energy.	1a. How is this developed?	1a. Teach this mechanism as a means of controlling stress.
1b. Content analysis: Two-person dialogues demonstrate that speakers influence each other's cognitive development and make it more creative.	1b. Coconstruction of reality leads to more adaptive consensual reality.	1b. Do speakers in dialogue *always* stimulate each other toward cognitive *growth?*	1b. Use dialogue in tactical ways during peace negotiations to lead to positive developments.
1c. Experimental study: Experience of respondents and social content in problems lead to more creative solutions.	1c. Interpersonal experiences lead to creative ways of processing reality that reduce over-stimulation.	1c. Is it experience or some other factor that releases creative cognition?	1c. Research how universities can promote creative cognition in their students.
1d. Experimental study: Postformal operations showing creative production of multiple solutions and a prioris were shown by about a third of the respondents, on average, and sometimes as	1d. Creativity is *commonly* expressed in a problem-solving context post-formally in mature adults.	1d. Does creative problem solving depend on other thinkers being present?	1d. Test whether corporations or nations can set up optimal groups for problem solving.

(continued)

Table 18.1. (*Continued*)

One main point/finding	One possible mechanism for the organism's regulation of midlife/aging stimulation	One future study needed	One application
high as 75% for interpersonal problems.			
1e. Content analysis: Group development is more creative and flexible when groups contain postformal participants.	1e. Multiperson co-constructed reality affects group dynamics so that groups handle complexity and stress better.	1e. What is the "natural history" of group cognitive dynamics, given that so many persons *can* think so creatively?	1e. Consider the setup of a classroom that would be needed to bring about creative group learning.

Source: Sinnott (1984a,b)

2. A synthetic model can be made for describing adults creatively co-constructing reality.	2. Postformal thought seems to describe this way to handle complex interpersonal experience.	2. Does postformal thought provide a model for studying the connection of complex, creative cognition and interpersonal/emotional factors? Where are the data?	2. Consider the emotional elements/roadblocks to learning and personal change.

Source: Cavanaugh et al. (1985)

3a. Experimental study: Mature adult creative postformal thought is reliably present.	3a. It is adaptive in some way for mature adults to think in a creative postformal way.	3a. Are there any conditions under which adults will *not* reliably produce this thought? If so, what are they?	3a. Optimal structures of think tanks, retreat centers, workshops, design of human resources materials.

Source: Sinnott (1987, 1989a, 1991a)

Table 18.1. (*Continued*)

One main point/finding	One possible mechanism for the organism's regulation of midlife/aging stimulation	One future study needed	One application
		Source: Sinnott (1987, 1989a, 1991a)	
3b. Correlational study: Health variables, such as blood pressure, do not seem to influence the presence of creative postformal thought.	3b. The use of creative postformal thought is a "durable" ability, a core skill, rather than a cognitive process used only when energy is over abundant.	3b. Does acute illness influence use of this creative thought?	3b. Compensatory training that would give patients these "survival skills."
3c. Correlational study: Memory and verbal ability are related to postformal creative problem solving.	3c. Creative postformal thought is part of an integrated package of adaptive cognitive skills.	3c. If memory changes over time, will postformal creative thought change?	3c. Remediation and training after head injury with memory loss.
3d. Model: Goal clarity and heuristic availability would seem to be related to postformal thought.	3d. Complex situations would be a prime occasion for use of creative postformal thought.	3d. Does manipulation of goal clarity in a real-life setting influence use of creative postformal thought? How?	3d. Improving economic forecasting, medical diagnosis.
3e. Correlational study: Older respondents produce general-creative-process-type answers to problems, though younger adults provide a larger sheer number of solutions.	3e. Process answers reduce overstimulation due to losses with advancing age.	3e. If older respondents are pressured to give *specific* answers, do they still prefer process answers?	3e. Teach different age groups in different ways.

(continued)

Table 18.1. (*Continued*)

One main point/finding	One possible mechanism for the organism's regulation of midlife/aging stimulation	One future study needed	One application
	Source: Sinnott (1987, 1989a, 1991a)		
3f. Experimentally manipulating emotion, mind wandering, and demand for production caused interpersonal logical problem-solving differences. Positive emotion led to greater productivity. Instruction to mind wander led to more postformal thought.	3f. Creative postformal thought is a synthesis of emotion and cognition in service to organism goals.	3f. Can induction of negative emotion ("depression") lead to lessened creative postformal thought?	3f. Adding emotional components to assist cognitive psychotherapy.
3g. Experimental study: Probes exploring set responses led to greater productivity and more creative postformal thought.	3g. Respondents limit overstimulation by deciding how much creativity to show.	3g. What criteria do respondents of various ages use to censor their responses?	3g. Obtaining better evidence from witnesses.
3h. Descriptive study: As many as 75% of respondents incorporated emotion or mind wandering into their creative problem-solving processes.	3h. Postformal creative thought is a synthesis of emotion and cognition in service to the organism's goals.	3h. Chart a descriptive taxonomy of noncognitive processes useful to cognition, especially postformal creative cognition.	3h. Adding more noncognitive elements to high-tech and high-stress workplaces.

Table 18.1. (*Continued*)

One main point/finding	One possible mechanism for the organism's regulation of midlife/aging stimulation	One future study needed	One application
		Source: Sinnott (1987, 1989a, 1991a)	
3i. Models: Individuals' models of creative, logical problem solving can be created and can demonstrate the points in the problem-solving process in which creative postformal thought has an impact on creative process or productivity or both.	3i. Individuals use their adaptive mechanisms at individual-specific points in their thinking processes.	3i. Can individuals' models form the basis of an artificial intelligence (AI) model of creative postformal thought?	3i. Create an interactive computer video game: Artificial Creator.
3j. Experimental study: Given a solver's creative or noncreative postformal or nonpostformal processing style, predictions can be made about the solver's errors and processes on later problems. There are age-related styles.	3j. Individuals show individual-specific patterns of weaknesses and strengths in this area.	3j. Can AI models be created for average performance of different age cohorts?	3j. Create user-friendly "watching myself get older" packages so individuals could explore predictable changes in their creative processes, if *they* change.

(*continued*)

Table 18.1. (*Continued*)

One main point/finding	One possible mechanism for the organism's regulation of midlife/aging stimulation	One future study needed	One application
	Source: Sinnott (1991c)		
4. Single-case experiment— Model: Postformal creativity can be seen in a mature adult's adaptive solution of a family mental health problem.	4. Creative postformal thought can bring order to crisis situations.	4. How do the cognitive levels of family members play into the genesis of the individual's problem?	4. Train clinicians and troubled families to deal with crises in this creative way.
	Source: D. R. B. Rogers et al. (1991)		
5. Experimental study: Married couples demonstrated more creative postformal thought when working together on problems if the couple was well-adjusted as a couple.	5. Creative postformal thought is adaptive in couples' interactions.	5. What *nonverbal* data correlate with creative postformal couple problem solving or with the lack of it? Does the couple's process influence their family's process?	5. Marital therapy.
	Source: Sinnott (1992, in press-a)		
6. Model: Creative postformal thought can be useful in the classroom.	6. Creative postformal thought can assist communication to prevent student overload.	6. Does teacher personality correlate with these skills?	6. Compare classroom outcomes for teachers with and without these skills.

Table 18.1. (*Continued*)

One main point/finding	One future study needed	One application
	One possible mechanism for the organism's regulation of midlife/aging stimulation	
Source: Sinnott (1992, 1993c)		
7. Model: Creative postformal thought can be used in the workplace for personal and group development during intragroup conflicts.	7. Does the social initial level of functioning influence the growth potential of the group member trying to be creative during this conflict?	7. Incorporate postformal training into spiritual practices.
Source: Sinnott (1995)		
8. A computerized version of the creative, postformal problem-solving test can be devised and used in place of other means, such as interviews.	8. Test the computerized version against paper-and-pencil and interview forms.	8. Predict weaknesses so individuals can get remediation for their complex cognitive lack.

Note: In the table above, "7. These skills can be useful for group development and personal development by ordering conflict situations." and "8. Average performance and norms can be created for these adaptive skills." also appear in the middle column region.

specific demands. The new ones are generated by the broader social identity usually created in midlife—and any adult with a full life can describe how overwhelming these may be! Some sets of demands come from family (children and older parents), community, social institutions, and work; others come from the sheer number of tasks to perform, bills to pay, items of information to assimilate. For example, in the past four hours this morning, while I was working on this chapter, I also had the following demands:

1. Assimilate and respond to printed matter in a 6-inch pile of mail.
2. Figure out the legalities and ethics of cat ownership versus euthanasia for warring neighbors and relatives of an 89-year-old neighbor who died 2 weeks ago (which resulted in my suddenly adopting the cat under dispute, *this* morning . . .).
3. Negotiate the administration of a part of our university's latest problem-focused center, taking into account interdepartmental rivalries.
4. Work out the specifics of a job offer for our 14-year-old daughter.
5. Try to apply the details and implications of a recent "intellectual property" court case in light of our recent book on reinventing the university (Sinnott & Johnson, 1996) (a case in which an undergraduate was actually sentenced to a chain gang for stealing his own research notes from a funded project).

Whew! Some other adult individuals may struggle with complex needs to refocus a career, mentor new workers today (which means first getting to know each of them), decide how to keep the crack dealers off the block, and come to terms with a divorce.

The formal logic system for carrying out any one of these tasks may not be logically compatible with that for resolving another. Generating more systems may help, since this productivity may provide more adequate answers to life's dilemmas. But the ante has been raised by life; there are too many contradictory demand and information systems. At this point of overload, the logic of postformal operations may help solve the ill-structured problem of life. In a best-case scenario, the cognitive demands could lead to a higher-level restructuring of logical abilities through which the problem is more easily solved.

If cognitive resources diminish with aging as time goes by, additional subjective overload may be experienced even with unchanging objective levels of demands. Such overstimulation must be regulated if the system is to function effectively and the "I" who can cope is to

continue. Postformal thought has potential for allowing a creative con-
solidation of ideas and experience that, in turn, lets the aging person
cognitively process what is perceived as overload for a longer time
without system breakdown.

The Overloaded Self

A situation of overload exists when the knower cannot effectively
process the amount of information that presents itself. The self who
processes is in danger of being fragmented. Although postformal
thought gives the knower *more* to think about and therefore has the
potential to *cause* overload, postformal thought is a powerful tool for
reducing overload adaptively.

Of course, there are *mal*adaptive and *non*creative ways to reduce
overload. For example, overloaded adults may limit their cognitive
stimulation by limiting their experience to those situations in which
only one formal logical system, or only concrete operational logic,
needs to be considered. In other words, they might rigidly interpret all
cognitive events through the filter of their limited system. In the realm
of personality, such a person might deny various aspects of the self
because there are no cognitive resources available to deal with the
complexity. Farrell and Rosenberg (1981) discuss the negative effects
on midlife development of having such styles. In earlier chapters of
this book, we saw the negative effects of such a rigid style on interpersonal relations in a group (Chapter 4) and on couple, family, and
workplace relations (Chapters 12, 13, 15, and 16).

The overload dilemma might be resolved more creatively and
adaptively, though, through postformal thought. These complex operations provide an advantage over formal operations by permitting con-
solidation across those conflicting systems of logical realities so that
more complex meanings and interactions might be available to the
thinker. Consensus understandings and maximal use of large amounts
of information would be possible. Sides of the self could be acknowledged and synthesized.

Maturity probably brings understanding and acceptance of the necessary subjectivity of knowledge (one of the characteristics of postformal
thought), whether it is knowledge of people, of events, or of objects. This
acceptance makes it easier to tolerate others' beliefs and ways of life. If
the knower has postformal thought, she or he looks with an empathic
eye, rather than with annoyance, on the younger person's painful struggles to make the truth of the world or of people into absolute, unchanging truth. The knower can sympathize with less skilled individuals'

defense of what they hope is the "right" way of doing something; the knower remembers when she or he was formal operational and felt the same way. Postformal thought can maximize the availability of information and at the same time minimize social conflict.

Coping with Overstimulation

If postformal thought is not available, various means of coping with overstimulation and overload might be used. Sometimes these creative coping strategies are available at the cost of adaptivity. Since adult coping is so often found in the realm of interpersonal cognition, let us look at examples of coping strategies in that domain. For example, consider a middle-aged adult with a family, a career, civic responsibilities, and a social life. This person is faced with endless demands to "fit" the data of this social world by choosing a viable formal operational system for interacting with each individual at an appropriate level. If this adult makes these choices and solves these interpersonal problems, he or she will not do so by means of formal operations alone. Postformal operations will provide the best possible match because postformal creative processes will provide the largest number of inclusive, real-life problem-solving possibilities for this ill-structured "fuzzy set" problem.

Here are some possible *un*creative, *non*-postformal solutions to overload in interpersonal midlife contexts:

1. The adult may reduce stimulation by limiting the self and retreating cognitively, perceiving all interpersonal relations at a lower level of cognitive or emotional complexity. Instead of "receiving" the behavior of others as the others have "sent" it, or trying to receive it at a higher and more integrated level, the adult might *interpret the behavior at a lower level,* that is, in a more simplistic way. For example, instead of trying to understand the relations that are possible with a certain individual, the adult may resort to dealing with him or her *only* as a member of a racial group because this limit lets him or her preserve the self.

2. The adult may reduce overload by *developing a rigid social identity* that permits only certain messages to be received. If, in such a case, the adult has a self-definition capable of only certain relations with others, other relational stimuli are ignored. All problems are oversimplified.

3. The adult can reduce overload by *focusing on only selected goals or interests,* again limiting the self. The effect of this tactic is similar to the effect of the second tactic. All levels of complexity are available to be used in analyzing an event, but the individual limits the types of content considered.

In contrast, here are some possible creative, adaptive solutions to overload and "self"-preservation that make use of postformal cognition.

1. The adult may reduce overload by understanding the *many* possible logical structures that can underlie a perceived interaction. This is an adaptive strategy that can come only from experience and familiarity with many types of systems and possession of postformal thought, which holds all logics as possible simultaneously. If the receiver can *match the message received by filtering it through the complex self) to the encoded level of the transmitted message,* conflict can be reduced. The key to this ability is to access a good system of transformations to relate the sets of coordinates using postformal operations.
2. The adult may reduce stimulus overload by making a *more efficient total integration,* again using the self as a *complex* filter. Developing the integrative skill is an adaptive solution to overload. It makes use of complex theorizing that is based on experience. No content or complexity is lost when this technique is used. The mapping surface is so large and the topography so varied that most messages fit in somewhere, through use of postformal thought. In the storage closet of the mind, overload clutter that has an interpretive place is no longer really "overload." Defined in relation to the fuller self, it has a meaningful place.

CREATING THE SELF

Creativity literature does not address one of the most difficult creative acts of all, that of creating the sense of who I am, the sense of myself. Clinical psychologists, developmentalists, and personality theorists seem to enjoy this existential topic more; it appears again in the next chapter of this book, which deals with psychopathology and psychotherapy. From a cognitive perspective, and especially from a postformal perspective, a concept of the self is created only gradually, as a unique configuration, by an individual in the context of his or her unique life events and biology. This act of creation may be the most complex and far-reaching creative experience any adult can perform, and it takes a lifetime. Integrity, Erikson wrote, is the culmination of that creation in the final-stage challenge of life. The creativity involved in this existential act is the kind that all adults must undertake (though with various degrees of skill) and the kind that demands complex cognition of a self-reflective sort to tie it neatly together as an integrated and *known* whole.

The postmodern industrial world demands that we create this entity called the self in part by responding to the demands of the many people who constitute our constituencies and who want us to "be" in a certain way (Gergen, 1991). But citizens of the nonindustrial world and humans with simpler philosophies at earlier points in history did not face that task of creating the self. In a tribal society, for example, my "self" is equivalent to the role I play in my social group; who I am is what I do, in relation to others. In any society with few choices and many rules, the self is less "created" and more "grown into" or "accepted." As one matures in such a society, one matures into a role (and therefore into a self) that is "given." That "given" may rest in part on one's biology, too, since social roles are often gender- and age-linked.

In the postmodern society, in contrast, choice is the blessing and the curse. We are not automatically granted roles or selves. Perhaps the closest we come to having "given" roles is the role of mother—one that some girls and women do use as a fallback position when they feel confused about their identity. While we are less likely to be trapped by roles, we are more likely to feel roleless, adrift, or disconnected, with a self that is undefined. That self is free, but that self is alone unless it chooses to define itself as existing in relation to others.

We can see that there is a continuum from socially and biologically given self to chosen self. For example, examine the gender-role-related selves inhabited by men and women in our own society over the last 50 years. Some of the creation of complexity of the masculine and feminine self has been considered an act of personal growth—for example, one involving the balancing of the *animus* and the *anima* (Jung, 1930/1971). Some of it has been a product of social forces and increasing social change. For example, industrialization freed males from rigid biological and social role selves earlier in history than it freed females. It continued to label certain traits such as aggression and compulsive sexuality as biologically necessary to the male self, but slowly eliminated parts of the male self that connected individuals to others. Females were not supposed to be totally free of biology, either, and they retained notions of self that had multiple connections to others. At one extreme of the currently acceptable masculine selves, then, might be a self who chooses to follow his lone ambitions with no obligation to family, company, or society. Even at an extreme of the currently acceptable feminine selves, however, the female is still expected to choose a self who is caring and connected, whatever other qualities she chooses.

The lenses through which an individual views the possibilities of self-creation, in gender-role-stereotypic terms, make a tremendous difference in the roles that individuals can enact and in the role studies that can be done by researchers (Bem, 1993; Sinnott, 1997). There is no single "right" lens; only the use of all of them gives a full picture. If the lenses are not interdisciplinary and complex, they cannot avoid the biological or societal or anthropocentric or heterocentric biases of simpler current gender-role-stereotype possibilities. To be complete, the lenses also must include a "view from the top," so to speak, a view that includes the point in development at which the person finds himself or herself. For example, if we study the gender roles of mature women, we must take into account the fact that mature women, because they are in the mature period of their lives, seek self-transcendence and communal, generative ties as part of all their roles. (Sinnott [1997] discusses the characteristics of current developmental life-span models, their biases, and how they might be expanded to include some of these lenses.)

Postformal thought could be an immense asset to a person's development of a concept of a complex, mature self. All the operations of postformal thought can be useful in changing the lenses through which one sees the self. The pitfall of viewing self as only one set of traits, unchanging, is avoided if the knower is postformal. The self also changes from a concrete, fixed set of polarized traits to a core set of qualities that shift their porous boundaries as needed. Eventually, the self is known as a predictable pattern of relations that can emerge only in *some context* and at *some point in history* (analogous to genetic factors, which can become meaningful only in *some environment*). This is the "postformal self" that can thrive in postmodern culture. As suggested in Chapter 14, the best analogy might be the chameleon, which is identifiable (does not lose its self), but is responsive to the context it is in.

ONE ASPECT OF SELF: SEX/GENDER ROLES AND POSTFORMAL THOUGHT

Over the course of my scholarly and research career, I have been fascinated by one type of role that has had a huge impact on my own life and on the lives of other women: sex roles. Sex roles will be defined here as stereotypically feminine and masculine behavior patterns. My career has taken place in a time of tremendous social change throughout the world, much of it related in some way to those roles. Even my study of middle-aged and older adults becomes a study of *women* as they age (since women survive longer than men), and much of women's behavior is influenced by sex roles and sex-role-stereotypical expectations. I have personally pushed the edges of my own sex role. First, I was married with children and a serious career when that combination was less common; then I made a second commitment to a life partner, this time to a woman, and am raising two children with her while continuing the career. So it seems that my interests, choices, and the social forces around me keep leading me back to the study of sex roles.

My study of sex roles has resulted in grants and publications over the years. My special focus has been on sex role complexity and the cognitive and other processes that underlie it (D. R. B. Rogers et al., 1991; Sinnott, 1977, 1981, 1982, 1984, 1985, 1986, 1987, 1989a,b, 1993b, 1997; Sinnott et al., 1980; Sinnott, Rogers, & Spencer, 1996; Windle & Sinnott, 1985).

Sex roles are defined as stereotypical behavior patterns identified by a culture with the label *female* or *male.* This means that sex roles are *not* the same thing as biological sex based on genes or genitals, sexual identity/preference, sexual behavior/sexuality, or the *actual* behavior of males and females (although in a given culture there is usually some similarity between roles and behaviors). The preponderance of evidence suggests that sex roles are most often created by a culture, although they may at some point in human history have some link (though perhaps a rather far-fetched one) with a biological factor.

In earlier times, sex roles were thought to be necessarily connected to biological factors and to be developed early in life as permanent characteristics of a healthy personality. Now we see that sex roles are connected with sex role identity, which is a cognitive concept created by the individual with the help of social feedback. We now know that sex roles are not necessarily laws of nature, and not necessarily healthy for the individual. Individuals' concepts of their sex roles vary in complexity, just as cognitive ability varies in complexity from person to person. Sex roles vary developmentally, too, in line with cognition. The infant has no idea of its sex role; the concrete operational child sees polarized roles of "masculinity" as distinct from "femininity"; the adolescent sees behaviors as flowing with formal logical necessity from accepted roles. The more mature adult might become androgynous (i.e., have access to the behaviors that belong to both femininity and masculinity), might display role reversal (Gutmann, 1964), or might even transcend sex roles altogether, seeing a behavioral opportunity at some higher level of cognitive conceptualization where sex roles no longer matter (Hefner, Rebecca, & Oleshansky, 1975).

What have all these considerations to do with postformal thought? It seems from these theoretical and empirical studies that complex thinking helps an individual work out complex sex roles. To create the androgynous or role-transcendent self requires the ability to coordinate logical systems of masculinity and femininity so that the most adaptive response for a given occasion might be chosen. If this is done consciously, postformal thought is a logical tool for the job.

Role conflicts may be seen as attempts to solve ill-structured problems. Consider this scenario illustrating a postformal complex sex role concept response made by one of the respondents in my studies: A 40-year-old woman who has lost her husband to cancer some months earlier is becoming aware that her house needs painting. Her husband used to be the one to do this. She knows from her childhood training and her neighbors' behavior when she mentions painting the house that her doing the job herself would not be considered feminine. She does recall that during the Depression and during World War II, her mother did such things for the sake of the family or the war effort, and she considered her mother feminine. She knows that the money she might pay someone to paint the house would be better spent for her more immediate needs and those of her children. She dislikes the idea of undertaking such a big job, but she would also enjoy working outside with her hands, for a change. If she paints the house, will she be too "masculine"? Should she do the job? Is her identity confused or slipping away?

Thinking about this scenario, we notice that the woman, her late husband, the woman's family of origin, and the neighbors all agree at some level that painting a house fits into a "masculine" sex role, but she and her mother sometimes seem to define such a job as "feminine," if the job is done for the sake of others. Thinking of her own needs and likes, and the needs of her children, she seems to want to act in both agentic, "masculine," ways and in communal, "feminine," ways.

She decides that if she is ever to resolve the situation, she must step back from it, *choose* a behavior on the basis of one of the logical systems of thinking about housepainting and roles, call it acceptably feminine in terms of her own self-image, and act. She must make a self-referential choice of the truth of her femininity. She must face the fact that this knowledge of what is feminine is partly a subjective choice of truth systems about femininity. She then chooses to know in a certain way and lets it influence her subsequent self-image and behavior. In other words, she uses postformal thought.

Thinking about the scenario in problem-solving terms, the woman seems to have had a clear subgoal (getting the house painted), but a fuzzy larger goal (keeping a coherent self-image). She therefore jumped out of the system to a higher level of decision making at which the main goal is to do something. That meant dealing with the potential relativity of the self-image by making a decision as to what is feminine for her, in relation to this situation and in view of her past history. The next step was to jump back into the problem-solving system and decide that she would still be feminine in this situation if she painted the house, since doing so would also be nurturing behavior and would feel a little like engaging in a hobby. She tested the workability of this solution on several neighbors and one of her children, and they did not respond in a way that threatened her self-image. Pleased with the results, she filed the process away as a good one to be used again.

Thinking about the scenario in terms of the evolution of society, decisions such as that of this woman, multiplied over many individuals and occasions, could change the nature of concepts of femininity and masculinity. Simple awareness that sex roles are relative would also have that effect. As we will see in the next chapter, using postformal thought can also change the human experience! The current phenomena of social change involving considerations of equity between the sexes attest to the fact that when individuals are aware that roles are not fixed to one truth system, they permit themselves role flexibility and become aware of the relative nature of other social rules. The use of postformal thinking can help individuals resolve their own role-related dilemmas and get that house painted; it can also help society rise above limited, crippling thinking about role-related issues. Yet the "self" of the individual or the society can be creatively enlarged without its losing its "self." This is a high-level form of creation!

In Chapter 19, we will explore more of the ways that postformal awareness can be part of a healing experience for the individual, the international community, and the planet. Psychotherapists have a special need to think postformally, as do negotiators or conflict resolution specialists. Being an ecological healer also seems to take some postformal skills.

Healing Minds, Bodies, Nations, and the Planet
The Value of Postformal Thought

Body is the outward manifestation of the mind.
CANDACE PERT

The truly reliable path to peace and creative cooperation must be rooted in self-transcendence.
VACLAV HAVEL

Whatever befalls the earth befalls the sons and daughters of the earth. We did not weave the web of life, we are merely a strand in it. Whatever we do to the web we do to ourselves.
CHIEF SEATTLE

Healers are those who can bind broken things together and make things whole again. Those who heal minds or bodies or nations arrive at their task with an extremely important asset. They have a larger vision of the *un*broken mind or body or nation in its state of wholeness, that "good" state that will obtain after the healing takes place. The psychotherapist, the medical diagnostician, the conflict resolution mediator, the peacemaker in the Middle East, the man or woman working toward *sustainable* ecological improvements must all envision a final outcome that brings together the different realities of the warring sides of the self, or of nations, or of differing resource needs in the global community. Without a way to imagine the fragmented realities together in some larger plan, no healing can take place. On a cognitive level, those realities seem to be bridged by means of postformal thought.

In this chapter, I will discuss how postformal thought is helpful to a healer and underlies our understanding of complex healing processes. We will speak of four types of healing: *psychological* healing, as in psychotherapy; healing of *conflicts,* that is, creating peace, between persons or nations; healing of the earth, as in concerns with *ecology and environment;* and healing the *body,* as in medicine, especially mind–body and complementary medicine. I will also suggest that postformal thought is useful for, and must be nurtured in, any client seeking *conscious* healing, or growth, or awareness of his or her own paradigm shift toward wellness (also see Chapter 20). These ideas about healing are grouped together in this way because these processes that look so different at first really share the same underpinnings and appear to mutually influence each other. New fields such as ecopsychology are developing to address these mutual influences.

Today, as I was preparing to work on this chapter, my glance came to rest on an article in the *Washington Post,* an article noting that Thomas Kuhn had died. Kuhn coined the now-popular phrases *new paradigm* and *paradigm shift,* and described such events in his book about the structure of scientific revolutions (T. Kuhn, 1962). His words "paradigm shift" and "revolution" are appropriate to describe what happens when we consciously move from a "diseased" (or less adaptive) to a healthy (or more adaptive) way of life. When Dean Ornish (1982) convinces heart patients to consciously and drastically change their lifestyles, emotions, and attitudes, or when Jon Kabat-Zinn (1990) gets patients suffering from stress or pain to consciously change the way they conceptualize those challenges, Ornish and Kabat-Zinn are nurturing such a paradigm shift. Those using imagery (e.g., Epstein, 1989; 1994) or Chinese medicine (e.g., Hammer, 1990) as healing systems demand even greater shifts in consciousness in service to the client's assuming control over her or his own health. The postformal thinker has the tools to use these new paradigms of holistic wellness.

But the postformal thinker is not immune to the personal conflicts of thought or emotion that psychologists call *psychopathology.* When psychopathology occurs in the behavior of a complex thinker, it takes on the special nuances, the coloration of postformal thought. Healing the psychopathology of the postformal client may take skills over and above those needed to heal, for example, the concrete operational client.

Postformal operations in the healer may be more useful for the treatment of certain psychological disorders than for the treatment of others if those certain disorders are dysfunctions of postformal thought itself. For example, a client with a multiple personality disorder, having the serious problem of integrating across the several logical systems of the various personalities, especially needs a therapist who can share those multiple realities at least during a session of psychotherapy. Since that complex-thinking therapist can "go home" again to an integrated reality, such a therapist can help that client select and make a commitment to one personality that can organize and integrate the others.

In this chapter, we will first explore the area of individual psychopathology by considering the nature of postformal psychopathology and the skills of the postformal psychotherapist. Then we will give some thought to conflict resolution and peacemaking, healing relations between individuals and nations. We will consider what this theory can bring to the understanding of how we can help heal the Earth by conceptualizing it in multiple ways. Finally, we will look at some ways in which new wellness approaches make use of postformal thought.

POSTFORMAL PSYCHOPATHOLOGY AND THE POSTFORMAL PSYCHOTHERAPIST

Postformal Psychopathology

One day at the university, I was speaking enthusiastically about how postformal thought is helpful to individuals' adaptation. A colleague of mine stopped me short with an unexpected question: Since the *mis*use and *over*use and distortion of any human skill causes problems, what are the problems connected with misuse or overuse or distortion of postformal thinking abilities? This question sent me back to ruminating about the clients I had worked with, all of whom suffered from psychological problems, but some of whom seemed to be postformal thinkers.

My usual practice was to focus on the thinking skills that a client needed to develop, not those he or she had already developed (in this case, postformal thinking skills). Of course, it was true that individuals' maladaptive ways of being usually were shaped by personality or cognitive patterns they already had and individual experiences they had survived. So it would make sense that being postformal would lend a certain quality to the defense mechanisms and problems of the client.

Thinking about individuals who had come to my office for therapy, and concentrating on the postformal ones (as determined by my judgment rather than by a test of any kind), I started to notice characteristics that might set them apart from non-postformal clients. Some key summary observations are presented here. In every case, the basic problem is that the postformal skill is overworked, used for the wrong purpose, not used when it should be used, or used "incompletely" (i.e., without any *commitment* to one of the realities). The intellectual skill misused this way then leads to behaviors that are maladaptive for the client personally or for the social groups to which the client belongs. For example, Chapter 16 and earlier chapters outline some of the ways such maladaptive thinking and behavior have an impact on intimate couples, families, and the workplace.

With respect to postformal thought, the first characteristic of pathological states that I noticed about my postformal clients in particular was overuse: These clients are much more facile at slipping among logics and belief systems, sometimes too facile for their own good or for the good of others with whom they interact. They can use reality shifts as a defense mechanism much more adroitly than the usual client. The postformal thinking that serves to handle overstimulation for the healthy person (see Chapter 18) serves instead to neutralize any outsiders' attempts to reframe reality more realistically for this troubled person. The personality-disordered clients who are sociopaths, who make such facile shifts of logic to change personalities in a chameleon-like way for their own purposes, have too fine a time shifting logics about their own self to be troubled by ethical, emotional, or consistency concerns. The individuals who intellectualize more than is useful have a hard time "getting out of their heads" because they enjoy postformal skills so much!

A second characteristic that is noticeable in clients who are *nearly* postformal, but not quite there yet, is their anxiety and depression when trapped in what they see as a world that to them is *overwhelmingly* relativistic. If they have not yet made the further leap to realization that one must become *committed* to a choice of truth and then live out that truth, they seem to remain stuck in a place where everything, even our therapeutic work together and their own sense of self, can be only relative. This trap usually is associated with some degree of existential despair and arbitrary feelings about relationships that would otherwise be important (emotionally salient) to the client.

The most extreme degree of a possibly postformal pathology can be seen, I believe, in the multiple-personality client. In such a person, the truth systems of the very concept of the self are shifted frequently,

Table 19.1. Ten Characteristics of Postformal Thinking, with Clinical Applications

1. Acceptance that there is more than one logical, valid understanding of events allows therapists to:
   * Shift between their own and their clients' realities and ways of knowing.
   * Work under conditions under which several realities must be balanced at once.
   * Be aware of more possibilities for clients' realities, with appropriate tools for reaching each.
2. Knowledge that contradictions, subjectivity, and choice are inherent in all observations, even logical, "objective" observations, permits therapists to:
   * See their role in creating the "reality" of the therapeutic situation.
   * Function under conditions under which there are clear limits to their objectivity and logic, and where they may influence what they are trying to observe.
   * Make a choice among logical tools used to study, understand, and influence a therapeutic situation.
3. Commitment to one of many possible sets of beliefs allows therapists to:
   * Develop priorities and make choices.
   * Be flexible enough to access many realities without being paralyzed by complexity.
4. Taking into account that contradictory multiple causes and solutions may be equally correct in real life (within certain limits) enables therapists to:
   * Function under conditions under which there is no absolute truth or reality.
   * Be open to changes in paradigms and examine the usefulness of new paradigms.
   * Be aware of the limitations of linear explanations in multicausal situations.
5. Recognition that an outcome state is inseparable from the process leading to that state lets therapists:
   * Focus more readily on change over time.
   * Understand that self and relationships are always in process and cannot be defined in a stable way until they end.
   * Use therapeutic techniques to encourage growth processes, rather than seek certain end states.
6. Awareness that the same manipulation of the same variable can have different effects due to changing contexts helps therapists:
   * Avoid burnout.
   * Moderate anxiety under conditions under which the "same" intervention never works twice in the same way.
7. Since postformal thinking, like any other cognitive mode, can be used in service of health or pathology, postformal therapists are aware that:
   * Any of the tools described above can be used as a defense against growth.
   * The client may be cognitively advanced, but still be in need of help from the therapist.

Source: Armstrong and Sinnott (1991).

but no one system is ever chosen in any permanent way. This kind of distortion can influence the non-multiple-personality postformal client in the same way, but to a lesser degree. Even though the general plight of the multiple-personality-disorder client may have come about through dissociation because of childhood abuse, the therapist's facilitating a postformal way of *intellectually* organizing knowledge of the formal systems of the self sometimes frees this patient to move forward and unite as one potential personality.

Helping these clients with problems in the development or use of postformal thought involves refining their postformal skills. The skills can then be used in the particular life area at issue.

The Postformal Psychotherapist

Possessing the intellectual operations of postformal thought can be of help to the psychotherapist. Table 19.1 is taken from a handout I prepared in collaboration with my colleague Judith Armstrong. It outlines seven characteristics of postformal thinking operations that are useful in the conduct of psychotherapy. As the table indicates, each aspect of postformal operations gives the clinician a tool that potentially changes interventions. Teaching postformal thinking to therapists in training is part of what a good doctoral program does. Interviews (as yet unpublished) with expert clinicians and with clinicians in training over the course of training suggest that improvement in postformal skills is part of what helps make an expert in this field. Recall for a moment the many levels of logical reality displayed in Milton Erikson's wonderful stories! Being a *postformal*-thinking psychotherapist obviously is helpful for addressing the types of problems discussed in the preceding section, problems that included adaptation-related complications of postformal thinking itself.

CONFLICT RESOLUTION
AND WORKING FOR PEACE

Conflict resolution and mediation are the art and science devoted to helping two sides to a dispute reach an agreement such that both feel understood and feel that they have won on the important aspects of the agreement. To achieve such a result, the mediator and the two sides must all be able to identify overarching considerations and values that the two sides share, understand, or accept. They then can make a commitment to some solution that is "true" or "correct" for them both. This basic pattern of events happens whether the warring factions are persons, groups, nations, or others.

Often, the only way warring factions can begin to reach an agreement is by taking the argument to a higher level of complexity. For example, in a small and mundane disagreement area, two intimate partners may be arguing over which movie to see in the evening. As the argument continues, more elements of their life together are brought into the picture, and they move even further from a resolution of the "which movie" question. Time passes. Eventually, they both notice that the evening is growing shorter. Soon they will have missed both movies. A more important concern on which they find themselves agreeing is that they have lately been spending too much of their time together arguing and that they don't like that way of life. The "which movie" debate is quickly settled by flipping a coin to avoid missing both movies (a higher-level concern). The debate is also settled by an agreement to begin discussing their ongoing tendency to argue (an overarching, higher-level concern), which has begun to worry them both. At the higher level of complexity, the initial impasse is resolved.

Moving to that higher level of complexity seems to require post-formal skills. The two competing formal logics are subsumed under a logic that involves elements of necessary subjectivity and a commitment to a chosen truth-of-the-situation.

A good conflict resolution resource person or a good mediator is able to facilitate this movement to that higher level of motives on which there can be agreement. Many of the guidelines for mediators involve the steps that make the movement to the chosen higher-level logical system more likely. For example, the negotiator or mediator listens uncritically to each individual giving her or his side of the story. Each one's logic is appreciated. This tactic serves to inform the mediator and to defuse the warring parties. At a higher level, however, it moves the conflict from a bad feeling state to a state of "being understood better"—a feeling that each party (if each is a reasonably well-adjusted human being) wishes to perpetuate. Moving to a higher-level (emotional) logic sets the stage for locating, among the issues cognitively associated with those happier feelings, some goal that the parties can agree they want to pursue. Bastick (1982) provides a good discussion of emotional associations used to shift idea states. Such goals are often hidden from the parties' awareness when emotions connected with the argument keep them in a negative state. United at the point of this chosen logic, the parties can then take steps to come to an agreement that satisfies both in terms of the higher-level goal.

The good conflict resolution facilitator is taught to avoid trying to solve the problem for the individuals who are at odds, even if the mediator has a better idea than the individuals are able to think of by themselves. This tactic makes sense from the "listening" point of view. It makes even better sense from the point of view that individuals cannot use their own postformal thought to rise above their formal logical systems if they are operating with the systems or the emotional states of the mediator rather than their own. In a similar vein, if the mediating session is conducted correctly, the room setup and the amount of time the mediator spends speaking with each participant facilitate the participants' being on an equal footing in their logics and emotional states so that the jointly generated overarching logical solution has equivalent weight for both. No one is judged.

Such an approach is obviously not the one taken in the usual alternative to conflict resolution, the courtroom, where actions are evaluated and labeled and conflict resolution in a true sense does not occur. It is not surprising, then, that no one thinks himself or herself to have really "won" in court! While appellate courts may be an exception, courts in general run on a formal operational model in which there is only one winning logic—that of the law. Appellate courts attempt to assume postformal logical resolution of conflicting truth and value systems. But then they deny that they ever did so, presenting findings as though they were the "real" law (the *correct* formal logic) all the time. King Solomon remains an eloquent exception.

International negotiations have a similar logic. They can be seen as conflict resolution resting upon a cognitive basis of postformal thought. Warring individuals in the example above can be replaced in this international example by warring nations. Using a shared emotional state to facilitate novel and more complex thinking, successful negotiators find a higher-level postformal logic to overarch the more formal, limited logics of the arguing nations. The Jungian psychologist Arnold Mindell (Mindell, 1992; Mindell & Mindell, 1992) is a successful international conflict resolution specialist who is expert at moving warring national interests from rigid formal positions, through accessed culturally shared emotional states, to postformal higher-order-logic resolutions.

The case of international negotiations is a tricky one, though, because the mediator is dealing with *shared* belief systems and culturally shared views of reality. He or she is also faced with the wider variety of cognitive skills, emotions, and shared assumptions brought to the negotiating table by the various negotiators, both as individuals and as representatives of the whole spectrum of views held by their nationals. It is easier to find common ground between two individuals than among these multiple views, many of which are unstated cultural assumptions.

The cognitive skills of the warring parties, especially whether or not they are postformal thinkers, are an important factor in the conflict resolution process. A postformal party to a conflict is inherently capable of getting to a higher-order logic about the problem; the non-postformal person may not be capable of getting there—at least with conscious awareness. In the case of warring nations or organizations, the national shared reality or the organizational culture may or may not include postformal ways of seeing truth. In groups such as this, a "critical mass" of persons who think postformally must exist for the culture to reflect awareness of the possibility of such thought during negotiations. One must at least hope that the representative of the organization or nation does have the skill and negotiations can go more smoothly.

Teaching peaceful problem-solving techniques may mean either teaching a *set of rules* or teaching a *postformal awareness* of connections and process along with those rules. The former can be used with individuals at any cognitive skill level; the latter demands a nurturing of or an induction of postformal thought. In Chapter 21, we will explore a few ways of facilitating postformal thought, ways that work with adults. Teaching peaceful mediation of conflict as a way of life and as a value system means teaching it in many situations and at many levels. But unless there is a critical mass of similar thinkers with a basic belief in the value of peace, or unless there is a critical mass of postformal thinkers in a culture, the nation or culture or organization will not seem to think and operate to reach a higher-level resolution. It does not fit their reality and their ideas of truth.

Consider the very practical situation that many of us are facing today: institutional reorganization. Reorganizations generate conflict among individuals and units in the organization. Finding the best way to reorganize a company, like finding the best way to negotiate any conflict situation, in part means finding the current level of cognitive skills of parties to the conflict, as well as the possible level of cognitive skills that might be attainable by those parties. Those enmeshed in conflict because they are trying to reorganize institutions (see Chapter 15), develop working teams, or otherwise change the institutional culture are faced with this task. They must, then, estimate the current and possible cognitive levels of the individuals or the groups to decide on the strategy for reorganization.

At this point, many companies call in highly paid consultants expecting the consultants to create a change of structures and "energy," which managers can then impose. Unfortunately, they usually find that no one "hears" the consultants because the present cultural tradition does not include that reality, even if it is potentially attainable for that organization or its people. Rather than waste the consultants' time (and the company's money), would it not be wiser to let the consultants assess the readiness for change (i.e., the current level of postformal skills in the context of human interactions as it is expressed on the job at the present time) and the potential for some day attaining a more complex level of interaction (postformal skills available to be exercised in *any* domain of life) by assessing the level of postformal thought in representatives of the culture? Appropriate strategies can then be devised to fit the situation, resolve the conflicts, and move to more complex and less conflicted levels of functioning as individual workers or as units. A simple assessment of the postformal thinking level of key decision makers (which wise managers automatically make) would be possible and would go a long way toward healing these conflicts and making conflict resolution and organizational reform successful and sustainable.

When we think about how the positive resolution of conflict improves the quality of interpersonal, international, and intraorganizational life, we begin to imagine what might happen if a *majority* of individuals used postformal skills to heal conflicts in all these domains. Chaos and complexity theories suggest that the development of greater numbers of such balanced individuals who operate postformally could be a source of group evolution! We will explore just one aspect of such group evolution in the next section, in the context of healing the earth.

HEALING THE EARTH

Some might argue that postformal thought has little to do with the ecology movement (as defined by Gore, 1992), the Gaia hypothesis, human evolution, or the earth-encompassing vision of thinkers such as philosopher-priest Teilhard de Chardin or doers such as Edgar Mitchell, who created the Institute for Noetic Sciences. Yet, when we talk about postformal thought, we are talking about the kind of thinking that permits us to see the Earth in more than one way, in more than one relation to us. The Earth can be seen as our home and our resource base, yet it can also be seen as a larger living organism of which we are just a part. It can be our creator, and we can be cocreators of it! In fact, ecopsychologists have argued quite successfully that mental health includes interaction with a healthy environment and that sanity must be redefined on a broader person-plus-planet scale (Roszak, Gomes, & Kanner, 1995).

The postformal way of looking at reality acknowledges at its core the possibility that the ground of our physical existence, the Earth, may be thought of in many ways, all of which may simultaneously be true ways of thinking of it. And there can be no new vision of our relation to the planet unless we thinkers at least permit the possibility that we can be in some additional new relationships with it. Without postformal thought, the ecology movement, Gaia, and other views of the Earth are just new orthodox formal logical positions. And if only *one* "true belief" about the nature of our relationship to the Earth can be held—that is, if we can*not* be conscious postformal thinkers about our relation to the Earth—then it stands to reason that our old dominating relation to the planet will be our automatic first choice. We will then keep a death grip on our dominating relation to the planet until we destroy our home.

Views of our possible relations to the Earth, and behaviors that should follow from those relations, have been becoming more varied in recent history. Of course, all the views we have of the Earth were held to some degree by earlier peoples, in the way that their historical context supported. We have "rediscovered" the view of the Earth as a living system that was held by ancient peoples. But we have rediscovered it with a 20th-century twist.

It almost seems that a critical mass of caring individuals who understand more about the nature of how the world works has been emerging at a faster rate in recent times. Increasing the critical mass might be accelerating group evolution and awareness of what Ferguson called "right relationship" between us and the planet.

POSTFORMAL CONCEPTS
OF MEDICAL CARE

Just as visions of psychological health, psychotherapy, and our relationship to the Earth have been evolving at a greater rate in recent past history, so has our understanding of what constitutes health and medical care. Just as our new understandings of psychological health and ecology seem to rest on our ability to think in complex postformal ways, so does our awareness of medical care. Our new holistic awareness of "physical" health as a wellness of body, mind, spirit, and relations, all involved at once, demands that we be able to shift realities about who and what we are as living beings. That *awareness* seems to require postformal thought, although simply *using* holistic medicine does not. One can be rigidly formal operational and a "true believer" in alternative holistic medicine, just as one can be a true believer in anything else!

In our new culture-wide interest in alternative medicine, we turn most readily to three approaches: Chinese medicine, effects of mind on body, and lifestyle changes that involve getting back to the "earthiness" of our physical bodies, which need well-paced exercise, food, rest. These three favorite approaches all demand that we reconnect the parts of our lives that have slipped out of right relationship to each other. Practitioners of the three all try to move a client to a point at which the client is aware of the postformal realities of her or his health and aware of her or his responsibility to create wellness in place of "dis-ease." This point of view does not "blame the victim"; the client is not told that it is all up to her or him or that illness is her or his fault. Rather, the client is gradually led to understand the postformal nature of wellness and the real power every individual has to create or change parts of personal reality, more than she or he ever expected.

In the Chinese medicine systems of acupuncture and acupressure, for example, symptoms are considered and treated directly, as needed, by stimulation of certain energy points. More important, however, the client is led toward seeing health as a free-flowing communication and transformation system based on energy operating in a body–mind–spirit–member of society. The client is encouraged to shift the reality of the health experience between Newtonian and new physics systems on all levels of the living systems (i.e., body, mind, interpersonal, spirit) that she or he inhabits.

In the system of guided imagery, too, the mind and body are expected to interact through images, which are responded to as real by the body. This demands conscious shifts between Newtonian and new physics reality systems. Only when the client "believes" (on the new physics level) that the image is "real" will the body then bring on the physical reactions that allow the image to have real physical effects. Only when I "feel" the warm sun and the gentle waves through deep visualization do I begin to relax as though I were really on that beach. The practitioner gradually helps me to see that the image has multifaceted realities that I can consciously visit—and must, if I want to stay "well."

The "healthy living" formal systems of our grandparents are also experiencing a new life at (one hopes) a postformal level in the new medicine. They go beyond rigid rules now, and are truly paradoxical. For example, we hear now that by resting more than we workaholics typically do, we can hope to accomplish more by feeling better in the time we are awake; conversely, by working either too little or too much, we produce less. Eating clean, healthful food is important, but eating less than we want helps us live longer and healthier. Exercising tires us out, but is necessary for building a metabolism that creates more energy for us later. The paradoxical rules make sense to the post-formal thinker, but can be interpreted only in a frustrating, guess-as-you-go rote way by the non-postformal thinker. The non-postformal thinker then declares the holistic medicine experience a fraud because he or she cannot decide (in formal operational terms) what, logically, to do next.

Postformal thinking makes sense of these holistic medicine approaches. It also permits us to turn the tools of these holistic approaches toward problems in the other healing areas we have dis-cussed (i.e., psychopathology; conflict resolution, both local and inter-national; healing the earth), using the same tools to help heal a wide variety of problems. The sample tools we have discussed—including unblocking the flow of energy, stimulating critical energy points, bal-ancing energy flow, imagining an event and then "moving into" the real reaction to the imaginal exercise, locating the personally optimal point for intervention—can be used with many other problems if we shift the logic that is in use so that it applies in another context. After all, all these realities, according to the new physics, are built on simi-lar transformable energy systems. For example, if one has the "tool" of "imagining," one can imagine change in many different contexts. Imagining a positive resolution for cancer, to heal a medical problem, can be used again by imagining oneself calmly flying, to heal a psy-chological anxiety problem, or yet again by imagining ways to conduct business that leave the Earth more whole, or yet again by imagining your opponent in a conflict as your eventual friend or your martial arts opponent so that possibilities for conflict resolution can emerge. The tools are very versatile (like "Multiple methods" in the list of postformal operations), but they must be used in appropriate ways. Healing is a powerful activity, but one that must be conducted like a dance, in balance with the partner, appropriate for the music being played. That balance demands deep understanding.

In Chapter 20, we will see the connection between postformal thought and humanistic psychology, a newer major branch of psy-chology that is philosophically attuned to the healing techniques described in this chapter. A postformal, new physics logic seems to form a logical underpinning for doing research in humanistic psychology. Since humanists have found it difficult to formulate a logical framework for research (or at least one that encompasses the richness of the humanist vision while being communicatable to more logical-positivistic branches of psychology), postformal thought might help.

CHAPTER 20

Some Uses of Postformal Thought in Humanistic Psychology

I speak of the Manifesto of the Person, the declaration of our sovereign right to self discovery.

THEODORE ROSZAK

The challenge articulated and accepted by the "third wave" of psychology, which includes humanistic, existential, and transpersonal psychology, is to make psychology whole again by putting meaning back into studies of human experience and by combining mind, heart, and spirit. Postformal thought seems to be one way that humans think about complex ideas such as the meaning of their existence, the split between mind, body, and emotion, the role of humankind in a universal or cosmic consciousness, and body–mind connections. It even seems *necessary* that we have postformal logic before we can *both* conceptualize the spiritually oriented subfield of humanistic psychology called transpersonal psychology *and* remain adaptively in touch with the "local" other-than-spiritual realities of our everyday existence.

A postformal, new physics logic also seems to form a logical underpinning for doing research in humanistic psychology. Humanists have found it difficult to find a logic that can encompass the richness of the humanist vision and still communicate with traditional branches of scientific psychology that are philosophically more attuned to logical positivism. Research on holistic humanistic topics, when it is done at all, tends to be qualitative, phenomenological, and oriented to case histories. Studies involving postformal thought might help bridge this philosophical gap.

We will examine the place of postformal thinking in humanistic psychology in this chapter. After examining the issue in a general way, we will look more closely at three areas and analyze examples of humanistic exercises and approaches in those areas. First among the three is the role of postformal thought in *existential* awareness, with existential psychotherapy as the example. Second, we will see how postformal thought permits us to bridge among representation systems and "speak" to various aspects of the mind and body, using as an example the familiar humanistic technique of *guided imagery.* Finally, we will see how postformal thought might help us study *mind–body connections* and interventions, using the example of biofeedback for control of blood pressure.

THE PROBLEM OF
THINKING HUMANISTICALLY

When we study cognition in psychology, we generally study what McLuhan (McLuhan, 1951; McLuhan & Fiore, 1967) termed *cold cognition,* that is, cognition that occurs only in the head. Humanism requires warm cognition and spirited cognition as well. Our culture, being a by-product of the industrial revolution and the rise of experimental science, does a great job of separating mind from other aspects of human experience. Analyzing how we think about mental abstractions, however, is only one part of the logic of human life. We are creatures with many evolutionary layers to our presence, and our task is to orchestrate all the layers into a working unit. In Paul MacLean's (1988) view, we humans come equipped with a triune brain: The portion that is reptilian (evolutionarily speaking) is hardwired for *instinctive* actions; the limbic system and associated structures give information an *emotional* valence and let us bond with each other; the neomammalian levels that constitute the cortex process *abstract thoughts* in the "big picture" relational style of the right hemisphere, the linear linguistic style of the left hemisphere, and the imaginal and empathic style of the prefrontal cortex (a possible fourth center that is still evolving). Thinking is more than a cortical activity and, even within the cortex, more than a simple cortical activity.

The questions and processes of interest to the humanist are often those that cross the hemispheric specialties of the cortex and traffic with all three of our poorly communicating brains, as well as with the hormone receptor and neuropeptide "brain" that is present all over our body, as Candace Pert (1986) and others remind us. To make these leaps of conceptualization with the humanists, then, and to do it *consciously*, requires a logic that can partly step out of logic and rise above it without losing its mind, so to speak.

Clients come to humanistic therapists when they can no longer do this balanced dance of humanistic knowing across these several moving spheres of influence that together constitute the thinking mind. Clients are often in conflict, and the conflict is often the result of one part of their mind not speaking with or listening to another part. Perhaps the feelings do not match the body sensations; the client's understanding of what he or she *should* do conflicts with what he or she does do (or feels compelled to do). It seems to make no sense, and the person visits the therapist. Some therapists take it as their role at this point to offer insight into the problem at the level of cortical mind alone. But the client may need ways to coordinate and continue to coordinate the cortical insight *and* the body or instincts or feelings or unconscious motivations to make life better. The difference between "clients" and "nonclients" is a matter of degree. All humans can benefit from knowing more of these coordination processes, because all of us are imperfectly balanced to some degree.

While some clients leave therapy knowing only that things *are* better without knowing *why* they are better, others leave therapy with an awareness of how to perform this coordination themselves, in the future, to keep things better. Workshop participants also acquire this awareness. The awareness is important, since it is a tool that gives considerable power to the individual to work her or his way out of future problems. The awareness involves operations like those of postformal thought. For example, the client may have learned through therapy that she or he can examine *any* stress-producing event in life with an eye toward multiple goals and multiple metatheories (both postformal operations), from which one goal or theory may pragmatically be chosen. In the three humanistic therapeutic approach examples we will discuss here, the client can come out of therapy with (among other things) conscious awareness of existential dilemmas and choices, a sense for orchestrating emotions, or the possibility of learning from the body's own physical logic. All three make use of complex thinking operations, as we will see below.

This conscious balancing act probably requires the ability to coordinate more than one logical system of thought and to rise above the logic of any one system. This set of "tools" benefits both nonclients (who have learned to do this balancing act on their own and need only refresh or enhance their skills) and clients (who have yet to develop the skills). The successful learner sees how the various contradictory logics fit together in a bigger picture of personal reality. The learner can then choose one or the other of the parts that overlap the several logics, ending a conflict by making a conscious choice of realities at a higher logical level. The humanistic traditions encourage this bridging of realities, or going beyond simple logics, and offer processes and exercises for clients and nonclients to use to learn to do this in an ongoing way. For example, Labouvie-Vief's (1982) learned self-governance, a balance of emotion and logic, seems to be an ongoing ability to use the tools or skills we have been speaking about.

It seems necessary that the humanistic therapist or workshop leader have postformal thought if he or she is not to become simply technique-driven and mechanical. It seems necessary that the learner have postformal thought in order to consciously continue the healing or growth process after leaving the therapist's office or the workshop.

Perhaps the best way to see how postformal thought is a root for humanistic thought and technique is to examine for a moment the humanistic emphasis on love as an important human process and a healing process (e.g., see Ashley Montagu, 1974, 1985). While we may not necessarily *like* what some of our fellow humans do (all that "unskilled behavior" out there is annoying and sometimes hurtful or deadly), the humanistic person or therapist can shift logically to see all individuals as *lovable* in the sense of *agape*, or unconditional positive regard. Being so loved may sometimes help heal even those unskilled persons at whom the love is directed; they may become lovable, accepting their "lovable" self-definition, role, and behavior. To think of this process logically requires that we think postformally and coordinate formal logical systems about "lovableness," consciously choosing one reality (the reality that, on a spirit or *agape* level, all, even the most unskilled humans, are lovable) and living as though it were truth. Recent books such as *The Celestine Prophecy* are immensely popular partly because they offer step-by-step rules for beginning to understand these important insights and for working with the postformal logic on which these insights are based.

EXISTENTIALISM AND POSTFORMAL THOUGHT

Humans have pondered the meaning of existence throughout the ages. If we suffer and ultimately die, and if we are conscious that we are going to do so, then how do we bear to live? Frankl considered these questions from the point of view of a Holocaust survivor. His resolution of the existential dilemma led him to create the system of logotherapy summarized in his extremely popular book, *Man's Search for Meaning* (Frankl, 1963). Yalom's work is more recent and focuses specifically on the conduct of existential psychotherapy (e.g., Yalom, 1980). For example, the fear of death can be said to underlie many other conflicts and concerns an individual might bring to therapy. The existential dilemma must be dealt with by the therapist before the other issues can be resolved effectively. The therapist might make use of exercises such as writing one's own obituary to enhance an awareness of these roots of the conflict to make the possibility of choice about one's existential logic seem more real.

Clients experiencing the existential dilemma of their own eventual death must make a major logical shift if they are to go on with life. They had been living within a logic that had this major premise: "If I stay alive, my life (my existence) can mean something, can be 'for' something." They must shift to a logic built on this premise: "My life has meaning even though it is finite and I must die." Further, each client, who may have come to the therapist in existential despair, must accept that it is his or her choice to select the logic of "meaning" or of "no meaning" on which to base his or her life. It is even a choice to be aware of death or to block death from awareness. Further, it is possible (within transpersonal psychology) to choose a logic for life that includes premises of life or consciousness existing beyond the individual at a universal consciousness level. Choice of one of these logical systems will profoundly influence the behavior and feelings of the individual during the remainder of his or her individual life. It is awareness of the choice that is frightening!

The cognitive operations needed for this problem solving are complex and postformal, as we define them. When individuals consider that there is more than one metatheory about the logic of life, they realize that they need to *choose* the logical basis for life. They must make a passionate commitment to the chosen logic and live it to completion, make it a reality. On a cognitive level, they use what we have throughout this book been terming postformal thought. The existential dilemma they face may have been the impetus for development of postformal thought, through interaction with the therapist. Later, postformal thinking skills may generalize from the existential dilemma to other areas of their lives.

Lesser existential dilemmas are the standard fare of psychotherapy within humanistic perspectives. For example, clients may be asked to think about what kind of person to be, or what sorts of stories they want their lives to tell. Postformal reasoning may be needed here, too, unless the therapist simply supplies the "right answer" in such a way that the client assimilates it, consciously or unconsciously. Overall, existential humanistic psychology seems to rest on the cognitive operations of postformal thought.

COGNITIVE BASES OF GUIDED IMAGERY

Imagery exercises form a powerful tool for humanistic psychology. They tap into our ability to create or experience an imaginary reality that combines the full spectrum of human experiences, just as the "real" reality does. In the imaginal realm, we can not only think, we can also feel sensations or emotions, see, hear, have relationships with others, relive past events, dialogue with parts of ourselves, and make time pass slowly or quickly. Through *visualization,* we even can imagine the future and "see" avenues we could take to arrive at that future. This gives imagery a "spooky" quality, but most practitioners who use the technique point out that, unlike hypnosis, visualization involves the continuing willful acts of the visualizer, who chooses to stay in the experience or leave it and chooses the direction that the experience will take. This imaginal experience differs from psychotic experiences, in which the real cannot be distinguished from the unreal and the client is "trapped" in the unreal state, sometimes against his or her will. Visualization has been used to address many types of issues and behavioral problems, including, to name just a few, relaxation, expanding human awareness and ability, smoking cessation, cancer therapy, peak performance in sports, relations with others in the client's life, prayer and contemplation, anxiety-based problems, meditation, and career transitions.

How does postformal complex thought matter for visualization? Again, the experiencer must choose to live out one or the other of a contradictory set of logics: One is the familiar everyday experience of some event; the other is the somewhat different (imaginal) experience of that same event. For example, if I am doing imaginal work related to smoking cessation, I now have two experiences, two "logics" of the event of smoking. One is what I have known for years, the whole set of beliefs, attitudes, sensations, conversations, rituals, and other aspects that are part of the experience of smoking for me in the real world. The second is what I know and am enlarging on about smoking in the imaginal experience going on at a cognitive–emotional–physical level. This second may include things about smoking that I have never experienced before, such as good feelings "experienced" *without* lighting up, unpleasant sensations "experienced" in relation to imaginal smoking, "experiences" of days when I had no interest in a cigarette, and "experiences" of my contentment during a long smoke-free lifetime. Now that imagery therapy has given me a sense of how things could be otherwise in my life, I can make a choice about the reality concerning smoking that I wish to inhabit. Then I can go on to live out that reality and elaborate upon it in real life. Again, these are the operations of metatheory choice, pragmatism, multiple methods, parameter setting, and other operations of postformal thought.

MIND–BODY CONNECTIONS AND THE POWER OF INTENTION

The essence of the humanistic philosophy is that the person is a whole, not fragmented into body versus mind versus emotions versus spirit. If this assumption is valid, what happens in the mind should have an impact on the body, and vice versa. In line with these beliefs, humanists of today, like the practitioners of Chinese medicine for thousands of years, pay attention to these interactions and devise modes of treatment that cross mind–body lines to take advantage of the relations. For example, Huang and Lynch (1992) discuss ways to achieve peak sports performance by using the mental–physical–emotional dance of tai chi. Epstein (1994) offers mental exercises to help heal physical illnesses. Hammer (1990) links psychology to the energy meridians of Chinese medicine.

These treatments and assumptions again involve the choice of logical systems of belief from two or more that are essentially incompatible, after a leap to a higher-level logical system that bridges across them. To believe that the body can be healed by the intentions of the mind is logically incompatible with the belief that intention, at best, can simply get you to visit the doctor. Realization that intention bridges these logics permits solution of the logical dilemma.

One of the simplest connections between mind–emotion–intention and physical well-being to see is the connection between stress and blood pressure. When individuals are stressed, blood pressure rises because of activation of the fight or flight response. That response is fine, some of the time, unless the person is already acutely ill with circulatory or cardiac problems and a blood pressure rise will be deadly. If that rise-in-blood-pressure reaction occurs much of the time or most of the time, chronic high blood pressure disables the individual by causing serious disease and may eventually prove fatal. The most interesting part of this dynamic to notice (for our purposes) is that the body does not care whether the stress is engendered by real dangers or imaginary ones. Its response is the same in either case: Blood pressure rises. When a person is taught to attempt to control pressure by mentally expressing an intention to be in a high-blood-pressure or a low-blood-pressure state, the body also responds to the mind's attempt, again irrespective of the actual stressors in the environment. Teaching people to orchestrate their physical responses to pain or stress by means of intention and selective attention has been successful enough to be practiced in clinics and medical schools around the country.

The humanistic psychology movement rests in part on the cognitive abilities associated with postformal complex thought. That it does is evident in existential psychotherapy, guided imagery, and biofeedback treatments. In Part IV of this book, I hope to do what the humanists value, namely, share with more individuals the experience of being a postformal thinker. This last part is divided into ideas on directly *teaching* postformal thought in university, classroom, or workshop settings, and ideas on *self-development* (by means of postformal thought) to achieve the holistic and spiritual goal of personally living in balance.

THE NEXT STEPS

Interventions—Teaching Postformal
Thinking and Using Postformal Thought
to Live in Balance

CHAPTER 21

Can We Teach Adults to Use Complex Postformal Thought?

educate: from Latin educare, from educere, to draw out

In Parts I and II, I described how it happened that the Theory of Post-formal Thought was created; I also outlined that theory. In Part III, I described applications of the theory to quite a number of situations and relationships of everyday life. In this first chapter in Part IV, I want to explore ways that I have seen adults taught to think postfor-mally as a result of interventions in classroom settings and in other formally structured interactions. In Chapter 22, I want to explore ways that I have seen individuals use postformal thinking to stimulate their own personal development as they struggle to reach their own poten-tial and to live in balance honoring mind, heart, body, and spirit.

Though these topics of Part IV are placed last, they are, in a way, the most important topics in the book. Understanding the richness of adult thought is fine in its own right, but being able to promote the development of that thought may be an even greater gift. What would our world, our relationships, our lives be like if we had larger access to this thinking? Living in a more complex world could be as exciting and enriching as acquiring color vision when before one had seen only in shades of gray or acquiring use of language when before one could only stand mute!

My hope has been that the very act of understanding postformal thought and its uses would lead to ways of giving the gift of postfor-mal thought to others, for their own sake and for the sake of the human future. We are a species in the process of becoming, as Teilhard de Chardin (1959) noted, and we can help construct ourselves through an awakened consciousness of our larger selves. I very much wish that this fourth part of the book could be longer, or even book-length in its own right. I wish that I could devote five years of my own life to doing nothing else but developing more techniques of teaching postformal thought and showing others how it can open doors for them in their personal growth. Teaching and sharing postformal thought is my own "next step" as I pursue this overall area of study.

Thought and research need not be separated from concerns about social change. It is a challenge, my own challenge as a human being, to join mind and heart in a vocational path. The postformal thinker has no troublesome, automatic split between what is good for the self and what is good for society. In terms of social justice, the postformal thinker can use this overarching logic to see ways to join forces for "win–win" situations. The postformal thinker is very practical and not at all naive, but can more easily see the path that is wide enough for "separate" groups to walk upon together. The postformal thinker can enter the larger story and address the needs of the group and at the same time enjoy what Hanh (1991) calls "this beautiful present moment" and serve the needs of the self.

In the years that I have been teaching college classes, doing workshops, and working with clients, I have created or stumbled upon some techniques that seem to lead students on the path to developing complex postformal thought. In this chapter, I want to share some of them with you. I suspect, from the criticisms I hear about college education, that we *do* want college students at all levels to develop complex, critical thinking such as is represented in postformal thinking. Workshop participants *do* want to see the world and their lives in more complex ways that capture the big picture of reality as they experience it. While trying to reach those goals, many individuals I have taught or worked with developed postformal thought, whatever else they "officially" were trying to study or work on with me on those occasions. While I can not yet provide a formula for creating postformal thinkers, I can suggest some approaches that seem to have worked in the past. Perhaps, in the future, writing an experiential handbook for getting to postformal thought designed for students and workshop participants would be a worthwhile effort for me to pursue.

Table 21.1 summarizes some techniques for leading members of a class or workshop toward their own postformal thinking. The table lists activities along with the postformal operation(s) each can lead to or the function it might serve in bringing about postformal thinking. One thing you may want to keep in mind: As I discuss this table and give examples below, I will use examples from the college classroom, a place with which I am very familiar. Let me emphasize, though, that the same sort of techniques can also be used in other types of classes, in workshops of all kinds, in office training programs, and in many other settings. Space limitations prohibit my giving specific examples of the activities in all of those contexts.

One difficulty in articulating any quick list of techniques, especially in an area such as complex postformal thought, is that the same activity may lead to different ends depending upon the teacher's intel-

Table 21.1. Activities for Teaching Postformal Thought in Formal Settings Such as Classes or Workshops[a] and Teaching Goals Emphasized in Each

Activity	Operations/goals
1. Jointly create a grading system.	1. All operations; see multiple logics, commit to one
2. Address a research question in several different ways.	2. Multiple methods, solutions; problem definition
3. Create naturalistic research projects.	3. Parameter setting
4. Shift from naturalistic to experimental studies.	4. Metatheory shift, pragmatism
5. Dialogue on existential questions.	5. Metatheory shift, problem definition
6. Analyze data and interpret results in many ways.	6. Multiple methods, process–product shift
7. Communicate the same ideas to many different types of audiences.	7. Multiple methods, solutions; parameter setting
8. Grade the process as well as the product.	8. Process–product shift
9. Write process papers as well as standard term papers.	9. Process–product shift
10. Tell paradoxical stories.	10. Paradox
11. Describe the logic of behavior from the point of view of the person taking action.	11. Metatheory shift
12. Paradoxical instruction, e.g., "We're here to *play* with these ideas" or "Do something silly."	12. Changing mood context
13. Group testing	13. Problem definition, multiple logical realities
14. Try "court cases," shifting logical arguments.	14. Directly addressing "what is truth"
15. Find six ways to ask any question or solve any problem.	15. Practice in using multiple realities
16. Open and close "problem space" repeatedly.	16. Parameter setting

[a]The activities are to be followed by discussions of multiple realities.

lectual and emotional qualities and upon how the teacher handles the material or the technique. This is especially true for teaching postformal thought. The essence of shifting to a more complex stage of thinking is that one views the "old" world in "new" ways, which implies that the *same* "old" reality can be viewed on higher and lower levels. It is less the technique than what one does with it. Give an aggressive preschool child a sophisticated calculator, and the child will probably just use it as a weapon. As the saying goes, if the only tool you have is a hammer, everything becomes a nail.

AN EXAMPLE—THE FIRST ACTIVITY: 'JOINTLY CREATING A GRADING SYSTEM'

Consider activity 1 in the table, class creation of a grading system. Any reader with experience in a classroom can imagine a way for students to create a grading system. Here are some examples—only some led to postformal thought: One instructor asked students at the end of the course what they thought of the system by which they were to be graded. Another had students discuss and then each cast a vote on her predetermined grading system. A third had students pick from among three existing grading systems that were carefully spelled out in a handout so as to avoid too much time-consuming discussion and feedback. A fourth gave students "free rein" in setting individual contracts, but was so angry-sounding and controlling that every student in that class "knew" what the "right" way was! All these instructors would have said they made use of the activity, but it is unlikely any of these four used it in such a way that much postformal thought was stimulated.

What were some main things wrong with their methods, as far as stimulating postformal thought is concerned? Let us look at the goal of this exercise of creating a grading system: *The goal is to promote students' thinking about and use of postformal operations* such as multiple methods, multiple goals, good process versus good products, metatheory shift, parameter shifting, paradox, and the other postformal operations we have identified. To do so, they need an occasion to do so, real freedom to do so, and a motivating emotional environment that reduces anxiety, demands, and the need to be controlling on the part of student or instructor. The first instructor, who wanted feedback on the grading system at the end of the course, provided an occasion but one without real motivation, since the course was over already. The first instructor will have minimal engagement of the students, who may be able to evaluate the class but will be afraid to be very negative since they are about to be graded. They also have no need to see multiple realities about the nature of grading systems or to make a passionate commitment to the "truth" or utility of one among many, since they are asked to judge only a single grading system, the one chosen by their own instructor. The students *may* become postformal thinkers, though, if they get angry enough about the question or the course and later begin to discuss it among themselves!

The second instructor would not stimulate much postformal thinking either. She would do so only if the students were to engage in incidental discussions fueled by anger at her having made only a single system available for a vote. Discussion makes other systems cognitively available to students. The controlling nature of the instructor's behavior (which is not inappropriate—*unless* the instructor's goal is to stimulate postformal thought) partly gets in the way of the development of postformal thought because students feel less free to access alternative goals and other aspects in the presence of instructor control. Recall from earlier chapters that productivity is reduced when negative emotions arise.

The third instructor, who avoided time-consuming feedback and discussion by giving students three carefully constructed alternative grading systems to vote on, derailed the process of creating postformal thought by doing all the postformal thinking for the students instead of letting them do it. They have permission only to evaluate and cannot have their thinking and logics challenged by the logics of others, here and now, in the heat of interpersonal interaction. Students in this setting *may* have a chance to compare logics of grading systems *if* those three systems have indeed been structured on three separate logical systems. If the three alternative systems really differ only on the basis of, let's say, how often exams are given, without exam dates being discussed as a reflection of *different logical philosophies* of student evaluation, then students are not specifically stimulated toward postformal thought by use of this exercise.

The fourth instructor made the mistake of causing an emotional shutdown of cognitive creativity, but otherwise—if *discussion* of the grading *logic* behind those individual contracts was encouraged—was headed for the goal of stimulating postformal thought. Students in this class could very well have been stimulated to challenge the logic of each other's proposals had discussion been part of the format and the discussion of grading logics (as opposed to the actual simpler discussion of 5 versus 10 points per quiz) been encouraged by the instructor.

Any of the four instructors could salvage the technique and teach postformal thought after all if, after the false start, they could themselves model postformal thinking about the logics of grading systems.

It would be valuable for teachers to learn how to do this in workshops designed for that purpose.

I hope the reader can begin to understand from this first example that, by definition, there can be no "cookbook" approach to teaching postformal thought in formal settings such as classrooms and workshops or, indeed, anywhere. Although serendipitous accidents that teach postformal thinking are useful, it probably takes a *postformal* instructor to *teach* postformal thought. The postformal instructor can guide the experience, in this case the experience of creating a grading system, to bring out issues and ideas that lead to gradual student awareness of complex logical thought *and* eventual student practice of it.

I have seen the exercise of creating a grading system work the best when it is done in the following way by an instructor familiar with postformal thought, either in theory or in practice: A new class of students is told on the first day of class that their first task at the next class meeting will be to jointly create a point system for determining their final grades and the value of class assignments. They are told that the instructor believes that there are several kinds of skills that might be rewarded in college, some of them, but by no means all of them, being "knowledge of content materials," "creativity," "effort," and "team participation." Assigning more or fewer points to a skill reflects how much one values that skill, and over the years colleges have had different value systems. The skills are reflected in assignments and the point system for determining grades. The instructor admits that instructors also have value systems, but suggests that, as students have noticed in many areas of life, "usually there is no single 'right' way" to do things. Their input is therefore valuable. The instructor then sets some parameters: Any system the students create has to be internally logical; total points earned in a given semester cannot be more than (here I give some large number, such as 500, so that there is ample room for students to allocate points); the nonnegotiable requirements of the class that appear in the syllabus must be honored in each system by the allocation of points; and additional requirements may be added by students and given points, within the total (not in addition to it). Students are invited to think overnight about this task of creating a grading system and to talk with others who have done this exercise before, especially those in the present class who have done the exercise with this instructor in earlier classes. A system that has been accepted in final form by a class may not be renegotiated during the semester.

The class is broken into groups of no more than 5 persons (any more, and some fall silent), each group to pick a reporter and a person to monitor that each member is allowed to speak. Each group develops a grading system. All systems are reported back to the entire class, where dissimilarities are discussed and resolved, or the groups again caucus among themselves. In the latter situation, new systems may be reported back. This sequence is performed as many times as needed to reach class resolution. While some fear that the discussion will never end, or never end in agreement, such an impasse has never come about, since the motivation to compromise seems to increase the longer the dialogue goes on. In these discussions, logical discrepancies are pointed out by the instructor as the groups are moved in a postformal direction. By the time a grading system is agreed upon, class thinking and interpersonal interactions have become much more complex and postformal, with the ongoing interpretations of the instructor.

OTHER EXAMPLES OF ACTIVITIES

Some of the activities listed in Table 21.1 mainly nurture one or a few postformal operational skills; others can be rich enough, in the right hands, to nurture all the operations. Some of the items in the list are context variables that can be created by instructors to provide a richer environment for postformal thinking to grow more readily. Because the activities are useful for these several different kinds of functions connected with postformal thought, additional purposes the activity is meant to serve are sometimes listed in the second column. The list of activities and purposes is *far* from complete!

Activity 2, addressing a single research question in several different ways, is carried out using logical brainstorming. For example, the activity may be used in research classes or content classes in which students are developing paper topics or applied/policy analyses. The instructions are simply to create several different logical research projects that will give some answers to this larger research question. Students may design an *experiment* to test the hypothesis that athletes have eating disorders more frequently than nonathletes, then design a *naturalistic study* to observe athletes and nonathletes in the cafeteria. Students can discuss the merits and the downside of each approach.

For activity 3, creating naturalistic research projects, students are asked to do some explorations "in the field," planned as a team, which means they need to decide which of the thousands of factors and events they will take into account in their finite (and short!) policy or research study. One of my favorite ways to conduct this exercise is to have a class study something at the ice cream parlor located on the first floor of the building in which I usually teach. After one quick visit, all teams quickly realize that they must narrow their options or be overwhelmed with information, since much more goes on in an ice cream parlor than one would imagine at first. Comparing projects later lets teams see the impact of wide or narrow options. All these events and choices can be discussed in terms of postformal thought.

Activity 4, shifting between the field and the structured experimental scientific world, can follow upon the third fairly easily, if a professor chooses to do so. "Before, you decided to observe the buying habits of ice cream parlor patrons to create a better marketing plan for ice cream franchise operations. You now have some information on buying habits. Let's see if you can influence buying habits to get men to buy as much chocolate ice cream as women do." The resulting project can be discussed and compared with the earlier naturalistic one in terms of metatheory shift, with examples of this operation from other areas of science and everyday life.

Activity 5, dialogues about existential questions, routinely stimulates postformal thought, since the meaning of life is an inherently postformal question. These discussions might occur in any number of college classes in many majors. Students who are formal operational thinkers often move to a postformal position when they consider the heartfelt logical beliefs of others in the class and ponder how one does make a choice of ways to live.

In contrast, even lower-level data-analysis activities (activity 6) can stimulate postformal thinking by analyzing numbers many different ways and looking at the "truth" that results when those analyses are interpreted. This activity also provides a chance to address the operation of process–product shift, since students can discriminate between having a good process (i.e., several statistical methods that can lead to an answer) and having a concrete answer to the hypothesis (often several contradictory ones!). For an example of the latter, results of a robust parametric statistical test like the t-test may be that "Women eat significantly more chocolate ice cream," while the results of a nonparametric χ^2 test are that there is no significant gender difference.

Communicating the same ideas to many different types of audiences (activity 7) demands that each student visit the logic of other adults, possibly deciding that those logical lenses for reality are better or worse choices than the one the student first used and reflected in his or her original communication. In my classes (which often are also advanced writing-in-the-discipline-of-psychology courses), students are asked to communicate some specific finding to TV viewers, magazine readers, PTA members, fifth-grade students, and other audiences, as well as in the standard journal article style. Doing so is fun—and a challenge. In another variation on this theme, students must use technical writing that is exact and detailed to express some everyday activity such as "how to tie a shoe" and, when the communication (inevitably) fails to some degree, find a better way to reach the logic of the listeners.

Activities 8 and 9 contrast process and product as part of the assigned term paper or writing activity in a class. Students may be asked both to describe in writing their process of, for example, "thinking through the ideas of a paper" and to submit the completed paper on a given topic (the product). Both process and product may be graded by the professor, separately. Similarly, the process of working on a project, perhaps cooperatively with a team, can be observed and graded separately from the project itself. Students can see how different processes can lead to the same product or how the same process can lead to two or more different products.

Activity 10, telling paradoxical stories, also shifts logics for consideration of metatheory shift. These can be modified to suit the content of the class or workshop. (Note that simply *going* to workshops leads to postformal thought because the logics of the several workshops can vary, but around the same topic. For example, "couples therapy" workshops may use a behavioral logic, a psychodynamic logic, or others.) What is a paradoxical story? Allan Chinen's book of elder (1989) and midlife folk tales (1992) contain many. One favorite story that I have heard often on the workshop circuit, with many variations, involves a farmer whose horse has disappeared. The farmer's neighbor comes to commiserate, saying "I pity you! What terrible luck!"

"You never can tell," replies the farmer.

Soon the horse returns, leading another wild horse! "What good fortune!" says the neighbor. "You now have *two* horses!"

"You never can tell," replies the farmer.

Soon the farmer's firstborn decides to break the wild horse and is immediately thrown to the ground, breaking his leg badly. "How awful, what terrible luck you've had! And you're so poor already!" laments the concerned friend, who knows quite well that farms need every worker, and more.

"You never can tell," replies the farmer, who is beginning to acquire a reputation for being a man of few words.

The very next day, the Cossacks ride into the village and conscript every able-bodied potential soldier and potential prostitute they can find. Young people with broken legs are not selected! The farmer smiles, but not as broadly as the neighbor does. "What amazing luck, how fortunate you were to be able to save your child when so many were taken!"

Of course, the farmer replies, "You never can tell. . . ."

I could go on, but you get the idea. Was the farmer's luck good or bad? It depends on your definitions, and even more on the logic you choose.

Activity 11 involves making a case for the rationality of any behavior. For example, a psychology class might be asked to show how an athlete who is anorectic, and even near death from it, might, on another level, be doing something useful (psychologically).

Paradoxical instructions (activity 12), which open possibility by elevating mood, might include something as simple as asking students to write down five things they would *never* think worth studying in the ice cream parlor (see activity 3 above).

Activity 13, group testing, means that the team or small group must work on the test together and come up with a single answer. Again, the goal is a shift among logics.

Thinking of behavior from the point of view of a courtroom trial (activity 14) requires students to assemble facts and logic to enhance either the prosecution or the defense position. One of my midlife development classes, conducted the same semester that a disastrous, deadly commuter train accident occurred nearby, used this exercise to argue for or against the position that the conductors partially caused the wreck because of middle-age changes in their bodies and minds. A trial does involve a final passionate commitment to one of the logics, by at least the jury and the judge.

The idea of finding six ways to look upon any given problem or decision (activity 15) comes from Native American tradition as articulated by Underwood (1991). The task is simple: Give *six* explanations that effectively explain a given event. Some variations on this theme are to give six ways to solve a given problem, and to look at a situation from six points of view. For an example of the latter, when an environmental policy team looks at a land-use dilemma, one team member might ask how a given land use might affect wildlife while a second considers how it might affect developers. My classes sometimes use the Narings Liv exercises presented in Appendix B, with some groups answering "What if work were only for profit?" and other groups answering "What if work were for nourishment of the soul?" Again, problems are redefined and logics are contrasted.

The last activity (16), opening and closing problem space repeatedly, flows from traditional problem-solving literature. The area of assumptions, content, or processes in which the problem may be solved is the problem space. Parameters must exist to tell the problem solver what is in or out of consideration (the space) during work on this problem. The parameters may be internally or externally generated. For example, many of my research respondents asked me to limit the problem space for them by calling the problem in front of them either "abstract" or "everyday/realistic." If I had told them "abstract," I would have closed or limited the problem space; when I declined to tell them, I opened up the problem space and made it larger to include more content and processes. In class, a professor could close the problem space of term paper topic choice by stating that the topic *must* be one from the materials on the professor's "faculty reserve" list in the library. The professor could then open the problem space by saying that *all* topics related to the psychology of aging are acceptable. Opening and closing problem space repeatedly is best done in the process of guiding discussion groups. For example, one of my classes was discussing a specific question (relatively small problem space), namely, how older adults compensate for their slower learning of details and their emphasis on meaning. When the students had answers, I asked them to discuss now how *younger* adults compensate for too much loading in of details and too little emphasis on meaning (more open problem space). When they had solved that one, I asked them to focus on (narrower problem space) how college instructors should *teach* differently to older versus younger classes. Finally, they needed to address what this all implies for life-span cognition (a very large problem space). The opening and closing of the problem space allows logic to shift and allows one logic to be chosen as best at each occasion. Parameters must be set, multiple goals and solutions and methods must be used, and all the other postformal operations must be invoked.

In this chapter, we have scratched the surface of discussion of how to teach adults gathered in a structured setting to use their postformal thinking abilities. In the next chapter, we will briefly discuss how individuals might use postformal thought to help them develop personally by balancing their *own* body, mind, spirit, heart, and relationships with others, all within their own lives.

CHAPTER 22

Postformal Thought and Living in Balance

And, it doesn't hurt to have a sense of humor!
Elderly Buddhist priest,
discussing how a wise
person deals with the
circle of life and death

The book you are reading right now is about logical cognitive development in midlife and late life. But it is also about how an individual can both *understand* and actually *live* in balance, that is, a balance of mind, emotions, body, interpersonal life, and spirit.

There can be said to be a "logic" of the body, of the spirit, of the emotions, and of the relations among individuals, just as there is said to be a cognitive "logic." These several "logics" often contradict each other, causing us conflicts on a day-to-day basis and leaving us miserably stuck in indecision and self-defeating actions. The Theory of Postformal Thought describes the general cognitive "steps forward"—the teachable, general, form of the advanced logic of adulthood—that overarches these several personal "logics." The advanced logic of adulthood can facilitate our living in balance, with fewer personal conflicts, during our adult years.

The general form or skill of adult logic has many personal, interpersonal, and societal applications, applications that can promote our living in balance, as we saw in the chapters in Part III of this book. But this one application, that of overarching our many personal "logics," embodies such an important synthesis that I have saved it for this final chapter. Put another way, the synthesis can be stated thus: *By accessing this type of postformal logic, an individual can think about and understand the possibility of personal balance (or imbalance!) among his or her own mind, heart, body, spirit, and interpersonal life "log-*

ics." What this statement means is that postformal thought allows us to *consciously* attempt to *live* in balance, in our own life, in addition to allowing us to *understand,* in the abstract, on a cognitive level, how such a balance might exist. How this balance comes about and what it implies are the focus of the remainder of this chapter.

When we talk about postformal understanding and living in balance, we are talking about a kind of heroism, a kind of living life to its limits, without denying any part of our larger self. We are talking about the man (a real person) who today has only an hour to do four hours of the work that puts bread on the table. He has only that one hour because he has three close relatives who are dying (one of them his wife, another his mother, a third his cousin) and his HMO wants more paperwork "right away" to keep pain medication coming for his wife, while his dyslexic son has just come crying to his desk needing help with schoolwork *now.* Quick memories cross his mind—of the last time he was hugged, of the last time he made love, and of the last time he slept five whole hours. A wave of grief washes over him. What was it, again, that he had planned to do with his life, once upon a time? He forgets to be thankful that he hasn't been "downsized," yet, and laid off entirely from his job because he needed to work at home some of the time. The demands of life seem impossibly large. Suddenly, something reaches his awareness. Coming ever closer outside, though the closed window, is the faint sound of geese honking, flying over in the V formations of fall migration, "talking" to each other as they fly toward something new. He grabs his son and goes to the window, throws it open, and points up at the story in the sky, the story of endings that are beginnings, and of bad days that are good days, as long as there are geese to call us into the clouds when we are tied too tightly to the earth. Then the man smiles, feeling himself an eagle. It all makes sense, but only from the eagle's visual perspective, even if you are tied to the ground. This is the kind of real life that must be wrestled into balance every day. These are the conflicted logics of the tired body, and the sadness, and the spiritual longings, and the demanding relations with others—all of which must be understood in terms of a very complex logic indeed if we are to go on *consciously!*

Notice that the consciousness he must use to resolve this difficult conflict flies in the face of the rationalism and the positivist logic that our shared "cultural trance" (Ferguson, 1980) tells us is the only logic that exists. Our cultural view that there is only one wisdom, a cognitive one, keeps us from framing questions that let us study the other types of logics or wisdoms. Our cultural view compartmentalizes the parts of self such as "mind" and "body." Postformal thought forms a bridge to let us represent the other "logics" (such as the body one) in the mind's language. (Note that the mind's logic can be represented in the language of any of the other systems, too—for example, in the language of the body or of the emotions.) Luckily, fields such as medicine have recently taken interest in "the wisdom of the body" (one of those alternative logics) in discussing preventive care. This increasing number of vantage points enlarges our types of questions by giving us cultural permission to look at the world in different ways. It also lets us see that we need postformal reasoning to consciously strive for flexible holistic wellness, rather than just learning the language and steps coming from the inflexible logic of a new, "absolutely right" single system of wellness.

What might this man in our example be doing, cognitively, while watching the geese and changing his attitude? Now we are back to abstract terms for a volatile, emotionally complex situation. He seems to be choosing to regulate his emotional (and other) reactions and their many logics by making his overriding logic about the moment more complex and postformal, using the thinking operations we have talked about in the cold-cognitive terms of earlier chapters. If he can continue to impose this regulation day by day, he will be able to avoid being completely overwhelmed by demands or emotions. Instead, he will be taking a broader logical view of them. Postformal thought permits an awareness of the other logics or the other types of "wisdoms" and provides a way to cognitively regulate them on a personal level. *He* will be the one making decisions about the meaning of his experiences and then regulating them on the level of behavior—but only because he dares to experience them fully. Of course, he will need behavior *skills,* too, to regulate them on a personal level, but he is more likely to develop such skills if he has the *knowledge* that such complex self-regulation is possible.

The synthesis involved in postformally living in balance involves being open to the spirit of possibility, as the existentialists are, open to creating the chosen meaning of your existence or even of one moment, and living that meaning out to a conclusion. This knower sees more clearly that we are a conflicted composite of body, mind, spirit, emotion, and social roles. But rather than bouncing from awareness of demands from one aspect of his life to awareness of demands from another—for example, from "what's good for body" to "what's good for emotions"—the postformal knower can maturely hold the various conflicting realities in awareness simultaneously. Rather than being pulled from one polarized response (serving only one of the aspects of awareness) to another (serving only some other aspect of awareness), the postformal knower has an overarching reality on which to stand and see larger patterns that lead to more useful choices serving the whole, complex situation.

Such a conscious living in balance using postformal thinking in daily life seems like the essence of integrity as Erikson envisioned it happening in the last developmental stages of life. The postformal part of that integration seems like a cognitive part that lets the integrated person become integrated at a *conscious* level. Wisdom, too, by any definition, implies living in balance. The wise person can (and does) balance the various demands and dimensions of his or her unique life-in-the-world, with all of its "logics," in such a way that they are integrated, usually consciously.

Living in balance pertains both to the individual's experience within the self (e.g., balancing internal conflicts over emotions or identities) and to the balance among individuals in the larger world that includes the self (e.g., balancing interpersonal or transpersonal conflicts). Psychologists historically have been more focused on what happens within the person than on what happens at any other level, and more psychologists are experts in the former types of questions than in the latter types. In the case of the complex postformal understanding that leads to balanced living, though, the same type of cognitive operations can allow us to understand the logics of both our in*tra*personal and our in*ter*personal realities, even when they conflict. Awareness of both types, and of their connections to each other, enhances the ability of the postformal individual to stay connected with the "real world" and with others, even while assimilating reality in very abstract and complex cognitive ways. Rather than experiencing the disconnection or distance of the subjectivist, or even of the meditator who forgets to come down from the mountain and live again in the real world, the postformal person, after achieving understanding, can be expected to return to the marketplace of practical, interpersonal life *because* his or her very understanding of reality automatically (potentially) includes consideration of, and a logical balance of, all the elements of any personal or interpersonal situation.

Postformal understanding also includes a built-in tolerance for and a built-in ability to hold a many-truth reality or the single realities of many less-developed persons whom one encounters, without being overwhelmed by stimulation and forced to resolve the situation simplistically, either by using simple, cynical relativism or by naming one single logical, "correct" truth. The postformal person can therefore live with a simultaneously macro- and microview of complex, ill-structured, problematic reality.

But the thinker must stay grounded on the Earth. The postformal person must be aware that abstract constructions of mind and the abstract words *are* abstract. They are reflections of our species' forms of cognition. Words are not enough to completely reflect real, grounded subjective reality. Seeing the connections among mind, body, emotions, spirit, and interpersonal interactions, the postformal thinker is aware that *all* of these realities coexist and matter. It is the *formal* operational person, the "expert" on abstraction, whose thinking ironically is dominated by the abstractions and products of the logical mind. The *postformal* thinker using the more complex logic, on the other hand, can be free to rise above abstraction while anchored to an adaptive reality involving body and emotions and other people.

In science and in academic life, we tend to talk about even complex, grounded, interpersonal life realities in terms that suggest only chilly, bloodless things. But the real life that makes demands on the postformal thinker usually comes crashing in with far more wrenching challenges and embodied immediacy. The real postformal thinker dances daily over hot coals near cliff edges while being distracted by threatening demands, piteous entreaties, and seductive pleasures. This dance is not an easy one. Balance, if it is achieved at all, is achieved by a wounded, limping warrior-dancer! Peaceful balance, if it is created, is created from the white-hot refinement of a life lived in relationship. The refined gold becomes cool and beautiful, but it becomes so very gradually through the "death" of its earlier forms.

Chungliang Al Huang is a wonderful, gifted teacher of tai chi, which is an Eastern martial art involving balanced movement (e.g., Huang & Lunch, 1992). He describes all of us as potential "tai chi dancers," able to orchestrate our energy movements. In one sequence of tai chi movements that he offers in workshops, he invites students to be like the legendary Buddha in the period in which he was reclaiming his preordained "Buddha nature." Workshop participants "dance" this spiritually important event, symbolically, by reaching up with one hand to access their spiritual nature and reaching down with the other hand to make contact with their roots in the physical reality of the Earth. The hands then meet at the heart and thereafter open to all the world of possibilities, the tai chi dancer balancing with arms outstretched while symbolically walking the tightrope of life's demands and keeping open to the learning experiences encountered along the way. What a wonderful movement metaphor for living in balance! The tai chi moves are designed to bring these complex relations to our conscious awareness, to deepen our understanding, especially by means of a body-centered knowing. *Postformal logical thinking might be envisioned as the tai chi of the mind that lets us move through the forms of the* understanding *of balanced mind, heart, interpersonal, body, and spirit logics.*

So this final application and synthesis involving postformal thought is both the simplest and the most important and far-reaching of them all. To reach this awareness signifies a quantum leap in logic and understanding on a personal level. Such an aware individual is eager to use the "tools" and personal growth/spiritual techniques that let growth continue indefinitely.

We thus come now to a final important question: What would be the implications for all of us if more and more individuals postformally balanced their lives? It is possible that more and more individuals, balancing their lives, can shift the balance of the mass of humanity? It seems there can be no internal peace without postformally living in balance, but that internal peace comes when one does so. There seems to be little peace for couples and families and organizations that cannot rise above lesser logics to the postformal level; peace is more likely to come when they do so. Perhaps the many of us, living in postformal balance, can cause shifts in nations and in the world community of nations. In this sense, individuals living in balance gradually may be able to change the world for the better.

Measures of Postformal Thought and Coding and Scoring Guidelines

MEASURES

ABC

Six letters of the 26 letters of the alphabet appear below. Imagine that you are making pairs of the letters, writing down all the possible ways of putting two different letters together. How many pairs will you have when you make all possible pairs of the six letters? (Remember, although any letter will appear several times in different pairs, the same letter should not appear twice in the same pair:

BB BC BD.

Use these letters:

A B C D E F

VC (Vitamin C)

Six foods appear in the list below. All six are good sources of Vitamin C. Your doctor has asked you to eat two different foods which are good sources of Vitamin C every day. (1) How many different pairs of foods might you eat when you make all possible pairs of the six foods? In other words, how many possible pairs are there? (2) In each pair you make, how many portions of each food must you eat to get at least 2 units of Vitamin C from that pair?

Vitamin C sources
1 portion and units of Vitamin C
in the portion:
1 orange, 1 unit
1 grapefruit, 2 units
8 oz. tomato juice, 1 unit
½ cup cabbage, 1 unit
20 grapes, ½ unit
1 cup greens, 1 unit

Find:
1. _____ possible pairs of different foods.
2. In each pair, how many portions of each to get at least 2 units of Vitamin C?

CAMP

You have six children who love to go camping. You have patience enough to take two children, but no more, on each trip. Each child wants a chance to camp with each of the other brothers and sisters during the summer. How many trips would be necessary to give each child a chance to camp with every brother and sister if you take only two children each trip? How do you know?

POW (Power Family Dynamics)

A family consisting of a father in his forties and a 15-year-old child live in the suburbs. They learn that a 70-year-old grandmother (the father's mother) will need to live with them due to her failing health. Right now, the family members have this "power relationship": The father runs the house and the child follows his rules (father-dominant, child dominated). The grandmother has made it clear that when she comes she may not want anyone, including the father, telling her what to do. If the grandmother moves in, what are all the possible "power relationships" that might develop among pairs of individuals in the household? (The possible power relationships are (1) *dominant–dominated* and (2) *equal–equal*.)

WK (Magazine Workers)

You are supervising the assembly of a magazine. Several workers are putting pages in order; others are binding the pages. The binders finish 20 magazines every hour. However, those putting pages together in order finish 40 in 2 hours. Some of your workers are idle part of the time. Equal numbers of workers are performing each task, and there are more than enough supplies in each area. All the workers can handle both jobs. What can you do to keep all the workers equally busy?

CAKE *(substituted for CAMP in the standard administration)*

A friend is having a birthday, and you are making a cake for the party. The cake recipe calls for 2 cups of flour, 1 cup of milk, and 1 cup of sugar, among other things. You have measured all the flour into a bowl and have added the sugar when the doorbell rings. You leave to answer it. When you return to the kitchen, you forget that the sugar is in the bowl and add 1 more cup of sugar, plus the milk. Suddenly, you realize your mistake; your cake will be too sweet. What can you do to solve the problem?

BR (Bedrooms)

A family consisting of a mother in her 40s, a father in his forties, a 10-year-old girl, a 12-year-old girl, and a 15-year-old boy live in a small two-bedroom house in Detroit. One of the bedrooms is large and well-decorated, and has a single bed; the other bedroom also has a single bed. This summer, the family learns that a grandfather who lives alone in a one-bedroom apartment two blocks away can no longer live alone. He might move in with the family. What are all the possible ways that the six persons can use the two bedrooms in the house?

CODING AND SCORING GUIDELINES

MERRIE STANDISH and JAN SINNOTT

Having access to any of these operations is evidence that the participant is shifting systems of logical reality to some degree. The degree of postformal thought shown by the participant is based on the nine different operations that follow. Each operation is one potential indicator of the use of postformal thought by the participant. In addition to defining how to code these nine operations, the scoring system is explaned and examples are given in order to clarify the coding and scoring system. The coding and scoring are usually recorded on a Postformal Reasoning Score Sheet.

Problem Definition

The coder should briefly indicate how the participant has defined the problem, listing the definitions. In defining the problem, the participant states or clearly implies that he or she is defining the problem in a given way, perhaps either as being a math problem and/or a social relations problem. This is a labeling of problem type. It is possible for the participant to indicate no ways or one or more ways of defining the problem. Problem definition is one potential indicator that the participant can shift logics.

Scoring. Defining the problem in two or more ways gives the participant a total of 1 point toward "being postformal" on the tally for this problem and/or on the tally across all problems. Therefore, the coder counts the definitions and enters the total number. If the number is 2 or more, 1 point can be added to the total postformal score, either for this problem or for the tally for all problems.

Examples. In the Bedrooms problem, the participant might state that this is a math problem asking for all possible permutations of people and bedrooms. Another definition by the participant might define the problem as asking for the possible arrangements based on optimizing the grandfather's well-being. A third might be that the problem is defined as "keeping the peace in the family." A second example can be drawn from the Vitamin C problem. One definition of the problem might assume that all foods are paired without any other restrictions; another definition might define the problem in terms of foods that are compatible or taste good together. A third definition of the problem might be pairing "using the foods you have on hand before buying any others, the oldest being eaten first."

Metatheory Shift

Metatheory shift by the participant takes place when she or he clearly indicates that it is possible to define the approach to the problem in more than one *major* way, that is, in an "abstract" manner *and* in a "practical" manner. Both terms are defined in a standard dictionary sense. Two or more practical definitions of the problem (or more than one abstract definition), a situation that would have sufficed to get points for "problem definition," does not constitute a metatheory shift because metatheory shift demands a larger paradigm shift. The participant either voices that the problem might be solved in more than one way or actually solves the problem in more than one way, showing this major shift. The participant is thereby "labeling her or his *logic*" by stating that there is more than one way to look at the problem, claiming it either for abstract logic or for practical logic. The issue is whether or not the participant can shift between two different *logics* with different and contradictory implications for the solution of the problem.

Scoring. The coder simply decides "yes" or "no" in this portion, after listing the metatheory(ies) used. If the score is "yes," the participant is given 1 point toward "being postformal" on the tally for this problem and/or on the tally across all problems.

Examples. In the Bedrooms problem, the participant states or clearly indicates that, although this may be treated as an abstract problem, there exists a second and practical logic of the problem involving the need to consider the people using the rooms or whether or not they have an intimate relationship, and other considerations. In another example, in the Family Power Dynamics problem, the participant may state or clearly imply that there is both an abstract logic that can be applied to this problem and a practical logic that can be applied to it that considers real-life limitations to developing power relationships, for example, age, health, and relational history.

Parameter Setting

Parameter setting involves the limiting aspects of the problem situation that are voiced by the participant or very clearly implied in the plan of attack used during problem solving. These may be any limits or any variables that are set and/or used by a participant to describe the conceptual space in which the solution will be worked out. However, that the larger dimensions of the logic and metatheory, or of the overall definition of the problem, may be taken for granted and left unstated during this (lower-level) parameter setting. The participant is deciding the (lower-level) rules of the problem-solving game. The parameters mentioned by the participant may be taken directly from the wording of the problem or may be added to the wording by the participant. Parameter setting must go beyond the mere reading of the problem, however. Parameter setting implies that the participant can increase and decrease the problem space in which the logic of the problem can then be worked out.

Scoring. The parameters that are expressed or clearly implied by the participant's attack on the problem are listed and counted. The listing of two or more parameters gives the participant one point toward "being postformal" either for the tally for this problem or for the tally across all problems.

Examples. In the Camping problem, the participant may decide that all numerical pairs are to be counted without any consideration that there are more pairs than weekends in the summer, or, conversely, the participant may decide that the number of pairs must not exceed the number of weekends in the summer. Another example of parameter setting applies to the ABC pairs problem. It is possible to set parameters that either allow reversals ("AB is not a duplicate of BA") or that disallow reversals ("AB is a duplicate of BA").

Multiple Goals

The coder should briefly list the goal(s) that the participant has indicated. Goals may be stated verbally by the participant or may be implied by a clearly and narrowly defined approach to the solution. What is the point or goal the participant is trying to achieve? What is/are the participant's stopping point(s) after which he or she considers the problem "solved" (by any definition)? These are the goals. Stating multiple goals implies that the participant can make use of more than one logic about the problem.

Scoring. The goals are listed and totaled. The participant also is given a point for two or more goals. This point may be added to the postformal tally for this problem or to the tally across all problems.

Examples. A restricted, that is, singular, example of a goal may occur in the ABC pairs problem when the participant's goal is only "to find the number of letter pairs." In both the Family Power Dynamics problem and the Bedrooms problem, not only is "finding the total number of combinations" often a goal of the participant, but also it is not unusual for there to be additional goals such as "that the solution be reasonable or socially acceptable within the respondent's parameters."

Multiple Methods

The coder needs to list briefly the methods that the participant has used to solve the problem. The methods are the general processes and/or the heuristic that have been used to reach a solution. These methods are general in nature so that they could be applied to any number of problems. For example, things such as formulas, multiplication, and addition are methods. General methods also include, for example, "seeking family counseling," "keeping the older person happy," and "putting together foods that taste good when eaten together." Sometimes "finding a method or a process that works in a lot of situations" is a *goal,* too, in the context of the operations called "process–product shift" (see [below]) and "multiple goals" (see [below]), because the participant considers the problem "solved" when a good method has been found. As before, using several methods to get to the same end implies the ability to shift logics and commit to one.

Scoring. The methods are listed and the total number of them is noted. If two or more are listed, a score of 1 point is given for this operation. This point may be added to the tally of postformal points for this problem and/or to the tally across all problems.

Examples. In the ABC pairs problem, it is possible methodologically to use pairing, to apply a math formula, or to use the answer from a similar previous problem to achieve the same numerical answer. If all of these methods are used by the participant, the participant is credited with three methods. An example of a general method that is often applied to the Bedrooms problem is to "base bedroom assignments on the furniture available and how it fits in the room."

Process–Product Shift

For process–product shift to be said to occur, there must be a shift in the type of solutions offered. With reference to the solutions provided, there must be at least one general process that is clearly seen as providing, in and of itself, a solution to the given problem. Therefore, in addition to a solution applicable to any of this sort of problem, similarly defined, there is at least one specific solution that would apply only to this particular problem. So the participant with process–product shift both (1) has clearly indicated the ability to define the solutions to a problem both in the sense of a generally applicable process and in the sense of providing a specific "product" solution and (2) has shown the ability to shift between these two types of "solutions," one a process and one a specific contexted product. This ability implies the ability to select logics.

Scoring. The two different types of solution should be written down by the coder. The coder needs to decide either "yes" or "no" as to the presence of the operation. A "yes" gives one more postformal point on the tally for this problem and/or on the tally across all problems. Simply having a method and an answer (together or alone) is not sufficient for getting a process–product point.

Examples. In applying process–product shift to the ABC problem, the participant may provide (solution 1) a math formula, clearly indicating that having the formula is itself a solution to this (and similar) problems. In addition, the participant may apply that formula and arrive at solution 2, a certain number of pairs of letters. These two steps together obtain a point for process–product shift. An example of process–product shift in the Camping problem could be the participant providing a general method as though it were one solution ("in these cases the answer is to draw up a round robin table like they use in a tennis tournament. . .") followed by a second solution that is context- and number-specific ("38 trips to camp").

Multiple Solutions

A solution is the answer that lets the participant reach her or his goal and stop solving the problem. If the participant acts as though she or he completed the process and reached a goal, but yet failed to voice the solution directly, it may be necessary for the coder to examine what the participant said or wrote. For example, the participant may have written down pairs of letters on the ABC pairs problem, yet failed to voice a specific number of pairs, after which it is clear that this array is viewed by the participant as "the solution." Yet if the number of pairs is on the scratch sheet, and the participant said she or he had reached a solution, this constitutes a solution. Creating *multiple* solutions implies that the participant can manipulate more than one logic.

Scoring. The coder lists all the solutions that are voiced and/or indicated and totals their number. If the total is two or more, the participant receives a point toward the postformal tally for this problem and/or for the tally for all the problems in the aggregate.

Examples. As noted earlier, for the ABC pairs problem, some solutions might include a formula, 15 pairs, and 30 pairs, which together constitute 3 solutions and are worth a postformal point for "multiple solutions." For the Bedrooms problem, the participant might give the specific final number of bedroom combinations and also, then, place all men in one bedroom and all women in another. This yields 2 solutions and a postformal point.

Pragmatism

For pragmatism to be found, the participant must have indicated more than one solution and then have chosen a best solution or a "clear winner" from the solutions given, thus permitting him or her to more on to the next problem. There must be evidence that the participant was able to make a choice between these competing solutions or realities and, having made a choice, was then able to move forward. This implies access to postformal logic. Pragmatism in this application differs slightly from the usual definition of pragmatism found in the dictionary.

Scoring. The coder indicates "yes" or "no." A "yes" code gives the participant one point toward "being postformal" on the tally for a single problem or on the tally across all problems.

Examples. In the ABC pairs problem, the participant might indicate both a formula solution and a specific number of pairs, but then clearly indicate that for this problem the best answer is the specific number of pairs. In the Camping problem, the participant may have given an answer of "15 trips" and an answer of "sending all the children to camp at the same time." After offering these two solutions, the participant then specifies that the single trip is the best choice based on the limited number of weekends in a single summer.

Paradox

Paradox, as an operation of postformal thought, is defined as a seemingly contradictory statement that may nonetheless be true. In this operation, the participant has noted that there is a contradiction present in the apparently simultaneous demands of the problem for (for example) simply looking for a mathematical solution and simultaneously creating a solution applicable to the real world. The participant appears to understand that there is a "double bind" quality to the demands of the problem. Often, this brings out the participant's sense of humor. Awareness of paradox implies awareness of multiple logical contradictory realities.

Scoring. The coder scores a "yes" or a "no" for paradox on this problem. The participant is given 1 point for "being postformal" if he or she obtains a "yes." The point may then be included in the tally either for this problem or for the tally across all problems.

Examples. In the vitamin C problem, the participant may note that, although it is possible to solve the problem mathematically, to do so leads to an ironic solution, since some of the food combinations are distasteful and no one would eat them anyhow. In the Bedrooms problem, the participant may note the paradoxical nature of "solving" a problem by creating new problems when people are "stacked in rooms like wood."

The Narings Liv Project at the Institute for Noetic Sciences

A form of free dialogue may well be one of the most effective ways of investigating the crises which face society. Moreover, it may turn out that such a form of free exchange of ideas and information is of fundamental relevance for transforming culture so that creativity can be liberated.

DAVID BOHM

What if the purpose of business is to provide nourishment for life?

In Swedish, the word for "business" is *narings liv,* literally, "nourishment for life."

The Swedish concept of business as nourishment for life inspired the Narings Liv Project at the Institute of Noetic Sciences. The purpose of the project is to explore the metaphor of business as nourishment for life at all levels of human activity—from the individual to the global—in the interest of contributing to a sustainable future.

Through dialogue and collaborative inquiry with interested individuals, groups, and organizations, the project seeks to expand international exploration of the creative role of business in a transforming world. The project asks such questions as these:

- What if the life of business and the business of living were based on principles and practices that nourish the long-term health of living systems?
- What if we as individuals, families, organizations, and communities considered our true business to be that of nourishment for life?

- Is it possible to implement the principles of nourishment for life and still create excellent personal and business results?
- What might be the effect on business *as* community and on business *in* the community?
- What organizations today consciously use *narings liv* sorts of approaches in guiding their strategic planning and daily actions? What have they learned?
- What deeply held assumptions and beliefs keep us from choosing to implement the principles of nourishment for life?

The Narings Liv Project welcomes collaboration with others who have common interests in this inquiry. It is part of the membership education program of the Institute of Noetic Sciences.

The goals of the Narings Liv Project are to:

- Support the development of dialogue groups among members and friends of the Institute of Noetic Sciences and among organizations or networks similarly interested in the creative role of business in a transforming world.
- Design and experiment with tools and processes to facilitate creative dialogue on the concept of business as nourishment for life.
- Identify, develop, and distribute resource materials to support self-managing dialogue groups, both within the institute's membership and in other organizations or networks.
- Share learning from *narings liv* dialogues with other dialogue groups in ways that allow for a continual deepening of the questions and the common "knowing" that may emerge.
- Experiment with appropriate database and groupware technologies to facilitate dialogue and to exchange ideas, information, insights, and understanding.
- Learn about the process of dialogue itself as a vehicle for transformative change.
- Develop strategic partnerships with others sharing common interests both in the United States and in other parts of the world.

Creative dialogue can help illuminate the values and beliefs that shape our experience and institutions, and thus help us learn to live and choose more wisely. While this project is not designed to take an advocacy stance, those engaged in this type of collaborative learning will be better able to make personal choices and commitments to public action that are more socially, economically, and politically aware. Inquiries may be sent to:

Director of Membership Education
Institute of Noetic Sciences
475 Gate Five Road   Suite 300
Sausalito, CA 94965
Phone: (415) 331-5650
Fax: (415) 331-5673

Some Readings in Existential, Humanistic, and Transpersonal Psychology and in Mind–Body Medicine

The books listed below may suggest the spirit of these approaches, although they *do not* represent *all* the thinking in any of the four approaches. Various journals and other materials are also available. The categories below are only "quick and dirty" ways to group the books, since most overlap categories!

Existential Psychology

Becker, E. (1974). *The denial of death.* New York: Free Press.
Bugenthal, J. F. T. (1990). *Intimate journeys: Stories from life changing therapy.* San Francisco: Jossey Bass.
Camus, A. (1947). *The plague* (fiction). New York: Vintage.
Deci, E. (1980). *The psychology of self-determination.* Lexington, MA: D. C. Heath.
Edwards, D. (1982). *Existential psychotherapy: The process of caring.* New York: Gardner.
Frankl, V. (1963). *Man's search for meaning.* New York: Basic Books.
Gould, W. (1993). *Frankl: Life with meaning.* Belmont, CA: Wadsworth.
Klinger, E. (1977). *Meaning and void.* Minneapolis: University of Minnesota Press.
Laing, R. D. (1959). *The divided self.* Baltimore: Pelican.
Laing, R. D. (1967). *The politics of experience.* New York: Ballantine Books.
May, R. (1953). *Man's search for himself.* New York: Signet.
May, R. (1969). *Love and will.* New York: Norton.
May, R. (1983). *The discovery of being: Writings in existential psychotherapy.* New York: Norton.

Monette, P. (1992). *Becoming a man: Half a life story.* New York: Harcourt Brace Jovanovich.

Pirsig, R. M. (1974). *Zen and the art of motorcycle maintenance* (fiction). New York: Bantam.

Quill, T. (1996). *A midwife through the dying process.* Baltimore: Johns Hopkins University Press.

Rinpoche, S. (1992). *The Tibetan book of living and dying.* San Francisco: Harper.

Sartre, P. (1957). *Existentialism and human emotions.* New York: Philosophical Library.

Tillich, P. (1952). *The courage to be.* New Haven, CT: Yale University Press.

Warschaw, T., & Barlow, D. (1995). *Resiliency.* New York: Mastermedia Books.

Wong, B., & McKeen, J. (1992). *A manual for life.* Gabriola Island, British Columbia, Canada: PD Seminars.

Yalom, I. D. (1980). *Existential psychotherapy,* New York: Basic Books.

Humanistic Psychology

Bateson, G. (1979). *Mind and nature: A necessary unity.* New York: Bantam.

Boldt, L. (1991). *Zen and the art of making a living: A practical guide to creative career design.* New York: Penguin Books.

Bolen, J. S. (1984). *Goddesses in everywoman: A new psychology of women.* New York: Harper Collins.

Bradshaw, J. (1988). *Healing the shame that binds you.* Deerfield Beach, FL: Health Communications.

Campbell, J. (1972). *Myths to live by.* New York: Bantam.

Campbell, J., & Moyers, B. (1988). *The power of myth.* New York: Doubleday.

Capra, F. (1988). *Uncommon wisdom: Conversations with remarkable people.* New York: Bantam.

Commons, M., Richards, R., & Armon, C. (Eds.). (1984). *Beyond formal operations.* New York: Praeger.

Feinstein, D., & Singer, J. (1988). *Personal mythology: The psychology of your evolving self.* Los Angeles: Tarcher.

Ferguson, M. (1980). *The aquarian conspiracy.* Los Angeles: Tarcher.

Goldstein, J. (1994). *The unshackled organization.* Portland, OR: Productivity Press.

Goerner, S. J. (1994). *Chaos and the evolving ecological universe.* Langhorne, PA: Gorden & Breach Science Publishers.

Hampden-Turner, C. (1981). *Maps of the mind: Charts and concepts of the mind and its labyrinths.* New York: Macmillan.

Harman, W., & Hormann, J. (1990). *Creative work: The constructive role of business in a transforming society.* Indianapolis, IN: Knowledge Systems Press.

Harman, W., & Rheingold, H. (1984). *Higher creativity.* Los Angeles: Tarcher.

Houston, J. (1980). *Lifeforce: The psychohistorical recovery of the self.* New York: Delacorte Press.

Huang, C. (1991). *Quantum soup: Fortune cookies in crisis.* Berkeley, CA: Celestial Arts.

Jung, C. G. (1933). *Modern man in search of a soul.* New York: Harcourt.

Kohn, A. (1986). *No contest: The case against competition.* Boston: Houghton Mifflin.

Kubler-Ross, E. (1969). *On death and dying.* New York: Macmillan.

Luce, G. G. (1979). *Your second life*. New York: Delacorte Press.
Maslow, A. (1968). *Toward a psychology of being*. New York: Van Nostrand Rinehold.
Masters, R., & Houston, J. (1966). *The varieties of psychedelic experience*. New York: Holt, Rinehart and Winston.
Maturana, H. R., & Varela, F. J. (1988). *The tree of knowledge: The biological roots of human understanding*. New York: New Sciences Press.
Mindell, A. (1989). *Coma: The dreambody near death*. New York: Penguin.
Mindell, A. (1992). *The dreambody in relationships*. New York: Penguin.
Mindell, A., & Mindell, A. (1992). *Riding the horse backwards: Process work in theory and practice*. New York: Penguin Books.
National Research Council. (1988). *Enhancing human performance: Issues, theories and techniques*. Washington, DC: National Academy of Sciences Press.
National Research Council. (1991). *In the mind's eye: Enhancing human performance*. Washington, DC: National Academy of Sciences Press.
National Research Council. (1994). *Learning, remembering, believing: Enhancing human performance*. Washington, DC: National Academy of Sciences Press.
Ostrander, S., & Sanderson, I. T. (1970). *Psychic discoveries behind the Iron Curtain*. New York: Bantam.
Pieper, M. H., & Pieper, W. J. (1990). *Intrapsychic humanism*. Chicago: Falcon II Press.
Robertson, R. (1987). *C. G. Jung and the archtypes of the collective unconscious*. New York: Peter Lang Publishers.
Rogers, C. (1961). *On becoming a person*. Boston: Houghton Mifflin.
Roszak, T. (1992). *The voice of the earth: An exploration of ecopsychology*. New York: Simon & Schuster.
Sankar, A. (1991). *Dying at home: A family guide for caregiving*. Baltimore: Johns Hopkins University Press.
Shorr, J. E. (1983). *Psychotherapy through imagery*. New York: Thieme-Stratton.
Sinnott, J. D. (Ed.). (1994). *Interdisciplinary handbook of adult development and aging*. Westport, CT: Greenwood.
Sinnott, J. D., & Cavanaugh, J. C. (Eds.). (1991). *Bridging paradigms: Positive development in adulthood and cognitive aging*. New York: Praeger.
Underwood, P. (1993). *The walking people*. San Anselmo, CA: A Tribe of Two Press.
Underwood, P. (1994). *Three strands in the braid: A guide for enablers of learning*. San Anselmo, CA: A Tribe of Two Press.
Whitmyer, C. (Ed.). (1993). *In the company of others: Making community in the modern world*. New York: Tarcher.
Williams, P. (1973). *Das energi*. New York: Warner Books.

Transpersonal Psychology

Abraham, R., McKenna, T., & Sheldrake, R. (1992). *Trialogues at the edge of the West: Chaos, creativity, and the resacralization of the world*. Santa Fe, NM: Bear.
Anderson, S. R., & Hopkins, P. (1991). *The feminine face of God*. New York: Bantam.
Bach, R. (19 *Illusions: The adventures of a reluctant messiah* (fiction). New York: William Morrow.
Brown, T., Jr. (1978). *The tracker*. New York: Berkley Books.

Capra, F. (1975). *The tao of physics.* New York: Bantam.

Castaneda, C. (1971). *A separate reality.* New York: Pocket Books.

Dossey, L. (1989). *Recovering the soul: A scientific and spiritual search.* New York: Bantam.

Feibleman, J. K. (1976). *Understanding Oriental philosophy.* New York: Times Mirror.

Fox, M. (1988). *The coming of the cosmic Christ.* New York: Harper & Row.

Gowan J. C. (1980). *Operations of increasing order, and other essays on exotic faculties of intellect.* Available from the author: 1426 Southwind Circle, Westlake Village, CA 91361.

Hanh, T. N. (1991). *Peace is every step.* New York: Bantam.

Hanh, T. N. (1992). *Touching peace: Practicing the art of mindful living.* Berkeley, CA: Parallax Press.

Harner, M. (1980). *The way of the shaman.* San Francisco: Harper & Row.

Houston, J. (1987). *The search for the beloved.* New York: Tarcher.

Ingerman, S. (1991). *Soul retrieval: Mending the fragmented self.* San Francisco: Harper Collins.

Jantsch, E. (1980). *The self organizing universe.* New York: Pergamon Press.

Joy, W. B. (1979). *Joy's way.* Los Angeles: Tarcher.

Jung, C. (1953). *Psychology and alchemy.* London: Routledge & Kegan Paul.

Keen, S. (1994). *Hymns to an unknown god: Awakening the spirit in everyday life.* New York: Bantam.

Khalsa, R. K. S. (1974). *Sadhana guidelines for kundalini yoga practice.* Los Angeles, CA: Arcline Publications.

Kopp, S. B. (1972). *If you meet the Buddha on the road, kill him!* New York: Bantam.

Kubler-Ross, E. (1991). *On life after death.* Berkeley, CA: Celestial Arts Press.

Miller, M., & Cook-Greuter, S. (Eds.) (1994). *Transcendence and mature thought in adulthood.* Lanham, MD: Rowman & Littlefield Publishers.

Mitchell, S. (1988). *Tao te ching.* New York: HarperCollins.

Moore, T. (1992). *Care of the soul.* New York: HarperCollins.

Moore, T. (1994). *Soul mates: Honoring the mysteries of love and relationships.* New York: HarperCollins.

Myss, C. (1996). *Anatomy of the spirit.* New York: Harmony Books.

Peck, M. S. (1978). *The road less traveled.* New York: Simon & Schuster.

Peck, M. S. (1983). *People of the lie: The hope for healing human evil.* New York: Simon & Schuster.

Prather, H. (1980). *There is a place where you are not alone.* New York: Doubleday.

Scotton, B., Chinen, A., & Battista, J. (Eds.). (1996). *Textbook of transpersonal psychiatry and psychology.* New York: Basic Books.

Shealy, C. N., & Myss, C. (1988). *The creation of health: The emotional, psychological, and spiritual responses that promote health and healing.* Walpole, NH: Stillpoint Publishing.

Sinetar, M. (1986). *Ordinary people as monks and mystics: Lifestyles for self discovery.* New York: Paulist Press.

Welwood, J. (1996). *Love and awakening: Discovering the sacred path of intimate relationship.* New York: HarperCollins.

Wilber, K. (1980). *The Atman Project.* Wheaton, IL: Quest Books.

Wilber, K. (1995). *Sex, ecology, and spirituality: The spirit of evolution.* Boston: Shambhala.

Zukav, G. (1979). *The dancing wu li masters.* New York: William Morrow.

Mind–Body Medicine

Achterberg, J. (1985). *Imagery in healing.* Boston: New Science Library.

Borysenko, J. (1987). *Minding the body, mending the mind.* Reading, MA: Addison Wesley.

Chopra, D. (1991). *Perfect health: The complete mind/body guide.* New York: Harmony Books.

Davis, M., Eshelman, E., & McKay, M. (1996). *The relaxation and stress reduction workbook.* Oakland, CA: New Harbinger Publications.

Dossey, L. (1985). *Space, time, and medicine.* Boston: Shambhala.

Drake, J. (1993). *Thorson's introductory guide to the Alexander Technique.* New York: HarperCollins.

Epstein, G. (1989). *Healing visualizations.* New York: Bantam.

Epstein, G. (1994). *Healing into immortality.* New York: Bantam.

Hammer, L. (1990). *Dragon rises, red bird flies: Psychology and Chinese medicine.* New York: Station Hill.

Huang, C. A., & Lynch, J. (1992). *Thinking body, dancing mind: Taosports for extraordinary performance in athletics, business, and life.* New York: Bantam.

Hultkrantz, A. (1992). *Shamanic healing and ritual drama: Health and medicine in Native North American religious traditions.* New York: Crossroads.

Locke, S., & Colligan, D. (1986). *The healer within: The new medicine of mind and body.* New York: Dutton.

Masters, R., & Houston, J. (1978). *Listening to the body: The psychophysical way to health and awareness.* New York: Dell.

Naparstek, B. (1994). *Staying well with guided imagery.* New York: Warner Books.

Ornstein, R., & Swencionis, C. (Eds.) (1990). *The healing brain: A scientific reader.* New York: Guilford Press.

Sheikh, A. A., & Sheikh, K. S. (1989). *Eastern and Western approaches to healing: Ancient wisdom and modern knowledge.* New York: Wiley.

Siegel, B. S. (1986). *Love, medicine and miracles.* New York: Harper & Row.

References

Abraham, R. (1985). Is there chaos without noise? In P. Fisher & W. Smith (Eds.), *Chaos, fractals, and dynamics* (pp. 117–121). New York: Marcel Dekker.

Alper, J. (1989). The chaotic brain: New models of behavior. *Psychology Today, 23*, 21.

Anderson, M. (1992). *Imposters in the temple.* New York: Simon & Schuster.

Arlin, P. K. (1975). Cognitive development in adulthood: A fifth stage? *Developmental Psychology, 11*, 602–606.

Armstrong, J. (1991). Keeping one's balance in a moving system: The effects of the multiple personality disordered patient on the cognitive development of the therapist. In J. D. Sinnott & J. Cavanaugh (Eds.), *Bridging paradigms: Positive development in adulthood and cognitive aging* (pp. 11–18). New York: Praeger.

Armstrong, J., & Sinnott, J. D. (1991, personal communication). Class handout on clinical aspects of postformal thought. Available from Sinnott at Towson University, Baltimore, MD 21204.

Augros, R., & Stanciu, G. (1987). *The new biology.* Boston: New Science Library.

Bach, R. (1977). *Illusions: Adventures of a reluctant messiah.* New York: Dell.

Barton, S. (1994). Chaos, self organization, and psychology. *American Psychologist, 49*, 5–14.

Basseches, M. (1984). *Dialectical thinking and adult development.* Norwood, NJ: Ablex.

Bastick, T. (1982). *Intuition: How we think and act.* New York: Wiley.

Beavers, W., & Hampson, R. (1990). *Successful families: Assessment and intervention.* New York: Norton.

Belenky, M. F., Clinchy, B. M., Goldberger, N. R., & Tarsule, J. M. (1986). *Women's ways of knowing.* New York: Basic Books.

Bem, S. (1993). *The lenses of gender.* New Haven, CT: Yale University Press.

Benack, S. (1984). Postformal epistemologies and the growth of empathy. In M. Commons, F. Richards, & C. Armon (Eds.), *Beyond formal operations* (pp. 340–356). New York: Praeger.

Benton, A. L. (1963). *The Revised Visual Retention Test: Clinical and experimental applications* (3rd ed.). New York: Psychological Corporation.

Blauberg, I., Sadovsky, V., & Yudin, E. (1977). *Systems theory.* Moscow: Progress Publishers.

Bohm, D. (1980). *Wholeness and the implicate order.* London: Routledge & Kegan Paul.

Born, M. (1962). *Einstein's theory of relativity.* New York: Dover.

Born, M. (1964). *Natural philosophy of cause and chance.* New York: Dover.

Brillouin, L. (1970). *Relativity reexamined.* New York: Academic Press.

Bronowski, J. (1974). *The ascent of man.* Boston: Little, Brown.

Campbell, J. (1988). *The power of myth*. New York: Doubleday.

Campbell, S. (1980). *The couple's journey: Intimacy as a path to wholeness*. San Luis Obispo, CA: Impact.

Capra, F. (1975). *The tao of physics*. New York: Bantam.

Cassirer, E. (1923). *Substance and function, and Einstein's theory of relativity*. New York: Dover.

Cassirer, E. (1950). *The problem of knowledge*. New Haven, CT: Yale University Press.

Cassirer, E. (1956). *Determinism and indeterminism in modern physics*. New Haven, CT: Yale University Press.

Castaneda, C. (1971). *A separate reality*. New York: Washington Square Press.

Cavanaugh, J. C. (1989). *The utility of concepts in chaos theory for psychological theory and research*. Paper presented at the Fourth Adult Development Conference at Harvard University, Cambridge, MA.

Cavanaugh, J., Kramer, D., Sinnott, J. D., Camp, C., & Markley, R. P. (1985). On missing links and such: Interfaces between cognitive research and everyday problem solving. *Human Development, 28,* 146–168.

Cavanaugh, J. C., & McGuire, L. (1994). The chaos of lifespan learning. In J. Sinnott (Ed.). *Interdisciplinary handbook of adult lifespan learning* (pp. 3–21). Westport, CT: Greenwood.

Chap, J. B., & Sinnott, J. D. (1977–1978). Performance of institutionalized and community active old persons on concrete and formal Piagetian tasks. *International Journal of Aging and Human Development, 8,* 269–278.

Chinen, A. B. (1984). *Eastern wisdom, Western aging*. Paper presented at the Annual Meeting of the Gerontological Society of America, San Antonio, TX.

Chinen, A. (1989). *In the ever after: Fairy tales and the second half of life*. Wilmette, IL: Chiron.

Chinen, A. (1992). *Once upon a midlife*. Los Angeles, CA: Tarcher.

Chowla, S., & Renesch, J. (Eds.). (1993). *Learning organizations: Developing cultures for tomorrow's workplace*. Portland: Productivity Press.

Churchman, C. (1971). *The design of inquiring systems: Basic concepts of systems and organizations*. New York: Basic Books.

Clayton, V. (1975). Erikson's theory of human development as it applies to the aged. *Human Development, 18,* 119–128.

Clinton, W., & Gore, A., Jr. (1993). *Technology for America's growth, a new direction to build economic strength*. Washington, D.C.: The White House, Office of the Press Secretary.

Commons, M., Armon, C., Kohlberg, L., Richards, F., Grotzer, T., & Sinnott, J. D. (Eds.). (1989). *Beyond formal operations III: Models and methods in the study of adult and adolescent thought*. New York: Praeger.

Commons, M., Richards, F., & Armon, C. (Eds.). (1984). *Beyond formal operations*. New York: Praeger.

Commons, M., Sinnott, J. D., Richards, F., & Armon, C. (Eds.). (1989). *Adult development II: Comparisons and applications of adolescent and adult developmental models*. New York: Praeger.

Crutchfield, J. P., Farmer, J. D., Packard, N. H., & Shaw, R. S. (1986). Chaos. *Scientific American, 255,* 46–57.

Csikszentmihalyi, M. (1978). Attention and the holistic approach to behavior. In K. Pope & J. Singer (Eds.), *The stream of consciousness* (pp. 335–358). New York: Plenum Press.

Davenport (1993). *Process innovation: Reengineering work through information technology*. Boston, MA: Harvard Business School Press.

Devaney, R. (1989). *An introduction to chaotic dynamical systems.* Redwood City, CA: Addison-Wesley.

Demick, J., & Miller, P. (Eds.). (1993). *Development in the workplace.* Hillsdale, NJ: Lawrence Erlbaum.

Dossey, L. (1982). *Space, time and medicine.* Boston: Shambhala.

Dossey, L. (1989). *Recovering the soul: A scientific and spiritual search.* New York: Bantam.

Efron, J. S., Lukens, M. D., & Lukens, R. J. (1990). *Language, structure and change.* New York: Norton.

Einstein, A. (1961). *Relativity: The special and general theory.* New York: Crown.

Eisler, R., & Loye, D. (1990). *The partnership way.* San Francisco: Harper.

Elias, D. (1987). *Implications of the postmodern world view for design in higher education.* Paper presented at the Third International Conference on Visions of Higher Education. Available from the author: California Institute for Integral Studies, San Francisco.

Epstein, G. (1989). *Healing visualisations.* New York: Bantam.

Epstein, G. (1994). *Healing into immortality.* New York: Bantam.

Ericsson, K., & Simon, H. (1984). *Protocol analysis.* Cambridge, MA: MIT Press.

Erikson, E. (1950). *Childhood and society.* New York: Norton.

Erikson, E. (1982). *The lifecycle completed.* New York: Norton.

Farrell, M. P., & Rosenberg, S. D. (1981). *Men at midlife.* Boston: Auburn House.

Ferguson, M. (1980). *The Aquarian conspiracy: Personal and social transformation in the 1980s.* Los Angeles: Tarcher.

Ford, D. (1987). *Humans as self-constructing living systems.* Hillsdale, NJ: Lawrence Erlbaum.

Fox, M. (1994). *The reinvention of work: A new vision of livelihood for our time.* San Francisco: Harper Collins.

Francis, J. B. (1992). Chaos models in higher education. In M. Michaels (Ed.), *Proceedings of the Annual Chaos Network Conference* (pp. 99–106). Urbana, IL: People Technologies.

Frankl, V. (1963). *Man's search for meaning.* New York: Washington Square Press.

Freedle, R. (1977). Psychology, Thomian topologies, deviant logics, and human development. In N. Datan & H. Reese (Eds.), *Lifespan developmental psychology: Dialectical perspectives on experimental research* (pp. 317–342). New York: Academic Press.

Freire, P. (1971). *The pedagogy of the oppressed.* New York: Herder & Herder.

Froman, L. (1994). Adult learning in the workplace. In J. D. Sinnott (Ed.), *Interdisciplinary handbook of adult lifespan learning* (pp. 159–170). Westport, CT: Greenwood.

Gandhi, M. K. (1951). *Satyagraha.* Ahmedabad, India: Navajivan.

Garmezy, N. (1976). *Vulnerable and invulnerable children.* Master Lectures in Psychology. Washington, D.C.: American Psychological Association.

Gergen, K. (1991). *The saturated self.* New York: Basic Books.

Giambra, L. (1983). *An idiographic, in depth approach to complex concept identification in adulthood.* Paper presented at the Gerontological Society of America Conference, San Francisco.

Giambra, L., & Arenberg, D. (1980). Problem solving, concept learning, and aging. In L. Poon (Ed.), *Aging in the 1980's: Psychological issues* (pp. 253–259). Washington, D.C.: American Psychological Association.

Gilligan, C. (1982). *In a different voice: Psychological theory and women's development.* Cambridge, MA: Harvard University Press.

Gleick, J. (1987). *Chaos: Making a new science.* New York: Penguin Books.

Godel, K. (1962). *On formally undecidable propositions.* New York: Basic Books.

Goerner, S. (1994). *Chaos and the evolving psychological universe.* Langhorne, PA: Gordon & Breach Scientific Publishers.

Goldstein, J. (1994). *The unshackled organization.* Portland, OR: Productivity Press.

Gore, A. (1992). *Earth in the balance: Ecology and the human spirit.* New York: Houghton Mifflin.

Gottman, J. (1991). Chaos and regulated change in families: A metaphor for the study of transitions. In P. A. Cohen & M. Hetherington (Eds.), *Family transitions* (pp. 247–272). Hillsdale, NJ: Erlbaum.

Gould, R. (1978). *Transformations.* New York: Simon & Schuster.

Grant, G., & Riesman, D. (1978). *The perpetual dream: Reform and experiment in the American college.* Chicago: University of Chicago Press.

Greeno, J., Magone, M., & Chaiklin, S. (1979). Theory of constructions and sets in problem solving. *Memory and Cognition, 7,* 445–461.

Guttmann, D. (1964). An exploration of ego configurations in middle and later life. In B. Neugarten (Ed.), *Personality in middle and late life* (pp. 137–158). New York: Atherton.

Guttmann, D., Sinnott, J. D., Carrigan, Z., Holahan, N. Flynn, M., & Mullaney, J. (1977). *The impact of needs, knowledge, ability, and living arrangements on decision making of the elderly.* Washington, D.C.: Catholic University Press.

Hanh, T. N. (1991). *Peace is every step.* New York: Bantam.

Hammer, L. (1990). *Dragon rises, red bird flies.* Barrytown, NY: Station Hill Press.

Hammer, M., & Champy, J. (1993). *Reengineering the corporation: A manifesto for business revolution.* New York: Harper Business Publishers.

Harman, W., & Hormann, J. (1990). *Creative work.* Indianapolis, IN: Knowledge Systems.

Harriger, C. (1994). Adults in college. In J. D. Sinnott (Ed.), *Interdisciplinary handbook of adult lifespan learning* (pp. 171–185). Westport, CT: Greenwood.

Havighurst, R. (1953). *Human development and education.* New York: Longmans.

Hayes-Roth, B., & Hayes-Roth, F. (1979). A cognitive model of planning. *Cognitive Science, 3,* 275–310.

Hefner, R., Rebecca, M., & Oleshansky, B. (1975). Development of sex role transcendence. *Human Development, 18,* 143–158.

Heisenberg, W. (1958). *Physics and philosophy.* New York: Harper & Row.

Hofstadter, D. R. (1979). *Godel, Escher and Bach: An eternal golden braid.* New York: Basic Books.

Hogue, A. T., Bross, L. S., & Efran, J. S. (1994). Learning in psychotherapy: A Batesonian perspective. In J. D. Sinnott (Ed.), *Interdisciplinary handbook of adult lifespan learning* (pp. 186–202). Westport, CT: Greenwood.

Howard, D. (1983). *Cognitive psychology.* New York: Macmillan.

Huang, C. A., & Lynch, J. (1992). *Thinking body, dancing mind: Taosports for extraordinary performance in athletics, business, and life.* New York: Bantam Books.

Hugo, V. (1938). *Les miserables* (Lascelles Wraxall, Trans.). New York: Heritage Press.

Hutchins, R. (1968). *The learning society.* New York: Praeger.

Inhelder, B., & Piaget, J. (1958). *The growth of logical thinking from childhood to adolescence.* New York: Basic Books.

Isen, A., & Shalker, T. (1982). Effects of feeling state on evaluation of positive, neutral, and negative stimuli: When you "accentuate the positive" do you "eliminate the negative"? *Social Psychology Quarterly, 45,* 58–63.

Johnson, L. (1991). Bridging paradigms: The role of a change agent in an international technical transfer project. In J. Sinnott & J. Cavanaugh (Eds.), *Bridging paradigms:*

Positive development in adulthood and cognitive aging (pp. 59–72). New York: Praeger.

Johnson, L. (1994). Nonformal adult learning in international development projects. In J. D. Sinnott (Ed.), *Interdisciplinary handbook of adult lifespan learning* (pp. 203–217). Westport, CT: Greenwood.

Johnson, L. (1996). Reorganization and institutional change. In J. Sinnott & L. Johnson (Eds.), *Reinventing the university: A radical proposal for a problem focused university* (pp. 123–134). Norwood, NJ: Ablex.

Johnson, L., & Sinnott, J. D. (1996). *Complex reasoning styles in expert research administrators.* Paper presented at the Society for Research Administrators National Conference, Toronto.

Jung, C. (1930/1971). The stages of life. In J. Campbell (Ed.), *The portable Jung,* New York: Viking Library.

Kabat-Zinn, J. (1990). *Full catastrophe living: Using the wisdom of your body and mind to face stress, pain, and illness.* New York: Dell Publishing.

Kahaney, P., Janangelo, J., & Perry, L. A. M. (Eds.). (1993). *Theoretical and critical perspectives on teacher change.* Norwood, NJ: Ablex.

Kauffman, S. (1993). *The origins of order.* New York: Oxford University Press.

Kaufman, W. (1973). *Relativity and cosmology.* New York: Harper & Row.

Kelly, K. (1995). *Out of control: The new biology of machines, social systems and the economic world.* Reading, MA: Addison-Wesley.

Kerr, C. (1964). *The uses of the university.* Cambridge, MA: Harvard University Press.

Kindervatter, S. (1983). *Women working together for personal, economic, and community development.* Washington, D.C.: OEF International.

Kinlaw, D. (1991). *Developing superior work teams.* Lexington, MA: Lexington Books.

Kitchener, K. (1983). Cognition, metacognition, and epistemic cognition. *Human Development, 26,* 222–232.

Koplowitz, H. (1984). A projection beyond Piaget's formal operational stage: A general system stage and a unitary stage. In M. Commons, F. Richards, & C. Armon (Eds.), *Beyond formal operations* (pp. 272–296). New York: Praeger.

Kramer, D. A. (1983). Postformal operations? A need for further conceptualization. *Human Development, 26,* 91–105.

Kübler-Ross. E. (1969). *On death and dying.* New York: Macmillan.

Kübler-Ross, E. (1991). *On life after death.* Berkeley, CA: Celestial Arts.

Kuhn, D. (1978). Mechanisms of cognitive and social development: One psychology or two? *Human Development, 21,* 92–118.

Kuhn, D. (1983). On the dual executive and its significance in the development of developmental psychology. In D. Kuhn & J. Meacham (Eds.), *On the development of developmental psychology* (pp. 81–110). New York: Karger.

Kuhn, T. (1962). *The structure of scientific revolutions.* Chicago: University of Chicago Press.

Labouvie-Vief, G. (1982). Dynamic development and mature autonomy: A theoretical prologue. *Human Development, 25,* 161–191.

Labouvie-Vief, G. (1984). Logic and self regulation from youth to maturity: A model. In M. Commons, F. Richards, & C. Armon (Eds.), *Beyond formal operations: Late adolescent and adult cognitive development* (pp. 158–179). New York: Praeger.

Labouvie-Vief, G. (1987). *Speaking about feelings: Symbolization and self regulation through the lifespan.* Paper presented at the Third Beyond Formal Operations Conference at Harvard, Cambridge MA.

Laughlin, P. R. (1965). Selection strategies in concept attainment as a function of number of persons and stimulus display. *Journal of Experimental Psychology, 70,* 323–327.

Laughlin, P., & Bitz, D. (1975). Individual vs dyadic performance on a disjunctive task as a function of individual ability level. *Journal of Personality and Social Psychology, 31,* 487–496.

Lee, D. M. (1987). *Relativistic operations: A framework for conceptualizing teachers' everyday problem solving.* Paper presented at the Third Beyond Formal Operations Conference at Harvard University, Cambridge, MA.

Lee, D. M. (1991). Relativistic operations: A framework for conceptualizing teachers' everyday problem solving. In J. Sinnott & J. Cavanaugh (Eds.), *Bridging paradigms: Positive development in adulthood and cognitive aging* (pp. 73–68). New York: Praeger.

Lee, D. M. (1994a). Becoming an expert: Reconsidering the place of wisdom in teaching adults. In J. D. Sinnott (Ed.), *Interdisciplinary handbook of adult lifespan learning* (pp. 234–248). Westport, CT: Greenwood.

Lee, D. M. (1994b). Models of collaboration in adult reasoning. In J. D. Sinnott, Ed.), *Interdisciplinary handbook of adult lifespan learning* (pp. 51–60). Westport, CT: Greenwood).

L'Engle, M. (1974). *A wind in the door.* New York: Dell.

Levine, R. L., & Fitzgerald, H. E. (Eds.). (1992). *Analysis of dynamic psychological systems: Vols. 1 & 2.* New York: Plenum Press.

Levinson, D. (1978). *The seasons of a man's life.* New York: Knopf.

Lipman, P. (1991). Age and exposure differences in acquisition of route information. *Psychology and Aging, 6,* 118–127.

Lock Land, G. T. (1973). *Grow or die.* New York: Random House.

Lorenz, E. (1963). Deterministic nonperiodic flow. *Journal of Atmospheric Sciences, 20,* 130–141.

Lorenz, E. (1979). *Predictability: Does the flap of a butterfly's wings in Brazil set off a tornado in Texas?* Paper presented at the annual meeting of the American Association for the Advancement of Science, Washington, DC.

Ludeman, K. (1990). *The work ethic: How to profit from the changing values of the new workforce.* New York: Dutton.

Luszcz, M. A., & Orr, R. L. (1991, April). *Constructed knowing and everyday problem solving in adults.* Paper presented at the 12th Biennial Lifespan Conference, West Virginia University, Morgantown, WV.

McLean, P. (1988). *Evolutionary biology.* Paper presented at the Gerontology Research Center, National Institute on Aging, NIH, Baltimore.

MacLean, P. (1990). *The triune brain in evolution.* New York: Plenum Press.

Mahoney, M. J. (1991). *Human change processes.* New York: Basic Books.

Marks, S. (1986). *Three corners: Exploring marriage and the self.* Lexington, MA: D. C. Heath.

Maslow, A. H. (1968). *Toward a psychology of being.* New York: Van Nostrand Reinhold.

Maturana, H., & Varela, F. (1980). *Autopoiesis and cognition: The realization of the living.* Boston: D. Reidel.

Maturana, H., & Varela, F. (1988). *The tree of knowledge.* Boston: New Science Library.

McLuhan, M. (1951). *The mechanical bride: Folklore of industrial man.* New York: Vanguard Press.

McLuhan, M., & Fiore, Q. (1967). *The medium is the massage.* New York: Bantam.

Meacham, J. A., & Boyd, C. (1994). Expanding the circle of caring: From local to global. In J. D. Sinnott (Ed.), *Interdisciplinary handbook of adult lifespan learning* (pp. 61–73). Westport, CT: Greenwood.

Meacham, J., & Emont, N. (1989). The interpersonal basis of everyday problem solving. In J. D. Sinnott & J. Cavanaugh (Eds.), *Bridging paradigms: Positive development in adulthood and positive aging* (pp. 7–23). New York: Praeger.

Merriam, S. B. (1994). Learning and life experience: The connection in adulthood. In J. D. Sinnott (Ed.), *Interdisciplinary handbook of adult lifespan learning* (pp. 74–89). Westport, CT: Greenwood.

Miller, J. (1978). *Living systems.* New York: McGraw Hill.

Mindell, A. (1992). *The dreambody in relationships.* New York: Penguin.

Mindell, A., & Mindell, A. (1992). *Riding the horse backwards: Process work in theory and practice.* New York: Penguin.

Mitchell, S. (1988). *Tao te ching.* New York: HarperCollins.

Montagu, A. (Ed.). (1974). *The meaning of love.* Westport, CT: Greenwood.

Montagu, A. (1989). *Growing young.* New York: Bergin & Garvey Publishers.

Neimark, E. (1975). Intellectual development during adolescence. In M. Horowitz (Ed.), *Review of child development research: Vol. 4* (pp. 000–000). Chicago: University of Chicago Press.

Newell, A., & Simon, H. (1972). *Human problem solving.* Englewood Cliffs, NJ: Prentice-Hall.

Nicholis, G., & Prigogene, I. (1989). *Exploring complexity.* New York: Freeman.

Ornish, D. (1982). *Stress, diet and your heart.* New York: Harper & Row.

Ornstein, R. (1991). *The origins of consciousness.* New York: Plenum Press.

Paul, J., & Paul, M. (1983). *Do I have to give up me to be loved by you?* Minneapolis, MN: Compcare.

Pearce, J. (1973). *The crack in the cosmic egg.* New York: Pocket Books.

Perry, W. G. (1975). *Forms of ethical and intellectual development in the college years.* New York: Holt, Rinehart & Winston.

Pert, C. (1986). The wisdom of the receptors: Neuropeptides, the emotions, and body-mind. *Advances, 3,* 8–16.

Peters, T. J., & Waterman, R. H. (1982). *In search of excellence: Lessons from America's best run companies.* New York: Harper & Row.

Phillips, A. Lipson, A., & Basseches, M. (1994). Empathy and listening skills: A developmental perspective on learning to listen. In J. D. Sinnott (Ed.), *Interdisciplinary handbook of adult lifespan learning* (pp. 301–324). Westport, CT: Greenwood.

Piaget, J. (1972). Intellectual evolution from adolescence to adulthood. *Human Development, 15,* 1–12.

Piaget, J., & Inhelder, B. (1969). *The psychology of the child.* New York: Basic Books.

Polanyi, M. (1971). *Personal knowledge.* Chicago: University of Chicago Press.

Pool, R. (1989). Is it healthy to be chaotic? *Science, 243,* 604–607.

Powell, P. (1980). Advanced social role taking and cognitive development in gifted adults. *International Journal of Aging and Human Development, 11,* 177–192.

Powell, P. (1984). Stage 4A: Category operations and interactive empathy. In M. Commons, F. Richards, & C. Armon (Eds.), *Beyond formal operations* (pp. 326–339). New York: Praeger.

Prigogene, I. (1980). *From being to becoming.* San Francisco: Freeman.

Prigogene, I., & Stengers, I. (1984). *Order out of chaos: Man's new dialogue with nature.* New York: Bantam.

Pruitt, D., & Rubin, J. (1986). *Social conflict.* New York: Random House.

Rathunde, K. (1995). Wisdom and abiding interest: Interviews with three noted historians in later life. *Journal of Adult Development, 2,* 159–172.

Read, P. P. (1974). *Alive: The story of the Andes survivors.* New York: Lippincott.

Redfield, J. (1993). *The Celestine prophecy: An adventure.* New York: Warner.

Redfield, J., & Adrienne, C. (1996). *The Celestine prophecy: An experiential guide.* New York: Warner.

Resnick, L., Levine, J., & Teasley, S. (Eds.). (1991). *Perspectives on socially shared cognition.* Washington, DC: Amerocan Psychological Association.

Riegel, K. F. (1973). Dialectical operations: The final period of cognitive development. *Human Development, 16,* 346–370.

Riegel, K. (1975). Adult life crises: A dialectical interpretation of development. In N. Datan & L. Ginsberg (Eds.), *Lifespan developmental psychology: Normative life crises* (pp. 99–129). New York: Academic Press.

Riegel, K. F. (1976). Toward a dialectical theory of development. *American Psychologist, 31,* 679–700.

Riegel, K. F. (1977). Past and future trends in gerontology. *Gerontologist, 17,* 105–113.

Robertson, H. P., & Noonan, T. W. (1968). *Relativity and cosmology.* Philedelphia: Saunders.

Rogers, C. (1951). *Client centered therapy: Its current practise, implications, and theory.* Boston: Houghton-Mifflin.

Rogers, D. R. B. (1989). *The effect of dyad interaction and marital adjustment on cognitive performance in everyday logical problem solving.* Doctoral dissertation, Utah State University, Logan.

Rogers, D., Sinnott, J., & Van Dusen, L. (1991, July). *Marital adjustment and social cognitive performance in everyday logical problem solving.* Paper presented at the sixth Adult Development Conference, Boston.

Roszak, T., Gomes, M. E., & Kanner, A. D. (Eds.). (1995). *Ecopsychology: Restoring the earth, healing the mind.* San Francisco: Sierra Club Books.

Rowe, H. (1984). *Problem solving and intelligence.* Hillsdale, NJ: Lawrence Erlbaum.

Russell, B. (1969). *The A B C of relativity.* New York: Mentor Books.

Satir, V. (Ed.). (1967). *Conjoint family therapy.* Palo Alto, CA: Science & Behavior Books.

Scarf, M. (1987). *Intimate partners: Patterns in love and marriage.* New York: Random House.

Scarf, M. (1995). *Intimate worlds: Life inside the family.* New York: Random House.

Schaie, K. W. (1977–1978). Toward a stage theory of adult cognitive development. *International Journal of Aging and Human Development, 8,* 129–138.

Schlick, M. (1970). Causality in contemporary physics. In J. Toulmin (Ed.), *Physical reality: Philosophical essays on 20th century physics* (pp. 83–121). New York: Harper & Row.

Schoenfeld, A. H. (1983). Beyond the purely cognitive: Belief systems, social cognitions, and metacognitions as driving forces in intellectual performance. *Cognitive Science, 7,* 329–363.

Scott, W., & Meyer, J. (1994). *Institutional environments and organizations: Structural complexity and individualism.* Thousand Oaks, CA: Sage.

Shank, R., Collins, G., Davis, E., Johnson, P., Lytinen, S., & Reiser, B. (1982). What's the point? *Cognitive Science, 6,* 255–275.

Sheldrake, R. (1981). *A new science of life.* Los Angeles: Tarcher.

Sheldrake, R. (1989). *The presence of the past: Morphic resonance and the habits of nature.* New York: Viking.

Sheldrake, R. (1990). *The rebirth of nature.* London: Century.

Shock, N., Andres, R., Arenberg, D., Costa, P., Greulich, R., Lakatta, E., & Tobin, J. (1985). *Normal human aging: The Baltimore Longitudinal Study of Aging.* Washington, DC: National Institutes of Health.

Sillars, A. (1986). *Manual for coding interpersonal conflict.* Unpublished manuscript, University of Montana, Department of Interpersonal Communications.

Simon, D., & Simon, H. (1978). Individual differences in solving physics problems. In R. S. Siegler (Ed.), *Children's thinking: What develops?* (pp. 325–348). Hillsdale, NJ: Erlbaum.

Sinetar, M. (1986). *Ordinary people as monks and mystics.* Mahwah, NJ: Paulist Press.

Sinnott, J. D. (1975). Everyday thinking and Piagetian operativity in adults. *Human Development, 18,* 430–444.

Sinnott, J. D. (1977). Sex-role inconstancy, biology, and successful aging: A dialectical model. *Gerontologist, 17,* 459–463.

Sinnott, J. D. (1981). The theory of relativity: A metatheory for development? *Human Development, 24,* 293–311.

Sinnott, J. D. (1982). Correlates of sex roles in older adults. *Journal of Gerontology, 37,* 587–594.

Sinnott, J. D. (1984a). Older men, older women: Are their perceived sex roles similar? *Sex Roles, 10,* 847–856.

Sinnott, J. D. (1984b). Postformal reasoning: The relativistic stage. In M. Commons, F. Richards, & C. Armon (Eds.), *Beyond formal operations* (pp. 298–325). New York: Praeger.

Sinnott, J. D. (1985). *The expression of postformal, relativistic self referential operations in everyday problem solving performance.* Paper presented at the Second Beyond Formal Operations Conference at Harvard University, Cambridge, MA.

Sinnott, J. D. (1986a). Prospective/intentional and incidental everyday memory: Effects of age and passage of time. *Psychology and Aging, 2,* 110–116.

Sinnott, J. D. (1986b). *Sex roles and aging: Theory and research from a systems perspective.* New York: S. Karger.

Sinnott, J. D. (1986c). Social cognition: The construction of self-referential truth? *Educational Gerontology, 12,* 337–340.

Sinnott, J. D. (1987). Sex roles in adulthood and old age. In D. B. Carter (Ed.), *Current conceptions of sex roles and sex typing* (pp. 155–180). New York: Praeger.

Sinnott, J. D. (1989a). Changing the known, knowing the changing. In D. Kramer & M. Bopp (Eds.), *Transformation in clinical and developmental psychology* (pp. 51–69). New York: Springer.

Sinnott, J. D. (Ed.). (1989b). *Everyday problem solving: Theory and applications.* New York: Praeger.

Sinnott, J. D. (1989c). General systems theory: A rationale for the study of everyday memory. In L. Poon, D. Rubin, & B. Wilson (Eds.), *Everyday cognition in adulthood and old age* (pp. 59–70). New Rochelle, NY: Cambridge University Press.

Sinnott, J. D. (1989d). Lifespan relativistic postformal thought. In M. Commons, J. Sinnott, F. Richards, & C. Armon (Eds.), *Beyond formal operations I* (pp. 239–278). New York: Praeger.

Sinnott, J. D. (1990). *Yes, it's worth the trouble! Unique contributions from everyday cognition studies.* Paper presented at the Twelfth West Virginia University Conference on Lifespan Developmental Psychology: Mechanisms of Everyday Cognition, Morgantown, WV.

Sinnott, J. D. (1991a). *Conscious adult development: Complex thought and solving our intragroup conflicts.* Invited presentation, Sixth Adult Development Conference, Suffolk University, Boston.

Sinnott, J. D. (1991b). Limits to problem solving: Emotion, intention, goal clarity, health, and other factors in postformal thought. In J. D. Sinnott & J. Cavanaugh (Eds.),

Bridging paradigms: Positive development in adulthood and cognitive aging. New York: Praeger.

Sinnott, J. D. (1991c). What do we do to help John? A case study of everyday problem solving in a family making decisions about an acutely psychotic member. In J. D. Sinnott & J. Cavanaugh (Eds.), *Bridging paradigms: Positive development in adulthood and cognitive aging* (pp. 203–220). New York: Praeger.

Sinnott, J. D. (1992). *Development and yearning: Cognitive aspects of spiritual development.* Paper presented at the American Psychological Association Conference, Washington, DC.

Sinnott, J. D. (1993a). Teaching in a chaotic new physics world: Teaching as a dialogue with reality. In P. Kahaney, J. Janangelo, & L. Perry (Eds.), *Theoretical and critical perspectives on teacher change* (pp. 91–108). Norwood, NJ: Ablex.

Sinnott, J. D. (1993b). Sex roles. In V. S. Ramachandran (Ed.), *Encyclopedia of human behavior: Vol. 4* (pp. 151–158).

Sinnott, J. D. (1993c). Use of complex thought and resolving intragroup conflicts: A means to conscious adult development in the workplace. In J. Demick & P. M. Miller (Eds.), *Development in the workplace* (pp. 155–175). Hillsdale, NJ: Erlbaum.

Sinnott, J. D. (1994a). Development and yearning: Cognitive aspects of spiritual development. *Journal of Adult Development, 1,* 91–99.

Sinnott, J. D. (Ed.). (1994b). *Interdisciplinary handbook of adult lifespan learning.* Westport, CT: Greenwood.

Sinnott, J. D. (1994c). New science models for teaching adults: Teaching as a dialogue with reality. In J. D. Sinnott (Ed.), *Interdisciplinary handbook of adult lifespan learning* (pp. 90–104). Westport, CT: Greenwood.

Sinnott, J. D. (1994d). The future of adult lifespan learning. In J. D. Sinnott (Ed.), *Interdisciplinary handbook of adult lifespan learning* (pp. 449–466). Westport, CT: Greenwood.

Sinnott, J. D. (1995). *A computerized test of complex formal thought.* Available from the author, Psychology Department, Towson University, Baltimore, MD

Sinnott, J. D. (1994e). The relationship of postformal learning and lifespan development. In J. D. Sinnott (Ed.), *Interdisciplinary handbook of adult lifespan learning* (pp. 105–119). Westport, CT: Greenwood.

Sinnott, J. D. (1996a). Postformal thought and mysticism: How might the mind know the unknowable? *Aging and Spirituality: Newsletter of American Sociological Association Forum on Religion, Spirituality and Aging, 8,* 7–8.

Sinnott, J. D. (1996b). The developmental approach: Postformal thought as adaptive intelligence. In F. Blanchard-Fields and T. Hess (Eds.), *Perspectives on cognitive change in adulthood and aging* (pp. 358–383). New York: McGraw-Hill.

Sinnott, J. D. (in press). Creativity and postformal thought. In C. Adams-Price (Ed.), *Creativity and aging: Theoretical and empirical approaches.* New York: Springer.

Sinnott, J. D. (1997). Developmental models of midlife and aging in women: Metaphors for transcendence and for individuality in community. In J. M. Coyle (Ed.), *Women and aging: A research guide.* Westport, CT: Greenwood.

Sinnott, J. D., Block, M., Grambs, J., Gaddy, C., & Davidson, J. (1980). *Sex roles in mature adults: Antecedents amd correlates.* College Park, MD: Center on Aging, University of Maryland College Park.

Sinnott, J. D., & Cavanaugh, J. (Eds.). (1991). *Bridging paradigms: Positive development in adulthood and cognitive aging.* New York: Praeger.

Sinnott, J. D., & Guttmann (1978a). Piagetian logical abilities and older adults' abilities to solve everyday problems. *Human Development, 21,* 327–333.

Sinnott, J. D., & Guttmann, D. (1978b). The dialectics of decision making in older adults. *Human Development, 21,* 190–200.

Sinnott, J. D., & Johnson, L. (1996). *Reinventing the university: A radical proposal for a problem focused university.* Norwood, NJ: Ablex.

Sinnott, J. D., & Johnson, L. (1997). Reinventing the university: A radical proposal for a problem-focused university for the next millennium. *Futurist.*

Sinnott, J. D., Rogers, D. B. R. & Spencer, F. (1996). Reconsidering sex roles and aging: Preliminary data on some influences of context, cohort, time. *ERIC.*

Smith, A. (1796). *An inquiry into the nature and causes of the wealth of nations.* London: Strahan & Cadell & Davies.

Smith, H. (1991). *President's address to the faculty.* Towson State University, Baltimore.

Smith, L. B., & Thelan, E. (Eds.) (1993). *A dynamic systems approach to development.* Cambridge, MA: MIT Press.

Solzhenitsyn, A. (1973). *The Gulag archipelago.* New York: Harper & Row.

Spanier, G. B. (1976). Measuring dyadic adjustment: New scales for assessing the quality of marriage and similar dyads. *Journal of Marriage and the Family, 38,* 15–28.

Sternberg, R. J. (1986). A triangular theory of love. *Psychological Review, 93,* 119–135.

Stevens-Long, J., & Trujillo, C. (1995). Individual experience and paradox in the development of small groups. *Journal of Adult Development, 2,* 265–273.

Sweller, J. (1983). Control mechanisms in problem solving. *Memory and Cognition, 11,* 32–40.

Sweller, J., & Levine, M. (1982). The effect of goal specificity on means–end analysis and learning. *Journal of Experimental Psychology: Learning, Memory, and Cognition, 8,* 463–474.

Sperry, R. (1987). Structure and significance of the consciousness revolution. *Journal of Mind and Behavior, 8,* 37–66.

Tanon, F. (1991). The influence of formal vs informal education on planning skills. In J. D. Sinnott & J. Cavanaugh (Eds.), *Bridging paradigms: Positive development in adulthood and cognitive aging* (pp. 221–236). New York: Praeger.

Tart, C. (1983). *States of consciousness.* El Cerrito, CA: Psychological Processes.

Teilhard de Chardin, P. (1959). *The phenomenon of man.* New York: Harper & Row.

Tinbergen, N. (1974). Ethology and stress diseases. *Science, 185,* 20–26.

Toulmin, J. (1970). *Physical reality: Philosophical essays on 20th century physics.* New York: Harper & Row.

Troll, L. (1985). *Early and middle adulthood (2nd ed.).* Monterey, CA: Brooks-Cole.

Underhill, E. (1961). *Mysticism.* New York: Dutton.

Underwood, P. (1991). *Three strands in the braid: A guide for enablers of learning.* San Anselmo, CA: A Tribe of Two Press.

von Bertalanfy, L. (1968). *General systems theory.* New York: Braziller.

von Neumann, J., & Morgenstern, O. (1947). *Theory of games and economic behavior.* Princeton, NJ: Princeton University Press.

Vygotsky, L. S. (1962). *Thought and language.* Cambridge, MA: MIT Press.

Vygotsky, L. S. (1978). *Mind in society.* Cambridge, MA: Harvard University Press.

Waldrop, M. (1992). *Complexity: The emerging science at the edge of order and chaos.* New York: Simon & Schuster.

Wechsler, D. (1955). *WAIS Manual: Wechsler Adult Intelligence Scale.* New York: Psychological Corporation.

Weibust, P. S., & Thomas, L. E. (1994). Learning and spirituality in adulthood. In J. D. Sinnott (Ed.), *Interdisciplinary handbook of adult lifespan learning* (pp. 120–134). Westport, CT: Greenwood.

Weiner, N. (1961). *Cybernetics.* Cambridge, MA: MIT Press.

Welwood, J. (1996). *Love and awakening.* New York: HarperCollins.

West, R. L., & Sinnott, J. D. (Eds.). (1992). *Everyday memory and aging: Current research and methodology.* New York: Springer-Verlag.

Whitbourne, S., & Weinstock, C. (1979). *Adult development.* New York: Holt, Rinehart & Winston.

Windle, M., & Sinnott, J. D. (1985). A psychometric study of the Bem Sex Role Inventory with an older adult sample. *Journal of Gerontology, 40,* 336–343.

Wolf, F. A. (1981). *Taking the quantum leap.* New York: Harper & Row.

Wood, P. (1983). Inquiring systems and problem structure: Implications for human development. *Human Development, 26,* 249–265.

Yalom, I. (1980). *Existential psychotherapy.* New York: Basic Books.

Yan, B. (1995). *Nonabsolute/relativistic (N/R) thinking: A possible unifying commonality underlying models of postformal reasoning.* Unpublished Ph.D. dissertation, University of British Columbia, Vancouver.

Yan, B., & Arlin, P. K. (1995). Nonabsolute/relativistic thinking: A common factor underlying models of postformal reasoning? *Jounal of Adult Development, 2,* 223–240.

Zukav, G. (1979). *The dancing wu li masters: An overview of the new physics.* New York: Bantam.

Index

An "*f*" suffix or a "*t*" suffix indicates that a term is to be found in a figure or table.

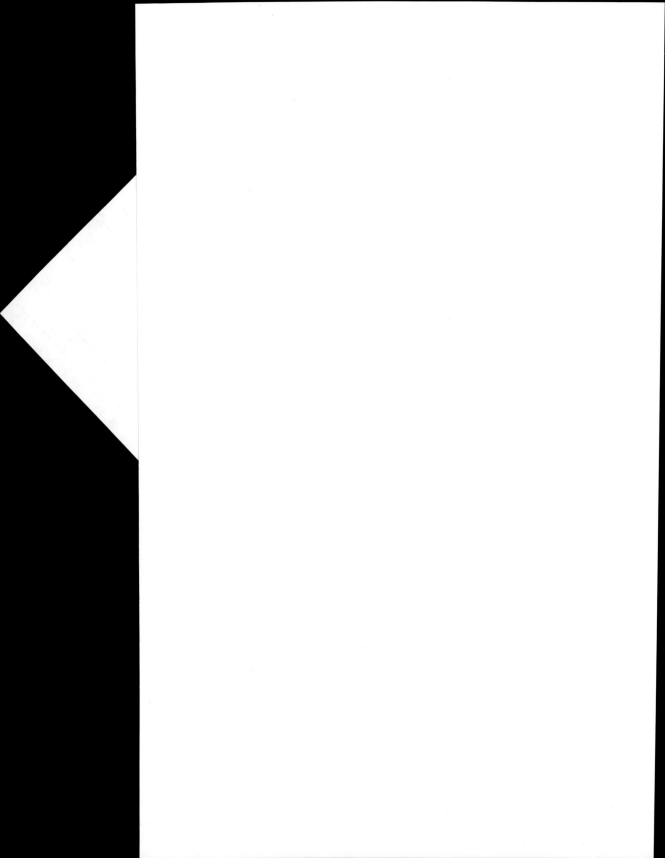

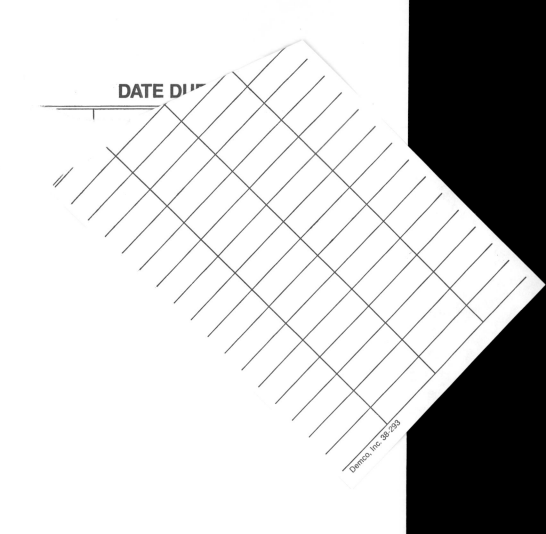

DATE DUE

Demco, Inc. 38-293